Ordinary Violence in Mussolini's Italy

Between 1926 and 1943, the Fascist regime arrested thousands of Italians and deported them to island internment colonies and small villages in southern Italy. *Ordinary Violence in Mussolini's Italy* analyzes this system of political confinement and, more broadly, its effects on Italian society, revealing the centrality of political violence to Fascist rule. In doing so, the book shatters the widely accepted view that the Mussolini regime ruled without a system of mass repression. The Fascist state ruled Italy violently, projecting its coercive power deeply and diffusely into society through confinement, imprisonment, low-level physical assaults, economic deprivations, intimidation, discrimination, and other quotidian forms of coercion. Moreover, by promoting denunciatory practices, the regime cemented the loyalties of "upstanding" citizens while suppressing opponents, dissenters, and social outsiders. Fascist repression was thus more intense and ideological than previously thought and even shared some important similarities with Nazi and Soviet terror.

Michael R. Ebner is Assistant Professor of History at the Maxwell School of Citizenship and Public Affairs, Syracuse University. He is the 2000–1 recipient of the Rome Prize in Modern Italian Studies from the American Academy in Rome. From 2001 to 2002, he was a Whiting Fellow at Columbia University.

Ordinary Violence in Mussolini's Italy

MICHAEL R. EBNER
Syracuse University

 CAMBRIDGE
UNIVERSITY PRESS

CAMBRIDGE UNIVERSITY PRESS
Cambridge, New York, Melbourne, Madrid, Cape Town, Singapore,
São Paulo, Delhi, Dubai, Tokyo, Mexico City

Cambridge University Press
32 Avenue of the Americas, New York, NY 10013-2473, USA

www.cambridge.org
Information on this title: www.cambridge.org/9780521762137

First published 2011

Printed in the United States of America

A catalog record for this publication is available from the British Library.

Library of Congress Cataloging in Publication data

Ebner, Michael R., 1972
Ordinary violence in Mussolini's Italy / Michael R. Ebner.
    p.   cm.
Includes bibliographical references and index.
ISBN 978-0-521-76213-7 (hbk.)
1. Italy – Politics and government – 1922–1945.   2. Mussolini, Benito, 1883–1945.
3. Fascism – Italy – History – 20th century.   4. Political violence – Italy – History –
20th century.   5. Political persecution – Italy – History – 20th century.   6. Deportation –
Italy – History – 20th century.   7. Imprisonment – Italy – History – 20th century.
8. State-sponsored terrorism – Italy – History – 20th century.   9. Italy – Social
conditions – 1918–1945.   I. Title.
DG571.E315   2011
323'.044094509043 – dc22   2010019594

ISBN 978-0-521-76213-7 Hardback

For Alceste Alvi

Contents

Tables and Figures

Tables

Figures

Acknowledgments

I researched and wrote this book in New York City, Rome, and Syracuse, New York. In all three places, and beyond, I found people who took interest in my project. I thank them all for their time and assistance. What follows is an attempt, however inadequate, to express my gratitude to the people and institutions that helped me the most. Victoria de Grazia supervised my dissertation and has continued to be steadfastly supportive, always offering critical insights just when it was difficult to see the way forward. Lewis Bateman at Cambridge University Press calmly and graciously guided me and my book through the publication process. Countless other advisors and colleagues provided advice and encouragement along the way, especially Eliza Johnson Ablovatski, Lorenzo Benadusi, Ruth Ben-Ghiat, Jennifer Bethke, Mauro Canali, Paul Corner, John Davis, István Deák, Jonathan Dunnage, Mia Fuller, Paul Garfinkel, Mary Gibson, Jennifer Hirsh, Adrian Lyttelton, Edward Malefakis, Benjamin Martin, Mark Mazower, Silvana Patriarca, Stanley Payne, Frank Snowden, Mark Von Hagen, and Perry Willson. I am also grateful to my mentors and colleagues in the History Department of the Maxwell School at Syracuse University, all of whom have nurtured this project and my professional life in so many ways. In particular, Frederick Marquardt and Subho Basu offered valuable comments on earlier versions of the manuscript. Finally, I thank my extremely capable, efficient graduate research assistant, Martin Gutmann.

A number of institutions provided me with material and financial backing. The Council for European Studies sponsored an initial short research trip to Rome, and the American Academy in Rome housed, fed, and funded me for an additional, splendid year. Fellowships from the

German-Marshall Fund and the Trinity College Barbieri Grant in Italian History enabled me to conduct further research. The Whiting Foundation, Columbia University's Institute for Social and Economic Research and Policy, and Columbia's Institute for the Study of Europe all supported me during various stages of writing. I am very grateful to the employees of the State Central Archive in Rome, particularly the staff members who had to retrieve all of those boxes! Finally, the Maxwell School at Syracuse University, thanks to Deans Mitchell Wallerstein and Michael Wasylenko, provided me with both the resources and time off to complete the book. At the Maxwell School, the Appleby-Mosher Fund sent me to Rome for one final research trip, and the Pigott Fund paid for the usage rights for many of the images in this book.

My family has always offered love and encouragement, especially my mother Cynthia, my brothers Christopher and David, and my grandparents Lois and Robert Schneider. My father, John Ebner, read the manuscript several times, catching all sorts of errors. Perhaps more importantly, as the only other person who really knew the manuscript well, he gave me someone to talk to during what was otherwise a very lonely process. I thank my wife's family, Joseph, Ginevra, and Kim Porcelli, for their support and enthusiasm.

Although this project has sometimes taken me away from my wife, Lesley Porcelli, it has mostly left us with happy memories, mainly involving our long and short stays in Rome and other parts of Italy, from before we were married up to the present. Most recently, in 2008, when our son Franklin was just three months old, we went to Rome for a month so that I could finish research. The picture we took of him staring up in wonder at the cobalt blue ceiling of Santa Maria Sopra Minerva is perhaps our favorite image of him. No doubt a future project will soon bring our next child, due in just a few months, to Rome.

For me, the personal happiness and professional satisfaction that surrounded my trips to Italy always stood in stark contrast with the sad stories of the Fascist political detainees and their families who are the subject of this study. Alceste Alvi, to whom I have dedicated this book, was a Roman anarchist whose life was ruined by Fascism. The police sanctions inflicted on him by the Fascist regime precipitated the physical and economic decline of him and his wife. By repeatedly arresting, confining, and harassing Alvi, the regime condemned him and his family to years of unemployment, poverty, homelessness, and illness. One should not overly romanticize a figure like Alvi. He was probably not a very pleasant person and would have run afoul of the law even if Fascism had never come to Italy. However, he certainly did not deserve what befell him. More importantly, the physical and economic decline of Alvi and his wife reveal the subtle but insidious ways that the Mussolini regime used violence and coercion to rule Italy. When I first read Alvi's file in 1999, his case struck me as very sad, but also very ordinary. He was not tortured, imprisoned for decades, or shot. In 2008, I was in Rome gathering a few last bits of archival research when I came across a police report detailing Alceste Alvi's 1937 suicide attempt – he jumped off of a bridge into the Tiber – along with the letters that Alvi subsequently wrote to Mussolini. The strictures and stigma of political probation, he told his dictator, made finding employment impossible. Consequently, his wife had gone blind; he had an excruciating ulcer; and they now lived apart in separate public dormitories. In his letter, Alvi extolled Mussolini's greatness, particularly his founding of the Fascist empire after the conquest of Ethiopia. But the letter also made clear that Fascist repressive measures had broken Alvi physically, politically, and psychologically. He begged Mussolini to revoke his probation, but to no avail. Police surveillance of Alvi ended only in 1941, the year he died, certainly prematurely, of unknown causes. The discovery of this last batch of documents suddenly made clear to me the extraordinary and brutal power of ordinary Fascist violence.

Sections of this book have appeared in other forms. Part of Chapter 2 comes from "The Political Police and Denunciation during Fascism: A Review of Recent Historical Literature," *Journal of Modern Italian Studies* 11:2 (June 2006): 209–26 (http://www.informaworld.com). Parts of Chapter 4 come from "Dalla repressione dell'antifascismo al controllo sociale. Il confino di polizia, 1926–1943," in *Storia e problemi contemporanei* 43 (2006): 81–104. A few sentences and paragraphs throughout the manuscript first appeared in "Terror und Bevölkerung im italienischen Faschismus," in *Beiträge zur Geschichte des Nationalsozialismus*, vol. 21: *Faschismus in Italien und Deutschland: Studien zu Transfer und Vergleich*, ed. Sven Reichardt and Armin Nolzen (Göttingen, Germany: Wallstein, 2005): 201–24; and "The Persecution of Homosexual Men under Fascism, 1926–1943," in *Gender, Family, and Sexuality: The Private Sphere in Italy, 1860–1945*, ed. Perry Willson (Basingstoke, UK: Palgrave Macmillan, 2004): 139–56.

Common Abbreviations in Text and Notes

ACS	State Central Archive (Archivio Centrale dello Stato)
b.	Busta
Confinati politici	Personal files of political detainees
Confinati comuni	Personal files of common detainees
CPC	Central Political Registry
DAGR	Division of General and Confidential Affairs
DGPS	General Directorate of Public Security
EOA	Ente Opere Assistenziali (Fascist welfare agency)
Fasc.	Fascicolo
GIL	Fascist Youth Organization (Italian Youth of the Lictors), 1937–43
MI	Ministry of the Interior
MVSN	Fascist Militia (Voluntary Militia for National Security)
OCI	Capillary Investigative Unit (of the PNF)
ONB	Fascist Youth Organization (National Balilla Organization), 1926–37
ONMI	National Organization for the Protection of Motherhood and Infancy
OVRA	Organization for the Surveillance and Repression of Antifascism (secret political police)
PCI	Italian Communist Party
PNF	National Fascist Party
PSI	Italian Socialist Party
Sf.	Sottofascicolo
UCP	Political Confinement Office
UPI	Provincial Investigative Office (of the MVSN)

Introduction

The Fascist Archipelago

In the Mediterranean and Adriatic seas lie several archipelagos of small Italian islands, some measuring only a few hundred meters across: the Pontine Islands, southwest of Rome; the Aeolian Islands, north of Messina; the Aegadian Islands, west of Sicily; the Pelagie archipelago, some two hundred miles south of Sicily, closer to the shores of Tunisia; and, finally, the Tremiti Islands, off the coast of northern Puglia in the Adriatic.[1] A handful of these islands – Ponza, Ventotene, Lipari, Ustica, Favignana, Pantelleria, Lampedusa, San Domino, and San Nicola – have served as sites of confinement, exile, and punishment for thousands of years. In the time of the Roman Empire, most of them hosted political exiles, often bothersome family members of the emperor.[2] Throughout the nineteenth century, the Italian peninsula's various kingdoms used them as penal colonies. After Italy's Unification in 1860, the islands continued to serve as sites of punishment, exile, and, during times of war, internment.[3] Although today these places are beautiful, sun-drenched

---

[1] There are several useful local histories of these islands: Giovanni Maria De Rossi, *Ventotene e S. Stefano* (Rome, 1999); Silvio Corvisieri, *All'Isola di Ponza. Regno borbonico e Italia nella storia di un'isola, 1734–1984* (Rome, 1985); Enzo Mancini, *Isole Tremiti: Sassi di Diomede. Natura, storia, arte, turismo* (Milan, 1979).

[2] Xavier Lafon, "Les îles de la mer Tyrrhénienne: entre palais et prisons sous les Julio-Claudiens," in *Carcer: Prison et privation de liberté dans l'antiquité classique. Actes du colloque de Strasbourg, 5 e 6 décembre 1997*, ed. Cécil Bertrand-Dagenbach, Alain Chauvot, Michel Matter, and Jean-Marie Salamito (Paris, 1999), 149–62.

[3] For the history of these practices, see Davide Petrini, *La prevenzione inutile: illegittimità delle misure praeter delictum* (Naples, 1996); Leonardo Musci, *Il confino fascista di polizia. L'apparato statale di fronte al dissenso politico e sociale* (Milan, 1983); Richard Bach Jensen, *Liberty and Order: The Theory and Practice of Italian Public Security*

tourist destinations, at the beginning of the twentieth century most were desolate, desiccated, wind-swept rocks. Their coasts – high, jagged cliffs – rendered them virtual prisons amid vast expanses of rolling sea.

Between 1926 and 1943, Benito Mussolini's Fascist regime arrested and deported tens of thousands of Italians to these islands.[4] In the 1930s, when the island "confinement colonies" became too full, the regime exiled "less dangerous" detainees to small, isolated villages in the Mezzogiorno, Italy's impoverished south.[5] By the end of the decade, there were more exiles on the mainland than detainees on the islands. Placing a half-dozen anti-Fascists in one village, a few Jehovah's Witnesses in another, a homosexual here, a *mafioso* there, and so on, the Fascists implanted across southern Italy a vast, man-made archipelago: hundreds of islands of exile inhabited by the regime's political and social outcasts. Over the course of the dictatorship, institutions of punishment and confinement proliferated. By the time of Italy's involvement in the Second World War, there were concentration camps, political prisons, work houses, confinement colonies, and sites of internment scattered throughout the entire Italian peninsula.[6] This archipelago of repression was not only geographic but also social: the Fascist regime carefully focused state-backed violence and repression on select communities, classes, and public and private spaces. Within the sea of "normal" society, there were thus myriad islands of repression.

This book began as a history of the Fascist system of political confinement (*confino politico*) told through the experiences of political

---

Policy, *1848 to the Crisis of the 1890s* (New York, 1991); John A. Davis, *Conflict and Control: Law and Order in Nineteenth Century Italy* (Basingstoke, 1988); Guido Corso, *L'ordine pubblico* (Bologna, 1979); and Franco Molfese, *Storia del brigantaggio dopo l'Unità* (Milan, 1964), 344–60.

[4] The regime sentenced 15,000 Italians to *confino politico* (political confinement) and between 25,000 and 50,000 to "common" *confino*. See Michael Ebner, "Dalla repressione dell'antifascismo al controllo sociale. Il confino di polizia, 1926–1943," *Storia e problemi contemporanei* 43 (2006): 81–104; Adriano Dal Pont and Simonetta Carolini, eds., *L'Italia al confino: le ordinanze di assegnazione al confino emesse dalle Commissioni provinciali dal novembre 1926 al luglio 1943*, 4 vols. (Milan, 1983).

[5] There are many works on aspects of the Fascist *confino di polizia* system. Among the most useful are Ebner, "Dalla repressione dell'antifascismo"; Silverio Corvisieri, *La villeggiatura di Mussolini: Il confino da Bocchini a Berlusconi* (Milan, 2004); Alessandra Pagano, *Il confino politico a Lipari, 1926–1933* (Milan, 2003); Musci, *Il confino fascista di polizia*; and Celso Ghini and Adriano Dal Pont, *Gli antifascisti al confino, 1926–1943* (Rome, 1971).

[6] See Carlo Spartaco Capogreco, *I campi del Duce: l'internamento civile nell'Italia fascista, 1940–43* (Turin, 2004); and the essays in Costantino di Sante, ed., *I campi di concentramento in Italia* (Milan, 2001).

detainees.[7] However, the files state authorities kept on these people – which contain police reports, correspondence between state agencies, denunciations, letters written by detainees and their families, medical records, and other documents – revealed to me the history of more than just one institution of repression.[8] Individually and collectively, these sources told the stories of ordinary people, families, and communities living under a violent Fascist dictatorship.[9] By telling the history of the Fascist archipelago, this book seeks to establish that the Mussolini dictatorship ruled Italy through violence. I use the term *violence* in two, closely related senses. The first is "the exercise of physical force in order to injure, control, or intimidate others," typically by persons who were "acting illegally."[10] Fascists and police, according to official sources, regularly "killed," "beat," "clubbed," "punched," "slapped," "kicked," "hit," and otherwise used spontaneous "force" and "acts of violence" against citizens. Police reports also often used euphemisms for these types of violence and other methods of torture.[11] The second, broader meaning of *violence* in this book refers to state practices which, although technically legal, were so broadly defined in the legislation and applied with such executive discretion that they can hardly be said to have been bound

---

[7] Although this book draws primarily on the files of political detainees, both the "political" and "common" branches of the *confino* system are relevant (and are dealt with extensively, particularly in ch. 4).

[8] Excerpts of these sources have been published in Donatella Carbone, *Il popolo al confino: la persecuzione fascista in Basilicata* (Rome, 1994); Katia Massara, *Il popolo al confino: la persecuzione fascista in Puglia* (Rome, 1991); Rosa Spadafora, *Il popolo al confino: la persecuzione fascista in Campania*, 2 vols. (Naples, 1989); Salvatore Carbone and Laura Grimaldi, *Il popolo al confino: la persecuzione fascista in Sicilia* (Rome, 1989); and Salvatore Carbone, *Il popolo al confino: la persecuzione fascista in Calabria* (Cosenza, 1977).

[9] Much of the research for this study is based on a sample I conducted on the personal files (*fascicoli personali*) of political detainees (*confinati politici*) at the State Central Archive in Rome. The sample consisted of 549 files, or almost 4% of the personal files. I requested every fifth or sixth box (I had to increase the box interval because the sample was taking too long). The number of files in each box was divided by three, and the resulting quotient constituted the interval. I then chose three files at that interval. For each box, I took a new starting point to select the first file and counted the interval from there (i.e., starting with the first file in the first box, the second file in the second box, and so forth). Therefore, as much as possible, considering the restrictions of time (twelve months), the structure of the archive, and archival regulations, this sample was random and representative of the archival series in general. From each file, I collected roughly 100 pieces of quantifiable data and recorded a mass of qualitative research on each case.

[10] *Oxford English Dictionary*, 2nd ed., sv. "violence," n. (1a) and "violent," adv. (3a).

[11] Mauro Canali, *Le spie del regime* (Bologna, 2004), 77–8.

by the law: the summary removal of people from their homes in the middle of the night; confinement in dirty, vermin-infested jails and prisons, without explanation or access to law courts; the thirst, hunger, and disease that were rife within the island confinement colonies; the trauma of poverty, which the police state knowingly and sometimes deliberately inflicted on wives and children of detainees; the revocation of business permits for political motives; the intimidation of living under a one-party regime whose supporters shared in the state's monopoly on violence and truth; and the political discrimination practiced by Fascists in distributing employment, welfare, and other state assistance.[12] The regime used these two types of violence – one illegal, the other legal – to punish Italians or coerce them into conforming to certain standards of political and social behavior. In select cases, public-security authorities, Fascists, or militiamen applied legal measures in conjunction with physical assaults and criminal behavior. Broadly and ambiguously defined police powers often begot abuse, mistreatment, and torture, so that Fascists and police operated in a "gray zone" between legality and illegality. Finally, in word and deed, the Fascist regime constantly reminded Italians that although it did not engage in physical or lethal violence on a *mass* scale, it claimed the right to beat, torture, and kill *select* enemies with impunity. For the intended audience, this threat meant that one truly never knew what to expect from a knock on the door. The fear of punishment unfettered by the rule of law was, for many Italians, a form of terror. The twentieth century – the century of genocide, concentration camps, ethnic cleansing, and extreme evil – has perhaps obscured how little it takes to frighten large numbers of ordinary people. Violence, albeit an ordinary kind of violence, was central to the policies and institutions of Fascist rule.

This regime of ordinary violence profoundly affected the minutiae of everyday life under Fascism. Although only fifteen thousand Italians experienced political confinement, the fearful and traumatic episodes that preceded these sentences were familiar to vastly broader sections of Italian society: tense run-ins with feared Fascists; house searches conducted by police or Fascist militiamen; the arrests and interrogations of neighbors, family members, co-workers, and other witnesses in the wake of some trifling offense to Mussolini; the pressure to conform, to nod silently while angrily disagreeing; the fear of reprisals, repercussions, and discrimination, based on one's past behavior; and the economic decline of a

---

[12] Paul Corner, "Italian Fascism: Whatever Happened to Dictatorship?" *Journal of Modern History* 74 (June 2002): 325–51.

political suspect and his family, witnessed by friends, family, and neighbors. The case files of Fascism's political detainees reveal patterns of physical attacks, threats, intimidation, and discrimination that were so mundane, banal, and similar, that they can only have occurred repeatedly literally *ad infinitum*, hundreds of thousands, even millions, of times over the course of two decades. Consequently, public and private spaces – particularly the iconic spaces of public life (e.g., the bar or the piazza) – were transformed into sites of fear and intimidation.[13] State policies established parameters for coercive action wherever there were highly charged spaces of social conflict: bars and taverns, piazzas and streets, train stations, trams, courtyards, public dormitories, jails, factories and work sites of manual laborers, and sometimes family homes. Politicized social conflict almost always involved a member of one of Fascism's constituencies (e.g., Fascists and militiamen, white-collar workers, professionals, state employees, and bar and small shop owners) initiating processes that led to the punishment of a member of a vulnerable group (e.g., political suspects, citizens "indifferent" to the regime, and a whole host of "social outsiders," including the poor, the unemployed, alcoholics, ex-convicts, and the mentally ill).[14] Granting citizens coercive power – whether they used it in good political faith or not – created a mechanism that bound many Italians, particularly Fascists, to the regime. Once Fascists and others became accustomed to calling on the state to resolve mundane conflicts in their favor, there was no turning back. Anyone who attained power, wealth, status, satisfaction, or revenge by exercising authoritarianism became heavily and irreversibly invested in the system. Therefore, political confinement, formal proceedings, and imprisonment might have been inflicted on relatively small numbers of people, but political conflict, arrests, interrogations, intimidation, threats, and silent sufferings were quotidian – they were hyperordinary.

The Era of Extraordinary Violence

In addition to exposing the centrality of "ordinary violence" to Fascist rule, this book aspires to position the case of Fascist Italy within the

---

[13] On the significance of the piazza and other public spaces, see Mario Isnenghi, *L'Italia in piazza: I luoghi della vita pubblica dal 1848 ai giorni nostri* (Bologna, 2004).

[14] On "fascist constituencies," see Michael Mann, *Fascists* (Cambridge, 2004), 25–7; Canali, *Le spie*; Mimmo Franzinelli, *I tentacoli dell'Ovra: agenti, collaborator e vittime della polizia politica fascista* (Turin, 1999); and Franzinelli, *Delatori: spie e confidenti anonimi: l'arma segreta del regime fascista* (Milan, 2001).

scholarly literature on political violence and totalitarian terror, fields of study from which the Italian case is too often excluded.[15] In the period after the First World War, European states, Italy first among them, constructed legal and institutional apparatuses for punishing and confining unprecedentedly large numbers of political prisoners.[16] More than a dozen authoritarian regimes established special courts, executive tribunals, secret police, and new institutions of confinement and punishment. Governments segregated these institutions from the regular judicial and prison systems in order to tightly control the prosecution of political crime. In most cases, with the exception of the Soviet Union, these new apparatuses of political repression primarily targeted the Marxist left and its affiliated organizations. Over time, however, many governments introduced increasingly broad definitions of "crimes against the state." Political prison sentences and other sanctions were meted out to people for merely holding Socialist or "antinational" ideas. Introduced in most cases to defend the established capitalist order, these novel practices of mass political repression marked a radical break with

---

[15] In comparative studies of political violence and terror, the absence of the case of Fascist Italy and the undervaluing of the role that repression played in the dictatorship probably owe more to the lack of research by historians of Italy than any predisposition among historians of modern Europe. Nevertheless, Hannah Arendt, in *The Origins of Totalitarianism* (New York, 1994), argued that Fascist Italy was not totalitarian because, she alleged, it lacked a system of mass repression. The study of "denunciatory" regimes usually excludes Fascist Italy; see, e.g., Robert Gellately and Sheila Fitzpatrick, eds., *Accusatory Practices: Denunciation in Modern European History, 1789–1989* (Chicago, 1997). Too often facile generalizations of Fascist Italy are used to underscore the monstrosity of other regimes. In the introduction to *The Black Book of Communism* (Cambridge, MA, 1999), Stephane Courtois dismisses repression under Italian Fascism, noting that in the "1930s Italy had a few hundred political prisoners and several hundred *confinati*, placed under house arrest on the country's coastal islands" (14). Courtois misstates the numbers of political prisoners (a few thousand political prisoners and a few thousand *confinati* would be more accurate) and misrepresents the conditions in which some detainees lived (often in crude, squalid barracks). The introduction to a new comparative volume notes that Italian Fascism "remained largely a concentrated drive to stylize social life that more often than not refrained from cutting into the flesh of its own subjects." See Amir Weiner, "Landscaping the Human Garden," in *Landscaping the Human Garden: Twentieth Century Population Management in a Comparative Framework*, ed. Amir Weiner (Stanford, 2003), 266n46.

[16] On the primacy of Fascist terror as a "model of activist mass politics" that "depended heavily on the formative and coercive use of violence in defiance of conventional rules of political or social conduct," see Aristotle A. Kallis, "Fascism, Violence and Terror," in *Terror: From Tyrannicide to Terrorism*, ed. Brett Bowden and Michael T. Davis (St. Lucia, 2008), 190–204.

nineteenth-century liberal models of constitutional rule and criminal justice.[17]

A few interwar regimes – notably Nazi Germany, the Soviet Union, and, I argue, Fascist Italy – set themselves apart by heavily involving militarized political parties and ordinary citizens in the implementation of coercive policies intended to effect a utopian social transformation. Unlike conservative, military, or monarchical authoritarian regimes, these states – which scholars often compare using "totalitarian" or "fascist" paradigms – sought not to repress mass society but instead to mobilize their populations through propaganda, party-controlled participatory organizations, and police-state terror.[18] Although the utility of the totalitarian model as a comparative tool appears to be waning, connecting the case of Fascist violence to the literature on totalitarian violence – or, specifically, National Socialist and Soviet terror – highlights several important features of the Fascist repressive apparatus.[19] The Mussolini regime's police, party, prisons, and propaganda, together with the real and metaphorical archipelagos described in the preceding text, performed most of the same core functions as the terror apparatuses of the Nazi and Soviet regimes.[20] The police state crushed the political opposition and stifled dissent, and then went on to target "objective enemies" whose behaviors, tendencies, and inherent traits Fascists deemed inimical to the

---

[17] For an excellent overview of interwar institutions of political repression, see Polymeris Voglis, *Becoming a Subject: Political Prisoners during the Greek Civil War* (New York, 2002), 22–30.

[18] The literature on totalitarianism is massive, beginning with the earliest works by Arendt, Jacob Talmon, Carl Friedrich, and Zbigniew Brzezinski, not all of whom considered Italy truly "totalitarian." My point here is not to argue that Mussolini's dictatorship was "totalitarian" (for this argument, see Emilio Gentile, *La via italiana al totalitarianism* [Rome, 2005]) but simply to compare Fascist Italy to National Socialist Germany and the Soviet Union by asking the very useful questions presented by the totalitarian, and also fascist, paradigms. A good comparison of Mussolini's dictatorship with traditional, authoritarian regimes can be found in Stanley Payne, *A History of Fascism, 1914–1945* (Madison, 1995), esp. 3–19. See also Edward Malefakis, "La dictadura de Franco en una perspectiva comparada," in *Franquismo: El juicio de la storia*, ed. José Luis García Delgado (Madrid: Temas de hoy, 2000), 11–68.

[19] See Michael Geyer and Sheila Fitzpatrick, eds., *Beyond Totalitarianism: Stalinism and Nazism Compared* (Cambridge, 2009).

[20] Recent examinations of Fascist repression and violence in comparative perspective include, Sven Reichardt and Armin Nolzen, eds., *Beiträge zur Geschichte des Nationalsozialismus*, vol. 21: *Faschismus in Italien und Deutschland: Studien zu Transfer und Vergleich* (Göttingen: 2005); and Gerhard Besier et al., eds., *Fascism, Communism, and the Consolidation of Democracy* (Berlin, 2006).

regime.[21] The Nazi and Fascist regimes in particular operated in strikingly similar fashions, first "cleansing" the nation of Communists and anti-Fascists, then stepping up their campaigns against ethnic and religious minorities, homosexuals, alcoholics, common criminals, and other categories of enemies and "social outsiders."[22] Upon a few select groups, both regimes imposed suffocating surveillance and control.[23] By persecuting these groups, and spreading fear among others, both aspired to advance their projects of social transformation, forcing people to adapt their behaviors to the expectations of the national government and its ideology. Moreover, in order to penetrate society more deeply, these regimes involved the party, paramilitary organizations – in Italy, the National Fascist Party (PNF) and the Fascist Militia (MVSN) – and ordinary citizens in the implementation of repression and coercion through policing, spying, informing, and other denunciatory practices.[24] Consequently, as in Nazi Germany or the Soviet Union, contending with political repression and state-backed violence constituted a way of life for many people in Fascist Italy. How people acted in public, at work, and even at home were in part conditioned by their understandings of the regime's policies and the ever-present potential for violence and punishment.

Italian Fascists by no means ruled more violently than the National Socialists, the Bolsheviks, or even Franco's Nationalists, all of whom adopted more formalized systems of repression, more clearly defined utopias, and incalculably more brutal strategies of rule.[25] Nevertheless, more so than any of these regimes, violence was central to the ideology and practice of Fascism. The Fascists viewed violence as a vital force capable of bringing about a moral and physical regeneration, or "reclamation"

---

[21] Arendt, *Origins*, 421–6.

[22] Mann, *Fascists*, 2; Robert Gellately, *Backing Hitler: Consent and Coercion in Nazi Germany* (Oxford, 2001); Robert Gellately and Nathan Stoltzfus, eds., *Social Outsiders in Nazi Germany* (Princeton, 2001).

[23] Eric A. Johnson, *Nazi Terror: The Gestapo, Jews, and Ordinary Germans* (New York, 1999); Franzinelli, *I tentacoli*; Giorgio Rochat, *Regime fascista e chiese evangeliche: direttive e articolazioni del controllo e della repressione* (Turin, 1990).

[24] On Germany, see Klaus-Michael Mallmann and Gerhard Paul, eds., *Die Gestapo: Mythos und Realität* (Darmstadt, 1995); Robert Gellately, *The Gestapo and German Society: Enforcing Racial Policy, 1933–1945* (Oxford and New York, 1990); Robert Gellately, "Aspects of Self-Policing in the Third Reich and the German Democratic Republic," *Journal of Modern History* 68 (1996): 931–67. On Italy, see Canali, *Le Spie*; Franzinelli, *Delatori*; Franzinelli, *I tentacoli*.

[25] On Spain, see Michael Richards, *A Time of Silence: Civil War and the Culture of Repression in Franco's Spain, 1936–1945* (Cambridge, 1998).

(*bonifica*), of the organic nation.[26] Violence, for Fascists, was not merely a strategy or technique for achieving political goals, but also a "'positive' formative experience in its own right."[27] In many ways, Fascists compensated for their relative ideological and programmatic vacuity by ascribing immense transformative power to interpersonal and military violence. The biographies of the regime's hierarchs (*gerarchi*) or Ras (bosses) underscore the specificity of Fascist attitudes toward political and military violence. Virtually all of the Ras had orchestrated terror, murdered people in Italy, or committed war crimes abroad.[28] Italo Balbo, the Ras of Ferrara, pioneered the tactics of agrarian *squadrismo* (squad violence): selective murder, beatings, force-feeding of castor oil to political opponents, ritual humiliation, and arson.[29] In the two years before Mussolini became prime minister in 1922, the Ras led squads of Black Shirts, who carried out a campaign of political terror throughout northern Italy that killed several thousand people, wounded tens of thousands, and forced tens of thousands of others to leave their communities or Italy altogether.[30] Fascists murdered prominent political opponents – Giacomo Matteotti most famously – and used interpersonal violence in their everyday lives.[31] Following the consolidation of Mussolini's power and the suppression of *squadrismo*, Fascists were deprived of domestic arenas for large-scale paramilitary violence. However, with the outbreak of war in Ethiopia, most Fascist bosses eagerly rushed to East Africa. Giuseppe Bottai, who held several important ministries under the regime, recalled that Fascists regularly committed small-scale, "bestial" war crimes, and

[26] On the term *bonifica* (reclamation or improvement) and Fascism's overarching social and cultural objectives, see Ruth Ben-Ghiat, *Fascist Modernities: Italy, 1922–45* (Berkeley, 2004).
[27] Kallis, "Fascism, Violence and Terror," 190.
[28] R. J. B. Bosworth, *Mussolini's Italy: Life under the Fascist Dictatorship, 1915–1945* (New York, 2005), 7.
[29] On Balbo's exploits, see Paul Corner, *Fascism in Ferrara, 1915–1925* (London, 1975), esp. 37, 259, 263–6.
[30] Sven Reichardt, *Faschistische Kampfbünde: Gewalt und Gemeinschaft im italienischen Squadrismus und der deutschen SA* (Cologne, 2002); Angelo Tasca, *The Rise of Italian Fascism*, trans. Peter and Dorothy Wait (New York, 1965), originally published in French in 1938; Mimmo Franzinelli, *Squadristi* (Milan, 2003); Adrian Lyttelton, "Fascism and Violence in Postwar Italy: Political Strategy and Social Conflict" and Jens Petersen, "Violence in Italian Fascism, 1919–1925," both in *Social Protest, Violence and Terror in 19th and 20th Century Europe*, ed. W. Mommsen and G. Hirschfeld (New York, 1982). On anti-Fascist exiles, see Aldo Garosci, *Storia dei fuorusciti* (Bari, 1953).
[31] See Paolo Nello, *Dino Grandi: La formazione di un leader fascista* (Bologna, 1987), 126; Harry Fornari, *Mussolini's Gadfly: Roberto Farinacci* (Nashville, 1971), 18–19; and Bosworth, *Mussolini's Italy*, 126–8.

that, "naturally, even if one did not speak about them, everyone gossiped about them."[32] For Ras and rank-and-file Fascists alike, squad violence, political violence, and military violence were inextricably linked and had forged their very identities as Fascists.[33] For Bottai, Fascism provided the opportunity to profit from his desire, awakened by the Great War, "to live war in the depth of [his] consciousness." Bottai recalled, "war, this fact dominated my life after 1914. Twenty years and more of life inside war."[34]

Despite the special valence of violence for Fascists, several factors imposed restraint, at least domestically, relative to other interwar regimes. Fascism harbored no ideological or programmatic imperative to kill its own citizens. In Germany and the Soviet Union, the guiding political ideologies, extreme in their utopianism, explicitly demanded the liquidation of entire groups of people.[35] Even in Spain, the Franco regime displayed a powerful, singular determination to extirpate the "anti-Spain."[36] Mussolini's "revolution" also brought no changes to the class structure and did not effectively break down the parochialisms of Italian society, in part because Mussolini eventually tempered repressive violence, most notably by suppressing *squadrismo*. Moreover, Italy did not experience a true civil war, which certainly contributed to the escalation of killing in Russia and Spain. Finally, Moscow, and later Berlin, presided over vast, land-based empires, in which most populations viewed the Germans and the Soviets as hostile, occupying powers.[37] These immense spaces, far removed from the *metropole* and populated by ethnic "others," created fields of operation without moral limits.[38]

It should be noted, however, that when Fascist Italy acted outside of its borders – for example, in Libya, Ethiopia, Yugoslavia, and Greece – the military committed horrible, genocidal atrocities, fueled in part by

---

[32] E.g., Giuseppe Bottai alleged that Achille Starace, the *squadrist* leader who served as the Fascist Party secretary for most of the 1930s, when summarily executing prisoners of war in Ethiopia, shot his victims in the testicles first so that they might suffer more. Bottai, *Diario, 1935–1944* (Milan, 1982), 102.

[33] Reichardt, *Faschistische Kampfbünde*, esp. 696.

[34] Quoted in Alexander De Grand, "Mussolini's Follies: Fascism in Its Imperial and Racist Phase, 1935–1940," *Contemporary European History* 13:2 (2004): 137; Bottai, *Diario*, entry for December 4, 1935, 62.

[35] Michael Burleigh and Wolfgang Wippermann, *The Racial State: Germany 1933–1945* (Cambridge, 2007).

[36] Richards, *Time of Silence*.

[37] See Mark Mazower, *Hitler's Empire: How the Nazis Ruled Europe* (New York, 2008), and Peter Holquist, *Making War, Forging Revolution: Russia's Continuum of Crisis, 1914–1921* (Cambridge, MA, 2002).

[38] See Geyer and Fitzpatrick, *Beyond Totalitarianism*.

Fascism's propensity for deploying violence gratuitously.[39] In the colonies and at war, Fascists thus found their own spaces free from institutional or ethical constraints.[40] In a similar environment, precipitated by the collapse of the Fascist regime and the German occupation of northern Italy between 1943 and 1945, die-hard Fascists resurrected *squadrist* tactics against the anti-Fascist resistance and Jews. These atrocities – committed by the regime, its military, and individual Fascists – were extreme and illegal, even by the standards of the day. All told, the Fascist regime's seizure of power, repression, and wars left a "body count" of an estimated one million dead.[41] However, these acts of extraordinary violence occurred largely on the periphery, temporally and geographically removed from the Fascist regime that ruled the Italian peninsula and its people between 1922 and 1943. In the view of a great many scholars, Italy under Mussolini was a more or less "normal" police state that often governed with the consent of its citizens.[42] Not since the 1920s has a book on Mussolini's Italy featured the term *terror*.[43] Challenging this view, this study exposes the Mussolini regime's mechanisms of mass repression and positions them within the historical continuum of Fascist violence.

Mussolini's Italy

The political and social realities of early-twentieth-century Italy shaped the specificity of Fascist repressive violence in many ways. Although

---

[39] The bibliography on war crimes and other atrocities committed by Fascist Italy has grown quite large, although there are few works in English. Worth noting here are Davide Rodogno, *Fascism's European Empire: Italian Occupation during the Second World War* (Cambridge and New York, 2006); the *Journal of Modern Italian Studies* 9:3 2004, special issue devoted to war crimes and memory; the essays in Costantino di Sante, ed. *I campi di concentramento in Italia* (Milan, 2001); Carlo Spartaco Capogreco, *I campi del Duce: L'Internamento civile nell'Italia fascista, 1940–43* (Turin, 2004); and James Walston, "History and Memory of the Italian Concentration Camps," *The Historical Journal* 40:1 (1997): 169–83. Several general and older works on Italian colonialism are also indispensable: Angelo Del Boca, *Gli italiani in Africa Orientale*, 4 vols. (Rome and Bari, 1976–1984); Angelo Del Boca, *Gli Italiani in Libia*, 2 vols. (Rome: Laterza, 1986–8); and Giorgio Rochat, "La repressione della resistenza in Cirenaica, 1927–1931" and "L'attentato a Graziani e la repressione italiana in Etiopia 1936–1937," both in *Guerra italiane in Libia e in Etiopia. Studi militiari, 1921–1939* (Paese, 1991).
[40] De Grand, "Mussolini's Follies," 127–47.
[41] Bosworth, "Mussolini's Italy," 4.
[42] First and foremost, Renzo De Felice, particularly in *Mussolini il fascista*, vol 2: *L'organizzazione dello Stato fascista, 1925–1929* (Turin, 1968); *Mussolini il duce: Gli anni del consenso, 1929–1936* (Turin, 1974); and *Mussolini il duce*, vol. 2: *Lo Stato Totalitario, 1936–40* (Turin, 1981).
[43] Gaetano Salvemini, *La Terreur Fasciste, 1922–1926* (Paris, 1930).

Mussolini vocally championed the "virtue" (*morale*) and "supreme morality" (*alta moralità*) of political violence, he also repeatedly insisted that any Fascist actions resembling real political "terror" would be counterproductive, eroding the support his regime received from powerful state institutions (e.g., the monarchy, military, bureaucracy, and police), political elites, the middle classes, landowners, industrialists, and the church.[44] Additionally, the Fascist Ras were never wholly loyal to Mussolini, and the regime spent its formative years (particularly 1925–6) defeating rebellious, "intransigent" Fascists who wanted to perpetuate the golden era of *squadrist* criminality. Therefore, in his battle to consolidate his dictatorship, Mussolini stripped provincial Fascists of their prerogative to kill, assault, and terrorize enemies. The state, and not the party, became the final arbiter of how illegal and institutionalized violence was deployed. Mussolini regularly insisted that police and Fascists submit to his strategy of selective, "surgical violence," killing or imprisoning truly dangerous enemies, while employing other diffuse strategies of low-level repression in order to produce conformity among the general population. Mussolini did not eschew illegality, but he manufactured a great deal of ambiguity surrounding Fascist terror by harshly punishing Fascist violence that he did not control. The Italians, he claimed, needed to be "chloroformed." When awoken from their black sleep, he hoped, they would find an Italy without opposition, firmly in control of a self-proclaimed "totalitarian" state.[45]

Local contexts also significantly helped determine the scope and nature of repression. Provincial police officials, for example, operated with different understandings of which measures would best consolidate the regime's power and advance its policies. Mussolini's police chief, Arturo Bocchini, regularly inquired about the "impression" that a sanction, or a political pardon, would make on a given community. The regime might inflict a harsh sentence in order to send a message to one community, but somewhere else it might pass a light sentence or grant a pardon in deference to local opinion. Oftentimes Italian communities demanded that certain individuals, groups, or behaviors be punished, and the regime complied. Fascist coercion thus often acted upon preexisting prejudices and hatreds, largely to win public support for the regime.[46]

---

44 See, e.g., Benito Mussolini, *Opera Omnia*, 36 vols. [hereafter OO], ed. Edoardo e Duilio Susmel (Firenze, 1951–63), XIII:64–6; XXI:358; XVII:67–8; XVI:271; XI:8–9.

45 De Felice, *Mussolini il fascista*, II:671.

46 George Mosse, "Toward a General Theory of Fascism," in *The Fascist Revolution: Toward a General Theory of Fascism*, ed. George Mosse (New York, 1993), 20–2.

Mussolini's strategy of "surgical violence," his fretfulness about powerful institutions and social structures, and the parochial nature of Italian society, all led to the emergence of a highly personalized, case-by-case administration of punishments and pardons. Unlike their counterparts in Nazi Germany or the Soviet Union, the Fascist police personnel did not reduce individuals to numbers or view communities as abstract "populations." Even at the very top, Mussolini presided over the Fascist repressive apparatus with an astonishing degree of personal attention. Provincial police collected voluminous dossiers on absolutely insignificant political detainees, the contents of which were regularly perused and commented on by the dictator and his police chief. Mussolini met with Bocchini virtually every day to discuss public order and the cases of individual prisoners and detainees. When face-to-face conversation was not possible, Mussolini often had the Interior Ministry send over recent police reports and personal files by courier to his office at Palazzo Venezia or his residence at Villa Torlonia.[47] Similar practices in Nazi Germany or the Soviet Union were unknown. The idea of Hitler and Himmler, or Stalin and Ezhov, regularly conferring about whether joke-telling drunks or neighborhood rabble-rousers should be sentenced to three or five years is unthinkable. The personalized, carefully calibrated deployment of state violence was thus a central feature of Fascist repression, setting the regime apart from its Nazi and Soviet counterparts.

Mussolini intended this repressive strategy to assist in the "Fascis tization" of the Italian people. Reading the files of political detainees, Mussolini confirmed his own diagnosis of the failings and foibles of his people.[48] The Italians were, at turns, cowardly, rebellious, disorganized, and buffoonish. "The Italian race is a race of sheep," he once told his foreign minister, Galeazzo Ciano.[49] "You need to keep them lined up and in uniform from morning until night. And then they need *bastone, bastone, bastone* [the club, the club, the club]."[50] At a very minimum, Mussolini hoped to use social discipline to force the Italian masses to "adhere to the state" – in essence, he wanted to "make Italians" – something in his view

---

[47] All decisions regarding political detainees were subject to Mussolini's approval, and his handwriting can be found throughout the files of detainees. See Carmine Senise, *Quando ero Capo della Polizia, 1940–1943* (Rome, 1946), 88–90.

[48] For a short but useful discussion of Mussolini's view of the Italians, see Emilio Gentile, "'Un gregge di rammolliti': Come Mussolini giudicava gli italiani e in che modo pensava di trasformarli," *Il Sole 24 Ore*, October 31, 2004, 4.

[49] Galeazzo Ciano, *Diario, 1937–1943* (Milan, 2006), entry for January 29, 1940, 391.

[50] Ibid., entry for February 7, 1940, 394.

that sixty years of liberal rule had failed to accomplish.[51] Understood in a more ideological or "Fascist" sense, the purpose of the dictator's involvement in the work of political repression was not necessarily just to eliminate a few hated groups or behaviors but also to use state force to reclaim (*bonificare*) or transform the "race." Mussolini, Fascists, jurists, and state officials consistently presented coercive discipline as an essential strategy for changing the habits and character of the Italian people.[52] In the late 1930s, according to Ciano, a frustrated Mussolini contemplated even "harsher [repressive] methods" so that Fascism would "place its mark on the way of life of the Italians, who must learn to be less 'sympathetic', to become hard, implacable, hateful, i.e. masters."[53] On perhaps no other issue was Mussolini so consistent: violence, inflicted *by* and *upon* his people, would transform the Italians from a bunch of undisciplined, chattering "mandolin players" into fearsome, conquering warriors.[54] Mussolini thus meant institutional repression – together with face-to-face violence and war making – to whip the Italians into shape, preparing them for the Darwinian struggle between nations.

The proper functioning of Mussolini's apparatus of political repression required enemies. In the early years of full-blown dictatorship, roughly 1926 to 1934, the dictatorship heavily targeted clandestine anti-Fascist movements and the working-class communities that supported them. In areas with ethnic minorities – particularly Venezia Giulia, with its large Slavic population – state agencies engaged in a thoroughgoing process of "Italianization," a violent policy of cultural denationalization.[55] By the late 1920s, though on a very small scale, it was also already evident that Mussolini was using explicitly "political" repression as a flexible tool for communicating bans on a wide array of behaviors, not just organized anti-Fascism. For example, abortion was illegal in liberal Italy, but under Fascism it became a political offense, a crime against the state, because it sabotaged Mussolini's demographic policy, the so-called Battle of the Births.[56] Police sentenced suspected abortionists to

---

[51] Victoria De Grazia, *The Culture of Consent: Mass Organization of Leisure in Fascist Italy* (Cambridge, 2002), 1–23.

[52] This point is taken up in ch. 2.

[53] See Galeazzo Ciano, *Diary, 1937–1943*, trans. Robert L. Miller and Umberto Coletti-Perucca (New York: Enigma, 1980), 107.

[54] See Franklin Hugh Adler, "Why Mussolini Turned on the Jews," *Patterns of Prejudice* 39:3 (2005): 285–300.

[55] Stefano Bartolini, *Fascismo antislavo: il tentativo di bonifica etnica al confine nord orientale* (Pistoia, 2008).

[56] On demographic policy, see Carl Ipsen, *Dictating Demography: The Problem of Population in Fascist Italy* (Cambridge, 1996).

"political" confinement, and Italians understood the added significance. Finally, although the apparatus of explicitly "political" repression primarily operated in areas from Rome northward during this period, the south of Italy was not exempt from authoritarian, sometimes draconian, police measures. Bolstering the dictatorship's image as a regime of public order, the police applied their new powers virtually everywhere (particularly in the south), all of the time, in order to harass, arrest, detain, and sanction various categories of "social outsiders," including vagabonds, drunks, "habitual criminals," pimps, loan sharks, homosexuals, drug dealers, child molesters, and the mentally ill. As one Communist put it, it was "open season" on these types of suspects; the police arrested them, and they never saw the inside of a court room.[57] With the onset of the Great Depression, police measures became even more important for suppressing popular unrest, economic protest, and the rise in criminality brought on by unemployment.[58] In Sicily, meanwhile, the state conducted a campaign against the *mafia* with a harshness and brutality perhaps unsurpassed in the history of Fascist domestic repression.[59]

By the early 1930s, the focus of Mussolini's repressive apparatus turned away from clandestine militancy and toward the mass of "ordinary" Italians. From 1935 onward, the regime prohibited a growing number of "political" activities, opinions, and behaviors. This dilation of the category of "political" crime coincided with several important developments. Having rooted out the forces of anti Fascism, imposed his authority on the PNF, and weathered several successive economic crises, Mussolini could now pursue the Fascist project of national renovation. State and party agencies would work toward the creation of a disciplined, hierarchical, militaristic society, obedient to a Duce who was, by his own admission, "always right." The regime's efforts to realize this project included the expansion and wider diffusion of the PNF and its organizations, involvement in foreign and colonial wars (e.g., Ethiopia, Spain, and Albania), the pursuit of an increasingly closer alliance with Nazi Germany, and the adoption of anti-Semitic race laws. These policies signaled a radical – even totalitarian, some historians argue – turn in the history of Mussolini's regime.[60]

---

[57] Altiero Spinelli, *Il lungo monologo* (Rome, 1968), 70.

[58] On social and political unrest during the Great Depression, see Marinella Chiodo, ed., *Geografia e forme del dissenso sociale in Italia durante il fascismo 1928–1934* (Cosenza, 1990).

[59] Salvatore Lupo, *Storia della mafia: dalle origini ai nostri giorni* (Rome, 1993), 203–25.

[60] De Felice, *Mussolini il Duce*, II:8, 82–90; Payne, *History of Fascism*, 212–44.

From 1935 onward, throughout the peninsula, political repression and politicized social conflict thus permeated broader segments of the Italian population. Whether in Milan or Messina, Como or Cosenza, an Italian who insulted Mussolini, criticized the invasion of Ethiopia, blamed the regime for unemployment, bemoaned the alliance with Nazi Germany, or engaged in any type of perceived "antinational" activity, might be beaten, arrested, interrogated, imprisoned, or confined. In the economic sphere, merchants and vendors who violated the regime's autarchic policies, introduced in response to the League of Nations sanctions, were investigated by the secret political police, the OVRA, and sentenced to political confinement. Some important regional differences persisted. In the northeast, ordinary (ethnic) Germans and Slavs were particularly vulnerable to political sanctions and spontaneous assaults. In the south, the regime punished individuals held responsible for *beghismo*, the factional feuding that so hampered local administration in small communities. In Rome and a few other provinces, the regime inflicted a wide array of political sanctions on small populations of Jehovah's Witnesses and Pentecostals.[61] Police chiefs persecuted homosexual men, particularly in cities with visible gay communities, such as Venice, Florence, and Catania (Sicily).[62] After the founding of the Fascist empire and the introduction of the racial laws, state authorities in Rome and Naples inflicted political sanctions on the few Italian women who had romantic or sexual relationships with African men from the colonies.[63] For the regime, all of these (and other) very diverse behaviors constituted threats to the state and nation. Within the context of war, foreign conquest, and empire, the regime deployed repression in order to advance its project of creating a disciplined, homogenous society, and imposing upon it a uniform national political culture.

Violence and Nation Building

As with all twentieth-century political utopias, the Fascist project of forging a militaristic, imperial society failed spectacularly. Notwithstanding, the regime had mixed results with its more modest aspirations to

---

[61] Rochat, *Regime fascista e chiese evangeliche.*

[62] On the persecution of homosexual men, see Lorenzo Benadusi, *Il nemico dell'uomo nuovo: l'omossesualità nell'esperimento totalitario fascista* (Milan, 2005).

[63] Gianluca Gabrielli, "Africani in Italia negli anni del razzismo di stato," in *Nel nome della razza: Il razzismo nella storia d'Italia, 1870–1945*, ed. Alberto Burgio (Bolgna, 1999), 201–12.

strengthen the central state apparatus, overwhelm local and regional parochialisms, homogenize the nation, and force the masses to "adhere to the state." In many ways, the regime failed to impose policies uniformly upon the provinces because Fascist rule so resembled the corrupt, clientelistic, parochial governmental system it intended to replace.[64] Although Fascists throughout Italy no doubt shared a few broad views – antiparliamentarianism, disdain for liberal-era political and social elites, and exaltation of the combat experience (*combattentismo*) – they primarily operated in discrete contexts.[65] The Ras developed their power bases by weighing in on local political and social conflicts, constructing loyal followings and clientele networks along the way. Under Fascist rule, although the state was vastly more centralized than it had ever been, one set of local or regional interest groups was replaced by another, albeit a new or reconfigured one. Whether "new men" or old elites, local power brokers still viewed politics as a means of advancing personal interests and managed to pursue goals that were often different from or at odds with those of the Fascist regime. To a much greater extent than Nazi Germany or the Soviet Union, the local, the factional, and personal self-interest were at the heart of Fascist politics.[66]

To say that Mussolini's project of fostering national cohesion and homogeneity through authoritarian centralization failed does not deny the profound and often uniform impact that Fascism had on ordinary people throughout Italy. For many decades, the debate over how Fascism affected the Italians centered on whether most people supported or resisted the regime. Scholarship has recently begun to move beyond this debate, without necessarily resolving the question. My own view is simply that some Italians, often (but not always) the most powerful, supported the regime and benefited from it at the expense of those Italians whose rights were suppressed, whose lives were filled with frustration and fear, and whose support the regime never won. By appearing to solve certain problems of Italian modernity, and engaging in wars of conquest, the regime drew larger numbers of Italians into the Fascist fold, but it alienated others as well. Ideologically and institutionally, the Fascist system of rule functioned and persisted precisely because there were categories, sometimes vague, of "winners" and "losers." From its

[64] Paul Corner, "Everyday Fascism in the 1930s: Centre and Periphery in the Decline of Mussolini's Dictatorship," *Contemporary European History* 15 (2006): 221.

[65] Salvatore Lupo, *Il fascismo: la politica in un regime totalitario* (Rome, 2000), 171–84.

[66] Corner, "Everyday Fascism," 200.

origins, Fascism defined and redefined *nation* and *antination*, repeatedly pitting one against the other. As the regime's ideologically driven policies proliferated and radicalized, so did the surveillance and punishment of political suspects and enemies. The most extreme manifestation of the Mussolini regime's using strategies of negative integration to galvanize the nation was the anti-Semitic racial laws of 1938.[67] The Italian Jews were the first group under Fascism to be completely stripped of their citizenship and rights in anticipation of some final separation from the Italian population.[68]

This much too schematic model (nation/antination) ignores that most people do not simply support or oppose – inflict or be victimized by – a given political and social reality. Such a stark view of life under Fascism does not take into account the effects the regime's policies had on mentalities and behaviors that did not necessarily fit neatly into a dichotomy between empowered "winners" and victimized "losers." Vulnerable or subaltern groups sometimes used state violence to resolve conflicts in their own favor, though other guiltless bystanders (e.g., spouses, children, and elderly parents) almost always suffered. Victims could be perpetrators, just as Fascist bosses regularly fell victim to interparty campaigns of character assassination and personal destruction.[69] Finally, the pressure to conform, rendered acute by the threat of punishment and discrimination, affected how people raised their children, spent their leisure time, and conducted other, often mundane aspects of their daily lives. Whether they suffered, prospered, or just got by, most Italians had to adapt to Fascism.

The interactions between the Fascist police and Italian society described in this book show the extent to which Mussolini's regime forcibly injected the state, politics, and ordinary violence into everyday life. Italians who previously – in the liberal era – did not feel particularly "Italian," and might never have dreamed of seeing the inside of a jail cell, were persecuted by the state because they had transgressed

---

[67] Lupo, *Il fascismo*, 425.

[68] See Liliana Picciotto Fargion's excellent *Il libro della memoria: Gli ebreideportati dall'Italia, 1943–1945* (Milan, 1991); in English, see her "The Persecution of Jews in Italy, 1943–1945: A Chronicle of Events," in *The Jews of Italy: Memory and Identity*, ed. Bernard D. Cooperman and Barbara Garvin (Bethesda, 2000), 443–54.

[69] The best treatment of factional fighting within the Fascist state is Lupo, *Il fascismo*; in English, see Corner, "Everyday Fascism."

an unwritten code of "political" conduct. For many Italians, particularly those belonging to vulnerable social or political groups, locating the ever-fluid parameters of acceptable, as well as obligatory, political and social behavior became critical. Failing to do so was to court trouble, even disaster. Once the authorities acted against an individual, he or she then had to figure out how to mitigate the effects. Financially and materially dependent on the Fascist regime, detainees had to formulate appeals, request subsidies, seek permissions for family visits, obtain authorizations for medical care, and, most importantly, win their freedom. Usually deprived of a breadwinner, families now had to solicit assistance from the state, extended family, and friends. In particular, because most detainees were men, Fascism drew women into the public sphere of politics and propaganda by forcing them to pursue constant interaction with state officials. Wives and mothers sought audiences with local officials and wrote letters directly to Rome. Saying the right thing in an appeal to Mussolini or another powerful figure could yield a cash handout to pay the rent, thereby staving off eviction. Likewise, assistance from the party-run welfare agencies (*Ente opere assistenziali* [EOA]) or another charitable institution might mean the difference between putting food on the table and going hungry.

In their appeals to Mussolini and other state officials, poor, ordinary Italians demonstrated strategies, practiced by millions of Italians, for surviving or thriving under Fascism. In particular, Italians who had conformed to Fascism revealed their expectation that they should have been exempted from political sanctions. Although it did not provide absolute immunity, superficial conformity could constitute real political and social capital. Welfare, jobs, cash handouts, pardons, and other forms of patronage and clemency went to Italians who had fought in the Great War, joined the party (the earlier the better!), enrolled their children in the youth organizations, and attended political parades and patriotic celebrations. When police made any decision regarding a political detainee, they took into account these positive factors as well as other negative "moral" failings (e.g., alcoholism, poor work ethic, criminal behavior, homelessness, the abandonment of one's family, and loose sexual morals).

However superficially, then, the Fascist state advanced a project of "nationalizing the masses." The police state repressed resistance and certain manifestations of social, religious, or ethnic heterogeneity. It then developed a uniform national political culture, which it attempted to impose on the Italian people through the party, its ancillary organizations, and propaganda. Though this project largely failed to create a population that would, as the slogan went, "believe, obey, fight," the regime's repressive rule disseminated fear, promoted conformity, and deeply affected the lives of ordinary Italians. Behind every decision to join the party, enroll one's children in the youth organizations, extol the Duce, praise the military, or otherwise display signs of "devotion" to the *patria* and the regime, laid the hope of protecting oneself from persecution, getting ahead, or shoring up one's already formidable social position. After two decades of thinking and acting this way, the masses certainly felt more "Italian" than they did in 1922, but they did not all necessarily think this was a good thing. Many still felt alienated from the state, precisely because the Fascists had imposed this "national identity" on them through two decades of divisive ordinary violence.

   Much of this study draws its evidence from the personal files of the Fascist regime's political detainees (*confinati politici*). These files were a depository, or clearinghouse, for all types of documents, often copies of originals generated by people and institutions inside and outside of the police bureaucracy, including prefects, central Interior Ministry officials, police officials of all ranks, *carabinieri*, medical doctors, party officials, detainees, family members, ordinary citizens, clergy, business owners, and the employees of many state agencies and ministries. Therefore, although relying so heavily on one set of files might appear to provide a too narrow archival base, these sources offer broad temporal, geographical, and social perspectives and thus warranted a lengthy and close reading. I spent one year carrying out a systematic sample (functionally similar to a simple random sample) that represented close to 4 percent of the entire series of approximately fifteen thousand detainee files – an enormous task, involving the close examination of 549 dossiers, some of which contained hundreds of documents, many handwritten.[70] Additionally, I looked at hundreds of other files in order to broaden my perspective on the experience of particular groups (e.g., midwives, homosexuals, Jehovah's Witnesses, and Pentecostals). The sample, which I organized in a large database, reveals how political repression changed over time, how it varied from place to place, whom it affected, and how it affected them. So, for example, a simple statement, such as "two-thirds of detainees with dependent families suffered serious economic deprivations," is supported by several dozen or even hundreds of hours of archival work, even if the

---

[70] For a description of the sample, see n. 9 in the preceding text.

discussion only offers two or three illustrative examples, citing just a few documents. In sum, although the book draws on several other important archival series, only the deep and systematic mining of the archive of the *confinati politici* revealed the ubiquity and insidiousness of "ordinary violence." Due to the recent curtailing of operational hours and the number of boxes one can request (per day) at Italy's State Central Archive, a study similar to this one probably could not be executed today, at least not by a foreign scholar with "only" a couple of years to do archival work.

Through the documentation largely associated with one institution (*confino di polizia*), this book narrates the history of a system of rule that enabled the few to control the many. The chapters that follow examine how this system worked, and to what end, across a span of almost two decades; as Fascist policies changed, repression and violence became more, not less, important. Chapter 1 describes the squad violence that brought Mussolini to power and explains how it shaped the regime's highly selective, localized, and personalized economy of violence. Chapter 2 discusses the main institutions of Fascist political repression, established in 1926, which subjugated individual rights to the priorities of the state and carved out the "gray zone" within which state officials and party members acted illegally. Chapter 3 examines the regime's campaign to suppress anti-Fascist resistance, the Italian Communist Party in particular, and the suffering and deprivations it inflicted on detainees, their families, and their communities. Chapter 4 offers a synoptic history of the island confinement colonies and sites of mainland exile, revealing a highly variegated detainee population subjected to a wide array of coercive regimes. In general, the system adjusted the conditions of confinement according to a given detainee's social class. Chapter 5 explores how Mussolini granted individual pardons and general amnesties in order to corroborate his claims about waning opposition and national reconciliation. In reality, though, pardons and clemency constituted forms of coercion because Mussolini granted or denied them based on very subjective evaluations of whether detainees had demonstrated evidence of "rehabilitation." Chapter 6 reconstructs the changing nature of "political" crime during the 1930s, showing how the regime subjected wider swaths of Italian society and also select groups to scrutiny and punishment. Chapter 7 describes how Fascist Party members and militiamen extended the regime's repressive policies further into the public and private spheres through practices that included formal patrols of urban neighborhoods, spontaneous assaults and denunciations, and discrimination in the distribution of welfare and public works employment. Chapter 8 similarly describes how Italians used their knowledge of the politics of ordinary Fascist violence either to punish others or to defend themselves against denunciations and politicized attacks.

I

Squad Violence

The Fascists devote themselves to manhunts, and not a day goes by in which they do not chase, confront, beat, and abuse those who belong to the socialist organizations.... And then there is no end to their breaking into homes, destroying furniture, documents, and objects, lighting fires, shooting into houses at night, [and] patrolling in armed groups; and all this in order to keep in a perpetual state of intimidation people who truly, in some places, are so traumatized and frightened, one could even say terrorized, that they completely avoid public places and never leave their homes.

Police Inspector, Province of Rovigo (April 1921)[1]

During the Fascist takeover, many Italians lived in a state of terror. Black-shirted *squadrists* beat, shot, ritually humiliated, and destroyed the property of peasants, workers, politicians, journalists, and labor organizers. Although Socialists and the working classes were the primary victims, the Fascists also targeted Catholics, liberals, Masons, state authorities, and even dissident Fascists. This unprecedented campaign of political violence, most intense during the years between 1920 and 1922, culminated with the March on Rome and the appointment of Benito Mussolini as prime minister. Thereafter, Fascist squads continued to perpetrate illegal violence, often with impunity, though with less frequency and intensity, enabling Mussolini to establish a full-blown dictatorship by 1926.

The experience of *squadrismo*, many scholars have shown, shaped the Fascist ideology, established the Fascist political "style," produced

[1] Guido Crainz, *Padania: il mondo dei braccianti dall'Ottocento alla fuga dalle campagne* (Rome, 2007), 188.

martyrs, and bequeathed a revolutionary mythology.[2] According to Sven
Reichardt, the violence of these years became central to Fascists' very
identity.[3] In practical terms, *squadrist* terror served to deny political
power to recently enfranchised groups, suppress industrial and agricultural wages, and impose labor contracts favorable to landowners and
industrialists. This pact among Mussolini's movement, Italian economic
elites, and the middle classes formed the bedrock upon which Mussolini
founded his regime. Not surprisingly, Fascists attached tremendous significance to the war they had waged on Italy's "internal enemies." They
interpreted *squadrist* violence as a creative, regenerative act that tran-
scended class. Their "punitive expeditions" were patriotic, cleansing, and,
like warfare, glorious. The destruction of working-class institutions and
ultimately the liberal state thus constituted Fascism's formative moment,
when violent action produced ideology and, in turn, belief. To maintain
its power, the regime had to continue to suppress the wages, rights, and
voice of the lower classes. To uphold their convictions, the Fascists could
never forget the initial violent struggle nor relinquish their duty to identify
and punish new enemies. To do so would be to deprive their movement
of meaning and purpose. For Fascists, the subjugation of enemies constituted a reaffirmation of the totalitarian project of remaking the Italian
nation.

Between 1920 and 1926, Mussolini clashed with the "intransigent"
wing of his party over the use of violence. For Fascist extremists,
autonomous squad violence should continue indefinitely, unabated, without interference from the state. Once in power, these radicals insisted, the
National Fascist Party (PNF), rather than the Interior Ministry, should
establish a "real revolutionary committee" that would "finally realize,
against all comers, the will of fascism."[4] By contrast, Mussolini and PNF
moderates wanted to "normalize" the dictatorship by quashing the spas-
modic, illegal activities of the squads and using state agencies to implement carefully calibrated, "surgical" violence, whether institutional or
illegal. Mussolini's formulation of the Fascist utopia – everything within

[2] The most thorough treatment of squad violence is Sven Reichardt's *Faschistische
Kampfbünde*. See also Petersen, "Violence in Italian Fascism," 278–9; Emilio Gentile,
Storia del partito fascista, 1919–1922: movimento e milizia (Bari, 1989); and Roberta
Suzzi Valli, "The Myth of Squadrismo in the Fascist Regime," *Journal of Contemporary
History* 35:2 (2000): 131–50.
[3] Reichardt, *Faschistische Kampfbünde*, 696.
[4] Quoted in Adrian Lyttelton, "Fascism in Italy: The Second Wave," *Journal of Contem-
porary History* 1:1 (1966): 96.

the state, nothing outside the state, nothing against the state – thus also applied to the deployment of political violence and repression. Yet, at the same time, for Mussolini, the Fascist Party and militia should both serve as revolutionary corps – one civilian, the other military – at the service of the Fascist state. Thus, when Mussolini finally suppressed the intransigent strain of Fascism during 1925 and 1926, he did not completely shut the party out of the work of identifying and punishing enemies of the Fascist order. Out of this clash between *squadrist* and statist conceptions of violence came a uniquely Fascist economy of violence that would preserve the regime's political power for nearly two decades.

Squadrismo (1920–1922)

During the high tide of *squadrismo*, the Fascists mobilized tens, even hundreds, of thousands of Italian men, who carried out thousands of acts of brutal violence within their own communities and neighboring cities, towns, villages, and hamlets. Before this "takeoff" in provincial Fascism, however, the Fascists were initially an urban phenomenon, motivated primarily by nationalism. They desired revenge against Socialists and others who had not supported Italy's participation in the Great War. Even before the war's end, veterans who would later become Fascists were calling for the extirpation of Italy's "internal enemies," whom they held responsible for Italy's crushing defeat at Caporetto.[5] For the leaders of the Arditi, Italy's shock troops, "the enemy was not only German" or Austrian but "also Italian." Veterans had a "divine duty" to "kill the monsters, both external and internal" who had "sabotaged the *patria*."[6] The defeat at Caporetto made clear the existence of an "internal front," and upon demobilization, there would be "a settling of scores," directed at subversives and the bourgeoisie.[7] Two pioneers of Fascist squad violence, the Futurist Filippo Marinetti and the Arditi leader Feruccio Vecchi, distributed a menacing manifesto throughout Milan declaring their determination to "add a few months onto our four years of war." Upon returning from the front in 1917, Roberto Farinacci, the future Fascist Ras of Cremona, insisted that he would now be "equally useful to the *patria* by fighting the enemies within, who are more cowardly than those

---

[5] See Angelo Ventrone, *La seduzione totalitaria: Guerra, modernità, violenza politica, 1914–1918* (Rome, 2003), 211–54.

[6] Quoted in Franzinelli, *Squadristi*, 15.

[7] Silvio Maurano, *Quando eravamo sovversivi...* (Como, 1939), 17–18. Quoted in Franzinelli, *Squadristi*, 15–16.

beyond our borders." Toward the end of 1917, Farinacci shouted at a Catholic, neutralist, parliamentary deputy, "German, sell-out, traitor, coward, the Germans have reached the Piave because of you!"[8] Fascist attacks against Socialists, according to Mussolini, were like assaults "on an Austrian trench." He declared, "This is heroism. This is violence. This is the violence of which I approve and which I exalt. This is the violence of Fascism."[9]

From spring 1919 onward, Fascist violence was a limited, urban phenomenon, with its epicenter at Milan, but there were also episodes in other northern cities. Wherever there were Arditi veteran organizations, there was conflict. Arditi, together with other Fascists and Futurists, disrupted speeches, physically attacked left-wingers and Catholics, and provoked altercations with Socialist or anarchist demonstrators. These fights led to serious injuries and even deaths. Because Fascists were commonly armed with daggers, truncheons, revolvers, and even hand grenades, they usually "won" these conflicts. To be sure, Socialists also attacked right-wingers, often without provocation, but the use of lethal, paramilitary force was unique to the Black Shirts. Public-security officials understandably viewed early Fascists as a serious threat to public order, and often arrested them. In Novara, there were about 150 organized Arditi who regularly sacked the offices of elected Socialists and provoked other violent clashes. Novara's prefect, Carlo Olivieri, later himself a Fascist sympathizer, asked Rome for authorization to remove the Arditi from his province, due to the population's general hostility toward them.[10] Early Black Shirts were also well armed. Police raids of the spaces that served as Fascist headquarters, including Mussolini's *Il popolo d'Italia*, yielded revolvers, hand grenades, machine guns, ammunition, and even artillery shells.[11]

In the newly acquired region of Venezia Giulia, the existence of large Slovene and Croat populations gave rise to a virulent Fascist movement, supported by urban middle classes and industrialists, who saw in Fascism an opportunity to advance their class interests and to affirm their own Italianess. The specificity of "border Fascism" was made clear by Mussolini in his visit to Venezia Giulia in 1920. The task facing the Fascists there was, for Mussolini, "more delicate, more sacred, more difficult, more

---

[8] Quoted in Lupo, *Il fascismo*, 81.

[9] Mussolini, *OO*, XIII:64–6.

[10] Franzinelli, *Squadristi*, 17–19.

[11] Ibid., 29; Reichardt, *Faschistische Kampfbünde*, 82–3.

necessary, the most necessary." In their dealings with Slavs, an "inferior and barbarous race," the Italians would have to rely on "the club."[12] In Trieste, the other main urban center of Fascist violence aside from Milan, Black Shirts launched attacks on the political and cultural organizations of Slavic nationalists and Socialists in the spring of 1920. Led by Francesco Giunta, Fascists burned down the Hotel Balkan, the seat of the main Slavic cultural association. The campaign against "Slavophiles" then radiated out into the provincial areas of Venezia Giulia. Within months, Social- ist headquarters, labor exchanges, and cultural organizations, all with predominantly Slavic membership, were virtually eradicated.[13] Julian Fascists then began a campaign of Italianization that would later become state policy. In some areas, the Fascists banned the use of Croat and Slove- nian languages, in official settings and in the public sphere. The squads even attacked priests who continued to give sermons in Slavic languages or otherwise acted as rallying points for Slavic resistance to Italianization.[14] Early on, border Fascists came to constitute a sort of lobby within Ital- ian Fascism. In 1921, 20 percent of Fascists came from just two (out of 71) Italian provinces, Trieste and Udine,[15] and many of the regime's leading figures came from the region.[16] Moreover, for years to come, anti- Slavism would continue to mobilize support for the regime, particularly among the middle classes, and hold together the often-fractious coalition that made up the Fascist movement in Venezia Giulia. The eradication of *slavo-communismo* (a Fascist neologism) bound Fascists and other Italians together in common purpose.[17]

Although causing considerable consternation among Socialists and state authorities, Mussolini's *fasci di combattimento* initially had few adherents, and squad violence was limited to a small number of urban areas in northern Italy. In the fall of 1920, however, Fascism spread to provinces like Bologna and Ferrara, marking the rise of so-called agrarian

---

[12] Both quoted in Bartolini, *Fascismo antislavo*, 31, 33.

[13] See Elio Apih, *Italia: fascismo e antifascismo nella Venezia Giulia, 1918–1943* (Bari, 1960).

[14] Bartolini, *Fascismo antislavo*, 74–5, 93, 102.

[15] Mann, *Fascists*, 106–7.

[16] Two secretaries of the PNF (Francesco Giunta and Aldo Vidussoni), a minister of justice under the Salò Republic (Piero Pisenti), and Fulvio Suvich (secretary of Foreign Affairs, ambassador to the United States), to name a few. Moreover, many Fascist racists, who grew in prominence after 1938, like Attilio Tamaro, came from Venezia Giulia. Bartolini, *Fascismo antislavo*, 35.

[17] Ibid., 33–4.

Fascism.[18] Within months, the squads dominated communities throughout Emilia Romagna. A year and a half later, much of northern and central
Italy, as well as Puglia in the south, had powerful Fascist movements.

The rise of Fascism in the provinces of the Po Valley occurred in reaction to the remarkable postwar growth of Socialist power. During the
biennio rosso (red two years), between 1918 and 1920, Socialists made
huge electoral gains nationally and locally, while labor unions unleashed
a wave of strikes unprecedented in Italian history. In the Po Valley, the
Socialists established a virtual "state within a state," winning control
of municipal government, labor exchanges, and peasant leagues (unions).
Socialists also founded cooperatives, cultural circles, taverns, and sporting
clubs.[19] Such working-class organizations exercised their power largely
through legal means – elections, boycotts, strikes, and demonstrations –
which nonetheless often led to clashes with police, with injuries and deaths
on both sides. Premeditated, illegal violence was also not unknown. To
prevent strike breaking, self-appointed tribunals decided punishments
and "fines" against peasants who failed to show solidarity with the
leagues.[20] In newspaper articles, pamphlets and speeches, maximalist
Socialists continually called for a Bolshevik-style takeover, though no
such plan existed.[21] Finally, political culture and the social order had
been radically altered, with rough peasants and workers occupying the
halls of power and red flags hanging from town halls. For landowners,
life in this new "red" state meant higher wages, higher taxes, reduced
profits, lost managerial authority, deteriorating private property rights,
and the threat of social revolution. Moreover, displays of red flags, busts
of Marx, and internationalist slogans offended nationalist and patriotic
middle-class sentiments.[22] Conservatives denounced the "red terror" and
"atrocities" of this period, though the landowners and middle classes
were in little real physical danger.[23] They were not physically assaulted,

---

[18] On the rise of agrarian Fascism, see Adrian Lyttelton, *The Seizure of Power: Fascism
   in Italy, 1919–1929*, 2nd ed. (Princeton, 1987); Corner, *Fascism in Ferrara*; Anthony
   Cardoza, *Agrarian Elites and Italian Fascism: The Province of Bologna, 1901–1926*
   (Princeton, 1982); Frank Snowden, *The Fascist Revolution in Tuscany, 1919–1922* (New
   York, 1989); Frank Snowden, *Violence and the Great Estates of Southern Italy: Apulia,
   1900–1922* (Cambridge, 2003); Alice Kelikian, *Town and Country under Fascism: The
   Transformation of Brescia, 1915–1926* (Oxford, 1986).
[19] De Grazia, *Culture of Consent*, 6–10.
[20] Tasca, *Rise of Fascism*, 92.
[21] Ibid., 71–5.
[22] See Corner, *Fascism in Ferrara*, 76–84; and Lyttelton, "Fascism and Violence," 259.
[23] On the overstatement of "red violence," see Reichardt, *Faschistische Kampfbünde*, 70–1.

nor were their homes, offices, or private property damaged or destroyed. Yet, from their perspective, they lived in a world turned upside down. The Socialists had virtually "taken over," and the liberal state appeared to have lost control of law and order. This postwar surge in working-class militancy peaked in 1920. Socialist union membership spiked (the General Confederation of Labor had 2.2 million members in 1921), and thousands of strikes occurred in virtually every area of the economy. In September, the workers of Italy's industrial triangle (Milan, Turin, and Genoa) seized control of their factories, and strikes and occupations spread to other parts of the peninsula.[24]

This seemingly revolutionary situation administered a "psychological shock" to the Italian bourgeoisie.[25] For the landowners, the last straw was the agricultural strike during the spring of 1920. When the government refused to intervene, they turned to the newly formed *fasci* in order to protect their interests and property.[26] Provincial Fascism was born, at least symbolically, in Bologna in the fall of 1920. Leandro Arpinati, the chief of Bolognese *squadrism*, led his Black Shirts in two important episodes of anti-Socialist violence, sacking the Socialist Chamber of Labor on November 4 and then, on November 21, together with Fascists from Ferrara, attacking the Palazzo d'Accursio, the seat of municipal government, upon the occasion of the inauguration of the newly elected Socialist administration. The resulting melee between Fascists and Socialist "Red Guards" was a catastrophe, leading to the deaths of ten people. Though the incident was apparently provoked by Fascists, the enduring result was an association of a Socialist government with violence and disorder. The central government soon suspended Bologna's Socialist administration and established a prefectorial committee to govern the province. The so-called battle of Palazzo D'Accursio had repercussions beyond Bologna. The incident inspired Fascists from Ferrara to provoke a similar clash with Socialists. *Squadrist* assaults on municipal governments and working-class institutions soon flooded Emilia-Romagna, Lombardy, Veneto, Piedmont, Tuscany, and Puglia. By the end of the year, individual punitive expeditions mobilized dozens, even hundreds, of Black Shirts, who coordinated attacks on a provincial and interprovincial level.[27]

[24] See Paolo Spriano, *L'occupazione delle fabbriche* (Turin, 1964).
[25] Tasca, *Rise of Fascism*, 80.
[26] Cardoza, *Agrarian Elites and Italian Fascism*, 294–5.
[27] Ibid., 306–15. On expansion of movement, see Lyttelton, *Seizure of Power*, 42–76.

In the provincial centers, Fascist violence was initially used to break the Socialist hold on local administration and labor organizations. Fascists interrupted meetings, beat elected officials, and made impossible the work of local government. Socialists in particular were intimidated, threatened, and even beaten until they resigned. The consequences for the Socialist Party, which was entirely unprepared to counter organized, paramilitary violence, were disastrous. In the province of Bologna, one of "reddest" provinces in the entire Po Valley, where the Italian Socialist Party (PSI) received almost three-quarters of the vote in 1919, the Fascists demolished the Socialist Party in a matter of months. Between March and May 1921, the squads destroyed dozens of newspapers offices, chambers of labor, peasant leagues, cooperatives, and social clubs.[28] Throughout northern and central Italy, Fascists replicated this feat. Having conquered major provincial centers such as Ferrara, Bologna, and Florence, Fascists spread out into small towns and hamlets. Major cities provided launching points for attacking other cities. Florence, for example, was the staging ground for attacks on Siena and Pisa. Having consolidated power in these places, the squads then moved into more peripheral areas. Newly founded *fasci* were local initiatives, organized by Fascists who understood the life of the place. The leaders were often locals who bore a particular grudge against Socialists, whether economic, political, or personal. When necessary, stronger *fasci* nearby lent paramilitary support. After rooting Socialists out of a community, Fascists commonly held a public ceremony inaugurating the new *fascio*. As Fascism penetrated smaller rural communities, it became a mass movement without precedent in Italian history.

As Adrian Lyttelton has noted, the most immediate and powerfully symbolic form of *squadrist* violence was the annihilation of the offices, institutions, and property of the Socialist Party, "but the 'conquest' of Socialist organizations and municipalities was reinforced and made possible by terror exercised against individuals."[29] Despite the "internationalist" orientation of Socialist ideology, the peasant leagues, cooperatives, labor halls, and social clubs – the entire infrastructure of the Socialist "state" – were intensely parochial institutions, organized around popular, charismatic political and labor leaders.[30] Fascist squads thus practiced highly personal, localized strategies of violence and intimidation,

---

[28] Cardoza, *Agrarian Elites and Italian Fascism*, 340–1.
[29] Lyttelton, "Fascism and Violence," 266.
[30] See Lupo, *Il fascismo*, 68–70.

attacking the most prominent and influential "subversives" within a given province, town, or *comune*. Communists, Socialists, and labor leaders – including workers who enjoyed a certain "ascendancy" among the masses – were the primary targets. Fascists sometimes beat these men, occasionally with homicidal intent, but perhaps more commonly intimidated them until they were forced to leave town, thereby decapitating their organizations. The Fascists published bans on certain individuals returning to their homes.[31] They spent their weekends chasing prominent peasant leaders across the countryside. Thus, life for labor leaders became terror-filled, especially because Fascists did not limit their attacks to the public sphere. Nowhere was safe. Late at night, ten, thirty, or even a hundred Black Shirts, sometimes traveling from neighboring towns, might surround a home, inviting a Socialist, anarchist, or Communist outside to talk. If they refused, the Fascists would enter forcibly or threaten to harm the entire family by lighting the house on fire. Fascists sometimes fired guns indiscriminately or threw hand grenades into homes in order to drive out the inhabitants.[32] In a small community in the province of Bologna, for example, a group of Fascists broke down the door of Emilio Avon, the secretary of the local Socialist Party. Armed with pistols, the Fascists took Avon outside and beat him senseless as his wife and children looked on, giving him fifteen days to leave town, which he did.[33] Although individual working-class leaders might have been willing to live under the constant threat of physical attacks, most were unwilling to subject their families to such danger. Deprived of leadership, meeting places, offices, records, and sympathetic Socialist town councils, the landless peasantry became subject to the landowners' conventional tactics of strike breaking and intimidation. Having broken the leagues, the Fascist then forced the laborers into "politically neutral" (Fascist) syndicates. Vulnerable peasants had little choice but to join. Landowners used their newfound position of power to restore labor relations to the nineteenth-century status quo. Even state prefects were shocked by the extent to which the landowners had been able to restore the worst excesses of capitalist agriculture.[34] Over time, the Fascist squads continued to watch over the peasants to make sure they adhered to the syndicates.[35]

---

[31] Lyttelton, "Fascism and Violence," 267.

[32] On home invasions, see Partito Socialista Italiano, *Inchiesta socialista sulle gesta dei fascisti in Italia* (Milan, 1963), esp. 21–4; see also Franzinelli, *Squadristi*, 73.

[33] See Cardoza, *Agrarian Elites and Italian Fascism*, 348.

[34] Crainz, *Padania*, 184–6.

[35] Cardoza, *Agrarian Elites and Italian Fascism*, 357–63.

In small towns, where everyone knew everyone, Fascists inflicted ritual humiliation on their enemies, a powerful strategy of terror understood by all. Black Shirts forced their opponents to drink castor oil and other purgatives, and then sent them home, wrenching with pain and covered in their own feces. In some cases, squads forced their enemies to defecate on politically symbolic objects – pages of a speech, a manifesto, a red flag, and so on. After administering a castor oil treatment, Fascists sometimes drove prominent anti-Fascist leaders around in lorries in order to reduce them in the eyes of their own supporters.[36] They also accosted their opponents in public, stripped them naked, beat them, and handcuffed them to posts in piazzas and along major roadways.[37]

The *squadrists* most explicit goal – destroying "Bolshevism" – was rapidly achieved, yet the violence continued unabated. Only by perpetuating this "revolutionary" situation could the Fascist movement undermine the liberal state and continue its push for political power. Additionally, at the local level, violence and criminality persisted more or less independent of any immediate larger political goals. The power of the Ras and the bonds of *squadrist* camaraderie depended on Fascists sustaining a state of lawlessness and initiating new attacks.[38] Illegal activities increased feelings of belonging and emotional interdependence among *squadrists*, making it more difficult for individual Black Shirts to pull out of the squads or refrain from violent acts. Any retreat, any return to normalcy, would have required dealing with potentially serious legal and psychological consequences.[39] Violence thus became cyclical and self-sustaining. Each "punitive expedition" was retribution for some earlier offense, and each attack contained the seed of a future act of revenge. If a Fascist was killed, his comrades would avenge him. When Fascists held a funeral for one of their "martyrs," the procession might deliberately cut through a Socialist neighborhood, leading to clashes and yet more punitive raids.[40] Squads perpetuated the environment of terror by constantly identifying new victims. Not surprisingly, due to its intimate nature, Fascist violence was shaped by local conditions: petty feuds, personal rivalries, and other motives beyond mere class warfare. Soon, Fascists even targeted rank-and-file Socialists distributing leaflets. Merely subscribing

---

[36] Franzinelli, *Squadristi*, 77–8.
[37] Lyttelton, "Fascism and Violence," 266–7.
[38] Ibid., 268–9.
[39] Reichardt, *Faschistische Kampfbünde*, 474–5.
[40] See Franzinelli, *Squadristi*, 75–86. E.g., see Pietro Alberghi, *Il Fascismo in Emilia Romagna: dalle origini alla Marcia su Roma* (Modena, 1989), 273–6.

to the Socialist daily *Avanti!* or some other publication that Fascists deemed "anti-Fascist" might bring a visit from a Fascist squad. When Fascists destroyed the offices of the party, the leagues, and other institutions, they often collected lists of names, which provided new targets for violence.

Having "conquered" and "pacified" Socialist communities, Fascists next asserted domination over the political and symbolic use of public space. With the rise of democracy and socialism, the economic and political elite lamented its loss of control over local government offices, piazzas, and political symbols. For landowners and the provincial middle classes, peasants and other manual laborers no longer "knew their place." When about town or conducting official business, the provincial bourgeois could no longer expect to be treated with deference, much less fear, by the lower classes. For the landowners of Bologna Province, the "simplest pleasures – strolls through the arcaded streets of the urban center, dinners in Bologna's elegant restaurants, or shopping trips in via Rizzoli – seemed to depend on the good will of the new provincial rulers."[41] The landowner, Angelo Tasca recounted, "had been the cock of the walk, head of the *comune*, manager of all local and provincial bodies." Now he had to deal with peasant-run leagues, labor offices, and Socialist cooperatives.[42] To correct this situation, the Fascists tore down red flags, busts of Marx, and Socialist slogans, replacing them with the Italian flag, busts of the king, and the fasces. Marches, parades, and political ceremonies reinforced the perception that the Fascists now dominated public spaces only recently occupied by Socialists. This "performance" of Fascist dominance intimidated real and potential enemies, while also fostering cohesion and solidarity among the Black Shirts.[43] It also served to reassure the provincial bourgeoisie that their dominant social position had been restored. Conservative and even moderate liberal provincial newspapers expressed support for the Black Shirts, praising their "patriotism" and respect for "law and order."[44]

By mid-1922, Fascists had not only defeated the Socialists, they had also undermined the liberal state's control over much of northern and

---

[41] Cardoza, *Agrarian Elites*, 289.

[42] Tasca, *Rise of Fascism*, 95.

[43] Reichardt, *Faschistische Kampfbünde*, 135–39; Lyttelton, "Fascism and Violence," 269.

[44] On the support of provincial elites, see Corner, *Fascism in Ferrara*, 113–15; Cardoza, *Agrarian Elites and Italian Fascism*, 309–10; Snowden, *Fascist Revolution in Tuscany*, 56–7, 226n158. For examples of moderate and conservative press coverage, see Alberghi, *Il Fascismo in Emilia Romagna*, 267–8.

central Italy. In the provinces of the Po Valley, Tuscany, and Puglia, Fascist bosses had deposed legally elected officers, and even commanded authority sufficient to bring about the transfer of centrally appointed officials, such as prefects and police chiefs. Many areas became private fiefdoms of local Ras, in some cases run as criminal enterprises.[45] The liberal state had lost its monopoly on legitimate violence. State institutions responsible for law and order – the magistracy, public-security forces, and the prefectures – were complicit in the demise of state authority on a massive scale.[46] In the wake of Fascist attacks, police and *carabinieri* arrested the Socialist victims, while allowing Fascists to slip away. Magistrates convicted Socialists at an absurdly higher rate than Fascists. Fascists also commonly "forced" police to release their comrades from jails and holding cells, meeting little resistance from their guards. In an environment of veritable civil war, many prefects used their considerable powers to tip the scales in favor of the Fascist camp.[47]

The new Fascist "state within a state" was very different from the preceding two years of Socialist hegemony. Through illegal violence, rather than elections, Fascists controlled government administration and destroyed the offices, newspapers, and cultural and social organizations of the Socialists, trade unions, and peasant leagues. Cyclical violence directed against local leaders prevented Socialists from reorganizing. Mass demonstrations, supported by the police and property-owning classes, were patriotic, reaffirming the primacy of the nation over internationalism. Politically, economically, and socially, traditional elites had reasserted their dominance over the laboring classes.

Despite its broad geographic impact and the importance of large, coordinated, interprovincial squad activity, the Fascist "Revolution," or reaction, largely consisted of thousands of intensely local episodes of violence. Although Fascists and their victims perceived *squadrism* as a continuation of the Great War, squads resorted to personal, highly symbolic, face-to-face violence and murder, rather than mass anonymous killing. In essence, although they could be exceedingly brutal, Fascist squads practiced a selective, calibrated, and choreographed economy of violence.

---

[45] Lyttelton, "Fascism and Violence," 267–9.

[46] Renzo De Felice, *Mussolini il fascista*, I: 27.

[47] This phenomenon has been documented in all of the classic works on agrarian Fascism. For a synthetic discussion, see Franzinelli, *Squadristi*, 96–117. See also Cardoza, *Agrarian Elites*, 308–9.

Turning Away from Liberal Italy (1922–1925)

Squad political violence started to erode the institutions of the liberal state even before the Fascists marched on Rome.[48] Inside the Parliament, deputies debated the legitimacy of *squadrismo*. Right-wing Fascist sympathizers deemed it patriotic, and therefore just, while Socialist and anti-Fascist liberals lamented the demise of the rule of law. Meanwhile, the governments of Ivanoe Bonomi (1921) and Luigi Facta (1922) seemingly failed to appreciate the scope of the phenomenon, issuing assurances that incidences of attacks against citizens and the state were "limited and isolated."[49] On one hand, this misperception seems justifiable. Accounts of murders, beatings, and arsons appeared, if at all, in local newspapers, often in the sections devoted to common crime.[50] Political elites with no personal connection to the localities affected by Fascist terror thus might be excused for failing to comprehend its magnitude. On the other hand, Fascist violence deeply affected national politics.[51] The elections of May 1921, which brought thirty-five Fascists into the Parliament, were preceded by a wave of squad violence that, in just two weeks, left seventy-one people dead and 216 wounded. Fascists attacked candidates in their home districts, in Rome, and even in the Parliament. At the convening of the new legislature, the Fascist deputies refused to allow the Communist deputy Francesco Misiano to enter the chamber. Fascists had thus successfully pushed for and attained a system in which state agents and political leaders tolerated and even legitimized illegal right-wing violence inflicted on Socialists, Communists, Catholic Popolari, and anti-Fascist liberal moderates. Though its success was not inevitable, the 1922 March on Rome was a Fascist coup against a system whose institutional integrity had already been severely compromised.[52]

The March on Rome (Figure 1) has often been portrayed as a comic opera, a "bluff." But as Giulia Albanese has shown, it was accompanied by serious, widespread violence. In provinces throughout Italy, paramilitary groups seized control of prefectures, telegraph offices, post offices, and rail stations. Where they encountered resistance from state

---

[48] Giulia Albanese, *La Marcia su Roma: violenza e politica nella crisi dello stato liberale* (Bari, 2006).
[49] Petersen, "Violence in Italian Fascism," 285.
[50] Ibid., 286.
[51] Franzinelli, *Squadristi*, 77–8.
[52] Albanese, *Marcia su Roma*, 36–41.

FIGURE 1. On the occasion of the March on Rome (1922), Mussolini flanked by Fascist bosses (from left) Attilio Teruzzi, Italo Balbo, Emilio de Bono, Cesare Maria de Vecchi, and Michele Bianchi. *Source:* Fototeca Gilardi.

authorities or workers, there were clashes and casualties.[53] In Rome, Fascists marched through popular neighborhoods and destroyed the offices and meeting places of left-wing newspapers, social clubs, and cooperatives.[54] In addition to attacking individual anti-Fascists, Fascists raided the homes of nationally prominent politicians, including the former prime minister, Francesco Nitti, throwing their books and furniture out the window and lighting the pile on fire. Meanwhile, in the provinces, Fascists seized control of local administrations that had resisted up until then. By the end of 1922, Fascists or pro-Fascists controlled virtually every communal administration in Italy.[55] Finally, the freedom of the press was severely curtailed. In the days following October 28, Fascists prevented most major dailies from publishing news of events.[56]

On October 29, 1922, the Italian king appointed Mussolini prime minister. Mussolini presided over a mixed cabinet, consisting of Fascists, Nationalists, Liberals, and Popolari. By taking the portfolio of minister

---

[53] On violence and March on Rome, see ibid., 102–15.
[54] Ibid., 117–18.
[55] Ibid., 119–21, 127.
[56] Ibid., 100–1.

of the Interior for himself, he controlled the Italian police.[57] Many political elites assumed that a Mussolini government would bring an end to two years of violent disorder, but it did not. Political violence in the years after the March on Rome continued to serve the same purposes as before: it suppressed opposition, replaced Socialist and non-Fascist administrations, and extended Fascist control over the rest of Italy.[58] Mussolini occasionally decried the illegal activities of the squads, but they operated as the motor that drove his government along the road to dictatorship. In December 1922, just weeks after the March on Rome, *squadrists* in Turin launched a bloody, three-day campaign of terror in an attempt to subdue the recalcitrant opposition to Fascism of the working classes, and even some industrialists and local political elites. Officially eleven people died, and scores were wounded, though the real numbers were probably higher.[59] That same month, administrative elections in Milan took place in an environment of intimidation, with squads stationed at polling stations to harass and intimidate voters.[60] Newspapers and journalists felt threatened to such an extent that a few simply stopped publishing news on politics, conceding that freedom of the press no longer existed in Italy. Fascists also exerted tremendous pressure on the non-Marxist dailies to take a pro-Fascist line.[61]

In the centers of agrarian Fascism, the vast majority of the rural population had already been cowed, but provincial Ras and their agrarian backers continued to face challenges. Liberals, Republicans, and Popolari who refused to support the Fascists provided rallying points for the opposition, and so they now faced the same fate as the Socialists before them.[62] Moreover, any sign of renewed opposition was ruthlessly repressed. In August 1923, after the release of several Socialists who had been in jail since early 1921, the Ras of Ferrara, Italo Balbo, ordered his Fascists to "explain to them [the Socialists] that it would be healthy for them to have a change of air and to settle down in some other province." He continued, "If they insist on staying you should beat them up, without exaggerating but with regularity, until they decide." Balbo also instructed that his letter be shown to the prefect, suggesting that "the police station would do

---

[57] Lyttelton, *Seizure of Power*, 8–9.
[58] Albanese, *Marcia su Roma*, 176.
[59] Antonio Sonnessa, "The 1922 Turin Massacre (Strage di Torino): Working Class Resistance and Conflicts within Fascism," *Modern Italy* 10:2 (2005): 187–205.
[60] Albanese, *Marcia su Roma*, 176.
[61] Ibid., 180, 194–6.
[62] See Corner, *Fascism in Ferrara*, 255–60.

well to persecute them with arrests at least once a week and it would be as well if the prefect makes the State Prosecutor understand that, in the event of beatings (which must be done with style), we do not want trouble with trials." These orders were carried out, and six of the eight men left Ferrara.[63] Significantly, Balbo, a major figure in the national leadership, sent these instructions from the Viminale (the Ministry of the Interior) in Rome, belying the Mussolini government's insistence that it was working to "reign in" the squads.[64]

National and local elections continued to feature spasms of squad violence. In the lead-up to the parliamentary elections of 1924, which won a Fascist majority, Black Shirts intimidated opposition candidates and voters. Their manipulation of elections was brutally straightforward. Explaining tactics that could apply to other elections of the era, Balbo instructed Fascists to seize the first elector to leave the voting booth "and break his head open – even if he has voted for us, too bad for him – shouting, 'Bastard, you voted for the socialists'. In this way we can be sure that, after this example, no one will risk not voting for the *lista nazionale*."[65] Although the Fascist list did not win everywhere in 1924, in some districts it miraculously received all votes, without a single person supporting an opposition candidate.[66]

In Rome, meanwhile, Mussolini's new government immediately began bringing the public-security forces into line with the Fascist project of eliminating anti-Fascist opposition. In December 1922, he abolished the four-year-old "Royal Guard," a public-security force that Mussolini considered hostile to Fascism. Many of its forty thousand personnel passed to the *carabinieri*, who Mussolini felt were more sympathetic to the Black Shirts. In its second meeting, the newly established Fascist Grand Council, a sort of shadow cabinet set up in December 1922, created a Fascist Militia (Voluntary Militia for National Security [MVSN]), which would organize the squads into a formal, hierarchical military structure, making them an official institution of the Italian state.[67] Despite the dubious constitutionality of the MVSN, many liberals accepted it as a necessary

---

[63] Quoted in ibid., 259 (Balbo to Beltrami, August 31, 1923).

[64] See Lupo, *Il fascismo*, 162.

[65] Corner, *Fascism in Ferrara*, 263.

[66] Ibid., 264–6.

[67] Lyttelton, *Seizure of Power*, 105. On the MVSN, see Alberto Aquarone, "La milizia volontaria nello Stato fascista," in *Il regime fascista*, ed. Alberto Aquarone and Maurizio Vernassa (Bologna, 1974), 85–111.

institution for controlling the squads.[68] For Mussolini, the creation of the MVSN constituted a strategy for reigning in the anarchic squad violence while establishing his own private political army. Emilio de Bono, the Fascist quadrumvir whom Mussolini had appointed director of public security (chief of police), also became the head of the MVSN. Thus, a Fascist controlled the police and the militia. De Bono authorized prefects to use militiamen to control "public order." In practice, militiamen still belonged to their squads, engaging in legal and illegal tactics in both capacities.[69]

The levers of state power firmly in hand, Mussolini's government increasingly began to perform the repressive function of the squads. With the Socialist Party demolished, the Interior Ministry targeted the Italian Communist Party (PCI), which had been founded the previous year. In early 1923, the police arrested thousands of Communist militants and politicians. The PCI's central leadership, federal secretaries, secretaries of the provincial youth organization, trade union leaders, and other national and provincial leaders were arrested and jailed for weeks, months, and even years, awaiting trial on vague offenses such as attempting to "overthrow the state" and "incite class hatred."[70] Mussolini's inner circle already clearly foresaw the suppression of all other parties but the PNF. Early on, he ordered prefects to compile lists of "subversives" and political opponents – Communists, anarchists, Socialists, Republicans, Catholic Popolari, and others – throughout Italy.[71] In one circular to prefects, Police Chief De Bono instructed the police not to focus solely on the Communists, because the state had "dangerous enemies, even among those men who display the most ostentatious devotion to the State itself."[72] These surveillance and intelligence-gathering activities, targeting all non-Fascist parties, would greatly facilitate future political repression.

---

[68] On the constitutionality of the squads, see Albanese, *Marcia su Roma*, 181–2.

[69] The position of director general of public security was soon changed to the more imposing "chief of police" (*Capo della Polizia*). See Paola Carucci, "L'organizzazione dei servizi di polizia dopo l'approvazione del testo unico di pubblica sicurezza nel 1926," *Rassegna degli archivi di Stato* 36 (1976): 95n1. Albanese, *Marcia su Roma*, 179.

[70] Official figures record the arrest of 2,000 suspected Communists during early 1923, while the Communists were reporting 5,000 arrests. These numbers do not include the victims of squad violence. See Paolo Spriano, *Storia del partito comunista*, vol. 2: *Gli anni della clandestinità* (Turin, 1969), 262–3n3.

[71] Franzinelli, *I tentacoli*, 5.

[72] Quoted in De Felice, *Mussolini il fascista*, II:395n1.

Whereas provincial Fascists targeted left-wing and Catholic politicians, in Rome Mussolini turned on moderate parliamentary deputies, and even dissident Fascists, who resisted his strategy of "legally" taking over the Italian state.[73] For example, parliamentary debates on the Acerbo Law, a proportional electoral reform that ultimately gave the PNF an overwhelming majority, were conducted under the watchful surveillance of Fascist militiamen, who had replaced the police officials normally responsible for security inside the chamber. During 1923 and 1924, MVSN officials working within the Viminale, the seat of the Ministry of the Interior, plotted attacks against select opponents.[74] In December 1923, the so-called Fascist "Ceka" attacked Giovanni Amendola, the prominent liberal and anti-Fascist. In May, Fascists in Rome savagely beat Alfredo Misuri, the *squadrist* leader of Perugia, after he had delivered a speech criticizing Mussolini's government. A year later, Fascists attacked Cesare Forni, a dissident Ras, in Milan. Undoubtedly the most notorious act of political violence was the abduction and murder of Giacomo Matteotti, a Reformist Socialist who denounced the results of the first post-Acerbo Law election. The Matteotti murder precipitated the most serious crisis in Mussolini's rise to power. Groups and institutions who were otherwise sympathetic to Mussolini temporarily abandoned him. In order to mitigate the crisis, Mussolini offered concessions to his flanking supporters. Several Fascists were forced to resign their government positions, including Police Chief De Bono. Mussolini also replaced himself as interior minister with a monarchist nationalist, Luigi Federzoni. Later in the summer, in August, he subordinated the militia to the military, and required militiamen to swear loyalty to the monarch.[75]

Mussolini's backpedaling offended many intransigent Fascists, who had envisioned a wave of revolutionary terror in the wake of the March on Rome. Instead, the Parliament still existed, opposition deputies and all. Working-class neighborhoods in Italy's largest cities remained no-go zones for Black Shirts. Opposition newspapers continued to be published in large cities. On the national stage, anti-Fascists freely denounced Mussolini's methods; when Fascists beat or murdered these critics, there was a public outcry. Impatient with the pace of the Fascist takeover, several dozen consols of the militia traveled to Rome and delivered an ultimatum to Mussolini: either he move the revolution forward by dispensing

---

[73] See Lyttelton, *Seizure of Power*, 145, 239.
[74] A reference to the Cheka, the earliest political police corps in the Soviet Union.
[75] Aquarone, "Milizia volontaria," 94–5.

with the liberal, constitutional order, or the Black Shirts would launch a "second wave" of *squadrism*. Politically weakened by the Matteotti crisis, and challenged by his own movement, Mussolini decided on dictatorship, a course he announced publicly in his January 3 speech to the Chamber of Deputies:

> If Fascism has been nothing more than castor oil and truncheons, rather than the supreme passion of the best of Italian youth, then the fault is mine! If Fascism has been a criminal association, then I am the boss. . . . If all acts of violence have been the outcome of a certain historical, political, moral climate, then the responsibility is mine, for I created this climate . . . through propaganda, beginning at the time of the *intervento* and lasting to the present day.[76]

By declaring that he and the squads were one and the same, Mussolini expressed solidarity with the most extreme and criminal elements within the Fascist movement. In his declaration, he also boldly challenged his opponents to prosecute him. Instead, this dramatic revelation was met with silence on the part of liberals like Giolitti and Salandra, as well as the Aventine Secession.[77] Meanwhile, despite the public backlash against the Matteotti murder, Fascist attacks on enemies continued, leading to the deaths of prominent anti-Fascists like Giovanni Amendola and Piero Gobetti.

Toward the Fascist State (1925–1926)

In the wake of the January *coup d'état*, Mussolini ordered police and *carabinieri* to shut down remaining opposition party offices, newspapers, and cultural circles.[78] Italy had become a de facto one-party state. Now the central problem for Mussolini was his own party, particularly the factions who continued to engage in anarchic, illegal violence. These extremists foresaw the creation of party-controlled institutions of purely Fascist political repression; for them, the police measures adopted by the dictatorship were either insufficient or entirely unwanted. One Florentine intransigent, Curzio Malaparte, demanded that Fascism "recall to its leader that the Ministry of the Interior is the least suitable organ for carrying out a revolution," calling for a party-controlled body to implement

---

[76] Mussolini, OO, XXI:238.
[77] Lyttelton, *Seizure of Power*, 266–7.
[78] Aquarone, *Organizzazione*, 48–9.

revolutionary terror against all enemies of Fascism.[79] Roberto Farinacci, the intransigent Ras of Cremona, explicitly called for the introduction of *confino di polizia* for political offenders, the creation of a Special Tribunal, and the reinstatement of the death penalty.[80] For many Fascists, then, squad violence should continue until such time as the state adopted a real apparatus of political repression. Regeneration of the nation through destruction of the "internal enemy" was, for some, seemingly the entire program.[81]

Mussolini continually insisted upon the Fascists' right to use violence. He openly threatened the opposition in speeches, even within the Parliament, and ordered attacks on his most vocal enemies. In a speech delivered in June 1925 and reprinted in *Il popolo d'Italia* under the title "Absolute Intransigence," Mussolini told the national conference of the PNF, "you know what I think of violence. For me, it is profoundly virtuous, more virtuous than compromise or agreement." At the same time, he remained at odds with intransigents, holding a very different view of what Fascist violence should look like. The supreme morality (*alta moralità*) of violence required that it be "guided by an idea" and not "crude self-interest."[82] Mussolini had insisted consistently throughout the early 1920s that Fascism was not an organization for "defending personal interests" or inflicting "violence for the sake of violence." "Our violence," he wrote in 1921, "must be chivalrous, aristocratic, surgical, and therefore, in a certain sense, humane."[83] Aggression against Fascists should be met with "swift and relentless retaliation," while at the same time "avoiding inflicting it on men and institutions uninvolved in the conflict." He concluded, "We repeat once more that Fascist violence must be reasoned, rational, surgical."[84] Mussolini also attached a stigma to "real" political terror, arguing that anarchic, mass killing was only practiced by Socialists and "Bolsheviks." Fascist violence was "child's play" compared to the actions of the French Revolutionaries, the Italian Socialists during the *biennio rosso*, or the Bolsheviks in Russia, where "two million people" had been executed and "two million more" were in prison.[85] Lenin's

---

[79] Quoted in Lyttelton, "Fascism in Italy," 96.
[80] Musci, *Il confino fascista di polizia*, xl.
[81] Lyttelton, "Fascism in Italy," 75–100.
[82] Mussolini, OO, XXI:358.
[83] Mussolini, OO, XVII:67–8.
[84] Mussolini, "La morale," in OO, XVI:271. From *Popolo d'Italia*, n. 93, April 19, 1921.
[85] "Continuando," *Popolo d'Italia*, August 6, 1922. Quoted in De Felice, *Mussolini il fascista*, II:672.

"politics of terror," which had wreaked "chaos," "disorganization," and "national catastrophe" on Russia, represented "the triumph of the most bestial instincts."[86] Socialism was bloody anarchy; Fascism represented order. Speaking to the party, Mussolini argued that a "second wave" of squad violence would be counterproductive. The elimination of Fascism's enemies would require a "delicate" and "subtle" strategy:

> We must chloroform . . . the Opposition and the Italian people. The state of mind of the Italian people is this: do anything but let us know afterwards. Don't tell us every day that you want to bring in firing squads. That annoys us. One morning, when we wake up, tell us you have done it, and we will be happy.[87]

During 1925 and 1926 and even beyond, squad violence still presented an even bigger problem for Mussolini than he let on.[88] In some places, *squadristi* continued to usurp the function of the police, investigating and punishing "subversion" on their own. In cities with a large working class (e.g., Turin, Genoa, and Rome), the squads remained particularly large and out of control. Urban districts known for anti-Fascism were attacked and occupied; all the while, Fascist "excesses" continued to be tolerated by local authorities. When Mussolini's Interior Minister, Luigi Federzoni, proved unable to deal with squad violence, the dictator appointed the Fascist boss of Cremona, Roberto Farinacci, as general secretary of the PNF.[89] Farinacci, an intransigent himself, issued a warning to the Fascist federations, telling them to tone down the violence, but he also made it clear that he expected the state to increase repression in return. With the collaboration of Farinacci, Mussolini pursued policies that undercut the power and autonomy of rebellious provincial Fascists bosses, while introducing laws and institutions of political repression that were controlled by the state, rather than the party.[90] Toward the end of 1925, a wave of anti-Freemason and anti-Catholic violence swept several Italian cities, particularly Florence and surrounding Tuscan towns, leaving several people

---

[86] Benito Mussolini, "Un documento terribile: le infamie e gli orrori del leninismo denunciati al mondo dagli operai socialisti russi," in *OO*, XI:8–9 (*Il popolo d'Italia*, n. 105, April 16, 1918).

[87] Quoted in De Felice, *Mussolini il fascista*, II:671.

[88] See the telegrams from Interior Minister Federzoni to prefects reprinted in Aquarone, *Organizzazione*, 382–4.

[89] Lyttelton, *Seizure of Power*, 271.

[90] See Aquarone, *Organizzazione*, 47.

dead.[91] These incidents represented, for Mussolini, "the degeneration of Fascism." He worried about "making a second Matteotti." The violence in Florence was "not Fascist, not Italian – not timely, chivalrous or surgical violence." Mussolini lamented, "All of this, under the eyes of 10,000 English and Americans."[92] Mussolini dismissed Farinacci over the matter, but by then he had already manipulated the Ras's moral authority to bring intransigents into line. The crackdown on Fascist extremism continued until most of the squads had been disbanded. Notorious leaders of particularly criminal squads were disciplined or transferred away from their power bases.[93] By the end of 1925, Mussolini had gained control of the party. Meanwhile, the dictatorship continued to deploy the militia in police operations in an attempt to quash heterodox networks of opponents and recalcitrant working-class neighborhoods. Spasms of squad violence still occasionally swept Italy.

Party-State Violence

On October 31, 1926, in Bologna, Mussolini escaped an assassination attempt – the fourth in a little more than a year – allegedly carried out by Anteo Zamboni, a teenage boy who was lynched on the spot by Fascists. As news of the event traveled throughout Italy, Fascist squads took retribution on persons associated with anti-Fascism, administering beatings and ransacking homes. An emergency meeting of Mussolini's Council of Ministers held on November 5 approved a series of "exceptional decrees" that had been drafted in the preceding months. The legislation, which included a new police code, dissolved all political parties and other anti-Fascist organizations, empowered provincial police commissions to order political confinement (*confino di polizia*) and other police sanctions, banned publications hostile to the regime, created a political investigative unit within the MVSN, and called for a total reorganization of the police.[94] With the creation of the Special Tribunal at the end of

---

[91] Fascist attacks on Masons, and opposition figures, also occurred in Bari, while in Modena, Forli, and Genoa the police restrained the Fascists from similar attacks. Lyttelton, *Seizure of Power*, 278–82.

[92] Ibid., 282–3.

[93] E.g., the exile of Florentine Ras Tamburini to Libya and the crackdown on Florentine *squadrism*. See ibid., 285–6.

[94] For a general discussion of the context into which these repressive measures were introduced in November 1926, see Aquarone, *Organizzazione*, 97–110, and Renzo De Felice, *Mussolini il fascista*, II:146–52.

November, the ethos of Fascist political violence had been definitively subsumed into the institutions of the state.

According to the orthodox historical interpretation of Fascism, the history of Fascist violence, at least in the domestic sphere, ended here, as the new authoritarian state definitively suppressed *squadrism*. The classic works on the Fascist seizure of power argue that after 1926, with the victory of Mussolini and his moderate "normalizers" over the intransigents, the Fascist Party was "defeated" or "liquidated." From that point forward, the PNF lost its revolutionary role and degenerated into a sterile, depoliticized bureaucracy. In this view, Mussolini had subordinated the party to state authority. One of the most significant documents supporting this interpretation is Mussolini's circular of 1927, which undercut the power of the party *federale* (provincial boss) by declaring that the authority of the prefect was supreme in the provinces.[95] Therefore, according to this interpretation, violence still remained central to the ideology of Fascism, but it would be directed outward in the form of warfare and territorial expansion. At home, Italy became a mildly repressive police state, where political power rested upon the "consensus" of the Italian population rather than any system of mass repression.

New studies have questioned the state's victory over the party, even doubting the utility of viewing the party and the state as separate entities within the regime. The relationship between the PNF and the state was complex and evolved over time. Giovanni Dolfin, a Fascist who served as both a PNF *federale* and a state prefect, recalled that the famous circular of 1927 was "very soon buried" by "later directives from the party."[96] Historian Salvatore Lupo has argued that Fascist party politics continued, only in different forms. Although always professing loyalty to Mussolini, rival Fascist blocs fought each other, using the power of state and party institutions. In these conflicts, the Fascist *federali* sometimes prevailed over career prefects and politically appointed prefects. As Marco Palla has noted, viewing the PNF as subordinate to the Italian state misses the point; one simply cannot imagine one without the other.[97] Without the PNF, Mussolini's regime would have been "invertebrate."[98]

---

[95] The circular is reproduced in Aquarone, *Organizzazione*, 485–8.

[96] Giovanni Dolfin, *Con Mussolini nella tragedia: diario del capo della segretaria particolare della duce, 1943–44* (Milan, 1949), 122. Quoted in Lupo, *Fascismo*, 392.

[97] Marco Palla, "Lo stato-partito," in *Lo stato fascista*, ed. Marco Palla (Milan, 2001), 1–78.

[98] Ibid., 8.

The regime, according to Palla, was a "party-state," with its own institutions, laws, and theoretical and juridical ideology. However, perhaps more than in other states, laws and institutions were not everything, thanks to the Fascist practice of "*ex post facto* juridical-legislative legitimization," which privileged action over law. State and party authorities engaged in practices that had no basis in law but were "legal" in that the state ultimately condoned them.[99] This practice of "legalizing illegality" had begun with squad violence, which then-parliamentary deputy Mussolini and his supporters argued was perfectly legitimate. During the seizure of power, they continued to assert this right, converting the squads into the MVSN, tolerating "pockets" of "Fascist illegality," and ordering savage beatings against select enemies.

Mussolini did not wage war on intransigents because of their radical politics or their use of violence per se. Rather, he suppressed them because they adhered neither to the main tenets of Mussolinian Fascism – centralization, discipline, and hierarchy – nor to the dictator's strategy of selective, "surgical" violence. For Mussolini, the practice of violence remained absolutely central to Fascist rule, and the PNF and MVSN had a critical role to play. Therefore, the Mussolinian economy of violence that emerged out of the seizure of power represented a synthesis between the dictator's strategy of carefully calibrated state repression and the *squadrist* ethos for spontaneous punishment of "internal enemies." After 1926, the state established narrow parameters within which Fascists could legitimately attack, harass, and call for state sanctions against their enemies. A Fascist state that did not provide these benefits to party members and did not institutionalize Fascism's ethos and propensity for violence and coercion, would have certainly never held the support of the PNF – it would have ceased to be Fascist. Institutionalized violence served a "ritual function," through which Fascists "renewed their faith."[100] More importantly, however, as will be shown in subsequent chapters, the Fascist police state would function so well precisely because it involved local Fascists in the gritty, day-to-day surveillance and intimidation of opponents and enemies. Fascists, including militiamen, provided the new party-state with a profoundly powerful instrument of political and social control. Socialists, Communists, anarchists, labor organizers, and other "antinational" elements would be suffocated by

---

[99] Ibid.
[100] Aquarone, "Violenza e consenso nel fascismo italiano," *Storia contemporanea* 1 (1979): 147.

the constant watchfulness, harassment, humiliation, and discrimination inflicted by authoritarian police chiefs and a voluntary corps of Fascist watchdogs. Although prefects and police chiefs rotated in and out of a province, the Fascists remained. As an institution, the *fascio* served as the depository of local memory, recalling every transgression against Fascism.

For those vulnerable to Fascist attacks and police sanctions, the memory of *squadrismo* was always just beneath the surface. The terror of the first half of the 1920s thus conditioned the experiences of Italians who lived under Fascist rule for the next twenty years. The victims of these acts of brutality had families, friends, and acquaintances who did not forget what had happened. The thousands who fled Italy to escape Fascist violence left behind lives full of people. Italians who witnessed, first- or secondhand, murders, beatings, and the destruction of homes and offices were affected profoundly. Any assessment of the role of violence under Fascism thus must take into consideration the initial terror upon which Mussolini established his dictatorship. Despite the diminution of illegal, open brutality, patterns of repression established during six years of squad violence continued under the police state. Memories of the beatings, ritual humiliation, and destruction of working-class institutions lingered on. The victors were empowered, while the "defeated" were cowed by residual fear and fresh acts of intimidation. Fascists continued to foster political and social divisions, old and new, which in turn nourished a culture of repression.

2

Institutions of Fascist Violence

> The police have heavy treads and firm voices. They entered the Via del Corno with the familiarity and self-assurance of boxers coming into the ring. It was the usual patrol, checking up on those not supposed to be out after nightfall [*gli ammoniti*].
>
> Vasco Pratolini, *A Tale of Poor Lovers* (1947)[1]

The exceptional decrees of 1926 marked the definitive institutional rupture between the liberal constitutional order and the new Fascist police state. The public-security code, although based largely on its liberal predecessor, nevertheless substantially curtailed individual rights, subordinating them to the interests of the state.[2] More than the legislation itself, it was the intentions of regime officials who implemented it that gave the dictatorship its Fascist character. According to Mussolini's new police chief, Arturo Bocchini, the police would now play a "more decisive and beneficial role in improving and transforming the habits of the Nation in keeping with the ethical and social principles that form the Fascist State." The new regime planned to use the public-security forces "to control activities once left to the initiative of individuals."[3] Police understood

[1] Vasco Pratolini, *A Tale of Poor Lovers* (New York, 1988), 18.
[2] For the debate over continuities between the liberal and Fascist police codes, see Jonathan Dunnage, "Social Control in Fascist Italy: The Role of the Police," in *Social Control in Europe, vol. 2: 1800–2000*, ed. Clive Emsley, Eric Johnson, and Pieter Spierenburg, (Columbus, 2004), 261–4.
[3] Arturo Bocchini, "Relazione a S E il Ministro," January 17, 1929; quoted in Italo Savella, "Arturo Bocchini and the Secret Political Police in Fascist Italy," *The Historian* 61 (1998–9): 792.

that, above all, the new legislation ordered them to ruthlessly suppress anti-Fascist groups and to facilitate the expansion of the National Fascist Party (PNF). However, police officials also correctly determined that the new law gave state authorities the right to intervene in an undefined set of public and private arenas in order to bring the nation into line with the "ethics" and "principles" of Fascism. The broadly defined jurisdiction of the police state meant that virtually no place was off-limits. Political expression, economic activity, employment, travel, sexuality, reproduction, religious practices, organized leisure, and other areas of national life could now be aggressively controlled by the police and other state agencies.

The theoretical basis for these new institutions relied on biological and organic metaphors that privileged society over the individual.[4] In his *Political Doctrine of Fascism*, Alfredo Rocco,[5] the nationalist theoretician and author of the Fascist state's legal codes, advanced the idea that an individual could pursue his own interests "only on behalf of the state." He wrote, "Society has historical and immanent ends of preservation, expansion, and improvement quite distinct from those of individuals." Abnormal developments, among individuals or classes, "would prove as fatal to society as abnormal growths are to living organisms."[6] He concluded, "Hence, the necessity, for which the older doctrines make little allowance, of sacrifice, even up to the total immolation of individuals, on behalf of society."[7] In addition to subordinating the individual to the state, the Fascist dictatorship also asserted its jurisdiction over activities and attitudes that had previously been protected, at least in theory, under the liberal regime. In a speech to Parliament explaining a new law that gave prefects the power to monitor and dissolve private associations, Rocco laid out the regime's prerogative to "watch over both the minds and the bodies of citizens." Accordingly, the state had a duty "to repress lies, corruption, and all forms of deviance and degeneration in public and private ethics."[8]

---

[4] David Horn, *Social Bodies: Science Reproduction, and Italian Modernity* (Princeton, 1994), 26.

[5] Alfredo Rocco (1875–1935) was a nationalist who joined the Fascist movement in 1923. He was minister of justice from 1925 to 1932 and authored much of the Fascist regime's founding legislation, including the public-security code, the criminal code, and labor laws.

[6] Alfredo Rocco, "The Political Doctrine of Fascism," in *A Primer of Italian Fascism*, trans. Jeffrey T. Schnapp, Olivia E. Sears, and Maria G. Stampino (Lincoln, 2000), 113.

[7] Ibid., 112.

[8] Quoted in Aquarone, *Organizzazione*, 70.

The role of the police in this project of national "preservation, expansion, and improvement" was explicit. Writing to prefects, the *carabinieri*, and the Fascist Militia (MVSN), Mussolini explained that the Fascist police code offered "the Public Security authorities new and more perfect weapons for performing the task . . . of controlling disruptive and malevolent elements and repressing any activity contrary to the physical and moral integrity and peaceful development of the national society."[9] Bocchini similarly instructed provincial authorities that the "new concept of police activity" should no longer be "considered as a mere limitation of individual rights, but as the development of a fundamental capacity of the state to act against citizens for prevailing reasons of public interest."[10] The primacy of state power over individual interests, Mussolini regularly emphasized, extended into the arenas of public and private morality. In a 1929 telegram to prefects, which he considered important enough to reprint in *Il popolo d'Italia*, Mussolini further articulated the role that the police should play in upholding and reforming the moral character of the Italians. "If the moral condition of the Italian people is in general reassuring," he wrote, "the authorities should nevertheless take care to prevent the germs of corruption from spoiling and annihilating vital energies." Although the regime would use "persuasion," relying on "educators of the people to attend to this task with assiduity," these efforts simply could not produce results "if the centers of infection" were not "neutralized and destroyed with diligence." Mussolini concluded, "And this is the responsibility of police authorities."[11]

The task of implementing the exceptional legislation and reorganizing the police apparatus was largely carried out by Bocchini. A career Interior Ministry official, Bocchini was promoted from vice-prefect to prefect in December 1922, just two months after the March on Rome. Mussolini assigned Bocchini to the province of Brescia, where he and Fascist boss Augusto Turati orchestrated the suppression of a powerful left-wing veterans' organization and the Catholic *Partito popolare*. Transferred to Bologna in December 1923, Mussolini charged Bocchini with

---

[9] Benito Mussolini to prefects, general command of the *carabinieri*, and general command of the MVSN, "Applicazione della nuova Legge sulla Pubblica Sicurezza," November 12, 1926, and November 29, 1930, n. 12982, 14, in ACS, MI, DGPS, DAGR, Massime D1, b. 24, fasc. D1/F.3, sf. 1/1928–9. See the list of abbreviations at the beginning of the book for definitions of acronyms used in the notes.

[10] Arturo Bocchini, "Relazione a S E il Ministro."

[11] Mussolini to prefects, February 20, 1929, OO, XXIV:380. Reprinted in *Il popolo d'Italia*, vol. XVI, n. 48, 1929.

FIGURE 2. Arturo Bocchini, here at his desk in 1926, served as Mussolini's chief of police from September 1926 until his death in November 1940. Mussolini then appointed Carmine Senise, previously the vice-chief of police, to the position. *Source:* Fototeca Gilardi.

ensuring the victory of the Fascist list in the 1924 parliamentary elections. In October 1925, as prefect of Genoa, he helped to break the maritime workers union, replacing it with a Fascist syndicate. In September 1926, with encouragement from both Roberto Farinacci and Augusto Turati, now secretary of the PNF, Mussolini named Bocchini chief of police (Figure 2), a position he held until his death in November 1940.[12]

Bocchini has often been depicted as an opportunist rather than a Fascist true believer. This interpretation problematically rests on the assumption that the regime consisted of a Fascist Party and a substantially non-Fascist

[12] Paola Carucci, "Arturo Bocchini," in *Uomini e volti del fascismo*, ed. Ferdinando Cordova (Rome, 1980), 65–103; Mimmo Franzinelli, s.v. "Bocchini, Arturo," in *Dizionario del Fascismo*, ed. Victoria de Grazia and Sergio Luzzato (Turin, 2002), I:173.

state apparatus. It also underestimates the coincidence between Bocchini's political views, to the extent that they can be intuited from his career in the Interior Ministry, and the nature of Fascist rule. His meteoric trajectory was, after all, based on his unique ability to obtain results favorable to the establishment of the dictatorship. He zealously carried out the regime's policies, including the ruthless suppression of anti-Fascism, the implementation of the anti-Semitic racial legislation, and the forging of links between Fascist Italy and Nazi Germany through his relationship with Heinrich Himmler. True, Bocchini clashed with factions within the PNF, but this was largely predetermined by the factional nature of Mussolini's regime rather than an absence of a "belief" in Fascism. At least for a time, he enjoyed good relations with two party secretaries, Augusto Turati and Roberto Farinacci, both of whom recommended him for the police chief position. Most importantly, Bocchini, perhaps more than any other figure, advanced Mussolini's policies, possessing an uncanny "ability to anticipate and interpret the intentions of the Duce with regard to the maintenance of domestic order, conferring upon them the coherence and clarity that Mussolini lacked."[13] In the absence of elections, free speech, and a free press, Mussolini relied heavily on Bocchini's political police, not to mention his judgment, to provide insights into the Italian public's opinion of domestic policy, foreign policy, the regime, and Mussolini. Mussolini consulted with his police chief in daily briefings, more than any other adviser. Unlike so many of Mussolini's collaborators, Bocchini was never dismissed, transferred, or sent off to administer an African colony. In conjunction with the dictator, Bocchini stood at the center of the Fascist state's power from 1926 until 1940.

The story of Bocchini's career in many ways reflects the regime's larger efforts to bring the Italian state police into accord with Fascist rule. Throughout the 1920s, Mussolini's police chiefs carried out significant purges of police personnel. In 1924 and 1927, enforced retirements led to the departure of hundreds of incompetent or politically unreliable officials, including seven police chiefs, four vice-police chiefs, sixty commissars, 320 vice-commissars, and dozens of administrative employees.[14] By the early 1930s, a total of 440 police officials and more than one thousand police agents had been removed from or forced out of their jobs.[15]

---

[13] Carrucci, "Arturo Bocchini," 77.
[14] Canali, *Le spie*, 31, 60, 680n125.
[15] Jonathan Dunnage, "Mussolini's Policemen, 1926–1943," in *Policing Interwar Europe*, ed. Gerald Blaney (London, 2006), 112–35.

In replacing state employees, the regime often gave precedence to party members. In particular, during 1928, competitions for state employment were held, and party secretary Augusto Turati sat on the appointment panels.[16] The regime thus clearly wanted to reward committed Fascists. In the 1930s, moreover, party members, particularly "Fascists of the first hour," were given preference in hiring and could count their years of service to the "Fascist revolution" when calculating seniority.[17] Yet more than ideological zeal, recent research has shown, the regime's reform of the police aspired to create a competent, efficient force. Even though the purges of the 1920s left the police understaffed, the Interior Ministry did not rush to fill these positions with unqualified Fascists.[18] More so than hiring Fascists or promoting ideological fervor, the dictatorship's renovation of the Italian police primarily involved promoting career state officials who, like Bocchini, could diligently and efficiently execute Fascist policies. Although many "first-hour" Fascists became prefects in the 1920s and, even more so, 1930s, the majority of the prefects during Fascism were career officials.[19]

As chief of police, Bocchini's first priorities were to expand Mussolini's security detail, introduce stricter protocols for his public appearances, and keep close track of suspected assassination plots. Having accomplished these tasks, he set about reorganizing the General Directorate of Public Security (DGPS), the central office of the state police. To some extent, all seven divisions of the police, as well as the *Carabinieri reali*, were actively engaged in repressing opposition and dissent. The two divisions most explicitly charged with conducting political duties were the Division of Political Police (*Divisione polizia politica*) and the Division of General and Confidential Affairs (*Divisione affari generali e riservati* [DAGR]). With offices inside the prefecture of each province, the *polizia politica* gathered information on anti-Fascist movements, PNF members, and public opinion through a network of informers. Deprived of institutions for gauging the public mood, Mussolini relied heavily on this information for governing Italy.[20] Meanwhile, the innocuous sounding DAGR contained the core operative institutions of political repression, including the Political

---

[16] See Aquarone, *Organizzazione*, 73–4; and Philip Morgan, "The Prefects and Party-State Relations in Fascist Italy," *Journal of Modern Italian Studies* 3:3 (1998): 254–5.

[17] Dunnage, "Mussolini's Policemen," 123–4.

[18] Ibid., 115–17.

[19] Morgan, "Prefects and Fascist Party."

[20] On the *Divisione polizia politica*, see Carucci, "Bocchini," 99–103; and Franzinelli, *I tentacoli*, 22–34, 229–60.

Confinement Office (Ufficio Confino Politico [UCP]), the Central Political Registry (Casellario Politico Centrale [CPC]), and the OVRA, the regime's secret political police. Moreover, the DAGR coordinated political repression nationwide through the prefects and the *questori* (provincial police chiefs). The offices of the *questura* (provincial police headquarters) were responsible for the very intensive work of political repression and social control. The personnel of the *questure* censored mail, recruited informants, performed interrogations, made arrests, monitored the Fascist Party and labor syndicates, conducted surveillance on suspects and ex-political detainees, and carried out a wide array of other activities.[21] Although the prefect and *questore* needed approval from Rome to sentence an individual to *confino di polizia*, they could arrest, detain, and assign political probation without any authorization from a court or the Interior Ministry in Rome.

Bocchini's secret political police, the OVRA, operated almost completely outside the law, effectively giving Mussolini a free hand over the state, the party, opponents, and dissenters. Beginning in 1927, the police chief began assembling an elite group of several hundred agents, known for several years as the Special Police Inspectorate. In 1930, in a terse paragraph printed in newspapers, the regime publicly, ominously announced the existence of a secret political police called the OVRA (which most likely stood for *Opera vigilanza e repressione antifascista*). OVRA solved two problems for Mussolini and his police chief. First, the limited provincial jurisdiction of Italian prefects was ill-suited for investigating clandestine anti-Fascist movements that operated on a national and international level. Accordingly, the early OVRA zones corresponded geographically to the Communist Party's clandestine structure. Second, the OVRA allowed Mussolini to monitor and circumvent the authority of state and party authorities in the provinces. OVRA inspectors general operated outside the Interior Ministry hierarchy and were empowered to investigate state and party officials. They could also intervene in or even stop ongoing police or state activities.

The OVRA's eleven zones were established on an ad hoc basis between 1927 and 1941. The first and second zones were most actively engaged in repressing the anti-Fascist movements, mainly the Communist Party (PCI) and the "Justice and Liberty" movement. Established in 1927

---

[21] On the *questori*, see Paola Carucci, "Il Ministero dell'Interno: Prefetti, Questori e Ispettori Generali," in *Sulla crisi del regime fascista, 1938–1943: la società italiana dal 'consenso' alla Resistenza*, ed. Angelo Ventura (Venice, 1996), 21–73.

and headquartered in Milan, the first zone covered northern Italy – Lombardy, Piedmont, Val d'Aosta, Liguria, and the Veneto. Police Inspector Francesco Nudi headed the zone from 1927 to 1937. The second zone, established in 1929 and directed by Giuseppe D'Andrea, covered Emilia-Romagna, Tuscany, and the Marches. The other OVRA zones were created and dismantled on an ad hoc basis and adapted their methods to the task and local conditions. The construction of a web of informants was standard practice, but their background varied, as did the ends to which intelligence was used. Outside the first and second zones, the OVRA primarily operated to provide Bocchini and Mussolini with information on public opinion as well as to take preventive measures against potential sources of dissent.[22]

OVRA and the *polizia politica* were separate institutions. The dozen or so high-level functionaries at the political police office in Rome served as "the brain of the entire investigative and repressive police system, the centralized memory of...knowledge accumulated in the fight against antifascism." If the *polizia politica* office in Rome constituted the brain of the regime's political policing apparatus, the OVRA offices, together with the provincial *questure*, functioned as its arms. While the OVRA was entrusted with investigating, infiltrating, and ultimately quashing anti-Fascist movements, the *questure* conducted these same activities in operations against "less dangerous" groups and individuals.[23] OVRA thus functioned as the secret, elite corps of a larger state police apparatus whose various other components – *questure*, provincial *polizia politica*, *carabinieri*, and so forth – were also conducting lower-level political repression.

Within Italy, the *polizia politica* coordinated the operations of the OVRA and the *questure*. Protocol prohibited the *questori* and OVRA zones from communicating directly with one another. If, for example, a *questore* discovered a potentially grave anti-Fascist plot, he alerted the *polizia politica* in Rome, which then activated the appropriate OVRA

---

[22] Additional zones were subsequently established in Puglia (1932), Umbria-Abruzzo-Molise-Rieti (1932), Sicily (1933), Sardinia (1937), Campania (1938) – including the provinces of Catanzaro, Reggio Calabria, and, in 1939, Potenza – and Littoria-Frosinone-Viterbo-Castelli Romani (1939). New OVRA zones were carved out of existing ones, and individual provinces shifted from one jurisdiction to another. In 1941, e.g., the OVRA established a zone for Tuscany, which was then reintegrated into the second zone in July 1941. Similarly, a tenth zone was established for eastern Sicily (June 1940–October 1941). Finally, a branch of the OVRA was established in eastern Italy, or Dalmatia, under Italian military occupation. See Franzinelli, I *tentacoli*, 245–51.

[23] Canali, *Le spie*, 70–3.

zone.[24] All three political policing corps often shared informants and other resources. Moreover, their agents all came from the same institutional culture and attended the same police schools. Overlapping jurisdictions and competencies required close collaboration but more often engendered intense institutional competition stemming in part from a general resentment, widespread throughout the state and party apparatuses, of the unfettered power of the OVRA. The *polizia politica* division was also very active in the centers of anti-Fascist immigration – such as Paris, London, Geneva, Barcelona, and Brussels – managing the political investigative offices installed in foreign embassies and consulates. The same political police functionaries responsible for these spy networks abroad also directed the web of informants within Italy, making clear the regime's appreciation of the interdependency between the anti-Fascists' leadership-in-exile and the domestic clandestine movements. Accordingly, *polizia politica* operatives abroad worked to infiltrate the exiled anti-Fascist groups and sever their links to their domestic counterparts.[25]

The regime's various political police forces conducted a wide array of intelligence-gathering activities within a context of absolutely arbitrary state police power, without warrants or judicial oversight. They recruited their informants from the ranks of old Socialists and Communists, often those who had been broken by prison sentences or had otherwise fallen on hard times. OVRA or police personnel would make contact with a former "subversive," offering a "friendly" admonishment to mend his ways. Later on, at another meeting, money or favors were offered in exchange for information. *Questori* sometimes employed subtle threats against family members, suggested possibilities for employment or career advancement, and kept information on criminal and sexual activity to use as blackmail.[26] Police also censored domestic and international mail, conducted house searches, and tapped phones. Four hundred stenographers listened in on the conversations of militants, suspects, Fascists, and government officials. Aware of these activities, Italians constructed the myth of an omniscient and omnipotent OVRA.[27] The myth was perhaps not entirely overblown, if one considers the interconnectedness of OVRA with the offices of the *polizia politica* and the network of informants surrounding the *questure*. The complicity of some Fascists, syndicalists, and state employees (including postal and telegraphic workers, railway men,

---

[24] Ibid., 68–75.
[25] Ibid., 41–59.
[26] See Franzinelli, I *tentacoli*, 245–5, 316–17.
[27] Ibid., 236–9.

and civil servants) further enhanced environments of suspicion and fear. Moreover, private businesses such as hotels were legally obligated to collect information on citizens, and houses of prostitution were randomly searched, their employees and customers detained. Doctors and other medical practitioners were required by law to report to police authorities any diagnoses of mental illness, psychosis, alcoholism, and venereal disease.[28] Bar owners received their business permits from the police and often served as police informants. Most of these modes of information gathering were not controlled by the OVRA, yet there was no way for ordinary Italians to know this. The myth of the OVRA thus reflected the public's experience with pervasive surveillance and authoritarian police actions.

Surveillance and intelligence gathering, particularly on individual political suspects, were at the heart of political policing strategy. In Rome, the *politizia politica*, Confino office, and the OVRA all compiled biographical files on opponents and dissidents, as well as on prominent individuals from various social strata. Provincial *questure* also managed their own archives of biographical information on local political suspects (*servizio informazioni riservate*).[29] Particularly dangerous individuals had files in the DAGR's Central Political Registry (CPC), which by 1943 had compiled 130,000 personal files, the majority between 1927 and 1932, during the campaigns against the Communist Party and the "Justice and Liberty" movement.[30] The police did not act upon most information but collected it in case some question should arise about an individual. The state also issued a mandatory "identity card," banned emigration, and required people to inform the police when they moved within Italy. Finally, the *questure* communicated with one another and Rome. Registration, surveillance, and interprovincial communication, not to mention widespread spying and informing, when introduced into the tightly knit social fabric of Italian communities, ensured that virtually no one was anonymous under Fascism. On the occasions that Italians moved about Italy for work or family, their criminal histories, political inclinations, and reputations followed them.

The centrality of gathering personal information on political suspects (broadly defined) fed the very personalized nature of Fascist political repression. Through traditional investigative techniques, police and other

---

[28] Ibid., 65.
[29] Ibid., 62–3.
[30] On the CPC, see Giovanna Tosatti, "L'anagrafe dei sovversivi italiani: origini e storia del Casellario politico central," *Le Carte e la Storia* 3:2 (1997): 133–50.

public-security agents gathered a remarkable amount of information on individual suspects' lives, including facts about their political and criminal history, social status, military service and honors, occupation, moral character, family members, physical health, membership in PNF organizations, and general attitude toward the regime. For *questori*, prefects, and even Mussolini and Bocchini, it was essential, in a sense, to "know" an individual in order to judge and sentence them. Especially for minor offenses, police reports focused less on the offense, evidence, or the veracity of accusations, and more on background information considered relevant to an individual's political, social, and moral character. These factors often determined the nature of their punishment, as did the economic status and character of the detainee's family. So, for example, an individual with no political precedents, "good moral character," and a family deemed supportive of the regime, but with unstable finances, might have been treated more leniently than a "subversive" with "bad moral character" whose family environment was "politically unhealthy." Fascist police officials, from provincial *questori* and prefects up to Bocchini and Mussolini, weighed these factors in their deliberations and decisions.

In the campaign to uproot clandestine opposition movements, agents and interrogators knew their anti-Fascist adversaries intimately and capitalized on the human dimension of clandestine militancy. Interrogators blended large amounts of truth with lies and deceptions, easily obtaining confessions from anti-Fascists who believed their comrades had betrayed them. At the conclusion of an investigation, after prison and *confino politico* sentences had been meted out, the political police forces then monitored persons who had been marginal to the investigation. A few known militants were also sometimes deliberately left out of the dragnet as a starting point for monitoring the development of new cells. In the case of the Communists, after a wave of repression, the PCI leadership-in-exile sent new operatives into Italy, and the cycle of surveillance and suppression continued. Although political investigations could be intimately personal, police agents harbored no pity. Communists, anarchists, and other militants were viewed as enemies, subversives, and even moral degenerates. Through slurs and aspersions regarding the sexual behaviors of female anti-Fascists, police investigators revealed their particular contempt for women militants, for their anti-Fascism and their activities as emancipated women.[31]

---

[31] Canali, *Le spie*, 76–8.

As during the years of *squadrismo*, the regime condemned unauthorized and inopportune violence, while nevertheless sanctioning the selective use of torture, beatings, and murder. State officials regularly denied the use of violence against political prisoners, a claim bolstered by the great many prominent anti-Fascists who recalled enduring only psychological abuse. The testimonies of anti-Fascists who accused the regime of inflicting violence were often discounted as hyperbolic propaganda. However, official sources attest to rough treatment, physical torture, and even murder, primarily in northern *questure* – Milan, Sondrio, Florence, Forlì, Trieste, and Perugia – where anti-Fascist networks were particularly robust. Such tactics may have been more widespread, considering the frequent use of euphemisms in police reports such as *"domande stringenti"* (tough questions). Not surprisingly, the police used violence discriminatingly. Prominent anti-Fascists, especially those who belonged to "moderate" (non-Communist) parties, were rarely abused. Ernesto Rossi, an anti-Fascist, claimed that "white-collar" militants were not tortured because police feared retribution from their families and friends.[32] Instead, the regime reserved the harshest treatment for working-class Communist militants, Slavs, and other marginal or subaltern groups whom police could assault or torture without arousing the ire of local communities or domestic and foreign opinion.[33] Additionally, police interrogators threatened suspects with devastatingly long prison sentences and physical violence. Political detainees obviously had every reason to fear the worst and only the most committed militants refused to talk.[34]

The regime's official attitude toward police who beat or tortured detainees further illuminates the very controlled use of violence under Fascism. For example, while posted in Genoa, Questore Pietro Bruno was widely considered responsible for the death (officially a "suicide") of a Communist militant. Bocchini described Bruno as an "authoritarian, impulsive and violent" official who did not "hesitate to use, and to order the use of, violence against antifascist detainees." Despite this frank assessment, Bruno rose through the ranks rapidly, becoming prefect in 1933 at the age of forty. Clearly he was useful to the regime. At the same time, the regime punished other public-security personnel for abusing detainees. Violence inflicted on the wrong type of detainee, or in such a manner as to provoke criticisms from certain communities or

[32] Ernesto Rossi, *La pupilla del duce* (Parma, 1956), 32.
[33] Canali, *Le spie*, 77–78. On the class dimension, see Rossi, *Pupilla del duce*.
[34] Franzinelli, *I tentacoli*, 241–3.

social strata, led to reprimands and punishment. Just as refraining from physically harming prominent anti-Fascists cast doubt upon the claims of rank-and-file militants who had actually been tortured, punishing provincial police officials for misusing violence preserved the veneer of legality the regime cultivated for domestic and foreign consumption.[35]

Institutions of Political Punishment

The gravest form of punishment available to police chiefs was *confino di polizia*. The provincial police commissions who passed *confino* sentences consisted of the prefect, who served as president, the police chief (*questore*), senior officers from the *carabinieri* and the MVSN, and a magistrate (*procuratore del re*), whose presence provided a veneer of judicial oversight. Occasionally, the Fascist *federale*, the provincial party boss, would sit in. Following an incident, arrest, or investigation, the *questore* presented his *confino* recommendation along with the results of an investigation to the commission. The *carabinieri* officer also submitted a report and a recommendation. The police chief and *carabinieri* official thus served as accuser and judge. The individual proposed for *confino di polizia*, who was granted no defense, could be arrested before or after the commission made its decision but was not usually present or even aware of the proceedings. The commission recommended the length of the sentence, ranging from a minimum of one year to a maximum of five years, but there was no limit to the number of times the sentence could be renewed if the individual did not demonstrate signs of "rehabilitation." In his report to the DGPS, the prefect was also required to indicate the nature of the individual's offense, which Mussolini and Bocchini used to determine whether the individual belonged in the "common" or "political" branch of the system. When it suited them, Mussolini and Bocchini exercised strict control over the decisions of the commissions.

In November 1926, Mussolini issued instructions to provincial public-security authorities regarding the application of *confino di polizia*, calling for the arrest and internment of any individual who demonstrated "the intent" of "subverting the national, social, or economic order" or who worked against the "activities of state authorities." Immediately alarmed by the high number of confinement sentences coming from some provincial commissions, the undersecretary of Mussolini's cabinet, Giacomo

[35] Canali, *Le spie*, 82–6.

Suardo, instructed Italian prefects to sentence to *confino* only those persons who constituted "local nuclei" of opposition, meaning those engaged in a "collective effort of action or propaganda, even clandestine, aimed at contradicting or impeding the work [of] State powers." The key was to identify those who led or inspired resistance. Suardo specifically instructed prefects to "abstain from a mass action which, while seemingly very easy, would not correspond with the goals of the legislation, but would instead ultimately compromise them."[36] Consistently throughout the first years of the system's operation, the regime made a concerted effort to portray *confino* as a very precise and limited measure of repression, revealing Mussolini's concern that foreign governments and domestic forces not perceive the Fascist style of rule as exceedingly authoritarian.[37] Moreover, Mussolini did not want to make anti-Fascism appear to be a mass phenomenon by deporting thousands of Italians.[38]

Italians sentenced to political confinement rarely served their entire sentences. Within ten days of sentencing, an individual could petition the Commission of Appeal, which was controlled by Bocchini.[39] Although around six thousand *confinati politici* submitted formal appeals during the entire period, the commission only commuted approximately five hundred sentences.[40] Far more common were the individual acts of clemency and the general amnesties granted by Mussolini on Fascist anniversaries, Catholic holidays (Christmas in particular), and important events such as the declaration of empire.[41] Frequent amnesties also fit well with the regime's larger strategy of repression, keeping numbers down and projecting an image of national reconciliation.

There was a gap between the carefully manipulated appearance and the harsh reality of a political system devoid of opposition or even dissent. Preserving the Fascist monopoly on power required mass repression, conducted through the widespread use of relatively subtle coercive measures and the selective utilization of harsher methods. Thus, while the regime

---

[36] ACS, MI, Ufficio Cifra-Partenze, November 15, 1926, n. 28555 and November 26, 1926, n. 29746. The latter telegram is reprinted in Aquarone, *Organizzazione*, 425–6.

[37] See Musci, *Confino fascista*, liv–lv.

[38] The regime kept no official statistics on the political detainee population until well into the 1930s. Official sources also sometimes provide conflicting estimates. At the end of 1926 there were 942 political detainees. In May 1927 there were approximately 950, and a total of approximately 1,200 assignments had been made. See ibid., lvii.

[39] On the commission, see ibid., lxvii–lxxv.

[40] See ibid., lxxiii.

[41] Ibid., lxxv.

regularly called attention to the small number of political detainees sentenced to *confino*, the provincial commissions were also empowered to impose probation (*ammonizione*), which required an individual to adhere to a curfew, report to the police every morning, and not arouse "suspicion," and police "warnings" (*diffide*), which officially informed an individual that he or she was under police investigation and surveillance.[42] The provincial commissions meted out somewhere between 200,000 to 300,000 probation sentences and warnings. The *confino di polizia* sentences, particularly political ones, thus represented the tip of an iceberg of a larger set of repressive practices. For example, in the first six months of 1927, the Provincial Commission of Naples examined 889 cases. Thirty-three were "politicals," and the remaining 856 were "common." The vast majority was sentenced to *ammonizione* (616), and fifty-two were sentenced to *confino di polizia*. The other cases were still pending, dropped, or sent to criminal prosecutors.[43] Therefore, judging the scope of police repression based solely on the number of political confinement sentences gives no sense of the very intense work of some commissions. These police sanctions also affected entire families, who either chose or were forced by circumstance to accompany the detainee to an island colony or village, or they languished at home, very often deprived of their primary breadwinner. For detainees sentenced to probation, finding and keeping employment became difficult, due to the curfew and the stigma that accompanied an *ammonizione* sentence. Meanwhile, "common detainees" were confined just as arbitrarily as politicals, and in much greater numbers: a total of twenty-five to fifty thousand throughout the course of the regime.[44] The arbitrary arrest and confinement of vagabonds, "habitual criminals," drunks, drug addicts, moneylenders, homosexuals, and other groups advanced the regime's project of upholding law and order. Moreover, some groups treated as "common" detainees, such as anarchists and homosexuals, were also treated as "political" offenders at other times or in other specific contexts.[45]

---

[42] *Enciclopedia dell'antifascismo e della resistenza* (Milan, 1968), s.v. "ammonizione," 1:61–2.

[43] See *questura* di Napoli, "Servizio del Confino e delle Ammonizioni dal 2.12.1926 al 28.6.1927," MI, DGPS, Divisione Polizia, *confinati comuni*, b. 8, fasc.: ammoniti comuni: quesiti, sf. "Servizio ammonizione in provincia di Napoli," "1930."

[44] Ebner, "Dalla repressione dell'antifascismo," 81–104.

[45] Michael Ebner, "The Persecution of Homosexual Men under Fascism, 1926–1943," in *Gender, Family, and Sexuality: The Private Sphere in Italy, 1860–1945*, ed. Perry Willson (London, 2004).

The Special Tribunal for Defense of the State, which began operating in early 1927, operated in much the same manner, at least in terms of its selectivity, as the provincial police commissions that passed *confino di polizia* sentences. The tribunal was staffed by Fascist military officers and worked according to military judicial procedures. Once denounced to the tribunal, an individual was held indefinitely in advance of their trial, which sometimes did not occur for months or even more than a year. The tribunal ordered executions and passed prison sentences of up to thirty years, but it is perhaps best known for the relatively few people it prosecuted: 5,619 were tried, 4,596 were convicted, and "only" forty-two received death sentences (with 31 actually carried out).[46] As with *confino* sentences, behind the official numbers lay wider patterns of repression. For example, the tribunal's investigating magistrates examined the cases of an additional nine thousand Italians but decided not to try them.[47] Instead, the investigators passed these cases off to regular courts and military tribunals or, in a large percentage of cases, declared them closed.[48] In the meantime, however, these suspects had spent months, and sometimes even years, in prison. Arrested, imprisoned, and having narrowly

---

[46] Adriano Dal Pont, Alfonso Leonetti, Pasquale Maiello, and Lino Zocchi, eds., *Aula IV: Tutti i processi del Tribunale Speciale fascista* (Milan: 1976).

[47] See Adriano Dal Pont and Simonetta Carolini, *L'Italia dissidente e antifascita: Le Ordinanze, le Sentenze istruttorie e le Sentenze in Camera di consiglio emesse dal Tribunale speciale fascista contro gli imputati di antifascismo dall'anno 1927 al 1943*, 3 vols. (Milan, 1980). Seventeen volumes cataloging the decisions of the Special Tribunal during each year of its operation have been published: Ministry of Defense, *Tribunale Speciale per la difesa dello Stato*, 17 vols. (Rome, 1980–99).

[48] Generally speaking, a solitary investigative magistrate (*giudice istruttore*) handled less important cases (offenses to the Duce, minor acts of propaganda), while an Investigative Commission (*Commissione istruttoria*) consisting of four magistrates handled more serious cases. The Special Tribunal's investigative magistrates were often highly competent and amenable to simply dropping a case if the evidence was insubstantial or if the act did not constitute a crime. In 85% of cases, investigative magistrates dropped the charges and the defendant was released from prison. They handled less serious cases, and so there was less executive pressure to impose a harsh prison sentence, even more so because the individual had already spent a considerable period in jail. The remaining 15% of cases examined by the investigative magistrates were referred either to the ordinary justice system (*magistratura ordinaria*) or, by far the least common option, the Special Tribunal. The Special Tribunal's Investigative Commission functioned in a similar manner. The commission's job was neither to convict nor to absolve but rather to judge the merits of the case and decide which court, if any, should hear it. Handling more serious political crimes, the commission referred cases to the Special Tribunal and ordinary courts more often than the solitary investigating magistrates: around 40% were dropped, 30% went to the ordinary courts, and the other 30% were sent to the Special Tribunal. Nevertheless, more than half of the cases investigated by the commission were closed or referred to ordinary courts. Dal Pont and Carolini, *L'Italia dissidente e antifascista*, 1:2, 5–6, 9.

averted being tried by the highest Fascist court in the land, an ordinary worker or peasant was unlikely to criticize the Duce or Fascism again.[49] Moreover, as some scholars have noted, the practice of dropping charges or moving cases to the jurisdiction of regular courts most likely functioned to "dilute" the appearance of political repression, minimizing the appearance of popular dissent by lowering the number of "political" victims.[50]

Ordinary Criminal Justice

As studies on Nazi Germany and the Soviet Union have shown, regular policing, criminal courts, and ordinary prisons played an important role in the pursuit of interwar political utopias. In these states, as in Fascist Italy, the repression of "ordinary" criminality simultaneously won public approval, enhanced the environment of fear, and advanced ideological policies of "negative selection" and "social cleansing."[51] Under Mussolini's dictatorship, manipulating the line between "common" and "political" crime allowed the regime to control strictly the apparent scope and meaning of "political crime" at home and abroad. Meanwhile, however, the Fascist penal code, the Rocco Code of 1930, criminalized all manner of activities remotely related to opposition and dissent. Regular criminal courts tried Italians for expatriation, forging documents, smuggling money and contraband, and other activities related to clandestine political activity. The Rocco Code also contained a series of "security measures" that allowed judges to condemn Italians who had been absolved of specific crimes to labor colonies, work houses, asylums, and other state institutions.[52] This aspect of the Fascist criminal code,

---

[49] The vast majority of people investigated and tried by the Special Tribunal were manual and agricultural laborers.

[50] Dal Pont and Carolini, *L'Italia dissidente e antifascita*, 1:11.

[51] Nikolaus Wachsmann, *Hitler's Prisons: Legal Terror in Nazi Germany* (New Haven, CT, and London, 2004). Robert Gellately and Nathan Stoltzfus, "Social Outsiders and the Construction of the Community of People," in *Social Outsiders in Nazi Germany*, ed. Robert Gellately and Nathan Stoltzfus (Princeton, 2001); Sheila Fitzpatrick, *Everyday Stalinism. Ordinary Life in Extraordinary Times: Soviet Russia in the 1930s* (New York, Oxford, 1999), 125–7; J. Arch Getty, Gábor T. Ritterspoon, and Viktor N. Zemskov, "Victims of the Soviet Penal System in the Pre-war Years: A First Approach on the Basis of Archival Evidence," *American Historical Review* 98:4 (October 1993): 1017–49.

[52] "Security measures" were assigned by judges and usually linked to an alleged crime. If the accused had committed crimes in the past ("habitual" or "professional" criminals); if he was found innocent of a crime due to insufficient evidence; if the act did not constitute a crime; if he was not considered responsible due to some condition; if the crime

influenced by Cesare Lombroso's criminology, operated on the premise that future crimes could be preempted through the preventive incarceration or institutionalization of individuals who represented a potential threat to the state or society.[53] Under a self-proclaimed totalitarian regime, in which most individual liberties and due process had been suspended, these "security measures" gave judges illiberal powers to mete out custodial (incarceration or institutionalization) and noncustodial sentences (such as *libertà vigilata*, a judicial sentence much like the police probation, *ammonizione*) to Italians who had not been found guilty of anything. Though decided by judges, these sentences were also administrative, because the victim was transferred to the jurisdiction of the Ministry of the Interior. Considering that each year, beginning in 1932, thousands of individuals were sentenced to "security measures," this aspect of state coercion under Fascism appears quite significant.[54] The Rocco Code thus largely embodied the political and ethical priorities of the new Fascist state. The code curtailed individual rights in favor of collective interests and established the primacy of state authority over legality. Political and common crimes were framed as threats to the nation. The right to mount a defense, or even be heard, diminished, while penalties increased.[55] By adhering to these quintessentially Fascist principles, and punishing activities related to opposition and dissent, the Italian judiciary occupied an important position in the regime's repressive apparatus.

Finally, the regime and its police often arbitrarily arrested and detained individuals, in some cases indefinitely. Acting on their own initiative

had not yet been committed; and if a judge ascertained a certain level of "dangerousness," or likelihood that the individual would commit a crime, a security measure might be assigned. Security measures could also be assigned in addition to a regular prison sentence. The duration of the sentence was limitless and dependent on the individual's "reeducation" (i.e., the cessation of their "dangerousness"). See Guido Neppi Modona, "Carcere e società civile," in *Storia d'Italia*, 5:2: *I Documenti* (Turin, 1973), 1901–98. See also Giuseppe Checchia, *Misure di polizia e misure di sicurezza* (Naples, 1934).

[53] See Mary Gibson, *Born to Crime: Cesare Lombroso and the Origins of Biological Criminology* (Westport, 2002); and Guido Neppi Modona, "Carcere e società civile," 1967.

[54] In the mid-1930s, the capacity of these "institutions for administrative security measures" (*stabilimenti per misure amministrative di sicurezza*) – agricultural colonies, work houses, asylums, *case di cura e di custodia, riformatori giudiziari, case di rigore*, and *case per minorati fisici* – increased greatly, from around 5,000 in 1933 to almost 9,000 in 1937. Accordingly, the population of these institutions during these years rose from approximately 3,000 to around 7,000 (6,322 males, 521 females, 6,754 total). See Ministero di Grazia e Giustizia, Direzione Generale per gli Istituti di Prevenzione di Pena, *Statistica degli Istituti di Prevenzione e di Pena e dei Riformatori* (Rome, 1928–37).

[55] Dunnage, "Social Control," 264.

or orders from Rome, police commissioners arrested suspects and kept them in prison for days, weeks, and months, without even intending to charge them with anything. Most commonly, the police arrested the same "usual" suspects over and over. One politically or socially "dangerous" individual might be arrested and released dozens of times. In the personal files of political detainees, it is also not uncommon to see the Interior Ministry order prison sentences of several months duration. These essentially constituted extrajudicial executive decrees of imprisonment, with no basis in law.

Although the Fascist state did not intern, imprison, or torture hundreds of thousands of Italians, it did employ a vast array of coercive measures of varying severity on a mass scale in its attempt to assert control over and transform Italian society. Moreover, by dispersing large numbers of troublesome Italians throughout the various police, penal, and public health institutions, as well as by putting many others on probation or simply "warning" them, the regime made political repression an almost impossible phenomenon to quantify. By successfully disguising politically motivated punishments, the regime could then manipulate and control its image at home and abroad.

Party and Militia

In Fascist Italy, as in Nazi Germany after it, paramilitary political militias, who had seized and consolidated power in part through illegal terrorist violence, became responsible for identifying, punishing, and controlling a great number of "enemies" of the state. Although the institutional and jurisdictional configurations differed in each case, the civil societies of both nations were inundated with members of militarized party organizations – identifiable by their uniforms, insignias, and reputations – whose right to intimidate, attack, and take custody of their fellow citizens was based primarily on their ideological zeal and capacity for violence, and not on any formal law-enforcement training. Though more so in Germany than in Italy, the police state's complicity in this extralegal violence created arenas in civil society that were lawless, in which party members and militiamen used intimidation, fear, and real physical violence to dominate their fellow citizens.

The role of the PNF and the MVSN in repressing dissent and punishing ideological enemies has never been clearly understood by scholars. Unlike Hitler's regime, where the state was, relatively speaking, "Nazified," the Mussolini dictatorship rebuked the Fascist Party's attempts to exercise direct, independent control over state institutions. At the same time, Mussolini charged the party with helping the regime penetrate and control Italian society, defining the PNF as a "civilian and voluntary force at the service of the State, just as the Voluntary Militia for National Security is an armed force at the service of the State." The party was "the capillary organization of the regime."[56] The degree to which the PNF was subordinated to the state has been an important point of debate among historians. As discussed in the previous chapter, one widely accepted view holds that after the establishment of a full-blown dictatorship in 1926, the party was rendered impotent by Mussolini's campaign to "normalize" his regime.

Interpretations of the role of the MVSN closely mirror those regarding the PNF. Established in 1923, the MVSN integrated the Fascist squads into a formal military structure. Mussolini's primary aim, in the view of most historians, was to tame the autonomous and anarchic violence of the *squadrists*.[57] The defeat of anti-Fascism and the institutionalization of the "revolution" in the late 1920s, undoubtedly cast the role of the MVSN into question. Although some Italians viewed the militiamen as *squadrists* by another name, many old-guard *squadrists* accused them of having lost their Fascist character. According to historian Alberto Aquarone, after Mussolini's definitive conquest of the state, the militia lost its "political bite and warlike party spirit" and was demoted to "normal police administration."[58] The MVSN's role as a "great political police," according to most historians, never materialized, and the regime relied instead on the state political police, the secret political police (OVRA), and the *Carabinieri reali* for the repression of opposition and dissent. At the same time, Mussolini refused to dissolve the militia. As Aquarone explains, "he was unable to renounce the militia as a tangible and living sign of the permanence of the Fascist revolution and its attributes of bellicose virility."[59] At least symbolically, the militia embodied the Fascist glorification of violence, male virility, discipline, and hierarchical sociopolitical organization.

Equally important for Mussolini, perhaps, was the MVSN's function of integrating Italian men into the regime. By 1930, there were almost four hundred thousand officers and militiamen in the MVSN, making

[56] Mussolini, OO, XXIV:141–2. See also Emilio Gentile, "The Problem of the Party in Italian Fascism," *Journal of Contemporary History* 19:2 (1984): 269.

[57] For a comparison, see Sven Reichardt, *Faschistische Kampfbünde.*

[58] Aquarone, "Milizia," 99.

[59] Ibid., 104, 109.

it larger than all branches of the armed forces (army, air force, navy, and *carabinieri*) combined. However, as a voluntary, national Fascist reserve force, most officers and militiamen were inactive. They lived as civilians, working at normal professions. Incentives for joining included material benefits and the less tangible but very real political privileges. The few thousand active members received discounted rail travel, free public transportation, and free admission to public facilities. The mostly inactive squad chiefs (sergeants), of which there were approximately twenty-five thousand, also received discounted train tickets and other benefits. The families of all MVSN members, militiamen and officers, received a pension in case of death.[60] In exchange, MVSN units could be called up for military service, and some were responsible for surveillance, security, and discipline in the political confinement colonies.

Although the power, autonomy, and revolutionary fervor of the militia was certainly curtailed by the late 1920s, viewing the MVSN as a depoliticized institution, created solely as part of a larger process of "normalizing" Fascism, mischaracterizes the novelty of this new corps. After all, the Fascist squads, made up of practitioners of brutal political violence, had been formally incorporated into the state. They swore their primary loyalty not to offices or institutions but to the person of the Duce. Moreover, the militia, although it served the state, was also connected to the Fascist Party through the person of Mussolini and, at the provincial level, the relationships between party *federali* and militia commanders.[61] In creating the militia, Mussolini intended not to return to some earlier state of "normalcy" but to permanently insert Fascism into the Italian state. Moreover, the MVSN, Mussolini hoped, would someday advance the project of "Fascistizing" Italy.[62] In theory and in practice, the Fascist regime valued the MVSN as a force for penetrating the authority and ideology of the regime deeply and diffusely into Italian society. The individual militiaman carried his commitment to Fascism into all areas of his life. Thus, although it is true that the violent exploits of the squads make the later activities of the MVSN seem tame by comparison, there was nothing "normal" about this new force.

[60] There were approximately 235,000 soldiers and 16,500 officers in the Italian armed forces. For the comparison, see Ricciotti Lazzero, *Il Partito Nazionale Fascista* (Milan 1985), 51–3.
[61] Elvira Valleri, "Dal partito armato al regime totalitario," *Italia contemporanea* 32:141 (1980): 31–60.
[62] Ibid., 34.

Whatever the failures of the Fascist transformation of society, militiamen had real power and legal jurisdiction to exercise state coercion and violence in their daily lives. In official documents, the militiaman was referred to as a "public official," "an official and agent of public security," and "an official and agent of the judicial police." Throughout the 1920s and early 1930s, contemporary jurists, writing in legal textbooks and public-security manuals, regularly remarked upon the high degree of "discretionary" power (*discrezionalità*) and "autonomy" with which militiamen acted, outside of any command structure, including the power to make arrests. This very wide field of action had been carved out for the militia in formal legislation and manuals.[63] "All of the members of the MVSN," according to one MVSN manual, "even if they are not wearing the uniform and have not been activated as the result of mobilization, are authorized to carry out their duties, safeguarding public order, impeding the perpetration of crimes, and repressing acts that the laws of the state prohibit."[64] The reformed Code of Penal Procedure also explicitly entrusted militiamen with arresting individuals in the act of committing crimes, including but not limited to suspected acts of anti-Fascism. The code also authorized militiamen to enter and search the homes of individuals who had committed a crime.[65] The militiaman, by Mussolini's exhortations and in training manuals, was encouraged to engage in "constant and continuous service" in his everyday life, even when dressed, and living, as civilian.[66] Above all, militiamen were ordered to look out for political opposition and dissent. The militia's chief function, according to the Grand Council of Fascism, was "to render impossible every disturbance of public order, every gesture or attempt at sedition against the Fascist Government, both independently and in conjunction with the ordinary police forces."[67]

The MVSN conducted its own political surveillance through approximately 170 Provincial Investigative Offices (UPI) responsible for recruiting

---

[63] Ibid., 46–8.

[64] Giuseppe Rabaglietti, *Le funzioni di polizia giudiziaria della Mvsn e delle sue specialità militizia forestale, stradale, ferroviaria, postelegrafonica, portuaria e confinaria* (Turin, 1933), 4. Quoted in Valleri, "Dal partito armato al regime totalitario," 47.

[65] The *Codice di procedura penale* names "the militiamen of the *Milizia volontaria per la sicurezza nazionale*" as "officials of the judiciary police" (Art. 221) and authorizes them to arrest, interrogate, and search the home of an individual caught committing a crime (Art. 222–4). See Italy, Ministero della Giustizia e degli Affari di Culto, *Codice di procedura penale* (Rome, 1930), 64.

[66] Valleri, "Dal partito armato al regime totalitario," 48.

[67] Quoted in Alberto Aquarone, "Milizia," 92.

informers and pursuing investigations into the activities of civilians from all social strata. Though technically subordinate to the provincial police chief, the UPIs often worked autonomously, ignoring police officials and reporting their findings instead to the general command of the MVSN in Rome. They also served as alternative repositories for denunciations from the public. When a UPI discovered any matter that required action against an individual under investigation, it was supposed to report to the provincial *questore*, because only the police could formally imprison, charge, sanction, or intern a suspect. However, in situations in which immediate intervention was required, members of the MVSN were authorized to use force and take custody of an individual.[68] Although the MVSN might deliver a suspect directly to the police, some offices – the UPI of Milan was notorious – frequently took suspects to their headquarters where they were interrogated, beaten, tortured, and, on rare occasions, murdered.[69] These types of spontaneous, public actions were perhaps more common, and certainly more visible, than UPI investigations that were quietly turned over to the police.

The PNF also conducted surveillance and intelligence-gathering activities, which increased in intensity from the mid-1930s onward. The *federali*, the provincial headquarters of the PNF, had always contained political offices, and beginning in 1935, the party introduced the Capillary Investigative Units (*Organizzazioni capillare investigativa* [OCI]), which operated at the neighborhood level. Even before the constitution of party investigative offices, local Fascists served as intermediaries between ordinary Italians and the police. They communicated their suspicions and desires to public-security authorities and received denunciations and complaints from citizens. Party members were technically responsible for reporting information regarding the activities of friends, acquaintances, and co-workers, but they performed this function selectively.[70] This relationship between the party, the state, and society bears some resemblance to the situation in Nazi Germany, where the Schutzstaffel (SS), Sturmabteilung (SA), Hitler Youth, and other party organizations were fully integrated into the terror apparatus at the local level.[71] In

---

[68] On the UPIs, see Canali, *Spie*, 114–18.
[69] Ibid., 86.
[70] Ibid., 122.
[71] Carl-Wilhelm Reibel, *Das Fundament der Diktatur. Die NSDAP-Ortsgruppen, 1932–1945* (Paderborn, München, Wien, Zürich, 2002), 271–377; Gerhard Rempel, *Hitler's Children: The Hitler Youth and the SS* (Chapel Hill, 1989).

the case of Fascist Italy, due to a dearth of scholarship and documentation, the degree to which the UPI and OCI – as well as branches of the party not specifically responsible for surveillance, such as the youth and women's sections – collaborated and were coordinated with the political police is unknown. However, particularly at the local level, the existence of these institutions obviously harbored great potential for informal contacts between the state, society, and the investigative offices of the PNF and MVSN.

Between 1926 and 1930, the Fascist regime created an entire constellation of party-state institutions responsible for political repression and social control. In particular, the reform and organization of the police gave the state unprecedented authority to intervene in the lives of ordinary individuals. In implementing these reforms, senior Interior Ministry officials made it clear that the new regime intended to use the police not simply to repress crime but to affect a transformation in the habits and attitudes of the Italian people. In practice, then, the Fascist police state laid claim to jurisdiction over an incredibly large, even unlimited, swath of public and private matters. At the same time, the regime deliberately worked to reduce the apparent scope of political repression. For political – not to mention economic – reasons, the regime preferred locally administered, noncustodial sanctions to mass imprisonment and confinement. Moreover, the regime punished a relatively small number of Italians for explicitly "political" offenses, while ordinary criminal courts meted out a wide array of sanctions against the regime's political and ideological enemies. The place of the PNF and MVSN within this repressive apparatus was somewhat ambiguous, perhaps intentionally. However, the enormous discretionary powers invested in the Interior Ministry and its DGPS meant that Fascists and militiamen could and often did operate as auxiliaries to the police and also act against anti-Fascists and other "suspects" in their daily lives. Mussolini repeatedly urged the party to act as a "capillary" force, penetrating Fascism more deeply into Italian society. When Fascists crossed the lines of legality, the police simply legitimized these acts *ex post facto*, implicitly falling back on the Fascist doctrine of state infallibility.

3

Breaking the Anti-Fascists, 1926–1934

> Always terror, fear. Either they took papa away or they went after the family. There you go: it was terror.
>
> A woman from San Lorenzo, a working-class district in Rome, recalls life under Fascism[1]

> They beat up Mario, they put Oreste in jail, they threw my brother out of his job. It is a leitmotiv. No one has ever forgotten.
>
> Igor Markevitch on the Tuscan peasantry[2]

For Italians who had been victimized by squad violence, the Fascist police state presented a new, even more potent form of terror. Viewed from below, all state institutions now appeared to rest in the hands of Mussolini and the Fascists. Even at the local level, Black Shirts held considerable sway over how the state punished anti-Fascists. Although illegal violence had diminished by 1926, systematic state violence in some ways functioned more efficiently. Individual anti-Fascists and recalcitrant working-class communities who had successfully fended off Fascist attacks in the past now had to contend with the police, *carabinieri*, courts, prisons, and other punitive institutions. The hostile practices of these and other state agencies – such as labor syndicates and welfare offices – ultimately overwhelmed Mussolini's opponents and the communities in which they operated. Eventually, the forces of anti-Fascism within Italy were broken. Italians who possessed the resolve to fight on usually did so alone, most often behind prison bars or inside of island *confino* colonies.

---

[1] Lidia Piccioni, *San Lorenzo, un quartiere romano durante il fascismo* (Rome, 1984), 108.
[2] Igor Markevitch, *Made in Italy* (Lausanne, 1946), 117.

Days after the introduction of the Fascist police code on November 6, 1926, Police Chief Bocchini sent out flurries of telegrams to police order-ing the arrest of prominent anti-Fascist politicians, party leaders, labor bosses, and intellectuals.[3] Police officials arrested the regime's oppo-nents in their homes, often waking them in the middle of the night and "accompanying" them to headquarters.[4] Some anti-Fascists were already on the run, in hiding, but police hunted most of them down. A few fled abroad. Following Bocchini's orders, public-security authorities first arrested Communist parliamentary deputies, like Antonio Gramsci, who stayed in Rome under the erroneous assumption that his parliamentary immunity would protect him. Socialists, Republicans, trade unionists, Freemasons, and other non-Communists of national standing also figured among the first to be arrested. Within weeks, however, Mussolini and his undersecretary of the interior, Giacomo Suardo, expanded the scope of the campaign, ordering provincial authorities – prefects and police chiefs – to arrest and sentence to confinement the "local nuclei" of opposition to Fascism. By the end of December, between five and six hundred Italians had been sentenced to political confinement, most of them from provinces where the violent clash between Fascists and anti-Fascists had been most intense – the north, the center, and Puglia.[5] State violence, just like squad violence, became intensely localized, albeit closely monitored by Rome.

The new Fascist institutions of repression served many purposes, but none more immediate than the suppression of individuals and groups who professed political beliefs contrary to, or simply different from, Fascism. The Fascist totalitarian utopia aspired to create a society without political opposition, dissent, or even a public memory of socialism, pacifism, and other forms of left-wing "subversion." Reaching this goal would require not just dismantling organizations, institutions, and movements. Subver-sion – socialism, anarchism, opposition to state authority – was deeply embedded in the social fabric of working-class communities, from the landless laborers of the Po Valley to the industrial workers of Turin. This *tradizione sovversiva* was sustained by informal social networks, families,

---

[3] For a description of the legislation, see Musci, *Confino fascista*, xli–liii.

[4] For firsthand accounts of the arrest, imprisonment, and transport of the first *confinati politici* (1926–7), see Luigi Salvatori, *Al confino e in carcere* (Milan, 1958); Jaures Busoni, *Nel tempo del fascismo* (Rome, 1975); Mario Magri, *Una vita per la libertà* (Rome, 1956); and Alfredo Misuri, *Ad Bestias! Memorie d'un perseguitato* (Rome, 1944).

[5] See Musci, *Confino fascista*, lvii.

and class solidarity.[6] Mussolini's police state thus set about breaking these bonds and conquering working-class strongholds. In most cases, arresting a few people completely neutralized opposition to Fascism. The suffering of detainees and their families provided "admonitory examples" for other members of the community, who quickly fell into line.

After years spent harassing and spying on local "subversives," provincial police authorities already knew whom to arrest. Throughout northern and central Italy, as well as Puglia and larger cities in the south, prefects passed confinement sentences on "fervent" Communists, "revolutionary" Socialists, "the most violent" anarchists, and "irreducible" subversives of indeterminate or crypto-anarchist political stripes. Particularly throughout the Po Valley, the police sought out local Socialist Party bosses, former mayors and councilmen, active rank-and-file Communists and Socialists, and labor organizers. In larger urban areas, especially Rome, police confined anarchists and lone "subversives" who, while not belonging to any organization, nevertheless constituted a threat to the "political and social order." In the villages and hamlets of the Po Valley, the targets were the leaders of the peasant leagues. In Bari and other larger cities in Puglia, police arrested peasants, anarchists, Communists, and other left-wingers who had participated in land occupations during the *biennio rosso*. Anyone held accountable for injuring or killing Fascists during the violence of the previous six years was also a likely target. Mussolini had finally begun carrying out the wave of "revolutionary justice" that intransigent members of his party had so ardently desired.

The Communist Party

The experiences of the leaders and militants of the Italian Communist Party (PCI) during the years from 1926 to 1934 reveal the difficulties of organizing meaningful resistance to the Mussolini regime. Well before 1926, the Fascist squads and police, often working in concert, had dismantled most of the major non-Communist anti-Fascist parties and movements – Socialists, Republicans, Catholics, liberal democrats, and others. The exceptional decrees then enabled the regime to mop up the remnants of such groups within a few months. Only the Communists managed to survive and rebuild in subsequent years, maintaining a national, centralized party structure. At the local level, particularly in working-class

---

[6] See Tobias Abse, "Italian Workers and Italian Fascism," in *Fascist Italy and Nazi Germany: Comparisons and Contrasts*, ed. Richard Bessel (Cambridge, 1996), 40–60.

communities, anti-Fascists of heterodox political faiths coalesced around the PCI. Accordingly, between 1927 and the early 1930s, the Fascist political police apparatus focused its efforts on penetrating and dismantling the Communists' clandestine network. Thousands of PCI leaders, cadres, and rank-and-file militants were arrested and prosecuted. With each wave of arrests, new, often younger militants stepped up to take the place of "fallen" comrades.

Large-scale repression of the Communists had already begun before November. Immediately after fifteen-year-old Anteo Zamboni's failed attempt to kill Mussolini in October 1926, Italian police arrested around two thousand, or approximately one-third, of PCI militants. Although authorities soon released many Communists, days later came the exceptional decrees. Acting upon their new authority, police immediately arrested current and potential leaders of the PCI, including parliamentary deputies.[7] Within months, PCI cadres still at large pessimistically concluded that maintaining the party network was neither possible nor advisable. However grim, the situation was not hopeless. After operating as a quasi-illegal organization for several years, the party had developed a robust clandestine network. Approximately one thousand Communists were in captivity, but the Central Committee calculated that, as of May 1927, about five thousand militants were still at large. In January, the first clandestine edition of *L'Unità* appeared, registering the continued existence of the party and its willingness to fight on.[8]

For Bocchini, the PCI's resilience was worrisome, and throughout 1927, the police state stepped up its campaign against the Communists. In some respects, the frenzied efforts to reconstitute the PCI and distribute propaganda actually assisted the regime in identifying Communist cells. The appearance of leaflets, manifestos, or graffiti in a given city, neighborhood, or factory helped police determine where to focus their efforts. Moreover, while rapidly reconstituting cells and recruiting new members, PCI cadres gave little thought to the possibility of infiltration by police informants, whom the regime began recruiting with great success. Despite setbacks, many Communists remained defiantly optimistic. Others were less so: the PCI's clandestine activity, according to one party leader, Pietro Secchia, was akin to carrying out a "frontal assault in front

[7] See "Provvedimenti adottati in dipendenza dell'applicazione delle leggi sulla difesa dello Stato," ACS, MI, PS, Anno 1926, b. 102, fasc. C2. On the arrest of parliamentary deputies, see Musci, *Confino fascista*, lvn115; Spriano, *Storia del partito comunista*, 2:67.

[8] Spriano, *Storia del partito comunista*, 2:68, 70–1.

of the machine guns."[9] In 1928, important operatives returned from France to reconstitute the PCI's Internal Center. Political police captured them within months.[10] An assassination attempt against the Italian king on April 12 led to the arrests of almost six hundred anti-Fascists, most of them Communists, even though the PCI had nothing to do with the plot.[11]

The regime imprisoned or confined the national and provincial leadership of the PCI as a temporary measure in anticipation of its formal prosecution before the Special Tribunal, which began operating in February 1927. The sentences inflicted on the highest-ranking PCI leadership were harsh. The tribunal condemned important, midlevel cadres to ten, twelve, or more years, while rank-and-file members received lesser terms. For the highest-ranking members, Mussolini insisted on draconian sentences. Between May 28 and June 4, 1928, the Special Tribunal conducted the so-called *processone* (big trial) of thirty-three Communists. Antonio Gramsci, Umberto Terracini, Mauro Scoccimarro, Giovanni Roveda, and many other PCI leaders appeared before a panel of six judges: five consoles of the Fascist Militia and one military general. Eight Communists, including Palmiro Togliatti and Camilla Ravera, were tried in absentia. At the trial, the prosecutor said of Antonio Gramsci, "we must prevent this brain from functioning for twenty years."[12]

Police originally arrested Gramsci, a parliamentary deputy and general secretary of the PCI, in Rome on the night of November 8, 1926. Sentenced to *confino*, he arrived on the island of Ustica on December 6 and remained there until January 20. Denounced to the Special Tribunal, Gramsci then spent more than two weeks in transit, stopping off in ten jails, before arriving at Milan's San Vittore prison on February 7. Determined to keep Communists and "irreducible" anti-Fascists in state custody indefinitely, the Fascist regime established a pattern of shuttling political prisoners like Gramsci back and forth between *confino* colonies and prisons. Executive punishment often picked up where the

---

[9] Ibid., 2:89–90, 95.

[10] In March 1928, four Communist leaders – Luigi Longo, Edoardo D'Onofrio, Girolamo Li Causi, and Giuseppe Amoretti – entered Italy to reconstitute the Internal Center, the party's domestic central committee. In less than two months, all but Longo had been arrested.

[11] Charles Delzell, *Mussolini's Enemies: The Italian Anti-Fascist Resistance* (Princeton, 1961), 150–1.

[12] Giuseppe Fiori, *Antonio Gramsci: Life of a Revolutionary*, trans. Tom Nairn (New York, 1990), 24.

Fascist judicial system left off.[13] The magistrate responsible for conducting the preliminary investigation of Gramsci's case completed his report in March 1927. During the next year, Gramsci remained in prison, while paid police informants posing as fellow political prisoners attempted to extract information from him. *Agents provocateurs* also tried to involve Gramsci in clandestine political plots. Failing to implicate the Communist leader in a crime against the state, the Special Tribunal tried him retroactively, for alleged crimes carried out before November 1926. Not surprisingly, the Fascist judges sentenced him to a term of twenty years. The next decade in Italy's inhospitable prisons took a serious toll on Gramsci's health. Around 1935, the regime authorized his transfer to a hospital, where he died in April 1937.[14] Had he been healthy, Gramsci would unquestionably never have been released from custody. Many of Gramsci's codefendants spent the entire regime in prison or confinement. Mauro Scoccimarro, for example, was arrested November 5, 1926, sentenced to *confino* on the island of Favignana, and then received a twenty-year prison sentence. In February 1937, Mussolini granted Scoccimarro amnesty, but then the police sent him directly into political confinement, first on Ponza, then Ventotene, where he remained until 1943. Dozens of other anti-Fascists followed similar trajectories. Mussolini had no real intention of ever releasing the Italians who actually posed a serious threat to his regime.

During 1927 and 1928, Fascist police repression devastated the PCI's clandestine network. By May 1928, its Foreign Center had almost no contact with the Internal Center. Communist publications appeared in Italy only sporadically.[15] Cells still existed, particularly in the north, but most had been compromised by spies and informants. During 1929, clandestine activity waned. In 1930, the acting PCI leader, Palmiro Togliatti, charted a new direction known as the *svolta* (turn), which largely reflected the influence of Stalin's Comintern. The PCI thereafter refused to cooperate with non-Communist, social-democratic anti-Fascists, labeling them "social-fascists." More importantly for the situation inside Italy, Togliatti concluded that the Wall Street crash signaled the definitive crisis of capitalism and Fascism. He ordered Italian Communists in exile to return to

---

[13] Twenty-three from the sample served Special Tribunal sentences, and another twenty-eight were investigated or tried, but their cases were dismissed or they were found innocent. While awaiting trial, the latter group would have been imprisoned for periods ranging from a few months to more than a year.

[14] Fiori, *Antonio Gramsci*, 220–33.

[15] Delzell, *Mussolini's Enemies*, 160.

Italy to resume opposition activities. The *svolta* thus brought experienced militants who had fled Fascism back into Italy. Many *svoltisti*, as they were sometimes called, were young, often working-class expatriates who had been trained in Marxist ideology and clandestine political operations at schools in Moscow and Leningrad. Italian Communists who opposed the *svolta*, and were consequently expelled from the party, warned that the PCI would be sending its best trained, most committed militants into Italy to be arrested and confined. They were soon proven right. Within days or weeks of entering Italy, most agents were arrested. Although this strategy was arguably ill-considered, the revolutionary impatience that drove the *svolta* was a reaction to deteriorating economic conditions. Rising unemployment, spontaneous strikes, and sporadic protests, accompanied by a resurgence of Communist propaganda on the ground, convinced the PCI leadership abroad that the revolutionary moment had arrived. Failing to have a network in place would, party leaders believed, mean abrogating the PCI's leadership in the resistance to Fascism. Precisely at this moment, the social-democratic opposition movement, Justice and Liberty, was establishing cells in the major cities of northern and central Italy. Justice and Liberty leaders also believed that the economic crisis provided an important opportunity to take direct action and turn Italians against the regime.[16] Beginning in 1930, then, the PCI devoted considerable resources and personnel to rebuilding the organization. The goal was to have a fully operational revolutionary network in place before the imminent collapse of the regime. As agents poured into Italy, new cells emerged, particularly in Veneto, Lombardy, Piedmont, Tuscany, and Emilia. Although the south saw little activity, Naples emerged as an important center.[17]

In Rome, Bocchini grew alarmed as police chiefs from all over Italy began noting the reappearance of anti-Fascist graffiti and pamphlets. He warned Mussolini that the PCI had increased its capacity for organization, propaganda, and fund raising. On May 1, 1930, for example, militants inside Italy distributed 32,000 newspapers and 150,000 pamphlets.[18] In response, the police stepped up surveillance and actions against suspected militants. During each week in December, the political police throughout Italy registered around twenty thousand operations – which included arbitrary arrests, warrantless searches of individuals and homes, spontaneous

---

[16] On the *svolta*, see Spriano, *Storia del partito comunista*, 2:187–9.
[17] Ibid., 2:239.
[18] Ibid., 2:232, 289–90.

inspections of public establishments, and the seizure of personal effects, propaganda, foreign publications, and arms. Political policing activities were particularly intense in the north, in cities and provinces with a notable Communist presence.[19] Compromised by informants and operating with negligible support from the population, the PCI's agents and cells were quickly ferreted out by the OVRA (secret political police) and the *polizia politica* (political police). In the second half of 1930, fifteen important functionaries were arrested, along with hundreds of militants. Between January 1931 and April 1932, police captured 1,595 militants and thirty-five higher-level functionaries.[20]

Though it displayed remarkable resilience, the PCI entered a period of dormancy by 1934, if not earlier.[21] Individual militants remained at large. Isolated cells survived. But Mussolini's political police had dismantled the PCI's centralized structure, and even localized propaganda became limited and difficult. Ironically, the Communist network only survived – even thrived – inside the prisons and the *confino* colonies. Smaller non-Communist movements that appeared in the 1930s, in particular Justice and Liberty, perhaps presented less of a threat to the regime. They were nevertheless pursued ruthlessly and effectively.

Breaking Subversive Communities

In its campaign to break anti-Fascist networks, the regime naturally focused on those areas of Italy – working-class quarters of major industrial centers, for example – where the sheer numbers of Italians hostile to Fascism offered safe havens and possibilities for carrying out opposition activities. During the years of *squadrism*, these communities had defended their neighborhoods, led by the *Arditi del popolo* (shock troops of the people). Men set up barricades and took up arms, and women threw rocks and boiling water out of windows onto the heads of Fascists. Subsequently, with the arrival of the dictatorship, opposition to Fascism and a more general "subversive tradition" persisted. Working-and middle-class families sympathetic to socialism offered assistance to

---

[19] De Felice, *Mussolini il duce*, I:83–4, esp. the chart in n. 1.
[20] Giovanni De Luna, *Donne in oggetto: l'antifascismo nella società italiana, 1922–1939* (Turin, 1995), 60. Among these were included several members of the Central Committee, including Camilla Ravera, Pietro Secchia, and Luigi Frausin, who were captured just weeks after arriving to reconstitute the Internal Center.
[21] Leonardo Rapone, *L'Italia antifascista*, in *Storia d'Italia*, vol. 4: *Guerre e fascismo*, ed. Giovanni Sabbatucci e Vittorio Vidotto (Rome-Bari, 1997), 519.

political fugitives. Workers found small ways to celebrate Socialist holidays and recall better times and places. Lone dissidents unfurled red flags and scrawled anti-Fascist slogans – "Viva Lenin," "Viva Communismo," "Abasso Mussolini" – in public places. The Fascist police state severely, often brutally, suppressed working-class opposition and the *tradizione sovversiva*, though it never entirely eradicated it.[22]

Determined to break these critical zones of working-class resistance, Mussolini's regime deployed an array of state agencies and strategies of violence. The assault on neighborhoods in cities like Rome, Turin, and Parma included not only police surveillance and repression but also urban renewal projects, labor and welfare discrimination, and Fascist infiltration. The overall goal was the "destruction of the social fabric" of "subversive" communities.[23] One of the regime's chief strategies for subduing working-class neighborhoods was eliminating or neutralizing local anti-Fascists who might provide leadership or points of reference for a resurgence of anti-Fascism. Following the October assassination attempt against Mussolini, police in Rome's San Lorenzo neighborhood arrested known Communists, anarchists, and other subversives. After the exceptional decrees, San Lorenzo's leading anti-Fascists disappeared into prison, *confino*, or exile. For other anti-Fascists, remaining in San Lorenzo simply became too dangerous. Moreover, many "subversives" lost their jobs, causing them to leave the area to look for employment or cheaper housing elsewhere. Others fled abroad. A younger cohort then replenished the ranks of the PCI, which initially thrived.[24] The residents of San Lorenzo had access to Communist publications and celebrated major Socialist holidays with dinners, or by wearing flowers or an article of red clothing. By 1930, however, unrelenting police actions began to erode anti-Fascist social cohesion. Moreover, notwithstanding Mussolini's attempt to "normalize" his regime, Fascists still engaged in violent and illegal behavior, creating an environment of constant fear and intimidation. In 1928 police reported that a group of Fascists in San

---

[22] See Antonio Sonnessa, "Working Class Defence Organization, Anti-Fascist Resistance and the Arditi Del Popolo in Turin, 1919–22," *European History Quarterly* 33:2 (2003): 183–218; Carl Levy, *Gramsci and the Anarchists* (Oxford, 1999); Eros Francescangeli, *Arditi Del Popolo: Argo Secondari e la prima organizzazione antifascita, 1917–1922* (Rome, 2000); Tobias Abse, "The Rise of Fascism in an Industrial City: The Case of Livorno 1918–1922," in *Rethinking Italian Fascism. Capitalism, Populism and Culture*, ed. David Forgacs (London, 1986), 52–82.

[23] Piccioni, *San Lorenzo*, 95.

[24] Ibid., 111–14.

Lorenzo committed crimes "without being punished, despite the notoriety of their acts of aggression, threats, assaults, breaking into homes, incurring debts, and more." Fascists intimidated and beat workers who criticized the regime, and generally mistreated San Lorenzo's inhabitants. One Fascist Militia (MVSN) officer led a group of Fascists around at night "stopping peaceful citizens, making demands, and using the pretense of an increase of subversive activity in the quarter as a justification for their violent behavior."[25] The same Fascists also extorted payoffs from shop owners and charged rent to the destitute inhabitants of a small settlement of tents on public property. Although the officer responsible was ultimately removed from his post, similar incidents involving other Fascists persisted throughout the 1930s.[26]

Reconstituting the PCI network after 1931 became difficult, as the social cohesion of San Lorenzo disintegrated. Party operatives traveled to Rome, but they were unable to establish contact with more than a few militants. Togliatti's strategy of flooding Italy with operatives ultimately did little to reestablish ties between the PCI and the population of working-class neighborhoods. As San Lorenzo's natural leaders disappeared into prison or retreated into private life, newcomers moved into the district, including the local offices of the National Fascist Party (PNF). Ordinary people not formally affiliated with the PCI, but who disliked, resented, or hated the regime, felt constantly watched, no longer certain whom to trust. Police and Fascist surveillance thus largely suffocated outward manifestations of the Socialist tradition. As a result, at least until the Spanish Civil War, anti-Fascism in San Lorenzo remained a very private affair.[27]

Further north, in Parma's Oltretorrente, a poor, working-class neighborhood, political militancy, and thus anti-Fascism, were so deeply imbedded in the social fabric that the Fascist squads were unable to penetrate the district before 1923. In August 1922, twenty thousand Fascists led by Italo Balbo failed to conquer Parma, thanks to the *Arditi del popolo* and the community that supported them. Once Mussolini assumed power, however, authorities simultaneously mobilized police repression and squad violence to subdue Parma. For state authorities, the Oltretorrente posed more than just a political problem. Officials reported that the district was "always dirty," the people were "always filthy," and

---

[25] Quoted in ibid., 89.
[26] Ibid., 89.
[27] Ibid., 114–18.

the population was "permeated by antifascism."[28] The prefect noted how people lived "in miserable houses and ignorance," while local subversives "inoculated" them with hatred for the regime and the bourgeoisie.[29] The solution to this set of problems, implemented between 1928 and 1935, was the "reclamation [*risanamento*] of the Oltretorrente." The state razed entire housing blocks, widened streets, and installed basic public utilities. Evicted from their homes, displaced workers resettled in peripheral areas of the city. Into the new, modern housing complexes moved the bedrock of the regime's social base – petite bourgeois families, civil servants, and white-collar workers.[30]

As expected, the "urban renewal" of the Oltretorrente thus helped destroy bonds of class solidarity. Additional waves of arrests brought an end to any meaningful connections between remnant Communist cells and the population. Old anti-Fascists who returned from prison and *confino* in the early 1930s found themselves lost and alienated in their own communities.[31] Red flags, graffiti, and other symbols still occasionally appeared, but the police and local Fascists quickly repressed such behaviors. Authorities continued to conduct constant surveillance on the population, endlessly compiling new lists of persons to arrest at the first sign of a resurgence of opposition. In particular, funerals of "subversives" provided an occasion to collect names of political suspects. An individual offering employment, housing, or an act of friendship to a known or suspected anti-Fascist might find himself the subject of a political police investigation, including unannounced house searches, phone taps, and investigative interviews with friends, family, and neighbors. Once an individual was subjected to such surveillance, there was no telling what might turn up.[32] As in San Lorenzo, the regime's tactics broke and nearly eradicated the anti-Fascist communities of the Oltretorrente by the early 1930s.

Though less commonly, agricultural laborers also displayed similarly stiff resilience in the face of a Fascist movement that had effectively declared war on their way of life. In 1923, in Molinella, farm laborers sent a signed petition to Mussolini, in which they explicitly rejected the Fascist syndicates, swearing to defend their labor leagues even "at the

---

[28] Franzinelli, introduction to Massimo Giufredi, ed., *Nella rete del regime. Gli antifascisti del Parmense nelle carte della polizia, 1922–43* (Rome, 2004), xvi.
[29] William Gambetta, "I sovversivi dei borghi," in ibid., 36.
[30] Ibid., 45.
[31] Ibid., 48.
[32] Ibid., 46–7, 49.

cost of dying of hunger with their families."[33] Throughout that year, Fascists subjected peasant families – including women and children – to a relentless onslaught of beatings, torture, and murder.[34] The leagues of Molinella were ultimately eradicated, but the workers remained bitterly opposed to the regime. According to a special prefectural commissioner,

> Thirty long years of uninterrupted subversive propaganda... have created an unhealthy environment that it would be vain to hope to cleanse in a brief time; it will require a long and patient process of detoxification, carried out by higher authorities with love and vigilant care, since the local [Fascist] forces are not up to the task.[35]

Authorities continued to fear this type of popular hostility toward the regime and the possibility of renewed Socialist activity. Throughout 1924 and into 1925, peasants engaged in wildcat strikes and protests. Squad violence and state sanctions ultimately failed to discipline the workers of Molinella. The regime then turned to tactics similar to those employed in Parma and Rome, forcibly evicting two hundred peasant families and resettling them in regions throughout Italy.[36] Although Rome, Parma, and Molinella represent harsh cases, they nevertheless reveal the regime's commitment to liquidating not just anti-Fascism but also the social bonds of working-class solidarity and outward expressions of socialism, both of which inhibited the infiltration of Fascism into Italian communities.

Impossible Resistance

For Communists and other militants active in the first half of the 1920s, continued resistance became nearly impossible under the regime. Year after year, anti-Fascists endured regular stints in jail, prison, and confinement. Even after the regime released political detainees, political activity still proved difficult for those who wished to fight on. Police surveillance, informants, the restrictions of political probation, and PNF vigilance largely impeded the activities of known anti-Fascists. Even "suspicious" activities, such as visiting old comrades or spending time in taverns, restaurants, or the local *piazza*, might lead to arrest and confinement.

---

[33] Cardoza, *Agrarian Elites*, 411.
[34] Giacomo Matteotti, *The Fascisti Exposed: A Year of Fascist Domination* (New York, 1969), 103–19.
[35] Cardoza, *Agrarian Elites*, 411.
[36] Ibid., 419.

In its struggle against the PCI, the OVRA and provincial police conducted long investigations into entire *milieus* of real and potential support for Communist activity in northern and central Italy. Police relied heavily on police informants and interrogations of captured suspects. One well-placed informant could cripple an entire network. Even the discovery of the identity of one Communist agent, followed by careful surveillance, could eventually compromise dozens of militants. Couriers who traveled from city to city, often carrying troves of false passports intended for their comrades, posed a particular danger for the PCI. If discovered and tailed by the OVRA, one courier could unwittingly betray cells in multiple cities. In August 1930, for example, the arrest of the Communist agent Guido Chiarelli in Rome led to the discovery of clandestine networks in four different cities. As a result, a total of fifty-eight Communists were denounced to the Special Tribunal, and many others were sentenced to political confinement. In Emilia, an interregional secretary was arrested, leading to the capture of twenty-four militants in Parma, seventeen in Modena, and eighty-seven in Ravenna.[37]

Once arrests had been made, the OVRA regional chief submitted a report specifying several categories of suspected militants. The ring leaders and principle militants were tried by the Special Tribunal. Individuals whose participation was "certain" but not actually demonstrable were sentenced to *confino*, and peripheral figures whose roles were unclear were nevertheless sentenced to probation or issued a "warning." For example, in November 1930, in the province of Bologna, a wave of arrests carried out in Imola led to eighty-nine suspected Communists being denounced to the Special Tribunal. In May of the following year, Fascist judges sentenced thirty-six of them to prison terms ranging from several months to six years, dropped charges against twenty-two, and found thirty-one innocent.[38] The Provincial Commission of Bologna immediately condemned the latter "innocent" group to either *confino* or political probation.[39] In addition to these eighty-nine suspects, another group had been sent directly to island confinement.[40] A final group, mostly individuals whose names came up in the course of the investigation, were sentenced to political probation (*ammonizione*) or issued a police warning

---

[37] Spriano, *Storia del partito comunista*, II:300.

[38] See Dal Pont and Carolini, *L'Italia dissidente e antifascista*, I:509–13.

[39] *Questore* of Bologna to Provincial Commission of Bologna, August 14, 1931, in ACS, *confinati politici*, b. 601, "Manaresi, Adelmo."

[40] E.g., see personal file of "Minarini, Giuseppe," in ACS, *confinati politici*, b. 673.

(*diffida*). In the end, more than one hundred individuals were imprisoned, confined, or sanctioned in Imola, a city in which the PCI could have expected to have no more than one or two dozen operatives.[41]

In many OVRA operations against the PCI, then, police confinement served as a preventive measure, inflicted on suspects against whom there was little, if any, evidence of anti-Fascist activity. Even ordinary social contact between former "subversives" or ex-political detainees might arouse the suspicions of the police. In Trieste, for example, police arrested ten suspected Communist militants. Two of the men, a PCI agent sent from Paris and his local contact, named Giusto Bonifacio, were denounced to the Special Tribunal. As for the eight others, OVRA Chief Francesco Nudi had found no "affirmative information and concrete proof with which to denounce them to the judicial authorities." However, he had "no doubt about their participation in the movement and about their consequent dangerousness."[42] One of the men, a forty-seven-year-old furniture upholsterer named Antonio Buttignon, had recently been released from prison after serving a sentence for belonging to the Communist Party.[43] The OVRA investigation identified Buttignon as a close friend of Bonifacio, the local PCI contact and the proprietor of a pastry shop. Under interrogation, Bonifacio admitted that when Buttignon and other men visited his shop, they discussed a variety of topics, including matters of a "strictly political nature." Nudi thus concluded that Buttignon and Bonifacio had at some point discussed "organization," because the subject was "so closely linked" to "politics." In the end, Nudi failed to find "specific evidence of punishable penal responsibility." Nevertheless, in language typifying official inclinations to define everyday activities as "subversive," he wrote, "there is sufficient evidence to confirm how Buttignon, while still under probation, continues to conduct himself as an irreducible, antisocial individual, and removing him from the environment in which he conducts his harmful activities would be a sound measure of prevention."[44] Bocchini conferred with Mussolini about Buttignon's case, and then ordered the *questore* of Trieste to propose him for *confino politico* to the Provincial Commission, which dutifully sentenced him to two years. He was then deported to Ponza. Soon

[41] In May 1927, the PCI counted 10 militants in Imola; see Spriano, *Storia del partito comunista*, 300–1.

[42] See Inspector General of Public Security Francesco Nudi to Bocchini, April 11, 1932, in ACS, *confinati politici*, b. 168, "Buttignon, Antonio."

[43] *Questore* to prefect of Trieste, April 25, 1932, in ibid.

[44] Nudi to Bocchini, April 11, 1932, in ibid.

after, Mussolini pardoned all ten political detainees and prisoners as part of the massive amnesty granted on the occasion of the Decennale (tenth anniversary of the March on Rome). Released after just seven months in prison and police confinement, these political suspects clearly posed little danger to Mussolini's regime. Pardoning suspected Communists also reflected the success of the regime's campaign to dismantle the PCI's network. Returned to Trieste and his family, Antonio Buttignon understandably ceased all political activity. By 1939, the General Directorate of Public Security (DGPS) in Rome had removed him from the central registry of political suspects.

By subjecting known Communists to intense surveillance, strict control, and multiple periods of confinement, police effectively neutralized the PCI's most experienced militants. Roberto Barsotti, one of the first Communists arrested in Pisa in November 1926, was a card-carrying member of the PCI who had "professed Communist ideals since his youth." During 1921, he served as secretary of the PCI in Pisa. His name was included on the PCI's list of candidates for the 1921 parliamentary elections, though he was not elected. When Fascist squads attacked Pisa, Barsotti organized a corps of *Arditi del popolo*, who led the defense of Pisa's working-class neighborhoods. After Mussolini became prime minister, the state fired Barsotti and dozens of other railway workers as retribution for their opposition to Fascism. Police deported Barsotti to Lipari at the end of 1926, and the following year, they arrested his wife, Elena Terrosi, for suspected Communist activity, leaving their five children completely alone. Two of their boys, ages sixteen and eight, went to live with acquaintances on Lipari; their two girls, ages seventeen and fourteen, moved in with an uncle; and the youngest, a five-year-old boy, was entrusted to another uncle.[45] More than a year later, authorities released Elena Terrosi from prison, and she reunited with her children in Pisa. The family soon found themselves living in poverty, prompting Pisa's prefect to request that Bocchini convert the remaining year of Barsotti's three-year sentence to probation. Mussolini approved the act of clemency in October 1928, and Barsotti returned to Pisa, where he lived under constant police surveillance.

Nearly two years later, in July 1930, police noticed Barsotti associating with "politically suspicious elements" and spending time in "public establishments," both violations of his political probation. Police also noted

---

[45] See Bocchini to Gabinetto di S.E. Il Ministro, "Appunto," February 13, 1928, n.793/ 2045, in ACS, *confinati politici*, b. 68, "Barsotti, Roberto."

that he spent sums of money that, "while not considerable, were not consistent with his poor economic situation." These "suspicious" activities prompted police to step up surveillance. In September 1930, police stopped and searched Barsotti on his way out of the post office, confiscating an envelope containing two hundred lira, which they believed had been sent from Paris by an unknown Communist. Police assumed that Barsotti was either the distributor, but more likely a recipient, of so-called red aid (*soccorso rosso*). Inside and outside of Italy, workers took up collections to help comrades and their families who had fallen on hard times. Such acts of charity toward ex-political prisoners or "subversives" could be construed by state officials as supporting anti-Fascism. In practical terms, outside financial or material aid undermined one of the regimes' main forms of political coercion: financial and material deprivation. In light of Barsotti's recent behavior, which included "associating with suspicious individuals," going to bars and taverns, receiving "red aid," and the general charge of "giving rise to suspicion" (expressly prohibited by the terms of political probation), Pisa's police commissioner recommended that he be interned on an island for five more years.[46]

At the end of 1930, Barsotti was returned to the island of Ponza, and there he contracted a grave form of tuberculosis that, according to the director of the colony, "undoubtedly threaten[ed] his life." Constantly mindful of its image at home and abroad, the regime went to great efforts to prevent political prisoners dying in custody, and so Barsotti obtained two months leave and returned to Pisa for medical treatment. After several weeks in the hospital, Barsotti was expelled for "disciplinary reasons." Patients and doctors there all used the Fascist "Roman salute," but Barsotti refused to do so. When a doctor rebuked him, Barsotti responded "forcefully," demonstrating, according to the prefect of Pisa, "Barsotti's arrogant character and his unwillingness to conduct himself in accordance with the directives of the regime." Booted out of the hospital, Barsotti had about two weeks left before he was to return to Ponza. The prefect reported that although he had made a satisfactory recovery, his infirmity "could become exacerbated and assume a progressively fatal course" if he were returned to Ponza.[47]

Debating Barsotti's fate, the prefect weighed health concerns against the fact that Barsotti and his entire family were "pertinacious subversives"

---

[46] See prefect of Pisa (Dentice) to DGPS (Bocchini), September 15, 1930, in ibid.
[47] See prefect of Pisa to Divisione Confino Politico, April 14, 1931, in ibid.

who gave "no sign of rehabilitating themselves." Moreover, if Barsotti were to stay in Pisa, as many as six police agents would be required to conduct nearly constant surveillance.[48] Bocchini ultimately decided to commute Barsotti's sentence to political probation. "Although we are dealing with an irreducible subversive," he wrote, "the measure of *ammonizione* is sufficient, especially if one considers his compromised physical condition." During Barsotti's confinement, his family had been reduced to "truly wretched conditions," such that the prefect twice advised Rome to pay them a three hundred lira subsidy.[49] Although Barsotti refrained from political activity after 1931, local police continued to watch and file reports on him until 1941. The Fascist regime had imposed a harsh existence on Barsotti. Unemployed, imprisoned, confined, afflicted with tuberculosis, and then released and kept under constant surveillance, Barsotti could hardly have produced propaganda, recruited party members, or engaged in other anti-Fascist activities.

The official duration of political confinement sentences ranged from a minimum of one to a maximum of five years, but provincial police commissions and the DGPS in Rome regularly confined anti-Fascists two, three, or more times, often successively.[50] Omar Conti, a young PCI militant, served five *confino di polizia* sentences during the period from 1927 to 1943. After serving his first sentence, three years on Ustica and Ponza, Conti was arrested after just four months of freedom. Recommending him again for confinement, police reported that he had contact with "anti-national individuals" and on April 23, 1931, had "dared appear in public in a red shirt with a clearly provocative purpose." Such scrutiny of wardrobes often provided a pretext for police and Fascists to harass or punish suspected anti-Fascists. Authorities viewed red or black ties, shirts, handkerchiefs, and lapel flowers as sufficiently unambiguous indicators of an individual's anti-Fascist political ideals. Conti spent the next seven years and eleven months in the Ponza colony as a result of his sumptuary offense. Though only sentenced to five years of confinement, the director of the colony incarcerated him an additional seven times (for a total of almost three years) for violating various regulations on Ponza. In 1939, the Provincial Commission of Littoria, which had jurisdiction over Ponza and Ventotene, summarily renewed his confinement on the very day his

---

[48] Prefect of Pisa (Dentice) to DGPS, March 5, 1931, in ibid.
[49] See "Appunto," April 18, 1931, in ibid.
[50] Thirty-eight *confinati* from the sample of 549 were sentenced two or more times. Most were suspected of anti-Fascist militancy.

1931 sentence ended. Conti's offense was "bad conduct" both inside and outside of the colony.[51]

The most intense strategies of political and social control operated at the local, rather than the national, level. Police and *carabinieri* repeatedly arrested, jailed, and generally harassed anti-Fascists, who spent hours, days, weeks, and months in local jails and prisons. When important personages – Fascists, state officials, members of the royal family – visited a city, authorities jailed dozens if not hundreds of "dangerous" persons. In anticipation of such events the Ministry of the Interior sometimes transferred police officers from other provinces to help with arrests.[52] Celebrations of national holidays or Fascist ceremonies likewise precipitated roundups of persons suspected of anti-Fascist activities. A single, major act of anti-Fascism or terrorism might lead police to arrest hundreds of political suspects throughout Italy. The same phenomenon played out in local contexts, where the appearance of one red flag could lead dozens of suspects to be arrested and held for days, weeks, or months. The files of political detainees are littered with references to "fermate per misure di sicurezza" (stops for security measures). These practices were so ordinary that memoirs and other sources mention them only in passing, if at all; they were part of the assumed backdrop to larger, more dramatic events. One Communist spent the periods from 1927 to 1929, 1936 to 1939, and 1939 to 1942 in island *confino* colonies and was then interned (as a war internee rather than as a political detainee) until the end of the war. During his intermittent years of "freedom," however, he spent time in jail. In 1934, for example, he was considered a "suspect in the exhibition of a red flag" and was jailed for two months. This jail sentence emanated by "order of the Ministry of the Interior," an executive order of imprisonment that was probably illegal. Then, in January 1936, a military tribunal ordered his arrest and imprisonment for two months, most likely for some offense related to the war in Ethiopia.[53] Thus, even for anti-Fascists not sentenced to life in prison, constant harassment by police made militancy impossible and life very difficult.

Although political police began their investigations with known anti-Fascists, they cast a wide net that snared Italians with no history of

[51] See Lieutenant Colonel of the *carabinieri* of Ancona (Pesaro Group), Pasquale Tammaro, to general command of the *carabinieri*, September 1, 1939, in ACS *confinati politici*, b. 277, "Conti, Omar."

[52] See Jonathan Dunnage, "Social Control in Fascist Italy," 270.

[53] See *questura* of Latina to DGPS, March 21, 1959, in ACS, *confinati politici*, b. 178, "Camarra, Natale."

political activity; even some whose membership in the PNF or MVSN should have placed them beyond suspicion. Anti-Communist actions often began with the surveillance of known militants and ex-political detainees and then "snowballed" as the suspect's comrades, friends, and family were drawn into the investigation. In Naples, for example, Manlio Rossi-Doria, a former seminary student now studying agricultural science, established one of Italy's most robust PCI networks together with Emilio Sereni, Giorgio Amendola (son of Giovanni Amendola, a former government minister), and Eugenio Reale. In July 1930, copies of the journal *L'Unità* began appearing among workers of several large metallurgic plants. This development, according to the *questore* of Naples, constituted "the first sign of renewal of the illegal activity of the Communist party."[54] In response, the police chief increased surveillance, including the use of paid informants, on the workers at four metallurgy plants – Ilva, Miani and Silvestri, Armstrong, and Silurificio. The suspected members of the Communist cells were soon identified, and through interrogations and informants, the police investigation revealed that two young doctors in agricultural science, Rossi Doria and Sereni, both Romans who had fellowships at the Agrarian Institute of Portici (Naples), were responsible for organizing the Communist network, as well as producing and disseminating *L'Unità*. Because both had been issued passports for professional reasons, they were able to travel to Paris and there received orders for implementing the PCI's new policy.[55] The *questore* of Naples reported, accurately, that Rossi Doria, while in Paris, had been ordered to infiltrate the metallurgic workers. By conducting small gatherings in rural areas outside of Naples, which often included seemingly "innocuous strolls," Rossi Doria and Sereni managed to establish a small network of about forty militants.[56] Although Rossi Doria and Sereni were ordered to keep a low profile, the police uncovered the organization by mid-September, and then made arrests. On November 15, the Special Tribunal sentenced them each to fifteen years imprisonment.[57]

The investigation did not end there, as authorities alleged that three other men – Giovanni La Greca, Luigi Amoroso, and Francesco Panico – were also important operatives. An employee at one of the metallurgic

---

[54] See *questore* of Naples (De Martino) to High Commissioner for Public Security, November 12, 1930, in ACS, *confinati politici*, b. 547, "La Greca, Giovanni."

[55] *Carabinieri* of Naples to Generale Command, December 31, 1930, in ibid.

[56] *Questore* of Naples (De Martino) to High Commissioner, November 12, 1930, in ibid.

[57] Dal Pont and Carolini, *L'Italia dissidente*, II:420.

plants under investigation, Giovanni La Greca seemed an unlikely political suspect, mainly because he was a Fascist. He had joined the PNF in 1922, at the age of sixteen, became a member of the MVSN in 1924, and had never been involved in subversive politics or demonstrated any animosity toward the regime or Fascism. Police and *carabinieri* alleged that La Greca accompanied Amoroso, his sister's boyfriend, on trips to the countryside and had "transported packs of subversive material which were entrusted to him because, as a militiaman, he was more easily able to elude the surveillance of Public Security [agents]." The *carabinieri* also reported that La Greca and Amoroso often went on "long bicycle rides to localities that have not been established," proving the closeness of their relationship and suggesting that they might have engaged in further political activities on their outings together.[58] Finally, authorities also alleged that Giovanni had developed a close "familial" relationship with his mother's relative, Francesco Panico, also an alleged "subversive."[59] In his defense, La Greca insisted that he had no knowledge of Amoroso's political activity. He admitted that he had once helped him transport packages but did not realize they contained subversive propaganda. From La Greca's file, it is difficult to judge whether or not he was telling the truth. The standards of evidence employed by the police, which included treating speculation as established fact, allowed a *questore* to write virtually anything he felt would convince the prefect to inflict *confino*. Because of his association with Panico and Amoroso, the Provincial Commission of Naples sentenced La Greca to five years of confinement, which he served on Lipari.

Giovanni La Greca's family had depended heavily on the twenty-two lira per day he earned at Ilva. His father Raffaele, fifty years old, received a pension of 340 lira per month from the Italian navy. The loss of Giovanni's income could not have come at a worse moment – the world economic crisis. His mother, two brothers, ages twenty-six and eighteen, and twenty-two-year-old sister were all unemployed. The family lived in a two-room apartment they rented for 230 lira per month, which left very little of his father's navy pension for food and other living expenses. Consequently, the family's situation quickly deteriorated and Raffaele became heavily indebted. In light of their circumstances, the Ministry of the Interior granted them a one-time living subsidy of 150 lira. However,

[58] *Questore* of Naples (De Martino) to High Commissioner, November 12, 1930, in "La Greca, Giovanni."

[59] See *carabinieri* of Naples to Generale Command, December 13, 1930, in ibid.

by December 1931, according to the High Commissar for Public Security of Naples, they had been reduced to poverty.[60] The family petitioned the Ministry of the Interior to move to Lipari, where they could at least combine Raffaele's pension and Giovanni's five lira per diem living subsidy, but their request was denied.

Just more than two years later, authorities included Giovanni in the Decennale amnesty, and he returned to Naples and set about putting his life back together. In light of the family's economic situation, he needed to find employment, a difficult task, as the Great Depression had now begun to affect Italian manufacturing. La Greca approached Ilva about returning to work, but the plant rejected him. He found it patently unfair that two other ex-political detainees, sentenced for belonging to the same Communist organization, had already returned to Ilva. In a letter to the Ministry of the Interior, he pointed out this inconsistency and asked for help getting his job back. The Ministry of the Interior refused to offer any assistance. The other two workers, wrote one official, "were more entitled to it because they are disabled veterans."[61] Significant discrimination in employment often awaited ex-detainees and suspected "subversives." Above all, employers, whether pro-Fascist or not, had difficulty justifying their decision to hire ex-political detainees instead of Fascist Party members or First World War veterans. Some employers were simply afraid to hire people notorious for anti-Fascist or subversive behavior. In other cases, however, employers wrote letters to police authorities in support of pardoning a detainee, attesting to their patriotism, work ethic, and devotion to family. This system of labor discrimination was thus not applied systematically or uniformly, but it did inflict further suffering on some former prisoners, detainees, and even anti-Fascists who had never been officially sanctioned.

Punishments and hardships inflicted by the regime on the friends, family, and acquaintances of political suspects created a *cordon sanitaire* around real and potential PCI militants, depriving them of necessary material, financial, and moral support. For an ostensibly apolitical individual to help a friend or family member was to risk being charged with complicity in Communist activity. The regime imposed an inverted burden of proof upon Italians who were associated by blood or by circumstance with Communists, "subversives," or other political suspects.

---

[60] See *Questore* of Naples (De Martino) to High Commissioner, November 12, 1930, in ibid.

[61] High Commissar of Public Security of Naples to DGPS, December 10, 1931, in ibid.

Family and acquaintances had to demonstrate unequivocally that despite their proximity to a political suspect, they were not able or inclined to provide assistance. By forcing Italians to keep up their guard against being "associated with known subversives," the regime's political policing isolated suspected militants. Cut off from local support, Communist networks withered. The PCI and other anti-Fascist groups operated in a "ghetto of illegality" that became increasingly hermetic with each passing year.

For Italians who inhabited the milieus of PCI militancy, without necessarily participating or even sympathizing, life in the Fascist police state thus became fraught with the risk of arrest or punishment. Cleofe Meroni, a forty-six-year-old housewife, had according to all observers abstained from political activity her entire life. She lost her husband in the Great War, and lived in Milan with her two children, a sixteen-year-old boy and a twelve-year-old girl, and her sister. In 1932, police arrested Teresa Meroni, Cleofe's forty-seven-year-old cousin, for Communist activity. Just before police deported Teresa to an island confinement colony, her brother came to San Vittore prison for one last visit. During the meeting, police thwarted Teresa's attempt to pass her brother a letter intended for her cousin, Cleofe. The letter gave Cleofe "tasks and instructions related to contacts with the Communist Party." Teresa informed Cleofe that her apartment would be used as a drop-off location for Communist operatives. The letter also instructed Cleofe to smuggle Teresa's son out of Italy to Russia. Police suspected that this operation would involve an employee of the local office of the Russian delegation who was renting a room in Cleofe's apartment. The letter offered no evidence that Cleofe would fulfill Teresa's requests – some authorities doubted her complicity – but the police arrested her the following day.[62] Under interrogation, Cleofe claimed not to even understand what her cousin's letter meant. Thus unwittingly implicated in clandestine political activities by her cousin's letter, Meroni admitted only that she had agreed to care for her nephew out of a "sense of humanity." Her Communist cousin, she maintained, thrust these other requests on her at the last minute, thereby betraying her trust. Whether Cleofe was complicit or not in her cousin's plans for her, she was almost certainly not a Communist. In a letter to the Commission of Appeals, she explained that she had never engaged in political activity, and, to the contrary, had inculcated her children with "sacred sentiment

---

[62] See report of Fabio Faggioni, Compagnia Milano Interna (*carabinieri*), to the *questura* of Milan, November 10, 1932, in ACS, *confinati politici*, b. 661, "Meroni, Cleofe."

and duties toward the *patria* [fatherland], so that they will not forget the heroic sacrifice of their father, who gave his life for it."[63] Such denials and oaths of loyalty were never offered by genuine Communist agents.

Despite these entreaties and the paucity of evidence against Cleofe Meroni, authorities sentenced her to political exile in southern Italy on the basis of a set of circumstances, rather than anything in her past or current political conduct. "While not being able to establish Cleofe Meroni's membership in the Communist party, nor the extent of the activities conducted by her in favor of the party before the present time," wrote an officer of the *carabinieri*, "it is legitimate to determine with certainty that she is not extraneous to the web of subversive intrigues plotted in this city."[64] That her cousin Teresa turned to Cleofe for help constituted evidence that she "was retained capable of performing the tasks and serving as a secure intermediary between the various communist elements." Whatever her political convictions or intentions, in the view of *carabinieri*, Cleofe was guilty not of action, or even of intent, but of the capacity to serve as a go-between for Communist operatives and employees of the Russian delegation. By penetrating the sphere of family relations and socialization, and denying the benefit of doubt to Italians who were "not extraneous to the web" of subversion, the regime's police made patently clear the dire consequences of any form of contact with political suspects.

Even for lone "subversives" who were not integrated into any formal structure, the regime's strategies of repression and control made life nearly impossible. In large urban areas, the first wave of political confinement sentences included individuals better known for their histories of petty crime, social protest, and clashes with police, than for any type of coherent, organized political activity. Anarchists in particular were arrested and interned not because of their adherence to a formal program of resistance but because of their beliefs, behavior, and general hostility to authority. Alceste Alvi, a forty-six-year-old anarchist from the Trastevere District of Rome, was first condemned to *confino* in September 1927. On March 18, 1926, Alvi and thirteen other "subversives" organized a dinner in a private room of a tavern on via Lungaretta, allegedly to honor the anniversary of the Paris Commune. Police cited this celebration, held eight months before the exceptional decrees went into effect, as evidence of Alvi's anti-Fascist "subversion." More generally, Alvi allegedly posed a threat to public order because he associated with "the most infamous

[63] See the "discolpa confino" of Meroni to the Provincial Commission in ibid.
[64] Fabio Faggioni to Questura of Milan, November 10, 1932, in ibid.

convicts [*pregiudicati*] and subversives of the District of Trastevere," with whom he frequented "the most infamous taverns." When drunk, Alvi allegedly provoked "incidents." He was "not fond of work," instead devoting himself to "sloth and wine," which rendered him "capable of impetuous acts." The *carabinieri* in Rome held an equally unfavorable opinion, reporting that Alvi had a history of property crimes, possession of arms, and acts of violence against the forces of public security. The Roman police chief concluded that Alvi was a "terrible subversive." Although possessing "scarce intelligence and the most limited culture," Alvi nevertheless engaged in "clandestine propaganda among his companions of faith." Put differently, Alvi talked politics and anarchism with his friends while out carousing in Trastevere.

Police and Fascists targeted Alvi for punishment because of his anarchist beliefs, which were widely known throughout Trastevere. However, authorities more strongly condemned his alcoholism, conflicts with authority, unnamed "subversive" associates, and history of petty crime. Most police reports calculated a political detainees' dangerousness in part according to a moral and legal arithmetic. In the eyes of public-security officials, a whole host of factors augmented or mitigated the threat an individual posed to the state or society: alcohol use, gambling, work ethic, comportment within their family, personal temperament, and other subjective factors. In the deliberations of authorities, these factors sometimes weighed more heavily than the suspect's active opposition to the Fascist regime or specific acts of political subversion. After 1934, as discussed in later chapters, provincial commissions would increasingly rely on these biographical evaluations in deciding police sanctions. Already, during the late 1920s and early 1930s, the regime had begun inflicting political punishments for erratic, lawless, or simply strange behavior, rather than political activities. In 1931, for example, the *questore* of Rome explained that an anarchist political detainee "could not be considered dangerous specifically for his ideas or his political beliefs." The police chief continued, "Nevertheless, because of his mental and psychological state, he constitutes a clear and constant problem for the organs of the police, such that he could easily be manipulated by subversive elements who could push him to commit ill-advised and criminal actions against state officials." *Carabinieri* similarly described the man as "mentally deficient."[65]

---

[65] On Alvi and Bonacci, see *questore* of Rome, December 15, 1927; Carabinieri Reali di Roma (Romolo di Furia) to Comando Generale, December 15, 1927; *questore* of Rome to DGPS, November 17, 1927, in ACS, *confinati politici*, b. 18, "Alvi, Alceste."

Despite the fact that police viewed anarchists primarily as threats to society and public order, it would be a mistake to view their arrest and confinement as essentially apolitical. In these cases, the interests of the police and *carabinieri* merged seamlessly with those of Fascists. Interned on Lipari, Alvi appealed his confinement, denying any political or criminal wrongdoing. His appeal was rejected. According to the Roman police chief and the *carabinieri*, an act of clemency "would create a bad impression" among the public and the "Fascist camp" of Trastevere.[66] Therefore, Alvi's case contained a political dimension in that his arrest appeased local Fascists and was more generally viewed positively by the public, at least according to police. As a veteran, Alceste Alvi qualified for a special amnesty granted by Mussolini on January 1, 1930. However, just thirteen months later, police arrested him again. Citing rehashed – verbatim – charges from Alvi's first sentence, police recommended him for yet another confinement term.[67] For local officials, individuals like Alceste remained forever subversive, even if the Duce had sent them home. Police resentenced anarchists proportionally more often than other political groups.[68] For many detainees, then, Mussolini's amnesties were fleeting.

Broken Families

Fascist strategies of dismantling opposition, stifling dissent, and suppressing public memory of socialism and other working-class political ideologies worked exceedingly well because of the trauma inflicted upon the families of political detainees. Police investigations carefully identified and evaluated the families of "subversives," commenting on their income, political leanings, morality, and the like. The regime fully recognized the importance of the family as a tool for controlling political opponents. In its efforts to break anti-Fascist networks and subversive communities, Fascist state violence knowingly and deliberately shattered families. At the same time, ever mindful of public opinion, Mussolini and Bocchini sometimes attempted to mitigate the consequences by offering families assistance or releasing a detainee. The attitude of authorities toward families thus cannot be neatly summed up. State officials knew that the absence of a primary breadwinner horribly eroded a family's

---

[66] See *questore* of Rome, December 15, 1927, in ibid.
[67] See *questura* di Roma to CPC, February 22, 1931, "Proposta di assegnazione al confino a carico di Alvi Alceste," in ibid.
[68] One-third (8) of anarchists sampled (22) from the years 1926–34 were reassigned.

already precarious financial situation. Police and *carabinieri* sometimes expressed callous disdain for a family, suggesting implicitly and explicitly that they deserved their fate. In other cases, authorities viewed families positively and urged that action be taken to ameliorate their suffering.

The complexities of the Fascist state's administration of these families can be illustrated by examining the case of Maria Bonacci, the wife of Roman anarchist Alceste Alvi. Alvi suffered little during his first political internment sentence, but the same cannot be said for Bonacci. During the first two years of his absence, she wrote often to the Ministry of the Interior seeking relief from the poverty caused by her husband's absence. Maria explained that Alceste, a bricklayer, had always paid the rent for their apartment at via dei Vascellari. She washed clothes and kept house for other families in Trastevere, but her income was insufficient to meet her expenses. She ate all of her meals with her husband's family and supplemented her small earnings with handouts from Alceste's brother.

From the outset, authorities displayed little sympathy for Bonacci, with various officials describing her as a woman of "depraved morals" (*costumi depravati*) and "dubious morality" who had no children.[69] These kinds of moral evaluations of families – and wives in particular – featured prominently in official assessments. From Fascist police reports emerges an "antimodel" of respectable femininity, that of the subversive woman.[70] Police routinely evaluated the education, intelligence, work ethic, and public behavior of men. For women, by contrast, authorities commented, usually negatively, on their morality, calling women "easy" and "immoral." Women who were not married but lived and had "illegitimate" children with men were referred to derogatorily as "lovers." Childlessness, too, was always presented within a larger discussion of sexual immorality. Such assessments were usually based on rumors and "public opinion" (*voce pubblica*), gleaned from the neighborhood gossip of small towns or cramped, working-class neighborhoods. Moreover, these evaluations of wives, companions, and daughters, were presented by police as a category of legitimate evidence. Just as having a "subversive" father, brother, or son reflected badly on an individual, having a "loose" wife effectively corroborated the "subversive" nature and inclinations of the husband.

---

[69] See *questore* of Rome, December 15, 1927; and Carabinieri Reali di Roma (Romolo di Furia) to Comando Generale, December 15, 1927, in "Alvi, Alceste."

[70] Brunella Manotti, "Un universo sommerso. Frammenti di vita di 'sovversive' parmensi," in *Nella rete del regime. Gli antifascisti del Parmense nelle carte della polizia, 1922–43*, ed. Massimo Giufredi (Rome, 2004), 136–7.

As Bonacci's situation continued to deteriorate, official attitudes softened, and slurs about her morality disappeared from subsequent reports. During her husband's absence, in her hour of greatest need, when petty theft, an affair, or prostitution might have lifted her out of absolute poverty, the police reported nothing to suggest the licentious behavior for which she was allegedly so notorious. In March of 1929, one year after Alceste's arrest, Maria fell into truly dire straits. The police chief reported to Bocchini that his agents had found Bonacci living in a horrible state, suffering from chronic bronchitis. Because of her poor health, doctors had forbidden her to work.[71] Worse still, her brother-in-law, on whom she had come to rely for so much assistance, had recently died.[72] Weeks later, Maria wrote to the DGPS, claiming to have suffered a nervous breakdown and complete physical exhaustion. The clear, careful handwriting of her earlier letters was now shaky and faint. The Roman police checked in on her once again, and the police chief reported to Bocchini that she was "effectively an invalid" living in "absolute misery." Over the course of Alceste's absence, Maria received a total of one thousand lira in subsidies from the Ministry of the Interior, due mainly to Roman police agents' accurate reporting of her dire economic straits and poor health.[73]

After Alceste Alvi's release from Lipari, life improved for the couple, mainly because he immediately found work. However, when police arrested Alceste again in February 1931, Maria immediately fell behind with the rent.[74] After 1930, moreover, the regime became considerably less generous with subsidies to families, and she received no further assistance from the Ministry of the Interior. Her sister was her only outside source of aid. By the end of May, Maria had been evicted from the couple's apartment, reduced to begging for food and sleeping under the staircase of an apartment building.[75] She was later admitted to a public

---

[71] See Bonacci to Mussolini, December 5, 1927; Bonacci to MI, March 26, 1928; Bonacci to Commissione d'Appello, October 22, 1928, March 21, 1929, October 2, 1929; all in "Alvi, Alceste."

[72] Telegram number 4957, January 8, 1930, in ibid.

[73] See *questore* of Rome to DGPS, "Istanza di sussidio della famiglia del confinato Alvi Alceste," April 12, 1926; *questore* of Rome to DGPS, November 29, 1928"; *questore* of Rome to DGPS, April 24, 1929; all in ibid.

[74] See *questura* di Roma to CPC, February 22, 1931, "Proposta di assegnazione al confino a carico di Alvi Alceste," in ibid.

[75] For Bonacci's ordeal after Alvi's second assignment, but before she joined him on Lipari, see letters of Bonacci to Mussolini, March 9, 1931; March 21, 1931; April 10, 1931; May 22, 1931; Bonacci to MI, June 1, 1931; Bonacci to Commissione d'Appello,

assistance facility. In September, after several requests, Bocchini and Mussolini authorized Maria to join her husband on Lipari. However, almost as soon as she arrived, the internment colony there was closed. Alceste, who was suffering from a severe ulcer, was transferred to the island of Ponza.[76] In accordance with the systemwide reforms that followed the escape of Carlo Rosselli from the Lipari colony, Ponza's director denied Maria permission to live with her husband. She returned to Rome. While on Ponza, Alceste was arrested and incarcerated twice for merely gathering with other internees.

On the morning of January 7, 1933, Maria Bonacci, barefoot and destitute, walked into the Roman office of the president of the Italian Red Cross, Filippo Cremonesi. Cremonesi had recently visited Lipari and Ponza to prepare a report on the political prisoners there. He largely gave the colonies his seal of approval. Shocked by the appearance of the woman, Cremonesi gave her one hundred lira and wrote to Bocchini, insisting that something be done.[77] Perhaps sensitive to the negative repercussions of the case, especially in light of the Red Cross president's positive report on Ponza, Bocchini immediately authorized Maria to join her husband. Together on Ponza, Alvi and Bonacci repeatedly implored officials for extra money to cope with their health problems. The director denied all but one. Alvi and Bonacci, he had decided, were alcoholics undeserving of monetary or material assistance. Alvi and Bonacci served out the remainder of the sentence on Lipari. Their last letters pleaded desperately for financial assistance and medical care. After release, their lives entered an even darker period. Maria went blind and, in 1937, unemployed and homeless, Alceste attempted to kill himself, an act motivated almost entirely by the desperation caused by years of Fascist political persecution.[78]

As Maria Bonacci's case illustrates, political internment could and often did have a devastating impact on families. Although detainees received a daily allowance of ten lira (five lira after 1930), a set of clothing

July 21, 1931; Bonacci to Corte di Apello per il confino politico, August 8, 1931; and Bonacci to Mussolini, September 16, 1931. See also prefect of Messina to DGPS, July 9, 1931; regarding the financial situation and health of Bonacci, see *questore* of Rome to DGPS, "Ogetto: Istanza di sussidio della famiglia del confinato politico Alvi Alceste," March 31, 1931; all in ibid.

[76] See diagnosis of Cristoforo Merlino, Seniore Medico, Dirigente il Servizio Sanitario, Lipari, December 31, 1931, in ibid.

[77] See Presidente Generale della Croce Rossa Italiana to Bocchini, January 7, 1933, in ibid.

[78] Alceste Alvi's case is taken up in the final chapter.

each year, and a roof over their heads, dependent spouses and children who had to pay rent and buy food and clothes were extremely fortunate if they received a one-time "subsidy" of two hundred or three hundred lira (roughly a month's rent) from the Ministry of the Interior over the course of several years. The consequent economic degradation caused poverty, stress, and illness, which in some cases contributed to the deaths of family members. The state recognized its responsibility for the plight of these families, as the deliberations over whether to grant subsidies make clear; still, officials were ultimately unwilling to check the downward spiral. As a last resort authorities sometimes allowed spouses and children to join husbands and fathers in the island colonies and villages of southern Italy. This solution, while potentially improving the condition of the family, exacerbated the usually grim but stable economic position of the husband. The histories of most families ended badly.

The scope of the deprivations and suffering endured by families cannot be overstated. A majority of detainees had dependent families, mostly wives and children but also elderly parents.[79] Of the approximately three hundred families (from the sample of 549 detainees) that had relied on the financial support of a political detainee, at least two-thirds suffered a verifiable, marked deterioration of their economic situation. The evidence of the deprivations brought on by political repression comes not from the multitude of personal letters of wives, mothers, and children that poured into state authorities, begging for help or leniency. Instead, in these cases, police and other state authorities visited families and reported in explicit terms that the forced absence of the primary breadwinner had taken families with previously stable economic situations – whether described as "excellent," "good," or "poor" – and reduced them to conditions described as "difficult," "miserable," "the most squalid misery," and "absolute misery." Because most political detainees were already poor, the consequences were harsh. In extreme cases, wives and children were evicted from their homes, forcing them to move in with relatives, enter charitable institutions, or become entirely homeless. More commonly, land laid uncultivated, family businesses were forced to close, and debts piled up. Families sometimes accompanied political detainees into exile or to live on an island. However, cohabitation during *confino*

---

[79] More than half (296 of 549, or 54%) of the political detainees from the sample had dependent families, and more than two-thirds of them (208 of 296) had dependent children.

was uncommon during the 1930s and was, overall, quite rare.[80] Stress and poor nutrition brought on illness for family members.[81] A minority of families (10%), most commonly families of veterans, received one or more cash payments totaling anywhere from a few hundred to one or two thousand lira.[82] These cash subsidies stopped the downward spiral for only a few families. In many cases, authorities recommended that the detainee be released – pardoned by Mussolini, that is – due to the family's dire financial straits.[83]

In a mix of political cynicism and irony, such pardons did not normally go to the neediest. Instead, detainees returned home when local authorities determined that it would make a "good" or "excellent" impression on the local population, when the detainee or family members belonged to the PNF and MVSN, or when the detainee was a veteran. Police officials also frequently deemed detainees or their families undeserving of a pardon or a subsidy due to their alleged political or moral conduct, even though they were often worse off than those who were pardoned. Antonio Buttignon, the Communist suspect in Trieste, lived with his wife Teresa, several children, and mother. During his absence, the entire family survived on one hundred lira per week that his wife Teresa earned working at a café. When she fell into "poor health," Teresa earned even less. "Without the presence of the head of household," reported the police chief of Trieste, "the family of Buttignon finds itself in awful financial straits, since it is the former who provides for the needs of the wife and children with the earnings from his work." Mussolini approved a one-time, three hundred lira living subsidy for Buttignon's elderly mother. When the family pleaded with authorities to pardon Buttignon, the police chief demurred. "The miserable condition in which the family of the *confinato* finds itself is worthy of particular consideration," he admitted, "but the political precedents of Buttignon do not warrant, for the moment, an act of clemency in his favor." In some cases it was the entire family that authorities found undeserving of aid or concessions. The prefect of Pisa seriously considered returning Roberto Barsotti to confinement in Ponza, even with a potentially fatal case of tuberculosis, because he and

---

[80] Only fifteen cases from the sample of 549 involved a wife, child, or other family member living with the detainee in *confino*.

[81] Thirty-one cases from the sample demonstrated a strong connection between political repression, economic degradation, and the illness of a family member.

[82] Fifty-four (out of 549) cases sampled featured families receiving subsidies from the state. In thirty-one cases, the detainee was a veteran.

[83] Fifty-three out of 549 cases sampled.

his entire family were "pertinacious subversives" that gave no "sign of rehabilitating themselves."

In several respects, political repression in the period immediately following the exceptional decrees represented a continuation of squad violence by other means. Mussolini's repressive tactics may have fallen short of the overtly violent revolutionary justice demanded by Fascist extremists, but state policies nonetheless targeted the same individuals, organizations, communities, and families. In many places, Fascists continued to play an important role in identifying "suspects" for the police to sanction, and squads of Black Shirts still engaged in illegal violence. Like *squadrismo* before it, state violence functioned locally, on a personal, intimate level, making admonitory examples of select anti-Fascists. Constant police harassment, surveillance, arbitrary arrests, and discrimination put anti-Fascists in a position where they could barely earn a living, much less conduct anti-Fascist activity. These systematic police actions and other coercive measures ultimately achieved what Fascist terror could not: the complete destruction or neutralization of anti-Fascist forces. The regime achieved this not by indiscriminately terrorizing Italians but by inflicting massive, low-level, localized repression. For the select communities, families, and individuals subjected to this repression, the regime's control over their lives was truly totalitarian. In working-class neighborhoods, where everyone knew too well the economic and social consequences of prison and *confino*, an ordinary knock on the door late at night was terrifying. "There you go," recalled a woman from San Lorenzo "it was terror" – an ordinary kind of terror, but terror nonetheless.

4

The Archipelago

I have been on Lipari for six months. . . . I am already sick of it, horribly sick of life in a chicken coop, of this false appearance of liberty: better prison, perhaps. In a prison cell, the impossibility of escape is evident and the suffering more clear. The confino is a cell without walls, all sky and sea: the patrols of militiamen serve as the walls. Walls of flesh and bones, not brick and mortar. The desire to climb over them becomes an obsession. . . .

Carlo Rosselli, 1928[1]

[*Confino di polizia*] is the masterpiece of the regime: the danger of being sent off hangs over everyone. For Fascism, this yields much more than just the punishments inflicted. The punishment is for the few; the threat is for everyone.

Emilio Lussu[2]

The network of islands and villages that constituted the Fascist archipelago represented a microcosm of the regime's deceptively violent strategies of rule. Fascist propaganda regularly characterized island confinement as a "*villeggiatura*" (seaside holiday), drawing particular attention to the colonies on Lipari and Ponza, where ex-parliamentary deputies lived comfortably in private accommodations. The reality of the archipelago was starkly different. On other islands, and even within the colonies on Lipari and Ponza, many detainees lived in squalid, vermin-infested barracks, without running water or electricity. The "common" colonies in particular were overcrowded, disease-ridden, awful places.

[1] Quoted in Alberto Tarchiani, "L'impresa di Lipari," in *No al fascismo*, 2nd ed., ed. Ernesto Rossi (Turin, 1963), 119.
[2] Emilio Lussu, *La Catena* (Milan, 1997), 44.

In the political colonies, the members of the Fascist Militia (MVSN) responsible for guarding the detainees usually left socially prominent Italians alone, but they regularly beat and tortured select anti-Fascists up through the early 1930s. *Squadrism* thus lived on. Once the regime had consolidated power and survived the Great Depression, keeping up appearances became less important. The police closed the Lipari colony in 1932, and the other islands soon came to resemble true internment camps, with most detainees living in common barracks. Whereas the common detainee population grew rapidly during the late 1920s and early 1930s, after 1934 the political population exploded, ultimately quadrupling. Ordinary Italians, rather than anti-Fascist militants, poured into the political branch, reflecting the increasingly pervasive presence of political policing in everyday life. Inside the island colonies, the living conditions and coercive regime became increasingly punitive, regimented, and harsh. Fascist militiamen no longer ran wild, but police officials now shared the MVSN's view that confinement was a punishment designed to "subjugate" detainees to Fascism. Instead of uncontrolled Fascist violence, the police and militia developed bureaucratized, routine practices for punishing and intimidating detainees. Finally, as the island colonies filled up beyond capacity, new modalities of confinement emerged. Exiling the "least dangerous" detainees to southern villages, a rare practice before 1935, became more common than island internment. Then, in 1939, in a malarial southern province, the regime established a large agricultural labor colony with the intention of combining the project of "land reclamation" with that of "human reclamation." Over all, the history of the Fascist archipelago reveals the Mussolini dictatorship's practice of inflicting more, and often harsher, repression on expanding categories of Italians.

To the Islands

The hundreds of political and criminal suspects arrested in late 1926 were brought to police headquarters, photographed, fingerprinted, and strip-searched. After relinquishing their personal effects (e.g., watches, cuff links, and belts) detainees could request a private cell at their own expense, but, most commonly, they shared cells with the general prison population. After the detainees had spent days, weeks, and sometimes months in jail, police officials delivered to them a half sheet of paper with a terse statement informing them of where they would be deported and for how long. Shortly thereafter, political prisoners left jail for the train station. At dawn, Fascists often gathered outside jails to jeer their defeated enemies. Detainees could request to travel at their own expense in third-class train cars, still in manacles, accompanied by two *carabinieri*. Such requests were only made by the wealthy, and the police often rejected them. Most political detainees, and virtually all common ones, were fitted with heavy manacles and chained to one another. They traveled down the Italian peninsula in special prison cars with individual cells, or third-class passenger cars.[3] Stopping at jails throughout the Italian south – often strip-searched upon arrival – detainees spent weeks in a series of vermin-infested holding cells. Once arrived at Naples or another port city, the deportees then traveled by steamship to one of several islands. Many detainees were transported in the hull, without fresh air or light, often in rough seas, still shackled to one another. As they sat or slept on the cold, wet steel floors, pools of vomit and urine formed, making the air putrid.[4] In letters to his family, the Communist leader Antonio Gramsci, who seldom complained about physical discomfort during his decade in Fascist prisons, repeatedly described the trauma caused by the Palermo-Ustica crossing.[5] Arrival on the islands was thus often a welcome relief.

The destination of these anti-Fascists were five small islands off the coast of Sicily – Ustica, Favignana, Lipari, Pantelleria, and Lampedusa – and two in the southern Adriatic, San Nicola and San Domino, both part of the Tremiti archipelago. When the regime introduced its public-security legislation in November 1926, most of the islands were classified as so-called *domicilio coatto* (forced domicile) colonies, a practice dating back at least to the nineteenth century. In the years since the First World War, however, deporting criminal suspects to these islands had become less common. Several colonies had been completely shut down, and when Mussolini came to power in 1922, only Lampedusa, Ustica, Favignana, and the Tremiti Islands were still active, holding a total of eight hundred detainees.[6] The practice, which had been much criticized by some Italian liberals, appeared to be dying a slow death.

---

[3] On *traduzione speciale* and *traduzione ordinaria*, see Misuri, *Ad Bestias!*, 181–2.

[4] For Naples-Palermo, see Magri, *Una vita*, 21; see also Salvatori, *Al confino*, 42; and for Porto Empedocle-Lampedusa, see Giovanni Monaco, "Traduzione ordinaria," in *Il prezzo della libertà, Episodi di lotta antifascista* (Rome, 1958), 120–1.

[5] Gramsci to Schucht, December 9 and 19, 1926; February 12, 1927; also, Gramsci to Sraffa, December 11 and 21, 1926, in *Lettere dal carcere, 1926–1930*, ed. Antonio Santucci (Palermo, 1996).

[6] See "Relazione sulla visita eseguita alle colonie di coatti di Pantelleria, Lampedusa ed Ustica," October 5, 1923, in ACS, MI, DGPS, Divisione Polizia, *confinati comuni*, b. 1: Affari generali e di massima, fasc.: ammoniti comuni: quesiti. sf.1: "Lavoro ai confinati nelle colonie."

By December 1926, however, the newly renamed "*confino* colonies" were inundated with hundreds of political and criminal detainees. Conditions on the islands were primitive. One Socialist sent to Favignana in December 1926 recalled living with twenty-seven other men in a stifling barrack without air circulation. Fifteen beds were packed tightly along one wall, and only twelve along the opposite wall, with the remaining space occupied by the "toilet," a hole in the floor.[7] Police inspectors confirmed these conditions and noted the "excessive rigor" of the coercive regime on Favignana. Each dormitory, one inspector reported, had an "internal latrine with a primitive closure that emits a foul stench." Barrack windows were bricked over or otherwise sealed off, preventing any light or air from entering. Ex-convicts and former parliamentary deputies slept shoulder to shoulder. Detainees with tuberculosis and syphilis were not segregated from healthy detainees, the inspector informed Bocchini.[8] Francesco Fausto Nitti, the nephew of a former prime minister, described his confinement on the island of Lampedusa, a "flat and sterile" island, "a few square miles in extent, a rocky strip of land without a tree, grass, or anything green." There he lived alongside the island's six hundred free citizens and among "some 400 ordinary convicts..., poor wretches demoralized by drink, misery and vice." According to Nitti, the overcrowded, stifling barracks had water troughs for drinking and bathing that were full of worms and open waste tubs for 120 men. During the daylight hours, detainees were allowed to circulate in the village, but from five in the evening until seven in the morning they were locked in the barracks.[9]

Conditions on Ustica and Lipari, where the most prominent detainees were sent, were apparently better. According to Gramsci's first impression, Ustica was "excellent in every way." The local population was "quite courteous," treating the political detainees "with the most proper manners." Gramsci was, however, a former parliamentary deputy and the general secretary of the Italian Communist Party (PCI). Like many other political detainees on Ustica and Lipari, he rented a house with other

---

[7] See Salvatori, *Al confino*, 65.

[8] Summary report in *dispaccio telegrafico*, Suardo to prefect of Trapani, February 3, 1927, in ACS, MI, DGPS, Divisione Polizia, *confinati comuni*, b. 19: Colonia Confinati, Affari Generali. Trienni 1930–3, 1934–6. See also Inspector General Capobianco, in MI, DGPS, UCP, 1927, b. 13, fasc. Relazioni. Quoted in Alessandro Coletti, *Il governo di Ventotene: stalinismo e lotta politica tra i dirigenti del PCI al confino* (Milan, 1978), 39.

[9] Francesco Fausto Nitti, *Review of Reviews* (London), September 14, 1929.

anti-Fascists, and thus was spared the miseries of the Ustica barracks.[10] Although hundreds of "common" detainees lived on Ustica, Gramsci made no mention of them. In contrast, the Fascist dissident Alfredo Misuri, also confined on Ustica, noted that common detainees and poor political detainees lived in "crude and squalid common dormitories," much like those on Lampedusa, Favignana, Tremiti, and Pantelleria, which were locked from sundown to sunrise.[11]

The rapidly growing detainee population, together with the mixing of political and common detainees, presented problems for the regime. As space on the islands became scarce, new transports were halted, leaving detainees sitting in jail cells throughout Italy.[12] In response, the General Directorate of Public Security (DGPS) began its efforts to expand the system. By August 1927 the islands had space for 1,310 common and 1,080 political detainees. Nevertheless, a high-ranking police official described the situation to Mussolini as "more grave" than ever. The number of common detainees, he explained, had risen beyond 1,600 and would "continue to rise because almost all of the Provincial Commissions pass sentences quite liberally." Southern provincial commissions, particularly those of Palermo and Nuoro (Sardinia), were passing a "staggering" number of sentences.[13] The "availability of posts" in the common branch, according to the official responsible for administering it, was "always insufficient."[14] In January 1928, with the common population approaching 2,200, Bocchini described conditions as "truly worrisome" in terms of "hygiene, discipline, and public order." The dormitories, in which conditions were awful under normal circumstances, were overcrowded by a factor of 33 percent.[15] The directors of the common colonies grew increasingly alarmed. One police official on Ustica warned Bocchini that the large number of common detainees posed a physical threat to the political population, a fact confirmed by the murder of a political detainee

---

[10] Gramsci to Schucht, December 9, 1926, in *Lettere dal carcere*.

[11] Misuri, *Ad Bestias*, 206, 237.

[12] For Ustica and Lipari, see prefect of Palermo to Bocchini (Ustica), April 28, 1927, UCP, b. 11, fasc. 710–12/1926–30, sf. 1927.

[13] Director of the Police Division (Section II), "Appunto," August 7, 1927, in UCP, b. 11, fasc. 710–12/1926–30, sf. 1927; director of the Police Division, "Appunto per DAGR," no. 1150, August 13, 1927, UCP, b. 11, fasc. 710–12/1926–30, sf. 1927.

[14] Chief director of the Police Division, "Appunto per DAGR," no. 1150, August 13, 1927.

[15] On Favignana, capacity was 250, with 333 present; Lampedusa: 784 capacity, with 879 present; Pantelleria: 180 capacity, with 390 present; Tremiti: 395 capacity, with 540 present. Direzione Generale, "Appunto per l'On Gabinetto di S.E. Il Ministro," January 12, 1928, UCP, b. 14, f. 710–24/33/Ponza/1930, sf. A.

in August 1927.[16] On orders from Rome, the DGPS began segregating
common and political detainees during the spring of 1927, in part because
the situation reflected poorly on the regime at home and abroad. Political
detainees were concentrated on Lipari and Ustica, and common detainees
on Lampedusa, Pantelleria, Favignana, and Le Tremiti.[17] The creation of
two different systems had no basis in the new public-security legislation nor did the very different confinement regimes imposed on the two
groups. Despite this policy of segregation, political and common detainees
continued to cohabitate in many island colonies thereafter. The two
groups were also linked by the permeability of the categories "common"
and "political." Many political detainees could have easily been labeled
"common" and vice versa, and the regime occasionally reclassified select
offenses.

Despite overcrowding in the islands, Bocchini and Mussolini labored
to expand the capacity of the system rather than curtail the number of
sentences.[18] In 1928, they established a new political colony on Ponza.
Within a short period of time, Lipari and Ponza would serve as the
two main political colonies, and Ustica would become a massive colony
for common detainees. Even before Ponza opened, Bocchini projected
a massive expansion of the system based on "sentences already passed,
those in process, and estimates for the future" (see Table 1). The seven
main island colonies, with a current capacity of three thousand posts,
would be expanded to hold six thousand detainees.

To deal with the shortage of posts, the regime also exiled a few of
the "least dangerous" common and political detainees to mainland villages in Italy's southern provinces, mainly Potenza, Nuoro (Sardinia),
and Matera.[19] Intended as a temporary measure, mainland exile became
increasingly common from 1935 onward. Authorities reasoned that
removing essentially "apolitical" political detainees from the islands prevented groups like the Communist Party from recruiting new militants.[20]
Mainland exile was also an inexpensive and elastic form of detention.
Exiles lived cheaply in the south, while existing police and *carabinieri*
provided security. By June 1927, at least fifty political detainees had been

---

[16] Director of the Police Division (Section II), "Appunto," August 7, 1927, in UCP, b. 11.
See also, Musci, *Confino fascista*, lxv.
[17] These transfers are discussed in Musci, *Confino fascista*, lxv, and Dal Pont, *I lager*, 41.
[18] Bocchini to Mussolini, October 1, 1927, n. 5458, UCP, b. 14, fasc. 710–16 sf. E.
[19] Bocchini to Mussolini, "Colonie di confino – Capienza," May 3, 1927, UCP, b. 1.
[20] Director Console to prefect of Messina, May 8, 1930, n. 630, UCP, b. 4, fasc. 710–
3/1932, sf. E/Ponza.

TABLE 1. *Projected Expansion of Confino Colonies*
(April 1928)

	Current Capacity	Projected Expansion
Lipari	215	700
Ponza	300	800
Favignana	250	1,000
Pantelleria	180	1,000
Lampedusa	784	1,000
Tremiti	600	600
TOTAL	2,124	5,100 (6,000)

Note: The capacity of Ustica (1,000) was not listed in Bocchini's memorandum.
Source: DGPS (Bocchini) to Ministero dei Lavori Pubblici, April 7, 1928, n. 11500, UCP, b. 1.

sent to southern villages, some for "socially dangerous" activities, such as usury and abortion, and others for isolated acts of dissidence, such as insults to Mussolini or slanders of the regime. Common exiles, ranging from *mafiosi* to homosexual men, soon began appearing in southern villages as well.[21]

In general, the provincial police commissions for the assignment of *confino di polizia* consistently sentenced more people than the system could accommodate.[22] Vacancies created by Mussolini's frequent amnesties were quickly filled by new and larger waves of detainees.[23] In the early years, between 1926 and 1934, the branch that handled "common" criminal suspects – "habitual" criminals, alcoholics, *mafiosi*, pimps, drug dealers and addicts, and vagabonds – grew remarkably (see Table 2). With the introduction of the police code in November 1926, the Fascist police immediately exercised its expanded powers in order to restore "law and order" and "clean up the streets" rather than to merely suppress anti-Fascism. Furthermore, the social consequences of Mussolini's deflationary economic policies and the great economic crisis that began in 1929 led the regime to rely even more on arbitrary arrest and confinement as a strategy for maintaining public order. By the early

---

[21] On *terraferma confino*, see Leonardo Sacco, *Provincia di confino: La Lucania nel ventennio fascista* (Fasano di Brindisi, 1995). For so-called pederasts in *terraferma confino* in 1929, see prefect of Potenza Ottavio Dinale to DGPS, December 28, 1929, in UCP, b. 11, fasc. 710–14, sf. C/comune.

[22] On the commissions, see Musci, *Confino fascista*, lviii.

[23] For a discussion of amnesties/clemency, see ibid., lxix–lxxv.

TABLE 2. *Common Detainees Assigned to Island Colonies, 1928–1937*

	Ustica	Ventotene	Favignana	Tremiti	Lampedusa	Pantelleria	Total
Jan. 1928	NA	NA	333	540	879	390	2,142
Nov. 1930	1,099	280	636	924	917	618	4,474
Nov. 1932	1,472	10	453	716	1,405	462	4,518
Aug. 1934	1,114		480	877	1,138	490	4,099
Nov. 1934	1,223		465	855	1,204	541	4,288
Dec. 1935	1,358		501	651	1,265	534	4,309
Nov. 1936	1,941		482	488	930	319	4,160
Dec. 1937	2,065		486	40	926	n.a.	3,517*

* Does not include unreported population of Pantelleria.

Source: Table compiled from tables and documents in MI, DGPS, Divisione Polizia, *confinati comuni*, b. 8, fasc. 10, 36, 38, 39; see also sf. "Liberazione condizionale" in MI, DGPS, Divisione Polizia, *confinati comuni*, b. 3; and Bocchini telegram to directors of *confino* colonies, November 7, 1932, "situazione numerica dei confinati comuni" in MI, DGPS, Divisione Polizia, *confinati comuni*, b. 3, sf. "liberazione condizionale."

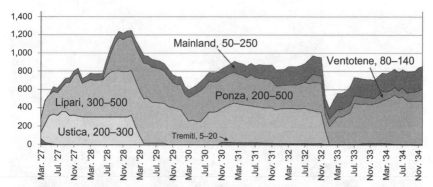

FIGURE 3. Political Detainee Population by Location, 1927–1934. *Sources:* "Situazione numerica degli assegnati al confino di polizia" series in MI, DGPS, UCP, b. 11, fasc. 710–14/1926–30, sf. A/Lipari, B/Ponza, C/Tremiti, D/Ustica, E/Terraferma; fasc. 710–14/1931, sf. A/Lipari, B/Ponza; fasc. 710–14/1932, sf. D/Ventotene; and "Capienza" series in UCP, b. 12, 710–14/1934, sf. 1/Ponza, 2/Ponza, 3/Tremiti, 710–14/1935, sf. 1/Ponza, 2/Ponza, 3/Ventotene, 4/Tremiti.

1930s the common *confino* population exceeded four thousand detainees (Table 2).[24]

During this same first period, between 1926 and 1934, the population of the political branch peaked at around 1,200 detainees, and then contracted slightly, as individuals serving shorter sentences were released and "less dangerous" individuals were amnestied (see Figure 3). The population of the political branch was relatively small and static for several reasons. First, although the suppression of anti-Fascist movements was a geographically limited phenomenon, the repression of common criminality occurred throughout the entire peninsula, particularly in the south. Second, detaining people on these islands was costly, and the large number of common detainees left little space for the political population. Finally, for the sake of appearances, the regime was deliberately avoiding a "mass action" against anti-Fascists, which "while seemingly easy" would have been "counterproductive." In its foreign and domestic propaganda, the regime consistently denied that it had to resort to "terror" to rule Italy.[25]

---

[24] For total common detainee population see "Elenco dei *confinati politici* suddivisi per provincia," November 13, 1937, in ACS, MI, DGPS, UCP, b. 2. For population of Ustica, see report of DGPS to Bocchini, November 7, 1937, in ACS, MI, DGPS, UCP, b. 2.

[25] Suardo to prefects, in ACS, MI, Ufficio Cifra-Partenze, November 15, 1926, n. 28555, and November 26, 1926, n. 29746. The latter telegram is reprinted in Aquarone, *Organizzazione*, 425–6.

FIGURE 4. Among this group of prominent political detainees being deported to confinement in 1927 was Carlo Rosselli (far right), who together with Emilio Lussu and Francesco Fausto Nitti would escape from the Lipari colony in 1929. *Source:* Fototeca Gilardi.

Lipari

In July 1929, three anti-Fascists – Carlo Rosselli (Figure 4), Francesco Fausto Nitti, and Emilio Lussu – escaped from the Lipari *confino politico* colony, fleeing by motorboat to France. Their accounts of Fascist political repression – arbitrary arrests, sham political trials, summary detainment, beatings, horrible living conditions, and torture – opened a debate in the foreign press about Mussolini's dictatorship.[26] Fascist apologists accused anti-Fascists like Rosselli, Nitti, and Lussu of lies and exaggeration, pointing to the "legality" of the repressive system, the small number of political prisoners, and the allegedly idyllic environs of the islands. Luigi Villari, the regime's chief English-language propagandist, explained to his readers that "political offenders are *confinati* in the islands of Ponza and Lipari, which are generally considered to be among the most beautiful spots in Italy." He insisted, "The places are not, as has been stated in the foreign

[26] Nitti, *Review of Reviews*, September 14, 1929.

Press, desert rocks, but thickly populated islands with large villages on them, inhabited by a numerous stable population, dwelling there by its own free will."[27] From this debate emerged two static images that have persisted to this day. Pro-Fascists, who had no direct experience with the colonies, sanitized the reality, sometimes beyond all recognition. The anti-Fascist version, though usually factual, focused on the worst instances of maltreatment, while often failing to acknowledge how factors like social class shaped Fascist political repression.

Lipari's physical beauty, public utilities, and civic life rendered it particularly well suited to the regime's strategy of presenting political confinement as exile in paradise rather than punitive internment. With a perimeter of sixteen nautical miles and a (free) population of fifteen thousand inhabitants, Lipari was the largest of the islands hosting *confino* colonies. In addition to cultivating grains, fruits, and vines, the inhabitants of Lipari generated significant revenue from pumice mining. The island's relative prosperity was reflected in its infrastructure and civic life. The town of Lipari was electrified and featured two large, paved roads with multiple intersecting streets, forming a lively city center with cafés, restaurants, hotels, and shops, not to mention gorgeous panoramas of the sea and other Aeolian islands. A municipal band performed a weekly concert in the central piazza during the summer. On the basis of this evaluation, the DGPS designated Lipari a suitable location for hosting former parliamentary deputies, intellectuals, and other prominent figures.[28]

As on Ustica and Ponza, state police administered the Lipari colony, but Fascist militiamen, led by a centurion, guarded the detainees. This arrangement led to clashes between police officials who thought that confinement should serve a "preventive" function and Fascists who viewed it as an institution of violent punishment. The director on Lipari, a police official named Francesco Cannata, who enjoyed the full support of Bocchini and other high-ranking DGPS officials, steadfastly maintained that punishing or restricting the liberty of detainees violated the public-security legislation.[29] Under Cannata, Lipari developed a reputation as the most

---

[27] Luigi Villari, *Italy* (New York and London, 1929), 231.

[28] On Lipari, see Inspector General Valenti to Gabinetto, "Colonie confinati di Ustica e di Lipari. Informazioni," September 2, 1927, UCP, b. 14, fasc. 710–16/1926–30, sf. B/Lipari.

[29] Inspector General Valenti to DGPS, August 30, 1927, UCP, b. 13, fasc. 710–15/1926–30; Ispettore Generale Biagio Ranalli to DGPS, "Ufficio di P.S. e Direzione dei confinati di polizia di Lipari," November 15, 1927, UCP, b. 4, fasc. 710–3/1926–30, sf. A/Lipari, 11.

comfortable of the *confino politico* colonies. Detainees either took a bed in a communal dormitory or found private accommodations at their own expense. Thanks to "la mazzetta" (the per diem living stipend, initially ten lira), not to mention the private resources of wealthy detainees, around 75 percent of Lipari's detainee population rented private apartments or rooms. Giovanni Ansaldo, an anti-Fascist journalist who later turned Fascist, arrived on the island during the spring of 1927. After meeting with the director, he encountered a Communist from Genoa, who invited him for breakfast at the Villa Diana, a large private residence on the island that had been rented by a few of the wealthier detainees and their wives. After breakfast, Ansaldo set himself up in an apartment with electric lights – a luxury, though not unheard of on Lipari – for 150 lira per month. He saw old friends, made new ones (as well as enemies), and went swimming and lay in the sun at least every other day. Ansaldo was a Fascist apologist, but memoirs from the other side of the political spectrum confirm aspects of this picture. Juares Busoni, a Socialist from Empoli, had suffered several months on Tremiti before being transferred to Lipari in early 1927, where he found "the conditions of life were more than tolerable."[30] Busoni fondly recalled that Carlo Rosselli and his English wife Marion regularly hosted afternoon tea at their home, where they lived with their newborn son and their Florentine domestic servant.[31] Director Cannata authorized detainees to send for their families, and about half did, bringing 120 children to the island by 1929.[32] Detainees were not forced to work, although a significant number found employment. Those who practiced a trade – barbers, cobblers, cooks, dentists, and mechanics – found work more easily than intellectuals or manual laborers.

Security on the island was relatively lax, perhaps intentionally. During the day, detainees circulated freely within a three kilometer security perimeter, the *zona di confino*, which included the city center.[33] However, the island's lush vegetation and hilly, rocky terrain left the perimeter quite porous, despite the garrisons manned by Fascist militiamen. A few detainees "escaped," easily evading the surveillance, but authorities soon

[30] Juares Busoni, *Nel tempo del fascismo* (Rome, 1927), 190.
[31] Ibid., 190–1.
[32] On families, see Pagano, *Confino politico a Lipari*, 171–7.
[33] Ispettore Generale Biagio Ranalli to DGPS, "Ufficio di P.S. e Direzione dei confinati di polizia di Lipari," November 15, 1927, UCP, b. 4, fasc. 710–3/1926–30, sf. A/Lipari, 11.

noted their absence and captured them elsewhere on the island. Police officials rejected all proposals to construct a physical barrier around the *zona di confino*. As the *vice-questore* of Messina explained, "The construction . . . of barracks grouped together and enclosed by iron gates" would turn the institution into "true detention . . . which is decidedly contrary to the spirit and letter of the new public security law." He explained, "The coercive system is a measure of prevention and social defense; it is neither a punishment nor a penalty against the *confinati*."[34] Even the general command of the MVSN declined to endorse such proposals due to "political repercussions that such an action might produce abroad, as well as the high expenditures which would certainly be incurred."[35] Surveillance and control were thus limited to guarding the perimeter, enforcing the curfew, convening a morning roll call, and conducting nocturnal house checks. Communal barracks were simply locked down at night.

Counteracting this rather light security regime were the approximately two hundred militiamen responsible for surveillance and discipline, who often created an environment of lawlessness and fear on Lipari. Police documents and firsthand accounts confirm numerous incidents of Black Shirts arresting or assaulting Lipari's citizens, harassing women, provocatively firing weapons in public, causing property damage, killing domestic animals, leaving unpaid debts, getting drunk and singing lewd songs, and beating and torturing detainees. Many MVSN officials and rank-and-file militiamen simply rejected the notion that their actions should be bound by the law. Moreover, although charged with the delicate task of controlling political detainees living amongst a free citizenry, the militiamen had no appropriate police or juridical training. As militiamen, their job was instead to "defend the Revolution" and their main qualification was "fascist zeal." Whether on or off duty, they arrested detainees and even free citizens for "provoking" or "defaming" them. Citizens of Lipari who criticized these arrests might be arrested for "petulance" or "offense" to the MVSN. When the local magistrate actually fined individuals for petty slights to the MVSN, the militiamen were invariably unsatisfied with the penalty. Even police agents and *carabinieri* clashed with militiamen,

---

[34] Vice-Questore Potito to chief of police (and Mussolini), October 6, 1928, in UCP, b. 16, fasc. 710–32/192, sf. 6–30.

[35] Undated, unsigned report on Ponza and Lipari to Comando Generale Milizia, Ufficio Politico Investigativo, in UCP, b. 4, fasc. 710–3/1932, sf. E/Varie.

who often made demands that violated official procedural codes and protocols. In sum, the MVSN disdained the rule of law on Lipari, viewing it as "un-Fascist," while many other of the island's inhabitants were understandably revolted by the MVSN's violent and often lawless behavior.[36]

MVSN and Fascist authorities regularly railed against the coercive regime on Lipari in letters to Interior Ministry officials. In a letter to Bocchini, Agostino Guerresi,[37] an old-guard *squadrist* who had been appointed prefect of Messina, indignantly complained that "The island, due to its mild climate, its natural resources, and its panoramic beauty, rather than being punishment for the confinati, is a vacation spot [*luogo di villeggiatura*]." Guerresi argued that the detainees "would reside here willingly, living communally with one another...behaving arrogantly and disdainfully toward the guards [and] brashly toward the peaceful population." He demanded that authorities on Lipari "modify the coercive regime" and "further restrict the liberty of the *confinati*." Fascists focused their anger and frustration on the colony's director, Cannata, whom they deemed an "anti-Fascist." Fascists alleged that Cannata indulged the political detainees, even befriending "well-bred" anti-Fascists such as Carlo Rosselli.[38] In response to these allegations, Bocchini ordered the *questura* of Messina to investigate. Rejecting Guerresi's claims, the *vice-questore* reported to Bocchini that "to remove an individual from his home, to interrupt his life, to keep him far from his family, to move him to an island and subject him to constant, daily, uninterrupted surveillance, cannot be considered an advantage for the *confinato*." Moreover, to increase the severity of the "coercive regime" would, he cautioned, "violate the laws of humanity" and fail to conform with the "fundamental spirit of prevention of the Public Security Laws: to put the subject in a position in which it is impossible

---

36 For a lengthy police report on these matters, see Ispettorato Regionale della P. S. per la Sicilia to prefect of Messina, July 18, 1928, in ACS, MI, DGPS, UCP, b. 16, fasc. 710–32/1926–30.

37 Agostino Guerresi (1880–1961). Along with Michele Bianchi, Guerresi was a principal proponent of Fascism and *squadrismo* in the province of Cosenza. He was appointed prefect of Cosenza in July 1923 and, five years later, was posted to the province of Messina, where he served for almost two years. He subsequently served in other provinces. See Mario Missori, *Governi, alte cariche dello stato, alti magistrati e prefetti del Regno d'Italia* (Rome, 1989), 461, 517, 520, 566, 586.

38 "Situazione della Colonia di Lipari," April 6, 1929, UCP, b. 13, fasc. 710–15/1926–30.

for him to do damage, not to punish or torment him."[39] Moreover, in several reports, high-ranking police officials consistently rejected the Fascists' characterization of Cannata, describing him as an exemplary official.[40]

Unfortunately for those confined on the island, the victory of these career police officials over Fascist appointees and MVSN officers was only temporary. In the wake of the Rosselli escape, Bocchini removed Cannata and several other police officials from Lipari.[41] More importantly, the DGPS discarded notions about the "preventative" nature of *confino*, introducing major reforms that would enhance security and drastically affect the lives of the detainees. In particular, Bocchini transferred "all services of surveillance and control of the confinati" from the jurisdiction of the director to that of the MVSN. Although the director was still the island's chief authority, the militia now had more autonomy and wider jurisdiction over the detainees. Police officials became less likely to challenge the militia and implicitly endorsed the view that *confino di polizia* was intended to operate as a measure of detention and punishment.[42] Within months, the number of militiamen on Lipari was increased from 180 to 260, reaching three hundred by December 1931.[43] The security perimeter was also to be reduced, more clearly delimited, and fortified with fixed guard posts, lights, telephone lines, and electric buzzers.[44] New, more invasive security protocols for patrols were established. Militiamen were now ordered to conduct house checks "with

[39] Guerresi's assessment and the vice-police chief's response are both included in the report of Vice-Questore Potito to chief of police, October 6, 1928, in ACS, MI, DGPS, UCP, b. 16, fasc. 710–32/192, sf. 6–30.

[40] Valenti to Bocchini, April 17, 1929, UCP, b. 13, fasc. 710–15/1926–30.

[41] Bocchini to Alto Commissario Napoli, Telegram, August 6, 1929, UCP, b. 4, fasc. 710–3/1926–30. For further dismissals, see Inspector General of Public Security Scalone to Bocchini, August 20, 1930, in ACS, MI, DGPS, UCP, b. 4, fasc. 710–3/1932, E/Varie.

[42] See director of Lipari (Console) to prefect of Messina, "Relazione sull'andamento delle Colonie di Lipari e Ponza," May 8, 1930, in UCP, b. 4, fasc. 710–3/1932, sf. E/Ponza.

[43] See *questura* of Messina to prefect of Messina, "Oggetto: Lipari – Colonia *confinati politici* – Notizie e proposte per l'assoluta sicurezza," September 8, 1929, UCP, b. 13, fasc. 710–15/1926–30. For 1931, see report of Inspector General Nazareno Musco to Bocchini, December 8, 1931, UCP, b. 16, fasc. 710–32/1931, sf. 1.

[44] See *questura* of Messina to prefect of Messina, "Oggetto: Lipari," September 8, 1929; inspector general to chief of police, "Oggetto: Ispezione alla Colonia Confinati Politici di Lipari," November 6, 1929, UCP, b. 13, fasc. 710–15/1926–30; Inspector General Nazareno Musco to Bocchini, December 8, 1931, in UCP, b. 16, fasc. 710–32/1931, sf. 1.

repeat visits, at difference times, from evening until morning," which meant multiple disruptions of sleep and privacy throughout the night.[45] Roll calls were similarly increased from one or two to three or more daily.[46] Police officials also began to address the problem of political activity among detainees. Anti-Fascists, particularly Communists, had maintained contact with their central leadership abroad and engaged in propaganda, proselytism, and collective resistance on the island. To disrupt such activities, police officers conducted searches, employed spies, and censored mail. Finally, the director more frequently inflicted sanctions, such as house arrest, reduced living subsidies, and short periods in jail. More serious violations were prosecuted by courts in Naples, often leading to long-term imprisonment.[47]

These reforms enhanced the environment of intimidation and fear on Lipari. The MVSN began punishing detainees for violating curfew, crossing the security perimeter, holding political discussions, possessing prohibited items, gathering in groups larger than three, and "provoking" or resisting the authority of the MVSN.[48] Not surprisingly, instances of violence and abuse increased. Walking too closely to the security perimeter or returning home just before curfew commonly provided militiamen with pretexts for arresting detainees. Once militiamen apprehended detainees, they sometimes brought them to their headquarters, where they were roughed up, beaten, or tortured. The doctor at Lipari's jail reported to police that most detainees delivered by the militia had contusions and other signs of maltreatment. A local judge reported hearing screams of pain coming from the MVSN holding cell at night.[49] Meanwhile, the chief of the MVSN's political office noted approvingly how the new coercive regime had changed "the outward conduct of the detainees." When approaching officials, he recounted, the detainees always appeared with "a jacket, without a hat, dressed decently and composed." "Certain displays (wearing of black ties, red flowers in button holes, spitting on the

---

[45] Inspector general to chief of police, "Oggetto: Ispezione alla Colonia Confinati Politici di Lipari," November 6, 1929, UCP, b. 13, fasc. 710–15/1926–30.

[46] Inspector General Scalone to Bocchini, August 20, 1930, UCP, b. 4, fasc. 710–3/1932, E/Varie. See Senise's response, attached to the Report of Inspector General of Public Security Scalone to Bocchini, August 20, 1930, UCP, b. 4, fasc. 710–3/1932, sf. E/Varie.

[47] Pagano, *Il confino politico a Lipari*, 106.

[48] See Capo dell Ufficio Politico UPI Console Ballabio to Bochini, March 27, 1930, UCP, b. 4, fasc. 710–3/1932, sf. E/Ponza.

[49] *Vice-questore* to Bocchini, January 14, 1930, ACS, MI, DGPS, UCP, b. 16, fasc. 710–32/1926–30, 5.

ground when passing a figure of authority, etc.)" had "almost completely stopped."[50]

Tensions between the MVSN and the local population also escalated.[51] In one incident, the MVSN, reacting to a totally unfounded, vague rumor of a detainee uprising, loaded their weapons and went on a rampage in Lipari town. Two dozen of Lipari's citizens were injured, many seriously, mostly due to blows from rifle butts. One pregnant woman was allegedly at risk of losing her child. Shortly thereafter, on Christmas Day 1929, one hundred militiamen got drunk and roamed the streets of Lipari singing offensive songs about women, the political detainees, and the population of Lipari.[52] The militia thus became, for many, a hostile and unwanted presence. The *vice-questore* of Messina reported to Bocchini that "the militia has gone well beyond its security duties, invading the jurisdiction of the direction and even the authority of Public Security Officials and the judiciary police." Often, "armed groups" took "to the streets without any request from public security officials, at times for simple, unnecessary demonstrations of force."[53] He wrote in a subsequent report, "In public, it is lamented how . . . all of the Officials of the Lipari unit are always equipped with long leather riding crops, and about these it has been said that they use them on the *confinati* and sometimes on individual citizens."[54] Even for one of the MVSN's own officials, aspects of the militia's behavior during 1929 and 1930 recalled "the time of *squadrismo*."[55]

Perhaps the most significant consequence of the Rosselli escape was the transfer of detainees out of private housing and into communal barracks. Prior to July 1929, less than 25 percent of detainees lived in Lipari's Bourbon castle.[56] Months after the escape, the number doubled, and

[50] See Capo dell Ufficio Politico UPI Console Ballabio to Bochini, March 27, 1930, ACS, MI, DGPS, UCP, b. 4, fasc. 710–3/1932, sf. E/Ponza.

[51] *Vice-questore* to Bocchini, January 14, 1930, in ACS, MI, DGPS, UCP, b. 16, fasc. 710–32/1926–30.

[52] See report of *vice-questore* to Bocchini, January 14, 1930, ACS, MI, DGPS, UCP, b. 16, fasc. 710–32/1926–30.

[53] See report of Vice-Questore Potito to Bocchini, marked "Riservatissima Personale," January 4, 1930, 7, in ACS, MI, DGPS, UCP, b. 16, fasc. 710–32/1926–30.

[54] See Vice-Questore Potito of Messina to Bocchini, January 14, 1930, 6, in ACS, MI, DGPS, UCP, b. 16, fasc. 710–32/1926–30.

[55] See Comandante Nicchiarelli, "Incidenti della sera del 29 Dicembre," January 4, 1930, UCP, b. 16, fasc. 710–32/1926–30.

[56] Ebner, *Fascist Archipelago*, 522–3. Ispettore Generale di P. S. per la Sicilia Biagio Ranalli to DGPS, "Ufficio di P.S. e Direzione dei confinati di polizia di Lipari," November 15, 1927, UCP, b. 4, fasc. 710–3/1926–30, sf. A/Lipari, 5.

only lack of space in the dormitories prevented further transfers. Meanwhile, plans for new dormitories, along with the implementation of other reforms, stalled because, already in the spring of 1930, the MVSN and the director were calling for Lipari to be shut down. Lipari's size and topography, authorities believed, made the island ill-suited for a *confino politico* colony.[57] Lipari closed in December 1932.

Ponza

Even before Rosselli and his accomplices fled Lipari, the colony on Ponza featured stricter discipline and more frequent abuse of detainees. Ponza was, in many ways, better equipped to host an internment colony. A military facility, vacated for the occasion, offered important infrastructure, including electrification and telephone lines. A former monastery provided space for the colony's administrative offices. In addition to an old jail from the Bourbon era, the island also had a prison for twenty to twenty-five persons.[58] On Lipari the regime had to contend with vocal political authorities and an antagonistic population. On Ponza, by contrast, the Interior Ministry simply seized control of local political and administrative offices, removing top officials and replacing them with other men, sometimes outsiders, of "secure devotion to the Regime." Most significantly, the incoming centurion of the MVSN, Alberto Memmi, who had been transferred from the Ustica colony, was also made secretary of the local *fascio*.[59] To prepare the public, authorities distributed a poster warning Ponza's 9,200 fishermen, farmers, and merchants that the *confinati politici* were "the irreducible adversaries of the regime," with whom the Ponzesi should avoid "any sort of familiarity

---

[57] See Capo dell Ufficio Politico UPI Console Ballabio to Bochini, March 27, 1930, in ACS, MI, DGPS, UCP, b. 4, fasc. 710–3/1932, sf. E/Ponza.

[58] Report of MVSN Centurion and Commissar Agg. of P.S. to DGPS (Bocchini), April 29, 1928, UCP, b. 14, fasc. 710–24/33, sf. B/Ponza/1930.

[59] For documentation of this development, see "Deliberazione del Podestà," December 15, 1927, UCP, b. 14. fasc. 710–24/33, sf. B/Ponza 1930; PNF (Ponza) to MI, December 14, 1927, UCP, b. 14, fasc. 710–24/33, sf. B/Ponza 1930; Bocchini to Mussolini, "Appunto per l'On. Gabinetto di S.E. il Ministro. Oggetto: Isola di Ponza – Confino Politico," February 18, 1928, in UCP, b. 14, fasc. 710–24/33, sf. B/Ponza/1930. See also "Gruppo massonica antinazionale esistente nell'Isola di Ponza," July 16, 1928; and Alto Commissariato per la Provincia di Napoli to MI, DGPS, "Attività massonica antifascista nell'Isola di Ponza Rev. Tagliamonte Raffaele – Parroco dell'Isola," August 8, 1928, both in UCP, b. 14, fasc. 710–24/33, sf. B/Ponza/1930.

or assistance, which would render those responsible subject to exemplary and grave police sanctions."[60]

When the Ponza colony began receiving political detainees from Ustica on July 29, 1928, Centurion Memmi already exercised more authority than the colony's directors, who often spent just a few months in the position before moving on. Memmi was, according to one personnel report, "pushy" and "controlling." Directors were "always in a state of submissiveness in his presence" and "feared putting up any resistance to him" because they believed "he was very well protected," referring to his position within both the MVSN and the National Fascist Party (PNF). Directors even allowed Memmi to file criminal charges directly with judicial authorities, a function restricted by law to the director as chief officer of the judicial police.[61] Memmi's uncontested authority allowed the MVSN to exert strict control over the island, its population, and the detainees.[62] Not surprisingly, incidents of beatings, torture, and general harassment of detainees, and even the local population, were reported by official and unofficial sources. Mario Magri, a political detainee, who would be confined on virtually every political colony during his seventeen years in captivity, described Memmi as "without a doubt the worst," as well as "ignorant in the extreme and proud of the authority that had been conferred upon him." During the year 1928 to 1929, Magri claimed, Ponza had been "given over to the *squadristi*." Unwarranted arrests, beatings, torture, whips, riding crops, vandalism, drinking, and singing were the order of the day, Magri recalled.[63] Police officials from the DGPS regularly investigated such allegations but relied heavily on Memmi's version of events. In a report typical of these inquiries, the *questore* of Naples stated that Memmi and the MVSN "carry out their duties with praiseworthy zeal and diligence: diligence and zeal which some *confinati*

[60] "R. Ufficio di P.S. – Direzione colonia confino politico," July 19, 1928, UCP, b. 4, fasc. 710–3/1926–30, sf. B/Ponza; Report of Lieutenant Commander Carlo Alberto Rainone (Ponza) to DGPS (Bocchini), "Per L'istituzione di colonia di *confinati politici* a Ponza (Napoli)," January 29, 1928, in UCP, b. 14, 710–24/33, sf. B/Ponza/1930.
[61] Inspector General Valenti to DGPS (Bocchini), "Colonia confino politico di Ponza," January 29, 1929, UCP, b. 4, fasc. 710–3/1926–30, sf. B/Ponza.
[62] Inspector General Valenti to MI, DGPS (Bocchini), "Colonia confino politico di Ponza," January 29, 1929, ACS, MI, DGPS, UCP, b. 4, fasc. 710–3/1926–30, sf. B/Ponza. See *questore* of Naples De Martino to Alto Commissario for the Province of Naples, n. 19606, September 14, 1929, UCP, b. 4, fasc. 710–3/1926–30, sf. B/Ponza. See Maìenza to *questore* di Napoli, "La Camera Fortunato, confinato politico," October 3, 1928, in UCP, b. 4, fasc. 710–3/1926–30, sf. B/Ponza.
[63] Mario Magri, *Vita per la libertà*, 77.

misinterpret."[64] At the same time, the Director confidentially reported to the DGPS that there were "a few elements who... sometimes engage in reprehensible excesses, and do not even behave with appropriate correctness and seriousness in their interactions with private citizens."[65] One inspector general similarly described a group of "aggressive militiamen... belonging to a small group of Sicilians that Memmi brought with him from Ustica and allegedly protects," who should be immediately transferred off the island.[66] Public-security officials thus rarely challenged Memmi's word or authority by substantiating specific allegations of mistreatment. They nevertheless lobbied to remove particularly violent militiamen, who antagonized the local population and disrupted the operation of the colony.

The topography of Ponza was much better suited than that of Lipari for establishing a secure colony. The *zona di confino* included a three-kilometer stretch of rock cliffs that dropped precipitously to the sea, making passage onto or off the island virtually impossible. Additionally, Ponza is a long, narrow island, and the town of Ponza, together with the *confino* colony, were located at one end. By establishing a second security perimeter (*linea di sbarramento*) very near the town, at a narrow point of the island, the police cut the colony off from the majority of the island's landmass. Guard posts were connected by telephones and electric buzzers, and a section of the security perimeter was illuminated. Ponza's lighthouse swept the waters around the island, and a motorboat and a larger naval vessel patrolled the waters. After the Rosselli escape, police and MVSN officials proposed shoring up security with a "physical barrier" consisting of a "chain link fence and reinforced concrete." Such proposals were never realized, but the system of surveillance and control was progressively fortified and refined, creating a colony that was virtually hermetic.[67] By 1933, the security perimeter had shrunk to three kilometers, carving out an area about one kilometer long and only 250 meters wide. With four hundred detainees, hundreds of security personnel, and the local population circulating in this small space, Ponza's narrow streets became clogged

---

[64] See *questore* of Naples De Martino to Alto Commissario for the Province of Naples, n. 19606, September 14, 1929, UCP, b. 4, fasc. 710–3/1926–30, sf. B/Ponza.

[65] See Maìenza to *questore* di Napoli, "La Camera Fortunato, confinato politico," October 3, 1928, in UCP, b. 4, fasc. 710–3/1926–30, sf. B/Ponza.

[66] Inspector General Valenti to DGPS (Bocchini), "Colonia confino politico di Ponza," January 29, 1929, ACS, MI, DGPS, UCP, b. 4, fasc. 710–3/1926–30, sf. B/Ponza.

[67] *Questore* of Naples (De Martino) to Alto Commissario for the Province of Naples, September 14, 1929.

and often impassable.[68] Meanwhile, the number of security personnel increased from 180 to 300 militiamen and from twenty-four to fifty-three public-security agents (twenty regular agents and thirty-three maritime personnel). Thirty-four additional guard posts were constructed, bringing the total to fifty-four. Both security perimeters were illuminated and fortified with more militiamen. Guard posts were strategically positioned near beaches, the port, the central piazza, the main street, and all of the colony's structures. Additionally, militiamen armed with machine guns rode on the boats piloted by police and naval officers.[69] By 1933, an inspector general declared that it would be virtually impossible for detainees to reach the beach or otherwise leave the *zona di confino*.[70] Police agents now also began performing specialized, coordinated "political policing" functions, including undercover surveillance, rigorous mail censorship, and special security details for the "most dangerous" *confinati*. Some apolitical or pro-Fascist detainees were recruited as informers. The police also closely monitored relations between the detainees and the local population in order to prevent clandestine correspondence and other contraband from leaving or entering.[71]

As on Lipari, the housing of detainees underwent significant changes in the wake of the Rosselli escape. Before 1929, anywhere from one-third to one-half of detainees lived in barracks. During 1929, the population of the dormitories grew from 166 in July to 259 in September.[72] The communal dormitories were unpleasant places. Mario Magri, who was transferred to Ponza from Lipari in 1928, experienced them firsthand. "I was sent to sleep in the prison," he recalled, "which had been transformed into housing for detainees. It was a ground floor structure, extremely humid and without air. Since, in general, the *confinati* could rent rooms in the village, all of the drunks and the rabble slept in the barrack. I felt like a fish out of water in that environment and I felt horrible from the very first day in that sad place."[73] Police also reported that these dormitories left "much to be desired in terms of hygiene and decency." According to

---

[68] Inspector General Buzzi to Bocchini, "Ponza-Confinati Politici," October 24, 1933, UCP, b. 17, fasc. 710–33/1932, 3.

[69] IGPS to Bocchini, "Ispezione alla Colonia dei *confinati politici* di Ponza," March 14, 1932, in UCP, b. 13, fasc. 710–15/1932–3.

[70] Buzzi to Bocchini, "Ponza-Confinati Politici," October 24, 1933, UCP, b. 17, fasc. 710–33/1932, 3.

[71] IGPS to Bocchini, "Ispezione alla Colonia dei *confinati politici* di Ponza."

[72] See "capienza" in UCP, b. 11, fasc. 710–14/1926–30, sf. B/Ponza.

[73] Magri, *Una vita per la libertà*, 75.

one inspector general, only the second floor of the former Bourbon prison had "satisfactory hygienic sanitary conditions in terms of air and light, cleanliness of the walls, and susceptibility of the floors to cleaning." However, the MVSN refused to allow detainees to occupy the second floor, forcing them to live on the substandard ground floor, where the rooms were "truly uninhabitable, hardly distinguishable from large, antiquated, filthy stables."[74] The colony's medical doctor reported that the walls were filthy and the windows lacked glass panes, allowing bad weather to pass through them. The cracks and deep fissures in the floor collected debris and refuse, preventing them from being properly cleaned.[75] From the early 1930s onward, detainees suffered from all manner of illness and disease, ranging from intestinal viruses to tuberculosis, which occasionally led to death.[76]

Giorgio Amendola, who arrived on Ponza in 1934, recalled that "material conditions and the standard of living on the island were not bad," suggesting some improvement,[77] yet his observation was not likely true for all detainees, whether on Ponza or any of the other islands. Detainees of higher social standing usually had the best, most comfortable accommodations. Before 1929, most anti-Fascists rented private housing, while poorer detainees, usually the ones without political affiliations, lived in barracks. After 1929, as all detainees moved into barracks, police officials raised concerns about detainees "of a higher social level" cohabiting with the large number (approximately half) of political detainees who had criminal histories. Accordingly, the DGPS ordered the director of Ponza to separate the detainees "of a more civilized social condition" from "ex-convict detainees."[78] Not surprisingly, the anti-Fascists embraced this directive. The two large dormitories inside the prison were known as "Siberia" and "Manchuria," due to the terrible cold during the winter months. Anti-Fascist militants claimed "Siberia" for themselves. "Manchuria," the least hospitable of the two, went to the poor, apolitical, often alcoholic detainees, the so-called Manchurians, whom anti-Fascists

---

74 Buzzi to Bocchini, October 24, 1933, UCP, b. 17, fasc. 710–33/1932, 3–4.
75 Seniore Medico Andrea Buonsante, "Relazione sulle condizioni igienico sanitarie Colonia Confinati Politici – Ponza," October 18, 1933, in UCP, b. 17, fasc. 710–33/1932.
76 Of the 67 detainees from the sample confined on Ponza, twenty-one suffered health problems including serious gastrointestinal illnesses, respiratory illnesses, and tuberculosis (5 of the 21). Two detainees died.
77 Giorgio Amendola, *Un'isola* (Milan, 1980), 147.
78 See *questore* of Naples De Martino to Alto Commissario for the Province of Naples, n. 19606, September 14, 1929, UCP, b. 4, fasc. 710–3/1926–30, sf. B/Ponza.

derided for their "immorality" and obsequiousness toward authorities.[79] The Communist detainee Altiero Spinelli, though he did not agree with the opinion, wrote that most anti-Fascists viewed "the Manchurian" as "an impure being with whom any contact was prohibited."[80] Anti-Fascist militants and scholars have long struggled to discredit Fascist rule as brutal and oppressive. Yet, they have largely ignored the plight of the so-called Manchurians, as well as that of the common detainees on other islands. It is ironic, then, that political detainment was even worse than most anti-Fascists claimed it was, precisely because they were reluctant to fully examine the "political" role that persecuting "the dregs" of Italians society may have played in winning support for the regime among many Italians.

Ventotene and Le Tremiti

The emergence of a more punitive, custodial form of political confinement was most clearly reflected in the size and topography of islands chosen to host colonies after the closure of Lipari. New political colonies were established on the tiny, desolate islands of Ventotene (1932) and Le Tremiti (1936), where larger numbers of detainees were interned on smaller landmasses with fewer resources. As the first political colony established after 1929, Ventotene (Figure 5) reflected the regime's new focus on security and surveillance. Police officials chose the island for several reasons. The inspector general who prepared a preliminary report on Ventotene noted that with a total circumference of just seven kilometers (2,500 × 850 meters) the island could be "scoured inch by inch . . . in less than two hours." As few as five guard posts could secure the entire *zona di confino*, he believed, and the island could be circumnavigated several times per hour.[81] Moreover, Ventotene's approximately nine hundred farmers and fishermen were "very loyal to the institutions of the Regime" and would not compromise security. Commercial vessels were virtually absent, and the fishermen's small wooden boats were unlikely to facilitate escape attempts.[82] Most importantly, the inspector reported confidently, "The entirety of the island's coast drops vertiginously to the sea and is

---

[79] Alberto Jacometti, *Ventotene* (Milan, 1946), 40.
[80] Spinelli, *Lungo monologo*, 108.
[81] IGPS Francesco Meo to Bocchini, "Istituenda colonia di confino politico a Ventotene," April 18, 1930, UCP, b. 25, fasc. 42, sf. anno 32 e 33, 9.
[82] Ibid.

FIGURE 5. The regime chose Ventotene to host a political colony because of its small size and precipitous cliffs. Moreover, a few hundred meters away was the island of San Stefano (not pictured), which featured a political prison, where detainees could be sent as punishment for violating the regulations of the *confino* colony. The large structure on the top right housed the colony's administrative offices. In 1939, the regime constructed thirteen masonry barracks (top left) – twelve for male and one for female detainees – surrounded by a low concrete wall. *Source:* Courtesy of Giovanni Maria de Rossi, *Ventotene e S. Stefano* (Rome: Guido Guidotti Editore, 1999).

therefore inaccessible, while the few points of approach could easily be sealed off if necessary." Escape was deemed nearly impossible.[83]

In contrast with Lipari or even Ponza, Ventotene was neither physically beautiful nor was it equipped with utilities such as running water and electrification. In the early 1930s, Ventotene's Bourbon castle, which had one toilet and no running water, housed 130 common *confinati*. At night, during lockdown, the common detainees relieved themselves in chamber pots that they emptied each morning. For personal hygiene, they collected rain water from an outdoor cistern. Conditions for the political detainees who arrived in July 1932 were not much better. The first fifty political detainees received new, standard-issue beds and linens, but later arrivals, one *carabinieri* reported, were issued beds left behind by the common detainees that "besides not being regulation, were dirty and infested with insects."[84] Throughout the 1930s, Ventotene hosted around two hundred political detainees, mainly the "least dangerous" Communists, as well as ex-convicts and alcoholics, in primitive conditions.[85] Initially no MVSN units were assigned to Ventotene, and security duties were performed exclusively by police and *carabinieri*.[86]

Even more so than Ventotene, the Tremiti colony resembled a true concentration camp. In the fall of 1936, the DGPS converted Le Tremiti from a common to a political colony. San Nicola, the island that hosted most of the political detainees, has a total circumference of 3,700 meters. Lacking vegetation, the island has the form of a large rock. High atop its sheer cliffs sits a fortress, inside of which lies a courtyard with long row houses that served as barracks (Figure 6). At the back of the courtyard, on an elevation, are a church and a medieval castle, which also housed detainees. Surrounded by high embattlements, the courtyard and barracks occupied only a small part of the island. Thus, the habitable space, surrounded by high stone walls, measured not more than a few hundred

[83] Ibid., 8. See IGPS to Bocchini, "Oggetto: Ventotene – Colonia di confino politico," September 19, 1932, UCP, b. 25, fasc. 42, sf. anno 32 e 33, 7.

[84] *Carabinieri* to Bocchini, "Promemoria," October 3, 1932, in ACS, MI, DGPS, UCP, b. 25, fasc. 42, sf. anno 32 e 33. See "Ventotene – Sgombero colonia confino da parte di confinati comuni," July 22, 1932; Chief of Division of General and Classified Affairs to Division V, "Ventotene = Forniture per la colonia dei *confinati politici*," December 28, 1932; and telegraphs from prefect of Naples and High Commissar of Public Security (Naples) to DGPS in UCP, b. 25, fasc. 42, sf. anno 32 e 33/42.

[85] See Capo dell'Ufficio Politico UPI Console Ballabio to Bochini, March 27, 1930, UCP, b. 4, fasc. 710–3/1932, sf. E/Ponza.

[86] See the "forza pubblica" sf. for Ponza and Ventotene in UCP, b. 6, fasc. 710–6/1933– 710–6/1939.

FIGURE 6. Conditions in the *confino* colony on the Tremiti Islands were harsh, particularly on the small island of San Nicola, which featured nothing more than communal barracks surrounded by high stone walls, 1930. *Source:* Fototeca Gilardi.

square meters.[87] The Tremiti colony, like that of Ventotene before it, received many of the so-called Manchurians and some of the "least dangerous" anti-Fascists. The regime occasionally transferred anti-Fascist militants from Ponza or Ventotene to Le Tremiti in order to neutralize them among "apoliticals." The security force on Tremiti was quite small. In 1936 there were only seven public-security agents and forty *carabinieri* to guard the 410 common detainees and 190 political detainees.[88] MVSN units never worked on Tremiti. However, corrupt Fascists were often sent to the colony, and they frequently collaborated with the colony's administration against the other detainees. Although police officials complained of being dangerously short of personnel, the physical structure of the island rendered it secure and fairly easy to control.[89]

[87] See IGPS Capobianco to Bocchini, "Colonia di confino polizia – Isole Le Tremiti," December 31, 1936, UCP, b. 4, fasc. 710–3/1937, sf. 1/Tremiti.
[88] Ibid.
[89] See reports of Director Coviello, August 1, 1939, UCP, b. 5, fasc. 710–5/1940, sf. 2/Tremiti; prefect of Foggia (Ciotola), December 31, 1936, UCP, b. 5, fasc. 710–5/1937, sf. 1/Tremiti; IGPS Campobianco to Bocchini, August 21, 1937, UCP, b. 4, 710–3/1937, sf. 1/Tremiti; Campobianco to Bocchini, December 1, 1937, UCP, b. 13, fasc. 710/15/1937, sf. 1.

Routine Violence

During the period after 1932, the DGPS began a campaign to impose stricter discipline in the political colonies. Inspectors general of the police reigned in the arbitrary violence of the militia, supplanting it with a bureaucratized coercive system of regulations, permissions, and sanctions. The reform of the disciplinary regime necessarily began with a campaign to break the hold of Communists and other anti-Fascists over the internal life of the colonies.[90] In the years after Mussolini's general amnesty of 1932, the political population temporarily dropped to between five and six hundred detainees.[91] The militants remaining on the islands established strong cooperative institutions and further perfected strategies of collective resistance.[92] They ran successful cooperative kitchens, general stores, and libraries. Apolitical detainees often joined the anti-Fascist parties in order to secure a higher standard of living, an economic safety net, and camaraderie. Educated detainees also taught courses on various subjects. In the eyes of police and anti-Fascists alike, political *confino* was "a school of antifascism," in particular "a school of Communism."[93]

In 1935, the director of Ponza revoked all permissions for detainees to keep rooms, apartments, and private houses used for work, study, storage, and generally passing the tedious daylight hours.[94] As anticipated, this prohibition provoked a collective protest, with 250 political detainees refusing to attend the morning roll. Authorities arrested the detainees and deported them to Naples, where they were sentenced to prison terms of between eight and fourteen months for violating regulations. Meanwhile, the few remaining detainees in private housing, very often women, were either moved into the barracks or, in a few cases, forced to sign a pledge that they would not allow other *confinati* into their homes. The few families of detainees remaining on Ponza were sent home, and family visits were thereafter largely prohibited. In March, the cafeterias, general stores, bars, barbershops, and libraries were taken over by the police.[95]

[90] Buzzi to Bocchini, November 16, 1934, UCP, b. 17, fasc. 710–33/1935; Buzzi to Bocchini, December 4, 1934, UCP, b. 25, fasc. 42, sf. 1935a/1; "Misure di polizia e di amministrazione da adottare nelle colonie di confino di Ponza e Ventotene," December 11, 1934, UCP, b. 25, fasc. 42, sf. 1935a/1; Buzzi to Bocchini, March 30, 1935, UCP, b. 17, fasc. 710–33/1935, sf. A.

[91] On amnesties and clemency, see Musci, *Confino fascista*, lxix–lxxv.

[92] See ibid., lxxxii–lxxxiv.

[93] See report of IGPS to Bocchini, November 16, 1934, UCP, b. 17, fasc. 710–33/1935, 2.

[94] Buzzi to Bocchini, November 16, 1934, UCP, b. 17, fasc. 710–33/1935, 5.

[95] Buzzi to Bocchini, March 30, 1935, UCP, b. 17, fasc. 710–33/1935, sf. A.

Memoirs from this period on Ponza acknowledge the demoralizing effect this development had on detainees. Mario Magri returned to Ponza in late October 1935 to find "terror." The colony's authorities had sequestered all property belonging to the cooperatives and put the militia in charge of the mess halls.[96] As anti-Fascist detainees returned from prison, the director assigned them to a barrack and a mess hall, placing the most militant detainees among apoliticals and ex-convicts.[97]

Between 1935 and 1938, police officials advanced their campaign to assert dominance over a population of political detainees who were, in their opinion, "always ready to engage in insolence, protests and threats."[98] After a visit to Ponza and Ventotene, one inspector general informed Bocchini that the detainees harbored an exaggerated sense of entitlement, revealing their incomprehension of their position vis-à-vis the colony's administration and the Fascist regime. "To the numerous *confinati* who have asked to speak with me for family reasons, or to protest aspects inherent to the *confino* rules and regulations," he wrote to Bocchini, "I have stated clearly that times have changed and that from now on it will be necessary to submit to the restrictions that *confino* entails."[99] On Ventotene and Ponza, militiamen began guarding the mess halls and strictly controlling their funds and supplies. Police agents and militiamen were stationed inside the barracks, night and day.[100] Surveillance and control increased outside the barracks as well. "In order to better follow the tenor of life of the *confinati*," ordered Inspector General Capobianco, "aside from the surveillance conducted by the political squad, all of the police agents, militiamen, and *carabinieri*, whether on

---

96 Magri, *Vita per la libertà*, 149.
97 For documentation of the struggle over the *spaccio, mense,* and library on Ponza, see Prefettura di Littoria to DGPS, May 13, 1935, in UCP, b. 17, fasc. 710–33/1935, sf. A; Capobianco to Bocchini, November 6, 1935, in UCP, b. 5, fasc. 710–5/1935, sf. Ponza; Capobianco to Bocchini, June 28, 1936, in UCP, b. 13, fasc. 710–10/1936, sf. 3/Ponza. For Ventotene see, Baratono to DGPS (Bocchini), December 27, 1935, in UCP, b. 25, fasc. 42, sf. 1936/1; Direzione Ventotene to Questore Napoli, February 4, 1936, UCP, b. 25, fasc. 42, sf. 1936/1; Capobianco to Bocchini, March 18, 1936, UCP, b. 25, fasc. 42, sf. 1936/1; Direzione Ventotene (Fraticelli) to Questore Napoli, October 20, 1936, UCP, b. 25, fasc. 42, sf. 1936a.
98 See Buzzi to Bocchini, March 30, 1935, in ACS, MI, DGPS, UCP, b. 17, fasc. 710–33/1935, sf. A, 4.
99 Buzzi to Bocchini, May 20, 1935, MI, ACS, DGPS, UCP, b. 25, fasc. 42, sf. 1935/a, 2.
100 See Capobianco, "Norme sulla disciplina della colonia da adottarsi dal Direttore senza farne oggetto di speciali ordinanze da rendere note ai *confinati politici,*" January 10, 1938, UCP, b. 4, fasc. 710–3/1938, sf. 2/Ponza.

duty or not, who note a gathering or meeting of *confinati*, must stop and, with their presence, make them feel a certain subjection, so as to give them the impression that they are being continually watched."[101]

Rather than squad violence, detainees were punished by disciplinary commissions, which reduced subsidies, revoked the right to circulate freely during the day, and ordered short prison sentences. More serious matters, such as collective protests, resulted in mass arrests and formal trials. Meanwhile, the MVSN exercised tremendous psychological pressure on the detainees through constant observation and increasingly invasive control. Under orders from the director, the barracks were regularly ransacked by the MVSN in search of contraband. Police officials had, in essence, phased out the MVSN's brutal methods but adopted their overall view of *confino politico* as a punitive institution for breaking the will of detainees and forcing them to submit to Fascism. Speaking a foreign language, a dialect, or in an incomprehensible manner led to arrest and interrogation. The police also began to closely monitor the activities of the local population, including censoring their mail. The Provincial Commission of Littoria, which had jurisdiction over the two islands, sentenced several locals to *confino* and *ammonizione* for their improper or suspicious interactions with detainees.[102]

Expansion and Exile

Beginning in 1935, precisely in the moment when Mussolini's dictatorship entered what one historian has called its "totalitarian turn" – a radicalization of foreign and domestic policy[103] – the political population expanded significantly, more than tripling from 800 to 2,800 (see Figure 7). Moreover, with the anti-Fascist movements largely defeated, the social composition of the political branch of the *confino* system began to change. Against the backdrop of the invasion of Ethiopia, Italian intervention in the Spanish Civil War, Mussolini's declaration of the Fascist

---

[101] See ibid.

[102] See report on Ponza of Capobianco to Bocchini, May 25, 1938, ACS, MI, DGPS, UCP, b. 4, fasc. 710–3/1938, sf. 2/Ponza. For an official copy of the identical regulations introduced to Ventotene in January 1938, see Cav. Giuseppe Marino (Direttore) "Norme sulla disciplina della Colonia," January 15, 1938, ACS, MI, DGPS, UCP, b. 4, fasc. 710–3/1938, 1/Ventotene.

[103] De Felice, *Mussolini il Duce*, II:8 and 82–90; see also Payne, *A History of Fascism*, 212–44.

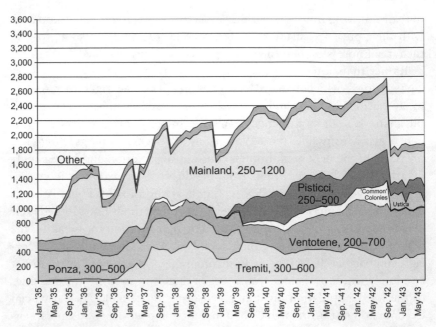

FIGURE 7. Political Detainee Population by Location, 1935–1943. *Source:* "Tabella dimostrativa del movimento confinati" series in ACS, MI, DGPS, UCP, b. 121.

Empire, and a series of policies promoting internal social mobilization, the Fascist apparatus of political repression began targeting a wide array of marginal social groups, including religious minorities, alcoholics, ex-criminals, homosexuals, prostitutes, and quite ordinary, often poor, Italians. In particular, police sentenced thousands of Italians, who posed no real threat to the regime, to political confinement for trifling speech offenses and other mundane behaviors committed in daily life: offending the Duce, defeatism, disobeying Fascists and other authority figures, and so on. Although the original offenses were usually vaguely political, police cited, in addition, an individual's alcoholism, mental illness, criminal record, unemployment, and other "moral" factors in their recommendations for confinement.[104] Anti-Fascists also continued appearing in the

---

[104] In the sample of 549 cases, one-third were sentenced for a simple phrase, conversation, or, in a small number of cases, a (subversive) song, most of these after 1934. Moreover, 81 of the 549 cases involved an individual who was intoxicated or an alcoholic; 65 of these cases occurred after 1934; 128 of 549 had criminal precedents; 36 of 549 were deemed mentally ill. Remarkably, 285 had no "political precedents." Regarding the

island colonies during this second period. Militants finishing their Special Tribunal prison sentences, Communists attempting to reconstitute their clandestine network, and Spanish Civil War volunteers repatriated by French authorities were all sentenced to the island camps during the 1930s. However, anti-Fascists constituted a small minority among the growing number of detainees.

The growth and diversification of the political detainee population led to the introduction of new modalities of political detainment – some harsher, others milder – and to the expansion of existing ones. Due to overcrowding in the colonies after 1935, the practice of assigning political detainees to the southern mainland, generally considered a "milder" form of punishment, soon became the predominant form of political confinement (see Figure 7).[105] Exiles could only circulate in a small area and had to obey the same regulations as Italians sentenced to political probation (*ammonizione*). Local authorities and detainees had to request permission from Rome for any actions not specifically authorized. Documentation for reconstructing the experience of mainland exile is much more diffuse, scattered throughout the personal files of the detainees and other local sources. Bocchini and Mussolini devoted many hours to manipulating the effect of island political internment but rarely intervened in the communities that hosted mainland exiles, who were generally considered harmless.

The central assumption of mainland exile held that Italy's rural southern provinces did not breed subversion (anti-Fascism) and "socially dangerous" behaviors (e.g., abortion, homosexuality, and alcoholism). Mussolini lauded the southern provinces for their high birthrate and the fact that their population had "not yet been infected by the many malignant trends of contemporary civilization."[106] More significantly, there had been very little organized anti-Fascism in the rural south. It was no coincidence that political exiles were not sent to Puglia, where the tradition of agricultural labor militancy rivaled that found in northern regions. The rural villages of the Mezzogiorno were cut off from the political and social conflicts that initially gave rise to Fascism in the north. In reality,

changing social composition of the *confinati politici* population, see ch. 6, and also Musci, *Confino fascista*, lxxiv.

[105] In 1935, Mussolini and Bocchini assigned most new political detainees to the mainland. In that year, about 600 persons were exiled to mainland villages, while only about 200 were interned in the island colonies.

[106] Mussolini, OO, XXII:366.

however, the regime sent detainees to the south primarily because it had nowhere else to put them. Because mainland *confinati politici* were usually not anti-Fascist militants, but rather "ordinary Italians" sentenced for a phrase, an insult, or a song, they posed little threat to the regime or to society.

Southern communities generally viewed most political detainees in a positive light. One prefect reported that "the *confinati politici*, in general, do not cause problems and are viewed by the people of these poor communities with indifference and sometimes with sympathetic commiseration." Prefect Ottavio Dinale, an old-guard Fascist, compared Fascist *confino di polizia* to Roman banishment: "the ancient undesirables from Rome explained their presence with the noted phrase – *hic potentia romanorum nos relegavit.*"[107] Locals viewed them neither as criminals nor as dangerous subversives. Political exiles, in Dinale's opinion, suffered from a "delinquency" of their "will and ideas," not something "congenital in their instincts and physiology," and so were not considered dangerous or likely to "cause infections."[108] For southern communities, there were certain economic advantages to hosting exiles, because they had to pay for room, board, and services. Moreover, like Carlo Levi, medical doctors and midwives exiled to the south often provided badly needed medical assistance to southern communities. Prefects petitioned Rome to have midwives sent to their provinces.[109]

Although there were few complaints about "respectable" political detainees, local people resented common exiles, along with political exiles who were alcoholics or ex-convicts. Dinale reported to Rome that "things are completely different with regard to the common *confinati*, each one of whom, due to physiological inevitability, is (and does not become) a most dangerous source of infection." Dinale could not resist pointing out to Bocchini the hypocrisy of a regime sending criminal or morally "infectious" individuals to live amongst the "good people" of southern provinces. "This state of affairs," he insisted, "constitutes a contradiction in terms for a regime which has created a marvel of institutions and organizations for the material and spiritual health of the race [*stirpe*]. I feel that I would be failing my duties as a fascist Prefect if I did not report

---

[107] Translation: "Roman power relegated us here."
[108] Prefect of Potenza Ottavio Dinale's report, December 28, 1929, in ACS, MI, DGPS, UCP, b. 11, fasc. 710–14, sf. C/comune.
[109] The cases of abortionists discussed in ch. 6 all contain evidence of state officials pleading for midwives and doctors to be sent to southern provinces.

this problem to the Government."[110] Dinale thus worried not only that the practice of mainland exile introduced sources of "moral infection" to the south. He and other officials knew that sending increasingly large numbers of anti-Fascists, alcoholics, pimps, homosexuals, abortionists, criminals, and usurers to his province reflected badly on Fascism. The most common problems these detainees brought to the south were public drunkenness or petty theft, but serious crimes committed by exiles, such as murder or rape, were not unknown.

In 1938, as the number of detainees exiled to the mainland reached one thousand, the regime renewed an earlier project to establish an agricultural labor colony for political exiles. Officials chose the Pisticci site in Matera for familiar reasons. It could be "guarded without excessive difficulty and without the employment of a substantial quantity of public security personnel." The Pisticci tract also conformed to the requirements of the regime's ongoing land reclamation projects. For Bocchini, the Pisticci colony combined land reclamation with "human reclamation." Updating Mussolini in the preliminary stages of establishing the work camp, Bocchini optimistically wrote, "If this experiment should be successful, and no one doubts that it will, other labor colonies could be established, even for *confinati comuni*, simultaneously performing agricultural reclamation and human reclamation [*bonifica umana*]."[111] Thus, for the regime, agricultural labor gave meaning to the otherwise depoliticized experience of mainland exile. As the regime's repressive apparatus increasingly targeted ordinary Italians, Mussolini and Bocchini used Pisticci to fill an ideological void in their campaign against anti-Fascist behaviors. In the abstract, Pisticci represented the realization of Mussolini's view of *confino di polizia* as an institution of "social hygiene" and "national prophylaxis."[112]

With the outbreak of war in 1939, mainland confinement became even more common, particularly because administering the island colonies had become more difficult. The DGPS shut down the Ponza colony, converting it back to military use, and transferred its detainees, personnel, and equipment to Ventotene, which became the regime's primary political colony. During the summer of 1941, Ventotene held between six hundred and seven hundred political detainees (*confinati*) as well as between

---

[110] Prefect of Potenza Ottavio Dinale's report, December 28, 1929, in ACS, MI, DGPS, UCP, b. 11, fasc. 710–14, sf. C/comune.
[111] "Relazione per S. E. il Capo del Governo: istituzione di una colonia confinaria," 21 August 21, 1938, in MI, DGPS, UCP, b. 32, fasc. 710–50.
[112] Mussolini, OO, XXII:378.

one hundred and two hundred wartime internees (*internati*). To accommodate the growing population, the regime constructed a veritable internment camp, "a *confino* citadel," in the words of one police official. Inside a low concrete wall were thirteen long, one-story stone barracks with small, iron-barred windows and a single door. In order to accommodate the growing number of female detainees, the director designated one barrack specifically for women. Finally, the regime installed electricity and public illumination.[113] On Le Tremiti, the sixty or so political detainees sentenced to San Domino for suspected homosexuality were sent home upon Italy's entrance into the war in order to make room for a wartime internment camp. Much like Ventotene, the Tremiti islands became a mixed confinement-internment camp, with three hundred to four hundred political detainees being interned on San Nicola and approximately two hundred wartime internees on San Domino.[114]

In 1940, with Italy's entrance into the Second World War, shortages, rationing, and the logistical problems of provisioning gave rise to malnutrition and starvation throughout the confinement archipelago. In January 1942, an inspector general reported, "the alimentary situation of the colony on Ventotene has become rather critical due to an absolute lack of potatoes and vegetables." The rationing of food did not prove "sufficient for the nutrition of the *confinati*."[115] Despite multiple requests during 1941 and 1942, Ventotene's detainees and population received no assistance. Milk shortages gravely affected infants, pregnant women, and the thirty or so detainees afflicted with tuberculosis. Disruptions in deliveries, often due to bombings, led to scarcity of fresh water, resulting in strict rationing and dehydration. In May, the director reported that "a notable number" of patients had been admitted to the infirmary because the "the alimentary restrictions imposed by the rationing of foodstuffs" had "greatly compromised the physical condition" of the detainees. Still nothing was done.[116] Anti-Fascists survived the war by pooling resources and renting cultivable land, but the Manchurians, according to the Communist Altiero Spinelli, were "abandoned in this cruel struggle for survival."

---

[113] For illustrations of the camp, see De Rossi, *Ventotene e S. Stefano*, 7, 69–72.

[114] See "Capienza Tremiti" series in UCP, b. 13, fasc. 710–14/1941, sf. 2/Tremiti; fasc. 710–14/1942, sf. 5/Tremiti; and fasc. 710–14/1943, sf. 3/Tremiti.

[115] See IGPS to Carmine Senise, "OGGETTO: Colonia di confino di Ventotene. Situazione alimentare," January 14, 1942, UCP, b. 27, fasc. 710–42/1942.

[116] See director of Section 2 of the DGPS (Perennetta) to DGPS, August 17, 1943, UCP, b. 27, fasc. 710–42/1943.

He claimed that some eventually died of hunger.[117] Another anti-Fascist also recalled "starving" Manchurians, whom he witnessed scrounging and begging for breadcrumbs.[118] On Tremiti, already considered the worst of the confinement colonies, wartime shortages only exacerbated the already poor conditions. Mario Magri described the winter of 1940 as a season of hunger, cold, and thirst.[119] Other detainees recalled how every living thing – rats, cats, and dogs – disappeared from the Tremiti islands during the war years.[120]

The Fascist archipelago of confinement exemplified the gray zone between legality and illegality established by the Fascist regime in 1926. Public-security legislation, implemented by state and party authorities, created an institution in which illegal or arbitrary abuse, torture, deprivations, and suffering were endemic. Over time, illegal Fascist violence diminished within the island colonies, as state officials adopted the Fascist view of confinement as political punishment. The DGPS and the MVSN then institutionalized the punishments and humiliations once inflicted illegally by the militiamen. Perhaps more significant than the scope of violence and suffering was the fact that anything was possible. Once the police arrested an Italian, the state could subject him or her to all manner of mistreatment, punishments, and neglect. Moreover, despite the tendency to view confinement as a static institution, virtually all detainees spent weeks and even months in jails and holding cells before reaching their destination. Once confined, police regularly inflicted short prison sentences and other punishments for alleged violations of regulations. A great number of detainees spent time in more than one colony, and sometimes passed from island confinement to mainland exile and back again.

By focusing the public's attention on colonies that hosted prominent anti-Fascists, the regime, its apologists, and later, inadvertently, the anti-Fascists, created an enduring image of Fascist political repression that is too simple and too benign. The tens of thousands of Italians sentenced to *confino di polizia* collectively experienced prison, filth, sleeplessness, exhaustion, malnutrition, thirst, disease, homesickness, illness, fear, physical violence, financial ruin, and pernicious uncertainty. Although

---

[117] Spinelli, *Lungo monologo*, 117.
[118] Jacometti, *Ventotene* (Milan, 1946), 31.
[119] Magri, *Vita per la libertà*, 178–80.
[120] See Armando Pilati's testimony in Luciano Bergonzini, *La resistenza a Bologna: testimonianze e documenti* (Bologna, 1967), 510.

the regime did not intend for detainees to die, the experience killed many of them and left many others gravely and chronically ill, often due to the negligence of politically vindictive officials. Finally, as revealed in the remaining chapters of this book, the very existence of this archipelago had effects that reverberated far beyond the sites of confinement and exile.

5

The Politics of Pardons

Zabaglione's local fame was based on his forensic eloquence. If it was known that he was going to plea at a criminal trial, the cobblers' and tailors' and carpenters' shops emptied, the concierges abandoned their lairs, and everyone who could went to listen to him. Many of his famous speeches had become proverbial. During the first years of the dictatorship he had had to make tremendous efforts to cause his rhetorical feats to be forgotten. He had transformed his old Mazzini-style beard, which he had worn since he was a young man, into a Balbo-style goatee; and he shortened and thinned his hair, changed the way he knotted his tie, and tried, though vainly, to lose weight. But if these were the most visible and hence the most painful sacrifices to which the former tribune of the people had had to subject himself, there was no counting the minor mortifications that he had to endure, such as having to sacrifice his ideas, being careful in what he said about the government, and breaking off relations with his suspect friends. In spite of the undeniable determination he had put into all this, he had not succeeded in completely rehabilitating himself, and he was consistently left out in the cold by the new institutions.

Ignazio Silone, Bread and Wine[1]

Mussolini's strategy of political and social control relied as much on releasing detainees as it did on confining them. Whether through individual pardons, or large, well-publicized amnesties, the dictatorship sent most detainees home before their official release date. There is no question, as we have seen, that the regime planned on keeping many anti-Fascists, particularly Communists, in custody, or otherwise subjugated to party-state authority, for an indefinite period. However, equally central

---

[1] Ignazio Silone, *Bread and Wine*, in *The Abruzzo Trilogy* (South Royalton, 2000), 327.

to the logic of the repressive apparatus was a process of reconciliation, both real and merely apparent, between the regime and its opponents. Releasing political prisoners – in addition to creating space for new detainees – provided fodder for propaganda that emphasized themes of national reconciliation and widespread acceptance of Fascism. Moreover, state authorities hoped that the release of some high-profile anti-Fascist leaders might be interpreted by their followers as evidence of their "capitulation," thereby deflating morale among rank-and-file militants. To win release, a detainee had to formally, and convincingly, pledge to refrain from political activity in a "letter of submission" (*sottomissione*). However, the process of winning Mussolini's consent to a pardon or some sort of clemency was also strongly influenced by local forces, particularly the desires of Fascists.

The influence of the National Fascist Party (PNF) over sentencing and pardons at the local level varied widely. In the north, Fascists regularly pressured state authorities to deny clemency requests from Socialists and labor leaders. The regime also extended preferential treatment to its own dissidents and intransigents, who had been confined for their refusal to accept the "normalization" of Fascism. In the south, the situation was dissimilar. Most *fasci* were founded after the March on Rome, and the forces of anti-Fascism were weak, so pressures for "revolutionary justice" were virtually absent. For Socialists and Communists, unless they were from Puglia, the path to freedom was blocked by fewer obstacles than in the north. Throughout the Mezzogiorno, the regime also commonly used political confinement to sort out the ubiquitous factional conflicts within newly formed Fascist institutions. In the eleventh hour, traditional southern elites scrambled to assert control over the *fasci*, often clashing with and displacing radical syndicalists and Socialists who, like some of their northern counterparts, had converted to Fascism. Radicals who continued to agitate against the dominant factions, which were invariably made up of traditional elites, often landed in political confinement. However, their early conversion to Fascism led Mussolini to pardon them, sometimes after serving only a few months in an island colony.

Pardons as Propaganda

With the exception of PCI militants, most of Fascism's opponents were willing to accept Fascism and move on with their lives. After all, the government of Italy had branded them political criminals and threatened to punish them for as long as they continued opposition activities. Before the exceptional decrees, anti-Fascists had been operating legally, within a nominal constitutional democracy, despite the harsh realities of illegal Fascist violence and state-sponsored repression. Now, with the birth of the police state, these Socialists, Republicans, liberals, and other groups had to contend with an entirely new constitutional order in which their activities were unequivocally illegal. Mussolini's critics adapted to this new situation in different ways.

Some anti-Fascists acquiesced to the regime immediately, and later even came around to fully supporting Mussolini. Giovanni Ansaldo, a journalist from Genoa, earned a reputation as a sharp-witted, outspoken critic of Mussolini's government. He headed his own daily, *Il Lavoro*, and associated with the regime's most strident critics, including Carlo Rosselli, Gaetano Salvemini, and Piero Gobetti, his close friend who died from a Fascist beating. He contributed articles to major anti-Fascist journals and signed Benedetto Croce's *Manifesto of Antifascist Intellectuals*.[2] After the Zamboni assassination attempt of October 1926, Ansaldo attempted to leave the country, fearing for his life. The police caught him near Como, jailed him for several months, and then deported him to Lipari.

Despite his earlier criticisms of Fascism, Ansaldo had little desire to become a martyr for the anti-Fascist cause. His memoir of this period reveals the psychological impact of being labeled an "outlaw." As police fingerprinted, photographed, and searched Ansaldo, he felt humiliated. Communists, and to a lesser extent Socialists, had long been subjected to arrests and incarceration and had more or less come to terms with their status as criminals. Liberals, Republicans, and many Socialists, by contrast, had never had to consider their opposition in terms of illegal behavior. Ansaldo recalled that he felt "inscribed in the ranks of the delinquent, the criminal, the subversive, the enemies of order." He knew he was a good citizen, but "the force of the words and methods" made him feel "subversive."[3] During the journey to Lipari, by train and steamship, in the custody of *carabinieri*, he felt "humiliation, in the sense of feeling shame from the stares of others, of attracting attention, handcuffed, the pity or disdain of others ... I was ashamed of myself." Ansaldo was now "defeated, beaten, mocked by destiny," especially when juxtaposed with the "clever," successful "fighter" he felt he used to be. He obsessed about the manacles, noting that it was psychologically less onerous if he asked

[2] See Giovanni Ansaldo, *L'antifascista riluttante: memorie del carcere e del confino, 1926–27*, ed. Marcello Staglieno (Bologna, 1992).
[3] Ibid., 281, 283–4.

for the cuffs to be put on his wrists rather than wait for the *carabinieri* to do so. The ordeal thus profoundly affected Ansaldo. He wondered empathetically what effect arrest and confinement might have "among the mass of people who had reverence for and fear of the authorities."[4]

For Ansaldo, the loss of freedom, coupled with his new status as a criminal subversive, constituted an unacceptable psychological trauma. On Lipari, in an effort to ingratiate himself with authorities, he deliberately disassociated himself from other "subversives" and exhibited strict, even zealous obedience to the regulations of the colony. He viewed fellow detainees who maintained their anti-Fascist stance with disdain. They were doomed to irrelevance in the new Fascist society, which he had now come to accept.[5] In a letter to the Ministry of the Interior, Ansaldo declared, "recognizing Fascism as a *fait accompli*, I pledge myself to cease fighting it in any way, [and], on the contrary, to never again engage in politics at all."[6] The latter part of this pledge turned out to be only partly true. Released in 1927, Ansaldo eventually joined the PNF, fought as a Black Shirt volunteer in the Ethiopian War, and contributed to *Il Telegrafo*, the newspaper of Mussolini's son-in-law and foreign minister, Galeazzo Ciano. Conforming to Fascism, he attained full rehabilitation, thereby regaining his professional and social status within Italian society.

For most political detainees, liberation was ultimately granted by the grace of Mussolini alone. Reviewing case files and pleas for clemency, Mussolini personally summarily granted individual pardons to more than a quarter of detainees from the sample (151 of 549), returning them home with a stroke of his pen during the course of a normal work day. Then there were the frequent, well-publicized amnesties, granted by the Duce on the occasion of the regime's milestones and anniversaries, as well as religious holidays: the tenth anniversary of the March on Rome (Decennale), the twentieth anniversary of the March on Rome (Ventennale), the Declaration of Empire, the birth of the new Savoyard Prince, and the perennial Christmas amnesties.[7] All told, Mussolini personally liberated well more than half the detainee population. Less than 20 percent of cases sampled served out their full term. The Commission of Appeals

---

[4] Ibid., 281.

[5] Marcello Staglieno in introductory essay to ibid., 34–5.

[6] See "Ricorso alla Commissione Centrale per le Assegnazioni al Confino presso il Ministero dell Interno," in ibid., 409–12.

[7] Decennale (22), Ventennale (36), Declaration of Empire (12), birth of prince (17), and Christmas amnesties (34).

occasionally reduced sentences by one or two years but rarely liberated detainees or overturned their sentences.[8]

Amnesties had a practical purpose: to make room for the ever-growing number of detainees. Publicly, however, the regime presented "acts of clemency" as evidence of diminishing opposition, growing consensus, and decreasing repression under Mussolini's dictatorship. Leniency and mercy were presented as signs of strength. On the tenth anniversary of the March on Rome, the front-page headline of *Il popolo di Roma* screamed out, "A Demonstration of Force and Generosity of the Regime," with several pages devoted to explaining the terms of a large amnesty, including a front-page article entitled "The Generosity of the Strong" regarding the 1,234 pardons granted to Italians detained for anti-Fascism.[9] In his diary, several years after his own release, Ansaldo noted that when he heard about the Decennale amnesty, he immediately thought of twenty or thirty anti-Fascists whom he had known on Lipari, men of principle who, like him, suffered only for their political beliefs. By releasing such men, Ansaldo believed, Mussolini would make a powerful statement: "After you plotted against me, I pardon you... I am strong and remain strong.... I am a bigger man than you because I have returned your liberty." A week later, after the newspaper coverage and the "applauding on command" had receded, Ansaldo admitted that the amnesty was "a bluff, like everything else." True, it was the largest amnesty in Italy's history but only because Mussolini wanted "to do everything better than everyone else." The most important anti-Fascists would remain in jail, while thousands of inconsequential political prisoners and common criminals would be set free. In the end, the amnesty could only be understood "as a symptom of the mentality of its author."[10]

Individual pardons granted to anti-Fascists willing to perform the "act of submission" served a similar propagandistic function, particularly during the early years of the system. Already by 1927, Mussolini was insisting publicly that the anti-Fascist movements were irrelevant and claimed untruthfully that the number of political prisoners was dwindling. He argued that many political detainees "did not want to be antifascists" and some seemed "to be Fascists." Mussolini bragged about the many "letters of submission" he had received, reading them aloud in the Chamber. As he read each one, the dictator belittled his vanquished opponents,

---

[8] Commission reduced 24 of 549 sentences and overturned only 15 of 549 sentences.
[9] *Il popolo di Roma*, November 8, 1932.
[10] Giovanni Ansaldo, *Il giornalista di Ciano: diari 1932–1943* (Rome, 2000), 27–8.

simultaneously mocking their capitulation and extolling his success in reconciling former enemies to Fascism. "I militated in the Communist Party until yesterday," quoted Mussolini from one letter, "[but] there not being a recognized Party . . . any longer, I quit." The Chamber roared with laughter. "Another promises 'to quit any form of political activity and to retire to Santa Margherita Ligure,'" Mussolini read from one letter. "A beautiful spot," he commented, and the Chamber of Fascists erupted with guffaws once again (Figure 8).[11]

Mussolini and Bocchini carefully monitored and controlled the cases of leading anti-Fascists, keeping truly dangerous individuals, like Antonio Gramsci, in prison, while granting special treatment to prominent figures whose freedom might somehow be exploited for propagandistic ends. Though the regime rarely granted freedom to leading Communist Party (PCI) militants, there were always exceptions. Amadeo Bordiga, the PCI's first secretary and the leader of its left wing, returned from confinement after serving just three years. During the wave of squad violence that followed the attempt on Mussolini's life in October 1926, Neapolitan Fascists went looking for Bordiga. Discovering that he had gone into hiding, the Black Shirts ransacked his home. Three weeks later, authorities caught Bordiga and deported him to Ustica, where he arrived on December 8, moving into a house with the current PCI secretary, Gramsci. Although Gramsci and Bordiga were rivals within the PCI, they regarded each other as friends. Stalin's Comintern, and thus the PCI, were becoming increasingly intolerant of heterodoxy, but Gramsci and Bordiga promoted an environment of free debate among the Communists on Ustica. Not long after his arrival in the internment colony, authorities arrested Gramsci and sent him to Milan to await his trial before the Special Tribunal. Because Bordiga had been ousted from the leadership of the party years before, and now played no role in its central direction, the Special Tribunal did not prosecute him in the so-called *processone* (big trial) of the PCI leadership in 1928. Nevertheless, Bordiga had a substantial following among left-wing Italian Communists, particularly in southern Italy.

On Ustica, Bordiga and his comrades organized themselves into a highly disciplined collective that dominated the life of the colony. The cohesiveness and militancy of these Communists – who established adult education courses, communal mess halls, and other collective organizations – alarmed the colony's director and ranking Fascist Militia (MVSN)

[11] Mussolini, OO, XXII:377.

FIGURE 8. An unknown political detainee returns home, escorted by a public-security official. *Source:* Copyright © Fototeca AAMOD/Database Fotoarchivi and Multimedia, Rome, 2010.

officer. Assisted by a large contingent of *carabinieri*, the militia arrested Bordiga and fifty-four other Communists, sending them off to Palermo's notorious jail, l'Ucciardone. The director and the MVSN centurion fabricated criminal charges and solicited false confessions from non-Communist detainees, claiming that Bordiga had conspired with PCI agents in Tunisia to organize a landing on the island. The Communists, according to the bogus plot, would kill the militiamen, *carabinieri*, and police agents, and set the detainees free. The serious nature of these fantastical charges – classified as an "insurrection against the state" – carried the (newly reintroduced) death penalty. The authorities on Ustica so poorly concocted the charges that the Special Tribunal's investigating magistrates refused to send it to trial. In a detailed brief, a magistrate completely discounted the testimony of the detainee-informants, which formed the basis of the charges.[12] Nevertheless, the incident hardly constituted a defeat for the director and the MVSN centurion, because Bordiga and his comrades languished for ten months in the inferno of the Palermo jail.

Released from prison and sent to Ponza in August 1928, Bordiga found a very different political environment. Trotsky and the left wing of the Soviet party had been expelled at the end of 1927. The Communists on Ponza passed an act of condemnation of Trotsky, but Bordiga voted against it. Alienated from the Communists, the former PCI leader spent the rest of his sentence associating with many non-Communists.[13] To improve his financial situation, he worked as an engineer with two other detainees, Giobbe Giopp and Giuseppe Romita. Neapolitan engineering firms that traditionally took projects on Ponza complained to the colony's director, who then revoked Bordiga's right to practice his profession. Bordiga protested to the Ministry of the Interior. Interestingly, General Directorate of Public Security (DGPS) officials quickly reversed the director's decision, and the Communist engineer continued his work.[14]

As Bordiga turned away from the party and attempted to move on with his professional life, Mussolini's police chief began to consider scenarios in which he might exploit the Communist leader's political and moral

---

[12] This discussion of Bordiga relies heavily on material presented in Arturo Peregalli and Sandro Saggioro, *Amadeo Bordiga: la sconfitta e gli anni oscuri, 1926–1945* (Turin, 1998), esp. 163–225.

[13] Such as Roberto Bencivenga, Giovanni Battista Canepa, Omar Conti, Mario Magri, Fioravante Mericone, Mario Neri, and Domenico Ritta. See ibid., 179.

[14] Ibid., 182–3.

authority. Writing to Mussolini in February 1929, Bocchini stressed Bordiga's "large following among the masses" and suggested that the regime might "discredit and cast a shadow of suspicion on a very influential and dangerous man – Bordiga – by commuting *confino* into *ammonizione* and carefully allowing a rumor that a compromise had been reached between Bordiga and Fascism to circulate among the milieu of the left, and among that of the centrists, of the PCI."[15] In the end, Mussolini did not pardon Bordiga, who only had nine months of his sentence remaining. His case would be manipulated to suit the interests of the regime nevertheless. In November 1929, just before Bordiga's release, the Fascist newspaper *La Stampa*, directed by Curzio Malaparte, sent its correspondent, Mino Maccari, to Ponza and Lipari to write a series of articles on the treatment of Fascism's opponents in the island colonies. Maccari described a fleeting glimpse of Bordiga, who was "busy, with a briefcase and files under his arms, followed by assistants armed with surveyors' stakes, pipes, and other instruments for measuring and marking." Maccari attested, "Occasionally, one caught him aboard a car, horn blaring." Bordiga had been granted permission "to travel freely throughout the island, far and wide, for reasons of work." He was "the engineer of the day, the engineer prince of Ponza."[16] The benign image of Bordiga, one of Italy's most militant Communists, bustling around Ponza with a team of assistants was surely invaluable for corroborating the regime's propaganda about the treatment of political detainees and the state of political opposition to his dictatorship. Rather than pardoning Bordiga, Mussolini and Bocchini opted for the subtler approach of simply letting his sentence expire.

Bordiga's behavior after his release in the fall of 1929 was perhaps better suited to the regime's purposes than Bocchini or Mussolini could have hoped. He devoted himself to family, work, and study, completely disengaging from anti-Fascist activities and the PCI, from which he was expelled in 1930. He returned to Naples and his engineering practice, and frequently visited Ponza to attend to projects begun during his internment. Communists there bridled at the sight of Bordiga, while they continued to suffer for the cause. As Bocchini had calculated, Communists in Naples, Bordiga's base, felt defeated. Although many explanations have

[15] See "Promemoria" from Bocchini to Mussolini, February 15, 1929, in ACS, MI, DGPS, Div. AGR, 1929, Massime, K I, b. 175, fasc. "PC. Servizio fiduciario." Quoted in Peregalli and Saggioro, *Amadeo Bordiga*, 184.
[16] The entire run of articles is reprinted in Mino Maccari, *Visita al confino: A Ponza e a Lipari nel 1929* (Marina di Belvedere, 1985).

been offered for his capitulation to Fascism, Bordiga allegedly told Luigi Longo, a member of the Comintern, that "there was nothing to be done."[17] Throughout the 1930s, the police diligently trailed Bordiga night and day, read his mail, and listened to his telephone conversations. Bordiga, like thousands of ex-detainees and anti-Fascists, had left his confinement, but he was not truly free. Authorities soon concluded that he had no intention of resuming political activity, though he sometimes met with former comrades. In similar circumstances, police would have arrested other anti-Fascists for "associating with known subversives," a vague charge that was nevertheless considered tantamount to political activity. In this special case, the police took no action to stop these encounters. As long as he refrained from outward opposition, Amadeo Bordiga served the regime's repressive strategy better as an ostensibly free citizen than as a prisoner.

How ordinary Italians actually understood these cases is far from clear, and open discussion of these matters in the press was forbidden. However, in the foreign press, anti-Fascists and pro-Fascists sparred over the treatment of Italian political prisoners and the regime's use of pardons. Silvia Terracini wrote a letter to the *Manchester Guardian* refuting the paper's assertion that Umberto Terracini, the PCI leader whom she claimed was her cousin, was "dying as the result of being in solitary confinement." On the contrary, she knew from "his family in Turin" that he was "enjoying good health" and had "adequate food and medical attendance." She also knew "as an incontrovertible fact that full liberty" had been offered to Terracini, but he refused a pardon.[18] Umberto Terracini's wife, Alma, responded from Paris, denying the existence of any relative named Silvia Terracini. After detailing her husband's solitary confinement on the island prison of San Stefano (a few hundred meters from Ventotene), his meager rations, and consequent weight loss, Alma Terracini refuted the idea that any amnesty had been offered her husband. "To a man sentenced to 23 years imprisonment," she wrote, "no one can offer liberty under any conditions." If it was true, moreover, it only proved "that those who have condemned him recognize that he is guilty of only his political opinions." If he refused such an amnesty, it attested to his character and not "the generosity of his gaolers."[19] Echoing Alma Terracini,

[17] Quoted in Peregalli and Saggioro, *Amadeo Bordiga*, 214.
[18] Silvia Terracini, *Manchester Guardian*, October 3, 1928.
[19] Alma Terracini, *Manchester Guardian*, November 21, 1928.

Francesco Nitti, the Lipari escapee, wrote his assessment of Fascist political pardons:

> It should be added that those wishing to be pardoned must write a letter in which they voice changed sentiment and a future good political behavior. Each time one of these "pardons" takes place the Fascist press lauds to the skies the "magnanimity and clemency of the beloved Duce." If one remembers that those men have committed no crime, that they have been undergoing arbitrary punishment, and that the liberty which they ought never to have been deprived of is hailed as an act of magnanimity when given back to them, one can form some opinion of the Duce's character and that of his propaganda agents.[20]

As Nitti reminded his readers, the manipulation of high-profile pardons and large amnesties only revealed the cynical, authoritarian nature of the Mussolini regime. If amnesties and pardons were so easy to attain, he queried, what were these men doing in prison and confinement in the first place?

Nevertheless, a common assumption, propagated by the regime domestically and Fascist sympathizers abroad, was that political prisoners and detainees were eligible for clemency if they simply pledged to refrain from politics.[21] The regime obviously made such offers to some anti-Fascists but certainly not to Communists in October 1928. Moreover, Mussolini and Bocchini knew that men of principle such as Terracini would never betray their ideals and humiliate themselves by formally accepting the legitimacy of the Fascist regime. The Communist Party generally forbade its militants to petition for clemency; to do so would mean expulsion from the party. Moreover, the criteria for determining what amounted to "refraining from politics" (the most important pledge of the *atto di sottomissione*) were also arbitrary. Prefects, police, and party officials consented to pardons only when detainees thoroughly subjugated themselves to the regime, by acting "obsequiously" in front of authorities and renouncing all ties to their "subversive" pasts. This meant devoting their lives to "family and work," staying out of "public establishments," and renouncing old friendships. Only by breaking with the party, severing ties to friends, comrades, and even sometimes family, all the while passively submitting to invasive police surveillance of private life, could

---

[20] Francesco Fausto Nitti, *Manchester Guardian*, September 4, 1929.
[21] For other examples, see the exchanges between the anti-Fascist Gaetano Salvemini, an anonymous anti-Fascist, and G. M. Palliccia, special Attaché to the Italian Embassy, in the *Manchester Guardian* in 1928 on the dates June 22 and September 8, 12, 15, 18, and 22.

anti-Fascists hope to definitively win release. Even after alienating himself from his social and political milieu, a detainee might have his amnesty request denied by state authorities. Thus ostracized from the party and persecuted by the state, such an individual would be deprived of the material and moral support provided by the Communists, anarchists, and other political groups in the island colonies and political prisons.

Political Pardons between Center and Periphery

Mussolini, Bocchini, and the regime's propagandists stage-managed the cases of nationally prominent anti-Fascists like Gramsci, Bordiga, Ansaldo, and dozens of others. However, the majority of political detainees during this period – local party bosses, former mayors, councilmen, rank-and-file party militants, labor activists, individual anarchists, and lone "subversives" – sought appeals and pardons that were subjected to a wide array of provincial and local influences. Prefects, police commissioners, and *carabinieri*, whose opinions carried the most weight, were operating in very diverse regional contexts. Fascists, from the federal secretary down to the local party directorate, also exercised influence. Further complicating matters, the director of the colony served as the judge of whether the detainee had "demonstrated signs of rehabilitation."

Mussolini's claim that some political detainees "did not want to be antifascists" and some seemed "to be Fascists" was actually quite close to the truth.[22] Most of the detainees sentenced in 1926 and 1927 had quit opposition activities before the introduction of the exceptional decrees.[23] At the local level, squad violence and police repression made opposition so dangerous that most anti-Fascists had withdrawn from political life after either the March on Rome (October 1922) or the Matteotti crisis (June 1924–January 1925). Some had even joined the PNF or the syndicates. Once arrested and interned, these detainees faced largely the same set of options as figures of national stature: submit to the regime, or resist and suffer the consequences. Of the cases sampled from the period from 1926 to 1928, most appealed, and at least 40 percent wrote letters of deference

---

[22] Mussolini, OO, XXII:377.
[23] Twenty-three were sentenced for pre-November 1926 political activities. Nineteen, including six Fascists, were sentenced for ongoing organized or individual political activities and six for general "subversion" or "offense to Mussolini." Additionally, there were three abortionists, three bank presidents or businessmen, two individuals who attempted to expatriate for apolitical motives, and 1 individual involved in an essentially apolitical conflict with local officials in Rome.

or submission.[24] Of those who submitted to the regime, many spent just a few months in confinement.[25] Many others who did not write letters of submission nevertheless had their sentences reduced by Mussolini or other authorities.

In theory, virtually all political detainees were considered for early release. Bocchini regularly solicited information from provincial officials regarding each individual's eligibility for clemency. One widely used fac-similed telegraph asked prefects to "take personal interest" in determining the "specific circumstances" and "concrete facts" relevant to a detainee's sentence, his "familial economic circumstances," and whether he had "any war decorations." Bocchini also requested prefects' assessments of the effect that an act of clemency would have on public opinion and whether the return of the individual "would require special measures in order to prevent violent conflict."[26] Bocchini wanted to know whether local Fascists would protest the pardon of an anti-Fascist or commit acts of violence against him upon his return. In the provinces of classic agrarian Fascism and urban centers from Rome northward, the disposi-tions of local Fascists proved decisive.[27] Mussolini decided against many

[24] See ACS, *confinati politici* (detainees sentenced in 1926): b. 211, "Caruso, Arturo"; b. 247, "Chioffi-Berni, Egisto"; b. 697, "Mucci, Vincenzo"; b. 703, "Nappi, Michele"; b. 715, "Nobili, Severino"; b. 793, "Piccioni, Paolo"; b. 1057, "Venturini, Ezechiele"; (detainees sentenced in 1927): b. 23, "Ameglio, Emilio"; b. 28, "Angelini, Tancredi"; b. 337, "Del Simone, Domenico"; b. 787, "Peyrone, Giovanni"; b. 973, "Spirito, Francesco"; b. 1045, "Vandelli, Roberto"; (detainees sentenced in 1928): b. 319, "De Ascentis, Pasquale"; b. 379, "Effernelli, Veronica"; b. 433, "Francolini, Annibale"; b. 445, "Galassi, Teobaldo"; b. 691, "Moretti, Ottavia"; b. 949, "Sicbaldi, Ettore"; b. 1069, "Viola, Giovanni."

[25] E.g., nine spent five months or less in island colonies, three spent ten months or less, and six others two years or less. See ACS, *confinati politici* (detainees sentenced in 1926): b. 697, "Mucci, Vincenzo" (four mos.); b. 703, "Nappi, Michele" (four mos.); b. 715, "Nobili, Severino" (two mos.); (detainees sentenced in 1927): b. 23, "Ameglio, Emilio" (less than one mo.); b. 28, "Angelini, Tancredi" (four mos.); b. 973, "Spirito, Francesco" (nine mos.); b. 1045, "Vandelli, Roberto" (five mos.); (detainees sentenced in 1928): b. 379, "Effernelli, Veronica" (four mos.); b. 445, "Galassi, Teobaldo" (two mos.); b. 691, "Moretti, Ottavia" (eight mos.); b. 1069, "Viola, Giovanni," (five mos.).

[26] Virtually all files have a copy of this request. For an example, see b. 697, "Mucci, Vincenzo."

[27] E.g., see ACS, *confinati politici*, b. 108, "Buccia, Arturo" (Vercelli); b. 183, "Campelli Oreste Vittorio" (Bergamo); b. 241, "Chesi, Giuseppe" (Forlì); b. 247, "Chiofi-Berni, Egisto" (Pavia); b. 295, "Cremaschi, Amedeo" (Modena); b. 337, "Del Simone, Domenico," (Sondrio); b. 361, "Di Mattia, Alessandro" (Ancona); b. 385, "Fab-bri, Gino" (Pistoia); b. 427, "Foschi, Guglielmo" (Spezia); b. 601, "Manaresi, Adelmo" (Imola); b. 673, "Minarini, Giuseppe" (Imola); b. 673, "Minghetti, Erminio" (Molinella); b. 787, "Peyrone, Giovanni Battista" (Savona).

individual pardons in part because they would have "produced an unfavorable impression, particularly among the fascist element." The return
of a Communist sharecropper to a small town in Modena province would
not have been "well received by the Fascists and, in general, by the right-
minded part of the population."[28] In Molinella (Bologna), the *carabinieri*
warned against the return of Erminio Minghetti, a leading organizer of
the intransigent peasant resistance to Fascism there: "such a measure
would without question not only make a horrible impression but would
also be dangerous for Minghetti himself, for if he were to return, he
would probably be eliminated by the most fervent Fascists."[29] Returning one Communist to his town in Tuscany would have made "a bad
impression among the public and the *ambiente fascista*," and would have
required "special measures in order to prevent unrest."[30] Pardoning a
Communist laborer in Savona (Liguria) would have required "special,
direct measures in order to prevent incidents" and would have made a
"horrible impression on public opinion, particularly among the *ambiente
fascista*."[31]

On the ground, then, Fascist political repression, like *squadrist* violence, was shaped by local factors, including history, memory, and
still-raw emotions. Socialist neutrality, the *biennio rosso*, and *squadrist*
vendettas cast a long, dark shadow over communities throughout the
north. Between 1920 and 1922, for example, the radical Socialist Egisto
Chioffi-Berni served as the mayor of the small *comune* of Chignolo
Po, near Pavia. Mayor Chioffi-Berni's major offense against the *patria*,
according to local lore, had been his relegation of the bust of Italy's
king from the main piazza to the cemetery, and its replacement with
busts of Marx and Lenin.[32] This type of substitution of national symbols
with Socialist ones in public spaces offended influential segments of the
population and ultimately garnered support for Fascists, who presented
themselves as the defenders of patriotism, law, and order.[33] Chioffi's
installation of Marx and Lenin was thus not easily forgotten. Like many
other Socialists in local political or administrative positions, Chioffi was

---

[28] See ACS, *confinati politici*, b. 295, "Cremaschi, Amedeo."
[29] *Carabinieri* of Bologna (Divisione Esterna) to Comando Generale, January 9, 1927, in
ACS, *confinati politici*, b. 673, "Minghetti, Erminio."
[30] Ibid.
[31] See ACS, *confinati politici*, b. 787, "Peyrone, Giovanni."
[32] See *Questore* of Naples to prefect of Pavia, December 5, 1926, in ACS, *confinati politici*,
b. 247, "Chioffi Berni, Egisto."
[33] Paul Corner, *Fascism in Ferrara*, 28–47.

"definitively thrown out" by the Fascists in 1922. Authorities believed that he subsequently withdrew from political agitation because he was "continually watched by the [*carabinieri*] and by local Fascist elements." *Carabinieri* remained skeptical, however, noting that Chioffi was clever and probably still engaged in secret propaganda. His house was searched on numerous occasions but with no result. In 1923 he was charged with defaming state institutions but was acquitted for lack of evidence.[34] At the time of his arrest in late 1926, authorities reported that he had abstained from political activity for at least eighteen months. He had even quit associating with other political suspects. Nevertheless, local authorities still believed that he had not "altered his profoundly subversive ideas," and they worried about his considerable stature within the community, particularly his popularity with the peasantry. The "subversive movement" in Chignolo Po had not been "completely subdued," and Chioffi might somehow inspire its resurgence.[35] Police arrested Chioffi on December 8, and he remained in jail in Pavia for fifty-four days. He was then deported to Lipari. Once settled on the island, according to Francesco Cannata, the colony's director, Chioffi lived entirely apart from the other detainees and abstained from political activity. Chioffi soon submitted a letter of submission, and Director Cannata was amenable to a pardon. Authorities in Pavia and Chignolo Po, particularly local Fascists, countered Chioffi's attempt to win release, insisting that he was "dangerous," "irreducible," and "capable of propaganda."[36] In the face of Fascist opposition, Chioffi remained on Lipari, but the Commission of Appeals, motivated by his good behavior and the deteriorating economic situation of his family, reduced his sentence from three to two years.

Meanwhile, as his wife, two children, and father-in-law suffered economic hardship and illness, Chioffi struggled to win release. Without anyone to work their land, wrote one *carabiniere*, the family of "the subversive" found themselves "in dire economic conditions." In early 1927, his wife and three-year-old daughter fell ill, the little girl very near fatally. Nevertheless, any leniency for Chioffi would, according to local *carabinieri*, "produce a bad impression in the Fascist camp."[37] Later

---

[34] See *carabinieri* of Alessandria (Pavia), Maggiore Angelo Barisone to Comando Generale, "Chioffi Berni, Egisto informazioni," March 9, 1927, in ACS, *confinati politici*, b. 247, "Chioffi Berni, Egisto."

[35] See prefect of Pavia to DGPS, March 12, 1928, in ibid.

[36] See Chioffi's appeal file, in ibid.

[37] See *carabinieri* of Alessandria (Pavia), Maggiore Angelo Barisone to Comando Generale, "Chioffi Berni, Egisto informazioni," March 9, 1927, in ibid.

that year, Bocchini asked the DGPS for the names of detainees who had been "rehabilitated" and might be pardoned by the Duce. Director Cannata once again affirmed Chioffi's eligibility, including his name on the list. The prefect of Pisa remained strongly opposed. Chioffi stayed on Lipari.[38] As a compromise, in early 1928, authorities granted Chioffi a leave of ten days. During his home stay, the political secretary of the local Fascist Party, the *podestà* (Fascist mayor), and other party hierarchs invited Chioffi to pay them a visit. At the meeting, the Fascist officials suggested that he request an act of clemency, which they assured him would be granted. Chioffi took their advice and returned to Lipari.[39] As local Fascists predicted, state authorities were disposed to set him free. According to the prefect, the regime had destroyed the subversive movement in the area, and most of the agricultural laborers, who were now "deferential" to the regime, had been integrated into the Fascist syndicates. The return of Chioffi therefore no longer constituted a threat to the "national order." The prefect believed that political confinement had led Chioffi to "modify his ideas." Chignolo Po's former mayor had made it clear to friends, local authorities, and the Fascists that "if he returned home he would refrain entirely from any political activity, and dedicate himself exclusively to his agricultural labor and to sorting out his economic situation, badly compromised by the long absence from his family." Finally, concluded the prefect, "a potential act of clemency in his favor would make a good impression on the population, and this office, sharing the favorable opinion of the [*carabinieri*], has no objection to the request."[40] Thus, in March 1928, nine months before his sentence would officially end, the path to liberation was open.

Or it would have been: learning of Chioffi's impending release, the very same Fascists who recommended that he request clemency again protested. According to them, one incident had left them unconvinced that Chioffi had rehabilitated himself. At their earlier meeting, the *podestà* had requested that Chioffi, an atheist, baptize his children. Chioffi replied that he could not because it contradicted his principles.[41] On these grounds, the Fascists deemed him "dangerous and unrepentant."[42] Even

---

[38] See telegram of Bocchini to prefect of Pavia, October 3, 1927; and Cannata to DGPS, "Chioffi Berni Egisto," October 16, 1927, in ibid.

[39] See prefect of Pavia (Baccaredda) to DGPS, March 12, 1928, in ibid.

[40] Ibid.

[41] Prefect of Pavia to DGPS, April 24, 1928, in ibid.

[42] See note of January 15, 1928, signed by the *podestà*, the political secretary, and the entire directory of the *fascio* of Chignolo Po, in ibid.

the *carabinieri* disagreed, contending that the refusal to baptize one's children did not constitute a threat to the state or public order. The prefect, "while retaining the opinion expressed previously in favor of granting the request," nevertheless withdrew his support for a pardon because he did not want to offend the "Fascist milieu."[43] In very explicit terms, the prefect acknowledged that state authorities were in favor of releasing Chioffi, and that the Fascists' objection was in no way grounded in the legal or public-security codes. Nevertheless, the wishes of local Fascists overrode the opinions of various state authorities regarding the personal freedom of a politically compromised individual. Bocchini approved the prefect's decision and Chioffi remained on Lipari.[44] He was released in December 1928, almost four years after he had completely abandoned political activity and had made every effort to demonstrate that he posed no threat to the regime.

Although released from confinement, Chioffi was still an ex-Socialist and his children remained unbaptized. Throughout the 1930s and early 1940s, police regularly reported that Chioffi was under "constant surveillance." During this time, he "attended exclusively to his family and work," visited neither "friends" nor "public establishments," and abstained "completely from any form of political activity." Nevertheless, in January 1930, police jailed him for two weeks during the celebration of the marriage of the Savoyard Prince and for another week in October 1932, when Mussolini paid a visit to nearby Pavia. In addition to these major sanctions, which were reported to Rome, Chioffi no doubt endured other acts of harassment, intimidation, and discrimination from state and party authorities. Without question, the searches, interrogations, and surveillance required to monitor men like Chioffi constituted forms of intimidation.[45]

Grounding Fascism in the Mezzogiorno

In the south and the islands, winning one's freedom frequently proved easier than in the north, in part because political confinement sentences there served somewhat different purposes. In the months after November 1926, few southern provincial commissions sentenced anyone to political

---

[43] See prefect of Pavia to DGPS, April 24, 1928, in ibid.
[44] Ibid.
[45] See "Notizie per il prospetto biografico di Chioffi Berni" for March 11, 1929; January 12, 1930; February 19, 1930; May 26, 1933; and December 30, 1937, in ACS, MI, DGPS, CPC, b. 1308, fasc. "Chioffi Berni, Egisto."

confinement, with the exception of those in Puglia and a few major urban areas.[46] For the most part, the working-class movement in the south was divided and weak. Long before the regime introduced the exceptional decrees, police had eradicated opposition to Fascism, including clandestine organizations. In many provinces, the police thus had only to neutralize a few isolated militants.

In a case mirroring that of Amadeo Bordiga, Fausto Gullo, a lawyer, a First World War veteran, and one of the most prominent Communists in Calabria (a *bordighiano*) was recommended for political confinement in November 1926 by Prefect Agostino Guerresi, a Fascist political appointee and a Calabrese. Guerresi cited Gullo's political and journalistic activities, and identified him as an inspiration to local peasants and Communists, whom he sometimes defended in court for free.[47] Bocchini sent Gullo to the province of Nuoro, Sardinia, rather than an island colony, most likely for reasons of health. Three months into Gullo's sentence, the prefect of Nuoro, Ottavio Dinale, an old-guard Fascist and political appointee, determined that Gullo could not "continue the life of *confino* without great damage to his own health." A recent doctor's visit revealed that Gullo was suffering from "debilitating rheumatism" and a "chronic skin disease."[48] Gullo had already written the obligatory "letter of submission," promising to refrain from politics and devote himself solely to work and family. Bocchini, after conferring with Mussolini, rejected Dinale's recommendation, entirely on the basis of Guerresi's opposition to the pardon.[49] Weeks later, Dinale wrote again, tersely warning that Gullo had become "frighteningly debilitated," walking only with great "pain and exhaustion" and showing "visible deformations in his hands," which he was no longer "able to articulate." Moreover, since arriving in Sardinia, Gullo had behaved well, living quietly and acting respectfully toward authorities.[50] Bocchini conferred again with Guerresi, who dropped his opposition, and Mussolini subsequently agreed to reduce the sentence to a mere "warning" (*diffida*), allowing Gullo to return to Cosenza.[51] Kept under close police surveillance during

---

[46] See Katia Massara, *Il popolo al confino: la persecuzione fascista in Puglia.*

[47] See telegram, Guerresi to MI, PS, December 23, 1926; and Emilio Gay, Tenente Colonnello, Carabinieri Catanzaro (Cosenza) to Comandante Generale, December 26, 1926, in ACS, *confinati politici*, b. 523, "Gullo, Fausto."

[48] Ottavio Dinale to undersecretary of state, February 28, 1927, in ibid.

[49] See handwritten note, Capo della Polizia to Prefetto of Nuoro, March 13, 1927, in ibid.

[50] Dinale to Mussolini, May 12, 1927, in ibid.

[51] Bocchini to Mussolini, March 9, 1927, and Guerresi to DGPS, June 2, 1927, in ibid.

the 1930s, Gullo "maintained his principles" and occasionally associated with his "old companions of faith," while conducting absolutely no political activity and devoting himself exclusively to his profession.[52] As demonstrated in earlier chapters, such conduct by a northern Communist might have led to further police sanctions. In Cosenza, the regime's purposes were better served by leaving Gullo at home, a living reminder of the impotency of Communism in Calabria.

Throughout much of the south, the regime had less to fear from the Communist Party and working-class organizations. Although local authorities sometimes sentenced Socialists or Communists to political confinement, central authorities in Rome quickly liberated those who had clearly already reconciled themselves to the regime. In Andria, one of Puglia's larger agricultural centers, authorities identified the *contadino* Vincenzo Mucci as "perhaps the only one" among the Socialist peasantry who was secretly "entrusted with tasks assigned by subversive organizations." Although the police had little documentation to support their claims, they alleged that Mucci operated as a trusted agent of the "communist movement." Sentenced to five years political confinement, Mucci appealed. The commission, with virtually no explanation, commuted his sentence from confinement to *ammonizione*, and he served only three months on Lipari. In another case, south of Naples, near the huge Ilva steelworks at Torre Anunziata, the mechanic Michele Nappi was one of the first "subversives" to be sentenced to political confinement in November 1926. Authorities labeled him one of the "major exponents of subversion" in the *comune* of Scalfati. Nappi not only worked for Ilva but also ran his own mechanic shop with a partner. *Carabinieri* reported that he had contact with local Communists, although he had not engaged in political activity since the advent of Fascism in October 1922. In 1923, police arrested and filed formal charges against him for a "crime against the state," but a judge ultimately acquitted him. In November 1926, after the introduction of the exceptional decrees, authorities arrested Nappi, insisting that he had retained his "proud and irreducible aversion to Fascism." Sent to a mainland village, Nappi immediately wrote to the Ministry of the Interior swearing loyalty to the regime and pledging to refrain from politics. Supporting his appeal were letters from a number of prominent people, the most important of which was the director of Ilva, where he had worked for eighteen

---

[52] See "Notizie per il prospetto biografico di Fausto Gullo," May 16, 1928; July 5, 1928; July 24, 1930, in MI, DGPS, CPC, b. 2595, fasc. "Gullo, Fausto."

years, since the age of sixteen. His employer characterized him as "diligent, intelligent, [and] vigorous," working overtime, even on weekends
and holidays. Although he and other workers had once held Socialist
principles, his political attitude had changed "profoundly" long ago. He
had never, to the knowledge of the director, "conducted political activity
inside the plant" or engaged in "Communist activity or any kind of subversion . . . not even outside the plant" (emphasis by Ministry of Interior
official).[53] Nappi's business partner, several Ilva workers who had won
the Ministry of Labor's "Star of Merit for Labor," and his wife all wrote
letters declaring his retirement from political activity of any kind. Four
months after his arrest, he was released and allowed to return home.[54]
He kept his job at Ilva and remained under police surveillance for the
rest of the regime. Police arrested and briefly detained him in 1937 for
suspected anti-Fascist activity but did not subject him to any other major
sanctions.[55]

In addition to repressing anti-Fascism, political confinement sentences
passed on southerners also commonly served to sort out the problems
that arose in the process of extending Fascism into the Mezzogiorno.
After 1922, local elites scrambled to preserve their political, social, and
economic positions by forming and joining *fasci*.[56] In some instances, two
or more *fasci* cropped up in the same community, or one faction sought
to build a power base within the Fascist syndicates or MVSN.[57] Many
former Socialists and syndicalists of minor statures, who had converted
to Fascism earlier than many traditional southern elites, found themselves
on the losing end of these struggles. Critical to the Fascist consolidation
of power after the March on Rome was securing the political (electoral)
support of southern elites and their clientele networks while asserting
greater control over local administration and founding local *fasci*. In the
north, Fascists accomplished these goals through squad violence. In the
south, by contrast, with the exception of Puglia and a few other areas
(Syracuse-Ragusa), this process began only at the end of 1922 and was
largely orchestrated by prefects, who dissolved locally elected councils

---

53 Letter from director of Ilva, no date, in ACS, *confinati politici*, b. 703, "Nappi, Michele."
54 *Carabinieri* (Salerno interno) to prefect of Salerno, December 21, 1926, in ibid.
55 "Notizie per il prospetto biografico di Michele Nappi," April 16, 1937, in MI, DGPS,
    CPC, b. 3487, fasc. "Nappi. Michele."
56 See Luigi Ponziani, *Il fascismo dei prefetti: amministrazione e politica nell'Italia merid-
    ionale, 1922–26* (Catanzaro, 1995).
57 Tommaso Baris, *Il fascismo in provincia: Politica e società a Frosinone* (Bari, 2007).

and sent special commissars to sort out matters.[58] These commissars could not simply choose the leader of the local *fascio*, because he might possess neither the support of local elites nor the requisite administrative skills.[59] From the perspective of state and party authorities in Rome, finding local collaborators with a sincere commitment to Fascism mattered less than installing local elites who had sufficient influence to rule their communities effectively. Consequently, the Fascist regime made serious compromises when establishing its institutions in the south. Meanwhile, the losing faction had to conform, continue to agitate against the local *fascio*, attempt to build a power base within the MVSN or the syndicates, or, as a last resort, turn to Fascist dissidence and even anti-Fascism.

The rather conservative character of southern Fascism thus left little room for individuals with left-wing backgrounds comparable to those of the northern leadership. Police in the south depicted Socialists and syndicalists who espoused Fascism, particularly after 1922, as opportunists merely seeking shelter from persecution. Severino Nobili, a journalist and labor militant, had served in several chambers of labor and published Socialist journals in and around Salerno and Bari since before the First World War. Salerno's *questore* described him as a "restless and ambitious soul, though uncultured." In 1919, Nobili was elected secretary of the Chamber of Labor of Cerato (Salerno), a position he held until the March on Rome. Fascists then "removed him" from office, and the police arrested him for "crimes against the powers of the state." Acquitted in 1923, after a full year in preventative imprisonment, Nobili returned home to Vietri sul Mare, on the Amalfi coast. During his incarceration, *squadrist* violence and police repression had crushed the forces of opposition in Salerno. Fascists primarily targeted the liberals loyal to Giovanni Amendola, a former government minister and opponent of Fascism, but they also attacked the leaders and burned down the headquarters of the Socialist and Catholic labor syndicates, forcing their members into the new Fascist syndicates.[60] During 1924, Fascists, with help from the police and Ministry of the Interior, violently ousted any remaining liberal administrations from the province of Salerno.[61] Despite this environment,

---

[58] Ponziani, *Fascismo dei prefetti*, 65–7.
[59] Ibid., 74.
[60] Delle Donne, Enrica Robertazzi, "Origini del fascismo a Salerno, 1919–1924," in *Mezzogiorno e fascismo: atti del Convegno nazionale di studi promosso dalla Regione Campania*, ed. Pietro Laveglia (Naples, 1975), I:225–8.
[61] Pietro Laveglia, "Fascismo, antifascismo e resistenza nel salernitano," in ibid., I:335.

according to the *questore*, Nobili continued his "antinational campaign" by "inciting the voters of Vietri to vote in opposition to the [Fascist] Block" in the elections of 1924. *Carabinieri* likewise believed that Nobili was operating as a "secret agent" of the Socialist Party. Never mind that he conducted his "secret," "anti-national campaign" to "incite voters" under a democratic parliamentary regime. After the Matteotti murder, Nobili founded the "Giacomo Matteotti Circle," joining the groundswell of protest that swept Italy. However, by early 1925, if not earlier, such opposition was no longer possible. *Squadrist* violence had cowed the provinces' population, and the main proponents of the opposition had withdrawn from politics or fled. In Tuscany, Fascists attacked Giovanni Amendola yet again in 1925, beating him so severely that he died months later.

During 1925, Nobili underwent an abrupt political transformation. The police chief of Salerno described how "the subversive" had "calmed himself" and "ceased ceased all political activity," even "seeking shelter in the local Fascist Corporations, . . . offering his services as an organizer."[62] In August 1926, months before his arrest, Nobili petitioned the local PNF for membership, offering a full explanation of, in his words, "the spiritual process which gave rise to my new political conscience." Nobili claimed that "The historic phenomenon of Fascism" had provoked in him a "crisis of conscience," instilling "a new breath of spirituality" that now rendered him "worthy of living in this marvelous epoch of spiritual rebirth, whose historic expression" was "Political and Syndical Fascism."[63] The local section of the PNF denied him membership but only because the rolls had been closed in April 1926.[64] Following the implementation of the exceptional decrees, the police and *carabinieri* still viewed Nobili as subversive. His political conversion, authorities alleged, derived "not from sincere rehabilitation, but from the desire to secure a safe position in case of reprisals, [while] even extracting advantages from the very Party which he hates in his own heart, ready to betray it and fight it even more energetically as soon as the occasion presents itself."[65]

---

[62] *Questore* of Salerno to the Provincial Commission, November 23, 1926, in ACS, *confinati politici*, b. 715, "Severino Nobili."

[63] Severino Nobili, "Agli On.li. componenti del Direttorio Fascista della Sezione di Vetri sul Mare," August 23, 1926, in ibid.

[64] See Segretario Politico del PNF (Vietri sul Mare) Rafaele Mauro to Nobili, September 24, 1926, in ibid.

[65] *Questore* of Salerno to Provincial Commission, November 23, 1926, and *carabinieri* to Questura of Salerno, November 23, 1926, in ibid.

The Salerno police commission sentenced Nobili to two years of confinement, and the DGPS assigned him to Lampedusa, where conditions were particularly harsh. Nobili immediately wrote to Mussolini, swearing loyalty to the regime. Bocchini reviewed his political history, taking special interest in his activity in Fascist labor organizations since 1924. After just two months, Mussolini pardoned Nobili, commuting his sentence to political probation (*ammonizione*). Upon his return home, he immediately composed a three-page letter to the "Duce of Fascism," expressing his "appreciative recognition for the act of reparative justice." He had quit socialism years before, he explained, and was now a devoted Fascist. Additionally, he requested that Mussolini lift his political probation. This final act of clemency would, he wrote, "cancel the last trace of a police measure that offends me, debases me, humiliates me, lumping me together with scum who deserve either pity or disgust."[66] Notably, the secretary general of the Salerno branch of the National Confederation of Fascist Syndicates wrote a letter in support of the full rehabilitation of Nobili.[67] Though his request was denied, Mussolini pardoned him the following year. Nobili sent a telegram to the Duce, expressing his "immense gratitude" for his "political [and] moral resurrection" and swearing anew his undying loyalty.[68] Although police judged Nobili's conversion to Fascism insincere, his ostensible conformity to his pledges convinced Mussolini and Bocchini that he posed no further threat to the regime. Upon his release, Nobili did not resume activity in the syndicates, probably because he was not readmitted. Instead, he drifted in and out of part-time administrative work, remaining unemployed for long periods during the 1930s. Authorities subjected him to "constant surveillance" but always reported that he had exhibited "good conduct." Finally, in November 1941, police informed Rome that Nobili had been interned in a concentration camp for his "bad political precedents" and unspecified "illegal activities" against public and private offices.[69]

Throughout the south, authorities similarly used their new powers to definitively end the attempts of syndicalists, Socialists, and other left-wingers to control or belong to Fascist institutions. For example, Vito Balzano, a lawyer from Carbonara (Bari), joined the Fascist movement

[66] Severino Nobili to Benito Mussolini, March 14, 1927, in ibid.
[67] Dino Andriani to prime minister, March 14, 1927, in ibid.
[68] Telegraph, Nobili to Mussolini, April 7, 1928, in ibid.
[69] "Notizie per il prospetto biografico di Severino Nobili" for October 11, 1928; June 2, 1929; May 19, 1933; and November 3, 1941, in ACS, MI, DGPS, CPC, b. 3552, fasc. "Nobili, Severino."

quite early on (1919, by his own account) and became a high-ranking officer of the MVSN. Like the squads in the north, he and a handful of militiamen engaged in attacks on the communal council of Carbonara, hoping to seize political power there. They failed, and the local elites, who had now become Fascists, forced Balzano to resign from several offices, including his position of *capo manipoli* of the MVSN. At this point, Balzano adopted a posture of open opposition to local Fascists, who in return regularly "visited" his law offices. The *carabinieri* frequently searched his home and offices but found nothing politically compromising. State authorities absolutely rejected Balzano's claims that he was a Fascist. The police noted that the lawyer "had always demonstrated subversive tendencies and participated actively in the antinational movement." In their view he "insinuated himself into fascism" in order to engage in practices of "disaggregation." Then, in the mid-1920s, according to the prefect, he became "one of the major exponents of the local communist group."[70] Contrary to the assessment of the prefect, the *carabinieri* reported that Balzano was a Republican who adopted subversive, antinational ideas after returning from the war. Whatever the case, after the introduction of the exceptional decrees, police sentenced Balzano to two years mainland exile, which he served in full, despite his long-standing Fascist credentials.[71]

Similarly, in Trapani, Sicily, Annibale Francolini, a Socialist railway man, converted to Fascism after October 1922, leading the transformation of the league of tram drivers into a Fascist syndicate. Despite Francolini's long, well-documented, active involvement in Fascist syndicalism, local authorities assessed him as an "unstable and turbulent" subversive responsible for "hundreds of disorderly incidents" and the formation of the *lega tranvieri* during the "sad years of subversion." The "complete triumph" of Fascism, police believed, had caused him to disguise his subversive, anti-Fascist beliefs by "camouflaging" his Socialist union in the trappings of a Fascist syndicate. Though the police and *carabinieri* offered no empirical evidence of continued subversive activity between 1922 and 1926, a search of the syndicate headquarters revealed a trove of Socialist paraphernalia, left over from the old league. Behind framed photographs of Mussolini and the king were hidden portraits of Karl Marx and the anarchist Andrea Costa. In Francolini's home, police

---

70 Prefect of Bari to DGPS, July 25, 1927, in ACS, *confinati politici*, b. 58, "Balzano, Vito."
71 Carabinieri Reali di Bari (Esterna), November 30, 1926; Vito Balzano to Commission of Appeal, November 30, 1926, in *confinati politici*, ibid.

found a red flag, an illegal handgun, and a portrait of Matteotti. In his appeal, Francolini noted, and police confirmed, that a faction within the syndicate opposed his leadership. He accused them of having planted incriminating materials in his home while he was attending a national convention of Fascist syndicates. Moreover, he insisted, the flags and journals at the syndicate headquarters had simply never been thrown out. In response, the *questore* argued that by failing to destroy the correspondence, flags, and emblems of the former Socialist league, Francolini revealed his true "subversive principles."[72] Contradicting provincial authorities' portrayal of Francolini, the director of Società Anonima Tramways, his employer of twelve years, issued a document certifying that Francolini was considered among "the best drivers" and had "always displayed impeccable conduct."[73] Francolini appealed his sentence and wrote several letters detailing his activities on behalf of both the syndicates and the *fasci*. Local authorities continued to defend their decision as "appropriate and just," because it was unacceptable that Francolini had "continued to preserve propaganda materials that espoused subversion meant to throw Italy into Bolshevik chaos." At the same time, "considering the pitiful condition" of his wife and five children, who had been reduced to the "most squalid misery," and "in order to not give exaggerated importance" to his case, authorities consented to reducing his sentence from three years to one. Such an act of clemency, they believed, might even bring about a "complete rehabilitation" of a grateful Francolini.[74]

Fully understanding the trajectories of left-wing Fascists sentenced to political confinement would be difficult without focused local research.[75] Few, if any, appeared to be actively intriguing against the regime. Instead, the political conflicts leading to their arrest and confinement were local in

---

[72] See Prefect Edoardo Salerno to DGPS, March 31, 1928; Captain Dante Caporali, *carabinieri* of Palermo (Trapani), January 21, 1928; Francolini to Prefect Edoardo Salerno, June 12, 1928; and official statement of Francolini, January 23, 1928, taken by Giuseppe Candia, all in ACS, MI, DGPS, *confinati politici*, b. 433, "Francolini, Annibale."

[73] See Direttore, Società Anonima Tramways (Andrea Marini), "Certificato," February 7, 1928, in *confinati politici*, ibid.

[74] *Carabinieri* of Palermo (Trapani) to Comando Generale, March 17, 1928, in *confinati politici*, ibid.

[75] One fine example, which would seem to support the argument being made here, is Salvatore Lupo, "L'utopia totalitaria del fascismo, 1918–1942," in *Storia d'Italia. Le regioni dall'Unità ad oggi. La Sicilia*, ed. M. Aymard and G. Giarrizzo (Turin, 1987), 373–482.

nature, or, more precisely, products of the new political dynamic between center and periphery, triggered by the arrival of Fascism in southern communities. As the regime sought powerful local collaborators, these radicals, despite their ostensibly legitimate Fascist credentials, were thrust aside. It might be tempting to view this process of grounding Fascism in the south as merely another chapter in the history of *trasformismo* – local elites adapting to yet another system in order to preserve their power and the status quo. However, the Fascist state was arguably embarking on a project that differed significantly from the liberal era practice of "buying off" southern elites. Instead, the regime was working to implant into southern communities a political party that was truly national in its structure. Moreover, many central and provincial officials presiding over this process were "new men," former *squadrists* and syndicalists, radicals from both the left and the right. In extending Fascist influence into the south, the regime mobilized prominent southern Fascists – Achile Starace (Puglia) and the Fascist Quadrumvir Michele Bianchi (Calabria) – who wielded great influence, recommending their associates for appointment to critical offices, such as prefectures. Their task was fraught with contradictions, because the regime had to win the support of landowners and elites who personified the very same legacy of corruption, clientelism, and factionalism that Fascism claimed to want to fight and ultimately eliminate.[76] Over time, Mussolini's regime hoped to improve administration, eliminate factional fighting (*beghismo*) and insert Fascism into the life of southern communities, thereby creating a centralized Fascist state.

The Socialists and syndicalists in the south who converted to Fascism may have simply been "taking refuge" within the *fasci* or the syndicates. However, whether their Fascism was genuine or ersatz, most of these detainees spent very little time in confinement, thanks apparently to their prior inclinations toward Fascism. Perhaps regime officials, including Mussolini, were reluctant to alienate radicals willing to adhere to Fascism. In the future, these grassroots labor organizers might have become "new men" capable of moving southern Italy out of the swamp of transformist corruption. However, whereas in the north ex-Socialists and syndicalists made careers as professional Fascists within the state and party bureaucracy, traditional southern elites monopolized most state and party offices at the local level, leaving little room for that type of social promotion.[77] As ex-political detainees, the individuals examined here

[76] Lupo, *Il fascismo*, 172–3.
[77] Ponziani, *Fascismo dei prefetti*, 13–15.

lived out their lives under regular police surveillance and discrimination. All were susceptible to further sanctions.

The release of political prisoners and detainees reveals several of the most elemental features of Fascist political repression. The consequences of confinement were sufficiently severe as to induce most of Mussolini's opponents to abandon their opposition to Fascism. The regime exploited their desperation, offering many of them pardons, which could then be used in propaganda to lessen the appearance of political repression and dishearten rank-and-file anti-Fascists. Moreover, by sending most detainees home, the regime made those who spent their lives in Fascist custody seem particularly dangerous and intransigent, deserving of their fate. The path to freedom, though perhaps not rehabilitation, was cleared or blocked by the political calculations of Mussolini, the whims of local Fascists, and the arbitrary opinions of state authorities. At the local level, Fascists strongly influenced whom the police punished and for how long, though state authorities made the ultimate determinations. Even after detainees returned to their families, they continued to live as second-class citizens under Fascism. Release from state custody was perhaps easier to obtain than liberation from the incessant regime of party-state surveillance, harassment, intimidation, and discrimination that operated at the local level. Finally, the politics of pardons reveals how confinement served different purposes in diverse regional contexts. As the cases of left-wing and dissident Fascists demonstrate, political confinement was not merely a tool of political repression. It also served to advance the regime's most critical priorities at the national and local levels. Fascist political repression was not simply reactive.

6

Everyday Political Crime

Mentre me leggo el solito giornale spaparacchiato all'ombra d'un pajaro vedo un porco e je dico: – Addio, majale! - vedo un ciuccio e je dico: – Addio, somaro! -	As I read my usual newspaper, relaxed in the shadow of a pile of straw, I see a swine and say: "Good day, pig!" I see a mule and say: "Good day, donkey!"
Forse 'ste bestie nun me capiranno,	Maybe these beasts won't understand me
ma provo armeno la soddisfazzione de potè di' le cose come stanno senza paura de finì in priggione.	but at least I'll have the satisfaction of being able to tell things straight, without the fear of ending up in prison.
Trilussa, "All'ombra" (1932)[1]	Trilussa, "In the Shade"

In October 1935, Fascist Italy launched a full-scale military invasion of Ethiopia. Thereafter, Mussolini thrust his nation into a series of military adventures: the Spanish Civil War (1936–9), the annexation of Albania (1939), and, during the Second World War, the attacks on France (June 1940) and, later, Greece (October 1940). For many historians, Ethiopia signaled the beginning of the regime's "totalitarian turn," a phase of Fascism in which warfare and radical domestic policies drove a "process of progressive 'totalitarianization'" and a "cultural revolution."[2] In the past, Mussolini had spoken about, and to some extent pursued, the project

---

[1] *Lo specchio e altre poesie* (Milan, 1938), 37.
[2] De Felice, *Mussolini il duce*, II:8, 82–90; see also Payne, *A History of Fascism*, 212–44.

of creating the new "Fascist man" (*uomo fascista*) but always as a long-term objective. Now, with Fascist rule well into its second decade, the moment had arrived to carry out the "moral reform" of the Italians, which in turn would allow Italy to fulfill its imperial destiny. Domestically, internal social mobilization accompanied this permanent state of war.[3] The expansion of the National Fascist Party (PNF), the promotion of the cult of the Duce, the cultivation of an increasingly martial society, the introduction of the anti-Semitic racial laws (1938), and other policies all served to imbue Fascism into the everyday lives of ordinary people. These increasingly radical domestic and foreign policies would, Mussolini believed, turn Italians' passive acceptance of Fascism into genuine faith.

During the run up to the Ethiopian invasion, the dictatorship entered its most repressive phase, turning state violence against broad sections of the Italian people, rather than just avowed anti-Fascists. The Special Tribunal, the regime's highest court for judging political offenses, sentenced 310 and 365 persons to prison during 1938 and 1939, the third- and fourth-highest totals per year after 1928 (636) and 1931 (519).[4] More remarkably, between June 1935 and April 1936, the number of political detainees and exiles (*confinati politici*) doubled from 800 to 1,600, and steadily increased thereafter, approaching 2,200 in September 1937.[5] By September 1942, there were almost three thousand political detainees. During every year from 1935 to 1943, the population of "politicals" was larger than *any* year during the previous period (1926–34), when the regime was still actively struggling to suppress organized anti-Fascist movements. By 1934, with organized clandestine opposition virtually eliminated, the population of political prisoners continued to grow, even despite large, sometimes biannual, amnesties. Finally, during 1939 through 1942, the steady growth of the confinement archipelago persisted alongside the parallel phenomenon of en masse internment. The regime set up concentration camps throughout Italy and filled them with many thousands of "political suspects," foreign Jews, common criminals, gypsies, and other "socially dangerous" individuals who might otherwise have been sentenced to *confino di polizia*.[6]

Increased political repression, military violence, and revolutionary radicalization were all linked within the logic of Fascism. For Fascists, the

---

[3] MacGregor Knox, "Conquest, Foreign and Domestic, in Fascist Italy and Nazi Germany," *Journal of Modern History* 56:1 (1984): 44.
[4] De Felice, *Mussolini il duce*, II:46.
[5] See fig. 2 in ch. 4.
[6] Capogreco, *I campi del duce*.

punishment and neutralization of "internal enemies" advanced the fascistization of the nation. War and territorial expansion, meanwhile, created the authoritarian environment in which harsher repression and revolutionary violence seemed necessary and justifiable. After the defeat of Italian forces by the International Brigades (which consisted of many Italian anti-Fascists) at the battle of Guadalajara, Spain, Mussolini bemoaned the "deficiency of the rank-and-file," who represented the "weak point of our military organization." Listening to Mussolini, Minister of Education Giuseppe Bottai thought of the disaster at Caporetto, in 1917, where the Italian army fell apart during an Austrian offensive. Mussolini then threatened that, after Guadalajara, the "repercussions in Italy" would be to see "if the wine of *squadrismo*," which had been "held in reserve for so long," was "still good." The regime would "uncork a few bottles," he predicted, and find it "still excellent." "We'll smash some heads, a few radios. Everything will be in order," concluded Mussolini. At the mention of cracking skulls, party secretary Achile Starace cheerfully exclaimed: "With style."[7] Around the same period, Foreign Minister Ciano recalled Mussolini threatening to construct a "concentration camp, with harsher methods than *confino di polizia*."[8]

In the wake of the First World War, the Fascists attacked Socialists and Slavs, as they consolidated their power over northern Italy. This violence was linked to war and expansionism. The Fascists were punishing Socialists for their neutralism, while agitating for the Italianization of Venezia Giulia and Trentino Alto-Adige and calling for Italian control of Fiume. In the 1930s, having consolidated power and weathered the Great Depression, the Mussolini regime relaunched the Fascist revolution with a state of perpetual war, imperial expansionism, and a repressive environment that would become, in the Duce's own words, "increasingly harsh." But now that the Bolshevik threat no longer provided a pretext for Fascist violence, who were to be the nation's "internal enemies," the new victims? Over the course of the 1930s, the dictatorship would continually expand the definition of *political crime*. The new "political criminals" represented yet another manifestation of the "antinational" elements against which the regime defined the Fascist nation. Above all, police and Fascists targeted ordinary speech offenses (often committed by poor, or otherwise socially marginal, Italians) throughout the Italian peninsula. In this sense, the regime targeted the lower classes more

---

[7] Bottai, *Diario*, April 12, 1937, 116.
[8] Ciano, *Diario*, July 10, 1938, 156.

broadly. Fascists and police also conducted harsh campaigns against ethnic minorities, homosexuals, Jehovah's Witnesses, Pentecostals, corrupt Fascists, and other groups, culminating with the regime's adoption of official racism, the anti-Semitic laws of 1938.

The Nationalization of Political Repression

To promote conformity to Mussolini's vision of Fascist society, the regime extended politicized repression to all regions of Italy. In the south, during the regime's first decade in power, the police state used its authoritarian powers to suppress common criminality and organized crime rather than political opposition. In their first eight years of operation (1926–34), provincial police commissions inflicted political confinement on only 842 Italians from the five southernmost regions (Sicily, Calabria, Campania, Puglia, and Basilicata). Of these, more than 40 percent (326) came from Puglia, the one region where agrarian Fascism, and anti-Fascism, had taken root before 1922. Only in a few provinces, usually major urban areas and mostly in Puglia, did provincial commissions regularly resort to political confinement prior to 1935. Some provincial commissions (Messina, Cosenza, Reggio Calabria, Catanzaro, Salerno, and Potenza) inflicted a wave of political sanctions, and then became relatively inactive.[9]

At the same time, southerners were not strangers to the regime's draconian measures of social control. The provincial commissions of southern Italy filled up the confinement archipelago at a faster rate than did their northern counterparts. The number of "common confinement" sentences coming out of Palermo and Nuoro (Sardinia) were "staggering," according to one police official.[10] Moreover, in western Sicily, the state conducted its campaign against the *mafia* with a harshness and brutality perhaps only matched by the combination of squad terror and police repression unleashed against the Socialists in northern Italy. State authorities deported thousands of people, held women and children hostage, and laid siege to entire villages and towns.[11]

---

[9] D. Carbone, *Il popolo al confino: La persecuzione fascista in Basilicata*, 262–4; S. Carbone, *Il popolo al confino: La persecuzione fascista in Calabria*, 520–7.

[10] Chief director of the Police Division, "Appunto per Onorevole Divisione Affari Generali e Riservati," no. 1150, August 13, 1927, MI, UCP, b. 11, fasc. 710–12/1926–30, sf. 1927.

[11] Lupo, *Storia della mafia*, 203–25.

By contrast, during the next eight years (1935–43), a great number of southerners previously unfamiliar with explicitly "political" repression would gain some sort of firsthand experience. From 1935 onward, the same southern commissions sentenced 2,157 individuals to political confinement.[12] In Ragusa (Sicily), for example, the Provincial Commission did not pass a single political confinement sentence before 1936; in subsequent years it passed thirty-one.[13] In Benevento (Campania), only four individuals were sentenced before 1935; thereafter there were twenty-one.[14] These examples were not exceptions but rather the rule. Even the Palermo commission produced only seventeen political sentences before 1935; thereafter it passed ninety-three.[15] Meanwhile, officials in Rome sent thousands of political detainees into exile in small southern villages, where they lived amongst southerners. Geographically speaking, Fascist political repression had been nationalized.

Despite these significant differences, drawing too stark a distinction between the rooting of Fascism in the north and south would be inaccurate. The Fascist movement was certainly strongest in the north, yet it was not unknown in the south. Moreover, much like the south, many northern provinces had no *fasci* until after the March on Rome. Accordingly, though approximately 3,500 Italians were sentenced to political confinement in central and northern Italy during the period from 1926 to 1934, some provincial commissions were relatively inactive.[16] Police in just a few major cities (Turin, Genoa, Milan, Venice, Trieste, Bologna, Florence, and Rome) generated the majority of political confinement sentences.

---

[12] Massara, *Il popolo al confino: la persecuzione fascista in Puglia*, 14n5.
[13] Carbone and Grimaldi, *Il popolo al confino: la persecuzione fascista in Sicilia*, 554–5.
[14] Spadafora, *Il popolo al confino: la persecuzione fascista in Campania*, 2:164–5.
[15] Carbone and Grimaldi, *Il popolo al confino: la persecuzione fascista in Sicilia*, 554–5.
[16] Most northern provincial commissions regularly sentenced at least a few people to political confinement each year. However, several notably passed no or very few sentences before 1933: in Piedmont, Aosta (0), Asti (0), Cuneo (12); Lombardy, Pavia (13), Sondrio (6); in Trentino-Alto Adige, Bolzano (8); in Friuli Venezia Giulia, Fiume (6), Zara (9); in Liguria, La Spezia (11), Savona (10 before 1934); in Tuscany, Arezzo (6), Grosseto (10), Lucca (9), Pistoia (9); in Le Marche, Ascoli-Piceno (11); in Abruzzi-Molise, Campobasso (6), Chieti (6), Pescara (9), Teramo (7); in Lazio, Rieti (6); Viterbo (11). Ferrara remarkably sentenced fewer political detainees between 1935 and 1943 (25) than the previous period, between 1926 and 1934 (27). The data for these commissions is somewhat flawed because the compilers excluded *confino politico* sentences unrelated to anti-Fascist activity or dissent. So Fascists, abortionists, homosexuals, Pentecostals, and Jehovah's Witnesses were excluded. Nevertheless, the overall pattern is significant. Adriano Dal Pont and Simonetta Carolini, eds., *L'Italia al confino*.

TABLE 3. *Political* Confino *Sentences, 1926–1934 (159 of 549 sampled)*

Political Affiliations		Motives for Sentences	
Communist	75	Pre-1926 political activity[a]	44
Anarchist	12	Communist Party activity	35
Socialist	11	Anarchist activity	4
Republican	7	Giustizia e libertà	5
Anti-Fascist	17	Other anti-Fascist activity[b]	19
"Subversive"	5	Expatriation/activity abroad	14
"Slavophile"	5	Fascists (dissident/criminal)	4
German (irredentism)	1	Labor abstention	1
Sardinian	1	Speech offenses (Duce/Fascism)	25
Apolitical	20	Economic/bank failure	5
Fascist	5	Abortion	3
TOTAL	159	TOTAL	159

[a] Includes 25 Communists, 7 anarchists, 6 Socialists, 2 Republicans, 2 "Subversives," 1 anti-Fascist, and 1 "Sardista."

[b] Includes contributing money to help political victims or their families, possessing or distributing anti-Fascist propaganda, corresponding with anti-Fascists, and other activities not specifically identified with a particular party.

After 1934, more police commissions in the north were active, sentencing approximately seven thousand individuals. Therefore, the introduction of a more politicized police repression to the south after 1934 was an experience shared by some northern provinces. By crushing anti-Fascism in select regions during 1926 through 1934, and then introducing the PNF and politicized repression to all of Italy, the regime eliminated some major differences between north and south. After 1934, the political landscapes of most Italian provinces would become strikingly, if superficially, similar, at least when compared to the preceding liberal era.

Fascist political repression before 1935 also fell most heavily upon specific political and social groups: mainly Communists, anarchists, Socialists, and, on a very selective basis, Republicans and anti-Fascist liberals (Table 3). Most detainees had spent years actively opposing the regime, even if they had abandoned militancy before 1926. However, a significant minority of detainees sentenced before 1935 were "apolitical" suspects whom the regime held responsible for abortion, clandestine expatriation, or bank failures. However limited, this use of politicized repression against essentially apolitical behaviors between 1926 and 1934 reflected, at this early stage, an essential feature of Fascist political confinement:

it served as a highly flexible tool of coercive political pedagogy, through which the regime communicated its priorities and expectations to the Italian people.

This phenomenon is well demonstrated by the two to three hundred political confinement sentences meted out to midwives and doctors suspected of performing abortions. In the early years of his dictatorship, Mussolini focused his energies on a small number of important priorities, which included consolidating political power, repressing anti-Fascism, and stabilizing the Italian economy. Equally important, in Mussolini's view, was the matter of demographic growth. For Mussolini, population growth was "the question of questions," the key to economic prosperity, military might, territorial expansion, and the overall progress of the "Italian race." The size of Italy's population would determine whether Italy would establish an empire or be colonized itself by the multiplying "hordes" of "black" and "yellow" peoples of Africa and Asia.[17] In 1925, he launched the "Battle of the Births," establishing the National Organization for the Protection of Motherhood and Infancy (ONMI), a network of pre- and postnatal health care. The demographic campaign also included coercive measures, such as the so-called bachelor tax, and even gimmicks, such as prizes for large families.[18] The regime outlawed birth control devices and information about birth control, labeling it "Malthusian propaganda." Finally, emigration, another source of population shrinkage, became illegal.

In support of the demographic campaign, the 1926 public-security code specifically called for police confinement (though not necessarily "political" *confino*) for doctors and midwives suspected of performing abortions. The Rocco Code, introduced in 1930, subsequently established much harsher penalties for abortion and made convictions easier to obtain. The guiding principle of both codes – one judicial, the other executive – was the view that abortion was a crime against the state.[19] Before the Rocco Code, the provincial police commissions played a more important role in punishing suspected abortionists. If the courts failed to convict suspected abortionists under preexisting legislation, police often levied

---

[17] See Mussolini's introduction to Richard Korherr's *Regresso delle nascite, morte dei popoli* (Rome, 1928). See also Carl Ipsen, *Dictating Demography: The Problem of Population in Fascist Italy* (Cambridge, 1996).

[18] Victoria de Grazia, *How Fascism Ruled Women: Italy, 1922–1945* (Berkeley, 1992); Anna Treves, *Le nascite e la politica nell'Italia del Novecento* (Milan, 2001).

[19] Nancy Triolo, "The Angel-makers: Fascist Pro-Natalism and the Normalization of Midwives in Sicily (PhD diss., University of California, Berkeley, 1989), 130.

executive sanctions. In Bologna province, for example, a *carabiniere* recommended confinement for a midwife because he could not find "sufficient evidence that could corroborate" an indictment, due to "the large number of obvious difficulties that hinder in every way the investigation of these crimes."[20] The Como Provincial Commission acted similarly against another midwife because, "in the investigative period, it was not possible to gather specific proof of her sinister activity." The report rather vaguely concluded, "Yet, definite convictions of her guilt have emerged."[21] For the police, the lack of evidence against suspected abortionists constituted an alarming sign of their "cunning," "slyness," and "cleverness," which, besides preventing the police from obtaining concrete evidence, made the suspects even more dangerous.[22] As with other political offenses, the police relied heavily on "public opinion" and hearsay in prosecuting abortionists.[23] To strengthen their cases, police resorted to unsubstantiated claims and sensationalism. Their reports almost invariably alleged that the suspect had conducted procedures resulting in hospitalization or death. In one case, police stated as a fact that a midwife was responsible for the death of a woman who was later discovered alive. Police recognized the impossibility of discovering every abortionist in their jurisdiction but expressed confidence that *confino politco* sentences served "as a warning to other unscrupulous professionals" and "those malcontents who impede the growth of the race."[24]

Although abortion was already a criminal offense, the demographic campaign provided even greater impetus to identify and punish suspected midwives and doctors. In many *questure*, police revisited their old case files, searching for "guilty" abortionists who had managed to avoid conviction. For police officials preferring to avoid such matters, the regime's demographic campaign, and the classification of abortion as a crime against the state, encouraged enthusiastic prosecution. Although police justified their actions on the basis of traditional notions of "morality," "decency," and the "sanctity of the family," they also characterized

[20] *Carabinieri* Reali of Bologna to Comando Generale, March 19, 1928, in ACS, *confinati politici*, b. 421, "Folli, Pasqua."
[21] *Carabinieri* of Milano to Comando Generale, January 29, 1929, in ACS *confinati politici*, b. 260, "Clerici, Maria."
[22] *Questore* to prefect of Como, October 17, 1928, in ACS *confinati politici*, b. 379, "Effernelli, Veronica."
[23] The standard indictment read "public opinion has found her habitually guilty of conducting abortions."
[24] *Questore* to prefect of Como, May 28, 1928, in ACS, *confinati politici*, b. 874, "Rodini, Isolina."

abortion as a "symptom of national decadence."[25] Authorities invariably cited the Duce, Fascism, and the "directives of the regime" as the impetus for their decision to pursue abortionists, parroting the rhetoric of the demographic campaign in their reports.[26] For the Venetian *questore*, abortionists "manifested the deliberate intention of impeding the activities of the powers of State with regard to the demographic defense of the nation."[27] For the *carabinieri* of Padova, the crime "openly violated the directives of the national government regarding demographic growth."[28] In Como, the police called the activities of one midwife "a direct attempt to inflict damage on the National interests of the State and in opposition to the directives of the Government itself."[29] Another midwife in Como actively impeded, authorities alleged, "the demographic growth of the race."[30] The regime's demographic campaign therefore lent urgency and cohesiveness to existing impulses to repress abortion. In Vercelli, Prefect Orlando D'Eufemia telegraphed Mussolini directly to inform him of an "emergency" meeting of the Provincial Commission to sentence a surgeon responsible for more than one hundred abortions. "Ever and always in every problem of the province," D'Eufemia signed off, "I obey the law of Fascism to believe and act."[31] Underlined and punctuated with an exclamation point by Mussolini, the prefect's telegram reflects how provincial authorities worked hard to repress activities that the dictator deemed inimical to Fascism. Truly, what Mussolini labeled "political" mattered, often spurring on prefects and police chiefs.

The recast Fascist ban on abortion also shaped the perceptions of ordinary people. Above all, the vigorous prosecution of abortionists served as

[25] *Questore* to prefect of Bologna, February 2, 1928; and *carabinieri* of Bologna, February 7, 1928, both in ACS, MI, DGPS, *confinati politici*, b. 801, "Piperno Francesco"; *questore* to prefect of Bologna, February 28, 1928, in ACS, MI, DGPS, *confinati politici*, b. 189, "Canova, Clementina"; *questore* to prefect of Bologna, February 8, 1928, in ACS, MI, DGPS, *confinati politici*, b. 1099, "Zappi, Ricordato."

[26] *Questore* to prefect of Bologna, February 28, 1928, in ACS, MI, DGPS, *confinati politici*, b. 189, "Canova, Clementina."

[27] Commissione Provinciale, in ACS, *confinati politici*, "Turchetto, Emma."

[28] *Carabinieri* of Padova to Comando Genderale, December 9, 1929, "Oggetto: Confinata di polizia GIORDAN Cecilia," in ACS, *confinati politici*, b. 483, "Giordan Cecilia."

[29] See statement of Rodini, Isolina, May 1928, in ACS, *confinati politici*, b. 874, "Rodini, Isolina."

[30] *Carabinieri* of Milano to *questura* of Como, March 16, 1929, in *confinati politici*, b. 64, "Barindelli Caterina"; prefect of Como to MI, March 9, 1929, and *questore* to prefect of Como, 26 March 1929, in ACS, *confinati politici*, b. 64, "Barindelli, Caterina."

[31] See telegram of prefect of Vercelli D'Eufemia to Capo del Governo, January 1, 1928, ACS, *confinati politici*, b. 949, "Sicbaldi, Ettore."

a deterrent by spreading fear and apprehension.[32] In Rome, for example, a wiretap set at a restaurant for a political operation caught one waitress telling another that there was "a terrible penalty" in place for abortion. "Mussolini himself put this penalty in place," she warned her friend, "and that's the trouble; if they come to suspect, we're fried."[33] Police also regularly reported on the public's impressions following the arrest and punishment of all political detainees, including midwives and doctors. In a small town in Bologna province, the punishment of abortionists was "well received, not only in the *comune*, but also in nearby [districts] and even Bologna." In the city of Bologna, the neighbor of a doctor who ran a clandestine abortion clinic out of his home in a respectable, bourgeois apartment complex went to the police after reading an article about the demographic campaign in the newspaper.[34] In Como, the "mainstream elements and fathers of families" led a "crusade" against a midwife suspected of performing abortions.[35] The regime thus appears to have tapped into a well of local hostility toward persons who provided abortions. At the same time, local people sometimes defended midwives, protesting their arrest. After all, these doctors and midwives provided other valuable services (including abortion) to poor, working-class women, who sorely missed their medical services. However, authorities characterized the authors of such protests as persons of "dubious morality" and even as "accomplices" in the nefarious activities of abortionists. The "mainstream" or "right-thinking" elements invariably held contempt for suspected abortionists, according to police.[36] Meanwhile, pragmatic southern prefects vigorously campaigned to have these political detainees sent to their provinces, which were often completely bereft of medical professionals.

The use of explicitly "political" repression against abortion, a completely apolitical act that the regime nevertheless believed impeded

---

[32] Triolo's interviews with midwives working in Sicily under Fascism bears out the hypothesis that police surveillance and sanctions served as a deterrent. Triolo writes "my own informants, which included an abortionist and women who casually helped at birth, admitted that fear caused them to limit their activities, though none had had a run-in with the law"; Triolo, "Angel-makers," 156.

[33] "Mozza, Elisa," in ACS, *confinati politici*, b. 696.

[34] *Questore* to prefect of Bologna, February 28, 1928, in ACS, *confinati politici*, b. 189, "Canova, Clementina"; see also n. 25.

[35] Prefect of Como to DGPS, October 27, 1928, in *confinati politici*, b. 960, "Soldati, Giovanna."

[36] See, e.g., the petition signed by the heads of families of Rome's Celio rione (San Giovanni in Laterano) for the release of a doctor assigned confino in ACS, *confinati politici*, b. 601, "Mammuccari, Nicola."

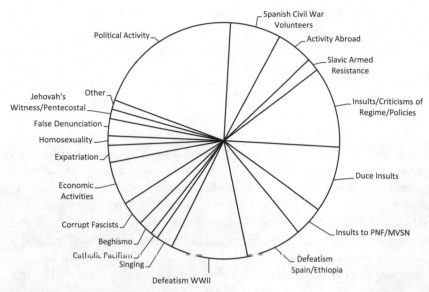

FIGURE 9. Political Confinement Sentences, 1935–1943 (388 cases from the sample of 549).

national renovation, sheds light on the use of political confinement during the 1930s. Beginning in 1935, Mussolini's police state began punishing a widening array of "offenses" unrelated to organized opposition (see Figure 9), most commonly committed by Italians with no history of political activity.[37] Only about one-fifth of the detainees were suspected of engaging in deliberate, sustained, organized opposition inside of Italy.[38] A small, though significant, minority was punished for suspected homosexuality, interracial sex, pedophilia, the practice of the Pentecostal and Jehovah's Witnesses religions, and violations of the economic prohibitions contained in the racial laws. Police punished the largest group (approximately 40% of the sample) for offensive speech or gestures: insults to Mussolini, Fascists, or militiamen; criticisms of domestic and

---

[37] Of the entire sample of 388 cases for this period, police identified 235 as "without political precedents" and, of these, 99 as "apolitical."

[38] I have designated "anti-Fascist political activity" as attempts to reconstitute the PCI (23), Justice and Liberty (9), or Masonry (2); contributions in favor of political detainees or the Spanish Republic (13); distribution or possession of propaganda (6); displays of flags, graffiti, or other anti-Fascist symbols (8); pro-German, pro-Hitler propaganda (6) in Trentino Alto-Adige; and house searches that revealed significant anti-Fascist propaganda or writings (10).

foreign policies; and expressions of "defeatism" with regard to the Ethiopian invasion, the Spanish Civil War, and the Second World War.

Of the people confined for politically offensive comments or gestures, very few had any history of political activity (anti-Fascist or otherwise).[39] Police largely targeted manual laborers, peasants, and, occasionally, white-collar workers, teachers, or other Italians from the lower-middle classes. Rarely were solidly middle- or upper-class Italians sentenced to confinement for trifling speech offenses, or any other behavior for that matter, save organized anti-Fascism or violations of the regime's economic policies. A disproportionate number of these detainees had histories of criminality, unemployment, alcoholism, and mental illness.[40] Many belonged to the Fascist Party.[41] Finally, more so than in the previous period, these detainees came from all over Italy. From the northernmost reaches of Piedmont and Trentino Alto-Adige, to the southern coasts of Sardinia, Calabria, and Sicily, the regime imposed a superficially uniform culture of political repression upon significant swaths of Italian society.

Defending the Cult of the Duce

In Agliè, a town thirty miles outside of Turin, a manual laborer named Antonino Prospero walked into the Trattoria Savoia carrying a live rabbit. He set the rabbit down on a table, gave it a slap on its haunches, and said, "Move it, Mussolini!" Two *carabinieri* witnessed the incident and promptly arrested Antonino. Investigating his past, police learned that both of Antonino's parents had died when he was still young, his father from alcoholism. He attended elementary school up to the fifth grade but had never excelled in his studies. He fought and was wounded

---

[39] Of 164 such cases, only 27 had "political precedents," i.e., they had once belonged to an anti-Fascist party or were known to hold ideas "contrary to the regime." Meanwhile, another 117 detainees had "no political precedents," meaning that they had never belonged to a "subversive" political party or engaged in anti-Fascist activity, and most had never "held ideas hostile to the regime," though some, police discovered upon investigation, were suspected of holding "subversive" or "Communist" beliefs. In short, most detainees sentenced for spontaneous insults and criticism had been uninvolved in anti-Fascist militancy.

[40] Of the 388 cases sampled from this period, sixty-six were alcoholics or at least drunk at the time of their offense. Ninety-one were ex-convicts or *pregiudicati*. Police identified thirty as unemployed, but the real number is probably greater. Twenty-seven had histories of mental illness.

[41] Fifty-nine belonged to the Fascist Party, including the twenty-one detainees sentenced due to corruption scandals or factional fighting within the PNF and its institutions.

in the First World War and had been punished several times for insubordination. After the war, Antonino drifted in and out of employment, never holding a job for very long; he had also been convicted of robbery and several other crimes against property. Police described him as "violent," "lazy," "alcoholic," and "fond of women," which explained why he suffered from "several venereal diseases, probably even syphilis." Though married, he lived separate from his wife, due largely to "his violent character." He now passed most of his days drinking in the company of "ex-convicts and alcoholics." Until the arrival of Fascism, he "professed advanced socialists ideas," but in recent years he had exhibited "indifference to the regime."[42] Without pondering the actual meaning of Antonino Prospero's remark to his rabbit, the police sentenced him to one year of political exile, which he served in the province of Matera.

Above all else, the Fascist project of totalitarian transformation was predicated on Mussolini's role as the infallible Duce of Fascism. The figure of Mussolini, like that of Hitler in Germany or Stalin in the USSR, held special valence in Fascist Italy. If Fascism was a "new, secular religion," replete with its own holidays, myths, rituals, and monuments, then the "symbolic universe" of the Fascist cult "centered upon the myth and cult of the Duce."[43] Over the course of the dictatorship, and particularly during the 1930s, the real and symbolic power of Mussolini within the party and state grew, becoming codified in law at each stage.[44] As the Duce's authoritarian power grew, fewer institutions inhibited his autocratic policy making. After 1935, his cabinet and the Grand Council of Fascism rarely met. In 1938, Mussolini had himself named First Marshall of the Empire, a status suggesting a military rank equal to that of King Victor Emanuel. Increasingly, Mussolini paid less attention to old-guard Fascists and advisers and demonstrated less concern for public opinion regarding his policies. The objective, to which his personal power was the means, was to instill Italians with an absolute faith in their "Leader." The "cult of the Duce" was propagated mainly by the party. During his tenure as PNF secretary, Augusto Turati (1926–31) began promoting Mussolini as Fascism's unifying figure, but it was Achile Starace (1931–9) who created the many new "rituals and formulae of devotion" that virtually deified

---

[42] See reports of *carabinieri* and *questore* of Turin, in ACS, *confinati politici*, b. 33, "Antonino, Prospero."

[43] See Emilio Gentile, *The Sacralization of Politics*, trans. Keith Botsford (Cambridge, MA, 1996), 132–52.

[44] Ibid., 135.

il Duce. Consequently, in the 1930s, for many ordinary Italians, Fascism and Mussolini became indistinguishable.[45]

The representation of the Duce as a secular god, a man of infallible genius and extraordinary abilities, who held the nation's destiny in his hands, necessitated the suppression of even the most casual insults, or blasphemy, directed against his person. Accordingly, a consistent thrust of political repression targeted Italians who expressed explicit or even indirect criticisms of Mussolini. Provincial commissions inflicted political confinement on Italians who called Mussolini a "pig" (*porco*), a "stinkpot" (*puzzolente*), a "villain," a "criminal," a "do-nothing," or an "imbecile." In the late 1920s, Duce offenders were predominantly anti-Fascists (e.g., Communists, anarchists, and Socialists), whose offenses were compounded by professions of their own political faith. For instance, in August 1927, Nicola Antonini, a manual laborer, stood in the main piazza of Cantalupo, a town fifty miles northeast of Rome, and yelled, "We're all reds, down with that pig Mussolini," leading to his arrest. Antonini, according to police, was an ex-convict and a "terrible subversive" who had "professed communist ideas" for many years.[46]

During the second half of the 1930s, the punishment of "offenses to the Duce" increased in relative and absolute terms.[47] Moreover, after 1934, such sentences were more commonly inflicted on Italians with no prior history of political activism or beliefs.[48] In Caltanisetta (Sicily), for example, a fifty-five-year-old drunken vegetable vendor with a long criminal record was arrested by the OVRA (secret political police) for saying "Mussolini's starving us, and we can't go on any longer; we'll need a revolution if this doesn't finish soon."[49] In Potenza, a drunken, unemployed music conductor at a café told two police officials that they should arrest Mussolini, whom he blamed for his unemployment.[50] After arresting the *maestro di musica*, a search of his pockets revealed a small metal effigy of the Duce, a sign of either a certain devotion to Mussolini or else a calculated conformity to his leadership cult.

---

[45] Ibid., 143–52, esp. 150–1.

[46] *Carabinieri* of Rome to Provincial Commission, August 6, 1927, in ACS, *confinati politici*, b. 33, "Tancredi, Nicola."

[47] The sample had 12 sentences involving an offense to the Duce between 1926 and 1934; 35 between 1935 and 1943.

[48] Of 12 cases before 1935, 8 had political precedents. After 1935, of 35 Duce offenders, 3 had histories of "subversive" political activity. Thirty-one had no political precedents or known political opinions.

[49] ACS, *confinati politici*, b. 1021, "Tramontana, Onofrio."

[50] ACS, *confinati politici*, b. 613, "Maranzana, Giuseppe."

Certainly the "political" nature of these "Duce offenses" cannot be easily separated from the drunkenness, unemployment, and criminal precedents of their authors. The strong, orderly, disciplined society that Fascism aspired to engineer had no place for drunks, the work-shy, "habitual" criminals, or erratic iconoclasts. To the regime, their disrespect for the Duce of Fascism was symptomatic of other character flaws or physical defects that rendered them ill-suited for the future Fascist utopia.

War, Empire, and the Axis

After Mussolini's person, ordinary Italians were most likely to criticize his regime's foreign policy. For the first ten years of Fascist government, the Duce's expansionist ambitions remained largely confined to bellicose rhetoric at home. In foreign affairs, Benito Mussolini the statesman regularly assured Britain, France, and the League of Nations that Italy meant to play the role of a dignified mediator. There were just a few exceptions. In August 1923, Mussolini ordered the Italian navy to bombard Corfu after blaming Greece for the death of an Italian general in Albania. Later, during the 1930s, in Libya, the Italian military arguably committed genocide, using poison gas, concentration camps, and forced marches across the desert to crush resistance to Fascist rule in Cyrenaica. Although at home Mussolini railed against France and Britain for making Italy a "prisoner" in the Mediterranean, his foreign diplomacy aimed at ingratiating Italy into the concert of great European powers. For Mussolini to achieve any of his expansionist goals, it seemed, he would have to deal with the Western democracies.

In 1933, the rise of National Socialism in Germany radically altered the diplomatic landscape of Europe. On the one hand, Hitler represented a challenge for Mussolini, who desperately wanted to avoid German unification with Austria. A mammoth, revanchist Germany on Italy's northern border represented a national security threat, and, at the very least, would make it increasingly difficult for Italy to govern and assimilate the large German population of Trentino-Alto Adige (Sud Tirol), a province acquired from Austria in 1919 and subjected to a harsh campaign of "Italianization" from the mid-1920s onward.[51] In July 1934, in a failed coup attempt, Austrian Nazis murdered Engelbert Dollfuss,

---

[51] Andrea di Michele, "Un prodromo emblematico: l'italianizzazione forzata del Sudtirolo, 1922–43," *Qualestoria* 30:1 (2002): 37–43.

the Christian Social chancellor of Austria, and a client of Mussolini. In response, Mussolini mobilized four divisions and moved military equipment to the border.[52] Subsequently, provincial commissions in the northeastern provinces (Trento, Bolzano, and Belluno) regularly sentenced ethnic Germans to political confinement for "antinational" (German) or pro-Nazi activities.[53] On the other hand, Hitler's bold, revisionist foreign policy opened up considerable diplomatic space for Fascist Italy to pursue territorial expansion, despite British or French opposition. For example, in the summer of 1935, with Hitler already dismantling the Versailles Treaty by rebuilding the German military, a diplomatic crisis erupted when Britain resisted agreeing upon terms by which Italy might take possession of Ethiopia. The conflict set Mussolini on a path that threatened to fatally undermine Italy's otherwise good relations with the Western democracies. By September, the League of Nations was threatening sanctions should Italy invade. Though perhaps not decisive, encouraging words from Hitler regarding the future of Italo-German relations may have further emboldened Mussolini to proceed with war against Ethiopia.[54]

Many historians believe that the invasion of Ethiopia, the League of Nations sanctions, and the Declaration of Empire won Mussolini great popularity among Italians. At the same time, the Ethiopian war poisoned relations with Great Britain, and moved Italy closer to Germany, a development that would prove increasingly unpopular. In October 1936, months after Mussolini and Hitler had sent military support to General Franco's Nationalists, foreign ministers Joachim von Ribbentrop and Galeazzo Ciano signed a treaty of friendship, leading Mussolini to describe Italy and Germany as an "axis" around which the rest of Europe revolved. In May 1939, the two powers committed to a formal alliance, a "Pact of Steel," as Mussolini later described it. The alliance would ultimately draw Italy into the Second World War, with disastrous consequences.

Between 1935 and 1943, support for these developments became mandatory for ordinary Italians. Nearly 20 percent of political confinement sentences in this period punished Italians for "defeatism" and other criticisms of the Duce's foreign policy. A common criticism of Mussolini's

---

[52] Renzo de Felice, *Mussolini il duce, 1929–1936*, I:501.
[53] Ten cases involved some sort of pro-German "antinational" activities, mostly from the provinces of Bolzano, Trento, and Belluno.
[54] Bosworth, *Mussolini*, 303.

Ethiopia invasion underscored the absurdity of conquering Africa when life remained so bleak in many parts of Italy. In his memoir *Christ Stopped at Eboli*, Carlo Levi recalled the reaction of Lucania's impoverished peasantry to the war in Abyssinia. "If they have money enough for a war, why don't they repair the bridge across the Agri," complained one peasant. "They might make a dam or provide us with more fountains, or plant young trees instead of cutting down the few that are left. We've plenty of land right here, but nothing to go with it."[55] Hundreds of miles away, in the extreme northeast of Italy, an impoverished street vendor stood in a piazza and posed the same question to a group of men: "It would be better if the millions that are being spent for this overseas expedition were used to carry out works here in the kingdom."[56] In two other cases, Italians hearing about the abolition of slavery in Ethiopia suggested that Mussolini should do the same in Italy![57] Despite the popularity of the Duce's adventure in Ethiopia, some Italians clearly opposed it.

The spike in political repression around 1935 should not be interpreted solely as a reaction to popular dissent to the war in Ethiopia or any other single policy. For the Fascist regime, coercion constituted a style of rule. New policies required new types of repression. The previous year, in a speech delivered in Rome and reprinted in *Il popolo d'Italia*, Mussolini bluntly declared that anti-Fascism was "dead." The new "internal enemy" of the Fascist revolution, he continued, was the *"spirito borghese"* (bourgeois spirit). For Mussolini, "bourgeois" was not necessarily a socioeconomic category; it was "a spirit of skepticism and accommodation, a tendency toward compromise, the comfortable life, careerism." The bourgeois was someone who believed that "there is nothing left to do, that enthusiasm is a nuisance, that the parades are too many, that it is now time to settle down, that one child is enough, that the household budget is the most supreme of all necessities."[58] Mussolini called for a "continuous revolution" in order to advance the "physical and moral transformation of the Italian people." The result, he claimed, would produce "integral fascists, that is to say born, raised and living entirely in our environment, provided with those virtues that confer on a people the privilege of primacy in the world." Fascism now had to

---

55 Carlo Levi, *Christ Stopped at Eboli*, trans. Frances Frenaye (New York, 1996), 133.
56 *Carabinieri* of Bolzano (Belluno) to general command, 9 October 1935, in ACS, *confinati politici*, b. 271, "Colotto, Riccardo."
57 ACS, *confinati politici*, b. 211, "Carturan, Giuseppe"; b. 271, "Colotto, Riccardo."
58 Mussolini, OO, XXVI:192.

exercise the strictest vigilance on the line dividing the "sacred" from the "profane" in order to preserve the "moral prestige of the regime." "One word, one reminiscence, one proposition, will be enough to make us suspicious," Mussolini warned ominously, "and the climate will be increasingly harsh." He concluded, "The latecomers, the irresolute, the nostalgic, we will leave them at the side of the road," and "the Italian people will go forward under the sign of the Littorio, which signifies unity, will, discipline."[59]

The echoes of such speeches resound in the files of detainees. A truck driver in Gorizia, for example, expressed feelings closely approximating the bourgeois complacency Mussolini so despised. "My belly's full," he exclaimed, "and if Mussolini wants land he can go conquer it himself; I don't want to go, nor will I." His outburst earned him three years political exile in the province of Matera.[60] Even mocking skepticism constituted defeatism. In the province of Fiume, a soldier buying a newspaper remarked to a store clerk, "our troops are advancing in East Africa." The clerk, Francesco Radan, responded, "Slowly though, because there are times when they want to turn back!" Radan was no anti-Fascist but had been convicted of several common crimes in the past. Moreover, his reputation, according to "public opinion," was "not good." After squandering his wife's dowry he left her to live with a married woman who had separated from her own husband.[61] Finally, like most Slavs who landed in prison or *confino politico*, Radan was alleged to be a "Slavophile" and "anti-Italian." Police sent Radan off to exile in Potenza, seemingly more for his "immorality" and "antinational" character than his relatively innocuous quip about the troops. In similar cases, Italians who were somehow already compromised politically, socially, or ethnically fell victim to police sanctions for essentially idle chatter about the war. Police punished Italians for spreading "false information" about the war, which included stories of lost battles, casualties, and war crimes.[62] In Lecce (Puglia), police condemned a poor, fifty-four-year-old merchant named Pietro Brunetti to five years confinement for mistakenly offering his condolences to the wife of a militiaman, who had not actually died. His gesture, as interpreted by local authorities, constituted a deliberate

---

[59] Ibid., XXVI:192–3.
[60] See personal file of "D'Andrea Antonio," in ACS, *confinati politici*, b. 313.
[61] *Carabinieri* of Fiume, January 1, 1936, in ACS, *confinati politici*, b. 841, "Radan, Francesco."
[62] ACS, *confinati politici*, b. 367, "Dobrilla Vittorio"; *carabinieri* of Vicenza, October 1935, in ibid.

attempt to depress morale and disseminate defeatism. Besides, Brunetti had a criminal history and his brother was a Communist.[63] In addition to punishing dissent, therefore, political repression also began targeting the attitudes and behaviors Mussolini deemed antithetical to his vision of a stoic, bellicose Italy.[64] With Italy's involvement in an increasing number of military conflicts, the punishment of such expressions of "defeatism" only became more common.

Although the Ethiopian war may have increased Mussolini's popularity, the Italian intervention in the Spanish Civil War proved quite divisive. Carlo Rosselli and several Italian Communists played a leading role in recruiting and organizing foreign anti-Fascist volunteers who fought for the Spanish Republic. Spain offered many anti-Fascists an opportunity to take up arms against Mussolini's regime by proxy. At home, political sanctions punished Italians who expressed sympathy for the Republic, deemed the Nationalists' cause unjust, lamented Italy's making war on workers, or discussed Nationalist setbacks.[65] Predicting that the Republic would prevail or that Barcelona would never fall were similarly deemed defeatist.[66] Italians caught listening to Radio Barcelona or other foreign radio broadcasts for news about Spain were accused of trafficking in "defeatist propaganda."[67] As with Ethiopia, spreading "tendentious information" about the war, even if it was true, constituted a political offense.[68] Italians suspected of organizing material support – usually donating a few lira in a bar – for the International Brigades were similarly the subject of intense police investigations and repression. Finally, after the defeat of the Spanish Republic, hundreds of Italians fled across the Spanish border, only to be interned by French authorities. Approximately 750 of them were repatriated to Italy, where police immediately deported them to political confinement colonies.[69]

---

[63] *Carabinieri* of Lecce, February 9, 1936, in ACS, *confinati politici*, b. 158, "Brunetti, Pietro."

[64] Twelve individuals from the sample were sentenced to *confino politico* for criticizing the war in Ethiopia. However, many more sentences were motivated by criticisms of the MVSN's performance in Ethiopia or figures and institutions with regard to the war.

[65] Fifteen cases in the sample were assigned for *defeatism* with regard to the Spanish Civil War.

[66] ACS, *confinati politici*, b. 517, "Gubernati, Alberto."

[67] See e.g., b. 108, "Bianchi, Augusto"; b. 247, "Chittaro, Ampellio"; b 505, "Graziosio, Linceo"; b. 265, "Colizzi, Ernesto"; b. 913, "Santurri, Mario."

[68] See, e.g., b. 799, "Pinna, Giovanni"; b, 895, "Russo, Salvatore"; b. 955, "Sinigaglia, Licurgo."

[69] There were 27 cases of 388 from the sample during the years 1935–43.

Some historians have argued that until as late as 1939, Mussolini positioned Italy diplomatically between the Western democracies and Nazi Germany, aspiring to act as a sort of "decisive weight" (*peso determinante*) in European diplomacy.[70] Whether true or not – and it seems unlikely – even ordinary Italians understood that Mussolini's real enemies were France and Britain. In the late 1930s, Mussolini and other Fascists stoked hatred for the European democracies, while disparaging Italian "xenophiles" (*esterofili*) who fretted that the Italian military was no match for that of Britain or France. "According to them," Mussolini told party leaders in 1938, "Italy is a small, poor country that must go to the school of French democracy and British aristocracy." Mussolini defiantly declared that he would dispel "the residual skepticisms of those fools [in Italy] and abroad who prefer the carefree, disordered, amusing, mandolin playing Italy of the past and not the organized, strong, taciturn, and powerful [Italy] of the Fascist era."[71] Many Italians thus understandably viewed war with England and France as highly likely, if not inevitable, and harbored a deep cynicism about Italy's chances in such a conflict. In Salerno, for example, a squad chief of the Fascist MVSN noticed two men engaged in an animated discussion in a public park. Upon moving closer, he heard one of the men say, "Italy is a poor state, incapable of sustaining a war against rich and powerful France. Italy is by now a vassal of Germany." The man spent the next four years in a small southern village.[72] Even before the outbreak of the Second World War, criticisms of Mussolini's foreign policy had become such a serious problem that the OVRA, once responsible solely for the repression of militant anti-Fascism, had been deployed to police everyday grumblings. Police subjected parks, piazzas, cafés, and other public spaces to increased surveillance, on the lookout for "defeatist" or "antinational" chatter. In 1939, the Sicilian OVRA investigated a group of middle-class professionals in Trapani, who gathered regularly at the Caffé Impero to discuss the Duce's foreign policy.[73] One of the men routinely engaged in particularly

---

[70] De Felice, *Mussolini il duce*, I:378; *Mussolini il duce*, II:681–2.

[71] Preface to "Il Gran Consiglio nei primi quindici anni dell'Era Fascista" (1938), in Mussolini, OO, XXIX:117.

[72] *Questore* to prefect of Salerno, October 6, 1938, in ACS, *confinati politici*, b. 703, "Napoli, Vincenzo."

[73] *Questore* to prefect of Trapani, October 10, 1939, in ACS, *confinati politici*, b. 343, "De Nobili, Gino." For similar cases, see b. 183, "Campelli, Oreste"; b. 319, "De Angelis, Mario"; b. 523, "Gusella, Secondo"; b. 763, "Patrioli, Angelo"; b. 799, "Pinfari, don Giuseppe."

strident criticisms, thus providing OVRA agents with "concrete proof of his inability to adapt himself to the new climate of the Fascist Revolution." According to the *questore*, "A severe police measure" was an "urgent necessity, not only as a just castigation of the anti-Fascist act that he committed, but also so that the example will serve as a discouraging lesson to others."[74]

Autarky

With the onset of war in Ethiopia, the regime also began to suppress what police officials characterized as "economic defeatism." The extreme politicization of select economic policies was not new. In 1925, Mussolini had launched the "battle for the lira" and the "battle for grain." Besides strengthening the Italian economy and making Italy self-sufficient in cereals, both campaigns served as nationalist propaganda. They were depicted as epic, militaristic struggles upon which the survival of the Italian nation depended. The *battaglia del grano* (battle for grain), for example, would "free the Italian people from the slavery of foreign bread."[75] Over time, the regime introduced price controls, protectionist quotas, prohibitions on imports, and currency controls for similar purposes. These showpieces of Fascist economic policy coalesced in May 1936, when Mussolini proclaimed "autarky," a program promoting total economic self-sufficiency. Introduced in response to the sanctions inflicted by the League of Nations, autarky intensified and expanded the protectionist policies introduced during the preceding period.

From its earliest years, the apparatus of political repression made considerable efforts to uncover violations of monetary, trade, and commercial laws the regime saw as vital to its program.[76] During the period from 1926 to 1934, provincial commissions punished suspected moneylenders and even presidents of banks whose institutions had failed, largely to mollify public anger when Fascist financial policy and the world economic

---

[74] *Questore* to prefect of Trapani, October 10, 1939, in ACS, *confinati politici*, b. 343, "De Nobili, Gino."

[75] Mussolini, OO, XXI:377–8.

[76] Not counting cases of corruption among Fascist and state officials, about 35 of the 549 cases sampled involved economic activity related to banking, money lending, currency exchange, illegal or clandestine importation of foodstuffs, raw materials, and other products, wartime rationing, and the black market. Projecting from the sample, the total number of *confino politico* sentences for these types of offenses would thus have been around 900.

downturn had lowered salaries, bringing hardship to many Italians.[77] Bank presidents in particular served as scapegoats. Though guiltless of any crime, the regime inflicted "political" punishments on them in order to deflect its own responsibility for the economy. Police also noted with approval how quick, streamlined punishment demonstrated Fascism's ability to act where the liberal judicial system would have done nothing.[78]

War in Ethiopia also brought the intensification of political repression in the economic sphere. Producers or merchants suspected of price fixing, hoarding, or selling on the black market fell under police scrutiny.[79] With the introduction of autarky, the regime established a Central Collection Office (Ufficio Centrale Amasso) for agricultural products.[80] Small producers, mistrustful of turning their crops over to a centralized authority often sold them on the black market instead. Large authorized distributors also traded grain and other agricultural products off the books; this practice only increased the mistrust with which small producers viewed the whole system.[81] Similar controls affected central markets selling fish, meat, and produce, and the regime punished small vendors who attempted to circumvent regulations.[82] Yet another area of economic activity subject to close surveillance was currency exchange. For Mussolini, according to one historian, the control of currency was "a veritable obsession, and the pivot of his entire economic policy."[83] In 1927, he established the "Quota Novanta," which fixed the Italian currency at a rate of ninety lira to one pound sterling, its value at the time of the March on Rome. Later, in 1934,

---

[77] See case of "Montemaggi, Antonio," ACS, *confinati politici*, b. 685.

[78] The collapse of the Neapolitan Banca di Credito Meridionale in 1928, according to the *questura* of Naples, had "grave repercussions on the southern economy, especially among the rural classes... undermining the Regime's efforts to safeguard savings as a principle factor in the well-being of the Nation." Judicial authorities had no evidence with which to prosecute the bank's president, Mario Bossi. However, the *questore* assured the prefect that Bossi's guilt was "beyond doubt." Provincial commissions similarly sentenced dozens of other bank directors from 1928 to 1930. But unlike most detainees, the bank directors were sent to mainland villages, including Amalfi, a picturesque Mediterranean resort town near Salerno. See *questore* (De Martino) to prefect of Naples, "Proposta di assegnazione al confino a carico di Bossi Mario," November 28, 1928, in ACS, *confinati politici*, b. 143, "Bossi, Mario." See also: b. 313, "D'Ammacco" and b. 1069, "Viola, Giovanni."

[79] See ACS, *confinati politici*, b. 721, "Odetti, Giovanni Battista" and b. 523, "Melchiore, Gunetti."

[80] Shepard B. Clough, *The Economic History of Modern Italy* (New York, 1964), 257.

[81] *Questore* of Bergamo (Monarca) to prefect of Bergamo, October 2, 1936, in ACS, *confinati politici*, b. 823, "Pozzoli, Goffredo."

[82] See, e.g., ACS, *confinati politici*, b. 607, "Manna, Salvatore."

[83] Shepard B. Clough, *Economic History*, 225–30.

the regime introduced legislation that funneled all currency exchanges through the Istituto Italiano Cambi. Italians were prohibited from sending or keeping lira abroad, except as payment in legitimate, authorized business transactions. Between 1936 and 1939, provincial commissions meted out approximately two hundred political confinement sentences for illegal foreign currency trades and illegitimate acquisitions of foreign products with lira.[84]

Provincial police chiefs characterized all of these illegal economic activities as "antinational," "defeatist" "sabotage," and contradictory to the "new commercial spirit" engendered by Fascism. Although these crimes could have been punished with judicial proceedings, police sanctions, according to one official, served as "an example, especially by the rapidity with which they are applied."[85] Therefore, as with the suppression of so many other activities, political police sanctions were not just applied in lieu of criminal proceedings but also when timely punishment would send a clear message to other potential offenders.

Border Fascism

In some regions and among some groups – the Slavic population of northeastern Italy, for example – the Fascist repressive apparatus struck more forcefully. Under the liberal and Fascist regimes, Slovenian and Croatian minorities living in the newly acquired region of Venezia Giulia were viewed as a problem, a dangerous foreign presence in a border region. The solution, Italians from all over the political spectrum agreed, was for Slavic minorities to assimilate into the Italian nation. The Slavs, most Italian commentators believed, possessed an inferior culture, while the superior Italian civilization (*civiltà*) had, since the time of ancient Rome, always had great success in integrating small minorities.[86] From the time that Italy took possession of Venezia Giulia, and also the predominantly German Alto-Adige, in 1918, liberal governments pledged to respect the

---

[84] See cases of b. 23, "Amici, Natale" (August 1939, Genova); b. 319, "De Angelis" (February 1939, Rome); b. 391, "Fano, Ugo," (January 1939, Rome/Turin); b. 463, "Gaudioso, Francesco" (November 1935, Napoli); b. 847, "Rapuzzi, Enrico" (August 1938, Milan/Bergamo); b. 997, "Tavecchia, Oreste" (June 1936, Milan); b. 1081, "Zaccaria Bortolo" (June 1939, Padova/Milan).

[85] *Questore* (Monarca) to prefect of Bergamo, October 2, 1936, in ACS, *confinati politici*, b. 823, "Pozzoli, Goffredo."

[86] Glenda Sluga, *The Problem of Trieste and the Italo-Yugoslav Border: Difference, Identity and Sovereignty in Twentieth-Century Europe* (Albany, 2001), 41–7.

language, culture, and rights of ethnic minorities. In practice, however, occupation authorities, state officials, and the central government began Italianizing these regions.[87] In their interactions with the Slavic population, bureaucrats, white-collar workers, police, and postal officials, without any provocation, began discriminating against Slovenes and Croats. Military officers, judges, and postal carriers arbitrarily banned the use of Slavic languages. Judges in Trieste spontaneously decided to ignore petitions to the court in Slovenian and Croatian and to ban their use in court proceedings. Postal workers simply threw out letters addressed in Slavic languages. At government offices, telegrams in Slovenian or Croatian were tossed, while those in German, French, English, or even Japanese were received in normal fashion. The central government ordered the transfers of Slavic civil servants, teachers, and priests who caused trouble by resisting this unofficial campaign of denationalization.[88]

The Fascist squads and, later, the regime, transformed these informal prejudices and practices of anti-Slavic discrimination into a violent, coordinated campaign of "cultural genocide."[89] The goal of local Fascists and the regime's central leadership was to achieve, within a very short period of time, a complete denationalization and Italianization of Venezia Giulia, eliminating all traces of Slavic language and culture. Beginning in 1923, Fascist legislation called for the Italianization of street names and monuments. Foreign-language publications had to publish Italian translations, and instruction in foreign languages was banned. Between 1924 and 1927, the regime forcibly converted hundreds of Croatian and Slovenian primary schools into Italian-language schools. Hundreds of schoolteachers who continued to teach in Slovenian or Croatian were arrested and removed to other parts of Italy. Language examinations served further to weed out civil servants and teachers who were unable or unwilling to speak Italian. In 1926, the regime decreed that Slavic surnames be changed to Italian-sounding ones. From 1926 onward, the forcible assimilation of minorities intensified, with the regime ordering police and *carabinieri* to shut down Slavic associations, search for illegal foreign-language publications, and break up groups that resisted Italianization.[90]

---

[87] Annamaria Vinci, "Il fascismo al confine orientale," in *Storia d'Italia: Le regioni dall'unità ad oggi*, vol. 17.1: *il Friuli-Venezia Giulia*, ed. Roberto Finzi, Claudio Magris, and Giovanni Miccoli (Turin, 2002), 394.

[88] Bartolini, *Fascismo antislavo*, 72–4.

[89] Ibid., 64; also, Enzo Collotti, "Sul razzismo antislavo," in *Nel nome della razza: Il razzismo nella storia d'Italia, 1870–1945*, ed. Alberto Burgio, 33–61.

[90] Sluga, *Problem of Trieste*, 47–8.

Once the regime had destroyed virtually all organizations and associations that bound ethnic Slavs together, only the Catholic Church remained. Slavic Church hierarchs, local priests, and churches constituted the last bulwark of Slavic languages and identity. In the wake of the First World War, even before the arrival of Fascism, the liberal state prevented the return of many Slavic priests to their parishes. With the arrival of Fascism in 1919, *squadrists*, nationalists, and soldiers attacked, harassed, and protested Slavic Church hierarchs. Fascists broke into the home of one bishop, sacked it, and forced him to resign. Fascists beat priests, destroyed churches, and defaced the images and monuments to Slavic saints. This type of activity continued throughout the 1920s and 1930s.[91] The eradication of Slavic culture from Venezia-Giulia garnered support from the Vatican. In 1930, Article 22 of the Concordat between Mussolini's government and the Vatican banned the use of any language besides Italian in Catholic services. The Vatican and Italian Catholic Church also removed, retired, or transferred out of Venezia Giulia any bishops, archbishops, and clergy deemed resistant to the Italian state's denationalization campaign. The Italian state, meanwhile, sentenced other "pro-Slav" clergy to *confino di polizia*. Instructors at seminary schools were removed or replaced. Into all of these vacant positions, the church installed nationalist or Fascist clergy, who viewed Italianization of Venezia Giulia as the mission of the church.[92]

The violence and rapidity with which the regime attempted to suffocate Slavic culture provoked strong, militant, organized resistance. Accordingly, the level of political repression in Venezia Giulia, particularly in cities like Trieste, where Italians and Slavs lived and worked in close proximity, was much higher. Although Slavs constituted a small minority of the Italian population, they constituted a full 10 percent of persons tried by the Special Tribunal. Forty of the tribunal's sixty-five death sentences were passed against Slavs. In the years before the war, five of the nine persons executed were Slovenes or Croats.[93] A similar pattern existed with *confino* sentences. Police commissions in Friuli-Venezia Giulia passed over one-tenth of all *confino* politico sentences.[94] The Provincial Commission of Trieste alone passed the third-highest number

---

[91] Bartolini, *Fascismo antislavo*, 102–4.

[92] Ibid., 109–15.

[93] These data are in ibid., 99n289, and were originally compiled in Sergio Dini, "Il tribunale speciale per la difesa dello stato e l'irredentismo jugoslavo," in *Qualestoria* 32:1 (2004): 65–80; see also Aquarone, *Organizzazione*, 103.

[94] Approximately 1,200. See Dal Pont and Carolini, *L'Italia al Confino*, 535.

of political sentences (585), considerably behind the commissions of Rome (1,482) and Milan (839) but ahead of those of Turin (507) and Bologna (544).[95]

Like most ordinary political crime in Fascist Italy, confinement sentences in Venezia Giulia often punished speech offenses. However, near Italy's border with Yugoslavia, the Fascist regime was engaged in a campaign to eradicate the culture of a clearly defined ethnic "other." Merely speaking a Slavic language, or otherwise publicly or privately exhibiting some form of Slavic cultural identity, was intrinsically antinational and anti-Fascist. So, for example, groups or individuals singing "popular songs" in Slovenian automatically came under suspicion. In the town of Prosecco (Trieste), one group of young men had drunk "abundantly" at a *trattoria* and "intoned in Slavic language songs exalting Slavism." Though the men had no history of political activity, singing these songs rendered them dangerous to "the national interest, given their irredentist sentiments and, therefore, hostility to the Italian nation."[96] In the eyes of authorities, the content of speech offenses was often corroborated by the form, not to mention the ethnicity of their authors. In another example, Luigi Sain sang a popular Slovenian song with an "irredentist bent." The offending lines, according to *carabinieri*, went "Slovenians, our voices cry as passionately as our hearts beat strongly for our people." The *questore* of Trieste, Peruzzi, denounced Sain for political confinement largely because "manifestations of a subversive and irredentist nature" were "unfortunately common in the small *comune* of Dan Dorligo della Valle," where the population was primarily Slavic.[97] In another example, police registered one Slovenian with absolutely no history of political activity as "of Slovenian origin" and "against Italy and the Regime." Other Italians of Slavic ethnicity drew attention for having large collections of Slavic language publications, refusing to speak Italian, or shunning the company of other Italians. Ermano Kinder, a small landowner in the hinterland of Trieste, was a "Slavophile" who had spit on the flag of the Fascio Giovanile di Combattimento. Among the other compromising details of his police file were the facts that his brother was a priest and that he "refused to speak the Italian language."[98]

95 Rome: 1482, Milan: 839, Trieste: 585, Torino: 507, and Bologna: 544; Dal Pont and Carolini, *L'Italia al confino*, esp. 233, 537, 1311.
96 ACS, *confinati politici*, b. 163, "Bukavez, Vittorio."
97 ACS, *confinati politici*, b. 901, "Sain, Luigi."
98 See ACS, *confinati politici*, b. 289, "Cosanz, Carlo"; b. 541, "Kinder, Ermano"; b. 775, "Peric, Francesco."

Disciplining the Mezzogiorno

In the south, authorities increasingly used police sanctions to put an end to factional struggles for political power in small communities (*comuni*). As during the 1920s, traditional elites still engaged in factional fighting over control of local offices.[99] In 1926, the regime had dissolved the elected councils of Italy's nine thousand municipalities, replacing them with one centrally appointed official, the *podestà*.[100] The position was not remunerated and required an advanced degree, a law degree, or service as an officer in the First World War. The *podestà* was not required to belong to the PNF, but by 1935, all but a few did. Arnaldo Mussolini, among other leading Fascists, had hoped that this type of authoritarian centralization would lift Italy's rural municipalities out of their traditional provincialism, putting an end to local feuds, power struggles, and contentious elections.[101] The new office would also link rural Italians to the regime, introducing them to Fascist ethical principles – above all, respect for hierarchical authority. By the early 1930s, most Fascists acknowledged that the *podestà* system had failed to realize these lofty goals.[102] In the Po Valley, for example, large landowners and their allies simply used the office to advance their economic interests, often at the expense of agricultural laborers.[103] In southern *comuni*, individuals who had been overlooked for the post wrote denunciations, organized protests, and engaged in elaborate schemes to discredit the incumbent *podestà*.

Beginning in 1934, to bolster the position of local authorities, including the *podestà* and the head of the *fascio*, the regime began sending the chief proponents of *beghismo* (factional fighting) to political confinement.[104] For example, on the night of October 21, 1936, in the

---

99 In addition to ACS, *confinati politici*, b. 415, "Fioredelisi, Pietro," see b. 13, "Aldaresi, Aurelio"; b. 178, "Camarda, Domenico"; b. 751, "Di Matteo, Armidoro"; b. 751, "Parente, Francesco."

100 In 1926, Fascist administrative reforms replaced local elective bodies (*consigli comunali*) with one central appointed official, the *podestà*. On the *podestà*, see Loreto di Nucci, "Podestà," in *Dizionario del Fascismo*, ed. Victoria de Grazia and Sergio Luzzato (Turin, 2003), II:395–8; Philip Morgan, "I primi podestà fascisti: 1926–32," *Storia contemporanea* 3 (1978): 407–23; Ettore Rotelli, "Le trasformazioni dell'ordinamento comunale e provinciale durante il regime fascista," *Storia contemporanea* 1 (1973): 57–121.

101 Morgan, "Primi podestà fascisti," 408.

102 Ibid., 416–17.

103 Ibid., 409–11.

104 E.g., see ACS, *confinati politici*, b. 595, "Maimone, Francesco"; b. 13, "Aldaresi, Aurelio"; b. 43, "Astorino, Attilio"; b. 223, "Cuali, Luigi"; b. 289, "Cosentini, Francesco";

comune of Quadrelle (population 900), in Avellino province, a lawyer named Giuseppe Magnotti killed the doctor Michele Magnotti (no relation) with two blasts from a shotgun. Writing to the prefect, the police chief of Avellino explained, "in the Comune of Quadrelle, as in many *comuni* of this province, various families, still imbued with feudal principles, and upon whom the purifying work of Fascism has not produced any benefit, have for quite some time competed with one another for power, both political and administrative." Life in the *comune* was tainted by "old hatreds" and *beghe* (feuds), which manifested themselves in the form of "denouncements, both anonymous and signed, and calumnious insinuations."[105] Giuseppe Magnotti was charged with homicide, but the police chief also insisted upon the punishment of other parties involved in their dispute. Foremost among them was a lawyer who had been scheming to make Giuseppe Magnotti head of the local *fascio*. Criminal charges were apparently out of the question because the man's uncle was a high-ranking magistrate. Nevertheless, in the view of the *questore*, the lawyer should be punished, "if not by the written Laws, then by the moral Laws of Fascism."[106] A confinement sentence would also serve as "a warning and example to those for whom *beghismo*" constituted "the sole purpose and scope of their existence."[107] During the 1930s, *beghismo* thus became "anti-Fascist." Agitating against centrally elected authorities was antithetical to the creation of an "organized, strong, stolid" Italy.[108]

Combating the Enemy of the New Fascist Man

Vincenzo Manzini, a prominent jurist during the Fascist era, in his seven-volume *Trattato di diritto penale italiano* (Treatise on Italian Penal Law) wrote that homosexuality, or "pederasty," represented a threat "to the stock, not only because it psychologically degrades whoever is affected by it, but also because it perverts the sexual instinct and therefore impedes

---

b. 403, "Ferrarese, Mario"; b. 409, "Ferri, Natale"; b. 451, "Galotti, Gaetano"; b. 553, "Lappererier, Osvaldo"; b. 967, "Spadaro, Antonio." Overall, approximately twenty cases of apolitical, noneconomic conflict appeared in the sample of 549 cases. In rare cases, political confinement was used to sort out similar problems in northern *comuni*. E.g., see b. 913, "Sanzin, Giovanni."

[105] *Questore* to prefect of Avellino, March 10, 1937, 1–2, in ACS, *confinati politici*, b. 415, "Fiordelisi, Pietro."

[106] Ibid., 10.

[107] Ibid., 11.

[108] Mussolini, "Il Gran Consiglio nei primi quindici anni dell'Era Fascista," OO, XXIX: 115.

procreation."[109] Fascism, according to Manzini, had demonstrated its
hostility to "pederasts" from its origins. He recalled that in Venice,
one well-known "conventicle" of homosexual men regularly gathered
at one another's homes. "Around 1925," he wrote in his legal textbook,
"the *squadre d'azione* violently rooted out those degenerates and forced
the police to take action."[110] Years later, in 1939, Mario Magri, a political detainee who spent seventeen years in captivity, noted the anomalous
presence of a group of homosexual men in the political confinement
colony on the Tremiti Islands: "There were about one hundred perverts,
almost all originating from Catania and other cities in Sicily. These poor
devils, among whom there were skilled artisans and even teachers, lived
in horrible conditions. They received four lire per day and were crammed
into two fetid wood barracks, surrounded by a metal fence that only
allowed a few square meters in which to move around."[111]

With its adulation of masculinity and its obsession with maintaining
strict gender differentiation, Fascism harbored an elevated level of hostility toward homosexuality.[112] As Lorenzo Benadusi has shown, at the
core of the Fascist totalitarian state's project to remake the Italian male
there operated an antimodel: the effeminate "pederast."[113] Unlike Nazi
Germany, where explicitly antihomosexual legislation and propaganda
drove brutal repression, Fascist Italy did not specifically proscribe homosexuality in its legal codes.[114] Neither the Rocco Code (1930), nor the Fascist Police Code (1926/1930) directly named same-sex sex acts as crimes
or threats to public security.[115] An article criminalizing homosexuality

---

[109] Vincenzo Manzini, *Trattato di diritto penale italiano secondo il codice del 1930* (Turin,
     1936), 7:253.
[110] Ibid., 7:252.
[111] Magri, *Vita per la libertà*, 175.
[112] See Rüdiger Lautman, "The Pink Triangle: Homosexuals as 'Enemies of the State,'"
     in *The Holocaust and History: The Known, the Unknown, the Disputed, and the Re-
     examined*, ed. Michael Berenbaum and Abraham J. Peck (Bloomington, 1998), 353; and
     George Mosse, *Nationalism and Sexuality: Middle-Class Morality and Sexual Norms
     in Modern Europe* (Madison, 1988).
[113] Lorenzo Benadusi, *Il nemico dell'uomo nuovo: omosessualità nell'esperimento totali-
     taria fascista* (Milan, 2005).
[114] Fascist and philo-Fascist journals attacked homosexuality and presented "scientific"
     inquiries portraying homosexuals as "degenerate." See Dario Petrosino, "Traditori
     della stirpe: il razzismo contro gli omossessuali nella stampa del fascismo," in *Studi sul
     razzismo Italiano*, ed. Alberto Burgio and Luciano Casali (Bologna, 1996), 89–107; and
     "Come si costruisce uno stereotipo. La rappresentazione degli omosessuali nell *Italiano
     di Leo Longanesi (1926–1929)*," in *Nel nome della razza*, ed. Burgio, 503–28.
[115] Art. 528 of the draft criminal code outlawed homosexuality, but the committee ulti-
     mately decided to delete the article on the grounds that even mentioning "the vice"

appeared in an early draft of the Rocco Code, but the jurists of the reform commission removed it, claiming that "the abominable vice" was not widespread in Italy and to include such an article might give foreigners the wrong impression.[116] "With certain things, the less one speaks of them the better," concluded one jurist.[117] Nonetheless, the commission recommended that the public-security code of 1926 furnished police with sufficient powers for controlling the activities of so-called habitual homosexuals – that is, men who engaged in consensual sex – who, the commission explained, were "in truth quite rare."[118]

Police and judges throughout Italy persecuted thousands of men they identified as homosexuals, or "pederasts," availing themselves of the greatly expanded powers and institutions of repression contained in the police and criminal codes. The provincial commissions established in November 1926 condemned hundreds of suspected homosexuals to "common" *confino* (*confino comune*), exiling them to small villages in the Italian south or interning them on island colonies for a renewable period of one to five years.[119] After 1934, Mussolini and Bocchini began regularly assigning homosexual men to political confinement, signaling to local authorities, communities, and gay men that homosexual activity, and even effeminacy, constituted anti-Fascist behaviors.[120] Evidence strongly suggests that the explicit "politicization" of homosexuality coincided with an intensification of the persecution of homosexual men. In Rome, Italy's elite policing school, located inside the infamous Regina Coeli jail, conducted research on criminality, including "pederasty." Between 1927 and 1933, the school's criminologists cataloged the cases of 346 homosexual subjects; in the subsequent six-year period

---

would bring shame upon Italy. See *Progetto preliminare di un nuovo codice penale* (Rome, 1927), 1:206.

[116] Italy, Ministry of Justice, *Lavori Preparatori del Codice Penale e del Codice di Procedura Penale*. 4 vols. (Rome, 1927–30), 4:4, 377; 4:3, 169; Manzini, *Trattato*, 254n2.

[117] Ibid., 4:3, 171.

[118] Ibid., 4:4, 377. See also Bruno P. F. Wanrooij, "Italy: Sexuality, Morality, and Public Authority," in *Sexual Cultures in Europe: National Histories*, ed. Frank X. Eder, Lesley A. Hall, and Gert Hekma (Manchester, 1999), 34.

[119] The files of common detainees, though not entirely available to scholars, attest to this. See Gianfranco Goretti, "Il periodo fascista e gli omosessuali: Il confino di polizia," in *Le ragioni di un silenzio: la persecuzione degli omosessuali durante il nazismo e il fascismo* (Verona, 2002), 72. See also prefect of Potenza Ottavio Dinale's report to the Interior Ministry, December 28, 1929, in ACS, MI, DGPS, UCP, b. 11, fasc. 710–14, sf. C/comune.

[120] There were officially ten cases of *confino politico* for "pederasty" from 1926 to 1937, and 67 between 1938 and 1941 (Goretti, "Il periodo fascista e gli omosessuali," 71).

(1934–9), they examined 647 men.[121] Moreover, political confinement
sentences also reflected larger ongoing campaigns to, in the words of one
official, "strike and inexorably crush ... pederasty."[122] In the second half
of the 1930s in Florence, Venice, Catania, and other cities, police conducted surveillance on cafés, dance halls, seaside and mountain resorts,
and other public areas where homosexuals gathered.[123] Police regularly
arrested and detained suspects, and once in custody, they were interrogated and often subjected to humiliating anal examinations (*visite sanitarie*) in order to determine whether they had engaged in "passive pederasty" or "anal coitus."[124]

The case of a twenty-two-year-old Florentine named Guglielmo, who
was regularly caught up in dragnets during the 1920s and 1930s, demon-
strates the types of repression and harassment inflicted on homosexuals
throughout Italy. Known to the authorities since the age of fourteen,
Guglielmo's lengthy criminal record consisted mainly of several charges
of extortion and numerous police citations for "pederasty." He had been
warned (*diffidato*) and sentenced to police probation several times in
the late 1920s for being a "vagabond" and a "pederast." Additionally,
between 1926 and 1939, police arrested Guglielmo thirteen times, lock-
ing him up for hours and sometimes days in their holding cell, usually
for being "in the company of" suspected "pederasts." On one occasion,
police forcibly hospitalized him. In 1939, a judge exercised his power
to sentence "potentially dangerous" individuals to "security measures"
(labor colonies, workhouses, asylums, hospitals, other state institutions,
and *libertà vigilata*, a type of probation) and sent Guglielmo off to an
agricultural labor colony on the island of Asinara.[125] Such sentences were
renewable indefinitely, enabling Italian magistrates to act as arbitrarily as
the regime they served.[126] Released from Asinara after only a few months,

---

[121] *Source*: Annual data from *Bollettino della Scuola Superiore di polizia e dei servizi
tecnici annessi* (Rome, 1927–39), fasc. 17 (1927), 121; fasc. 18 (1928), 103; fasc. 19–
20 (1929–30), 99, 107; fasc. 21 (1931), 114; fasc. 22–3 (1932–3), 106, 114; fasc. 24–6
(1934–6), 30, 36; fasc. 27–9 (1937–9), 27, 33.

[122] Prefect of Florence to MI, "Oggetto: Prevenzione e repressione della pederastia –
provvedimenti di Polizia," August 16, 1939, in ACS, *confinati politici*, b. 83, fasc.
"B.G."

[123] *Questore* (Molina) to prefect of Catania, March 29, 1939, in ACS, *confinati politici*,
b. 247, fasc. "C.G."

[124] See the *confino* proposal of the *questore* of Salerno to the prefect of Salerno, July 24,
1939, in ACS, *confinati politici*, b. 878, fasc. "R.D." On the widespread nature of this
practice, see Benadusi, *Nemico dell'uomo nuovo*, 149–50.

[125] On security measures see Neppi Modona, "Carcere e società civile," 1901–98; on the
courts' treatment of homosexuals, see Benadusi, *Nemico dell'uomo nuovo*, 187–216.

[126] Neppi Modona, "Carcere e società civile," 1967.

Guglielmo was immediately subjected to a five-year *confino politico* sentence by the Florentine Provincial Commission.

The actions of public-security authorities against homosexuals were motivated by public-security concerns, such as the repression of prostitution and extortion, as well as by predictable prejudices and visceral antipathies toward homosexuals or effeminate men and their presence in the public sphere. These anxieties and stereotypes have existed in many historical contexts. However, the Mussolini regime defined male homosexuality, as it did abortion, as a political threat to the state. Prefects and police, echoing the regime's rhetoric, claimed that homosexuals undermined Mussolini's larger project of strengthening the Italian "race" (*razza*) or "stock" (*stirpe*). The intensification of antihomosexual measures during the 1930s has been attributed to various factors. Some scholars have pointed to growing concerns about demographic expansion and, in the context of war and empire, racial health.[127] Other historians view the persecution of homosexuals as an integral component of Mussolini's project of creating the new *uomo fascista* within an increasingly totalitarian environment. Whatever the case, one should not underestimate the level of repression inflicted on suspected homosexual men during the entirety of Fascist rule. The appearance of so many homosexuals in repressive institutions in the period after 1934 was certainly significant. However, during the 1920s, particularly in the wake of the exceptional decrees of 1926, police heavily targeted criminal suspects and social outsiders, including homosexuals.[128] In the eyes of authorities, homosexual men, particularly prostitutes and flamboyantly effeminate men, belonged to the category of "dregs" that the Fascist regime sought to eliminate from public spaces.

Subversive Sects

In 1935, during the crisis that led up to the invasion of Ethiopia, Pentecostals and Jehovah's Witnesses suddenly appeared among the ranks of political detainees. As was the case with homosexuality, the practice of the two religions had not been explicitly proscribed in the Fascist criminal code. Absent such a ban, the regime instead utilized police sanctions, executive orders of imprisonment, judicial "security measures," and various

---

[127] See Ebner, "Persecution of Homosexual Men," 139–56.
[128] On the use of "common" *confino* against suspected homosexuals, see Benadusi, *Nemico dell'uomo nuovo*, 139–46, and for other measures (e.g., asylums, prisons), 187–216.

forms of low-level harassment. A major difference between the repression of abortion and homosexuality, on the one hand, and the campaign against Pentecostals and Jehovah's Witnesses, on the other, was that Christian religious minorities were largely tolerated during the 1920s. After Mussolini's Concordat with the Vatican, if not earlier, religious equality ceased to exist in Italy, as Catholicism had become the official religion of state. Pentecostals and Jehovah's Witnesses then became tolerated "sects." Later in the decade, the environment of war and internal social mobilization led Mussolini and other officials to classify the faithful of these religions as enemies of the state.

The Catholic Church had for many years urged the government to suppress non-Catholic Christian religions other than the mainstream Protestant faiths. At the local level and through the diplomatic channels formally established between the Vatican and Mussolini's regime in 1929, Catholic officials and parish priests pressured the Italian government and local police to outlaw evangelical groups. In Rome, the Pentecostal community consisted of about five hundred members. Throughout the 1920s and into the early 1930s, the Roman Pentecostals met for worship several times weekly in a space on via Adige rented by their leader, Ettore Strappavecchia, a relatively wealthy owner of a construction company. During 1927 and 1928, Catholic Church officials engaged in constant machinations to have Strappavecchia's congregation suppressed, even commissioning a medical report on the supposedly degenerative physical and psychological effects of Pentecostal rites.[129] However, the Roman *questore* repeatedly rejected the notion that church members constituted a danger to public order, the regime, or themselves.[130] Importantly, in early 1931, the state officially recognized Ettore Strappavecchia as a *ministro di culto*, which authorized him to convene religious gatherings.[131] At the same time, Pentecostals in Rome and elsewhere still endured harassment, including constant surveillance and arrests for convening unauthorized meetings.

---

[129] "Perizia Zacchi, 1931," in ACS, MI, DGPS, Massime, G.1/Roma/Pentecostali. Entire report published in Giorgio Rochat, *Regime fascista e chiese evangeliche*, 121–2, 124–6.

[130] Guido Bellone, the *vice-questore* of Rome, led an investigation of the Pentecostals in January 1927 and found nothing out of the ordinary. His report defended the behavior and good intentions of the group against the slanders of the Catholic Church. In 1928, at the request of police headquarters, a local medical doctor, Vincenzo Clerico, attended a service and concluded Pentecostal religious practices posed no threat to the parishioners; see Rochat, *Chiese evangeliche*, 113–17.

[131] For further explanation of the *ministro di culto* status, see Rochat, *Chiese evangeliche*, 127–45.

Then, in April 1935, Guido Buffarini Guidi, the Fascist undersecretary of the Interior Ministry, circulated a directive ordering the suppression of Pentecostal meeting places and the prosecution of those who continued to practice their faith. The official justification for the action was that the religion was "contrary to the social order and damaging to the physical and psychic integrity of the race."[132] Throughout central and southern Italy, police soon acted against approximately 150 Pentecostal groups, closing down their meeting halls and inflicting police sanctions on those who continued to gather and worship.[133] In Rome, on March 15, the police seized the meeting hall on via Adige. The Pentecostals nevertheless continued to gather in private homes to pray. In response, the police raided these unauthorized religious services, arresting the attendees and denouncing them to judicial authorities.[134] Even if the courts absolved a Pentecostal, Rome's police commission still sentenced them to police political confinement, probation (*ammonizione*), or admonishment (*diffida*).[135] Police reports contained no accusations of anti-Fascism or criminality. One Pentecostal was a veteran of the First World War and, according to the *carabinieri*, "had always held good moral and political conduct, demonstrating himself devoted to his family and dedicated to his work."[136] The accusations against him merely regurgitated the claims of Buffarini Guidi's circular.[137] In 1937, as the remaining Pentecostals of Rome engaged in clandestine religious activities, Bocchini ordered the *questore* to cease passing confinement sentences and, instead, to begin deporting them to their hometowns and villages because most were not originally from Rome.[138]

In the eyes of authorities, the Jehovah's Witnesses, who fell under similar scrutiny and persecution in 1935, posed a greater threat or obstacle

---

[132] Quoted in ibid., 246.

[133] Rochat offers many examples of this type of repression in various communities of central and southern Italy, many of which were established by the Roman Pentecostals who had been repatriated in 1937; ibid., 253–6.

[134] The results of criminal proceedings against Pentecostals are not known, yet there is some evidence that they were often absolved.

[135] The five cases are found in ACS, *confinati politici*, b. 142, "Bosco, Giuseppe"; b. 555, "Laudisa, Nicola"; b. 555, "Laudisa, Fiordisa"; b. 1024, "Tricerri, Elvira," and b. 1024, "Tricerri, Francesco."

[136] *Carabinieri* of Rome to comando generale, August 14, 1936, *confinati politici*, b. 142, "Bosco, Giuseppe."

[137] See, e.g., *Questura* (Palma) to prefect of Roma, "Denunzia per l'assegnazione al confino di polizia e per l'ammonizione a carico di aderenti al culto pentecostale," June 8, 1936, in ACS, *confinati politici*, b. 1024, "Tricerri, Francesco."

[138] See Rochat, *Chiese evangeliche*, 252.

to the Fascist project. A small group of Witnesses had existed in Pinerolo, a city in Piedmont, since early in the century.[139] In recent years, as immigrants returned to Italy from the United States and other European nations, small groups of Witnesses appeared in provinces through Italy, including Sondrio, Trento, Aquila, Teramo, Pescara, Benevento, Aosta, Ravenna, and Foggia. Even so, their presence in Italy was extremely limited, amounting to only 150 to 300 members by the early 1940s. Like the Pentecostals, the Jehovah's Witnesses initially attracted the antipathy of the Catholic Church, ordinary Italians, and even Fascists. In the fall of 1936, in a district of Trento province called Canal San Bovo, local authorities informed Rome of the existence of a "pseudo-religion," explaining that although the group did not engage in anti-Fascist behavior, their faith functioned "as an instrument of disaggregation" in the community. Moreover, their publications, emanating from the Witnesses' headquarters in Brooklyn, tended to "rebuke governments, men of Finance, Politics and Religion, and even Patriotism."[140] Provincial authorities also blamed Jehovah's Witnesses for a lack of enthusiasm for Fascism among the general population, particularly in provinces with ethnic German minorities. The *carabinieri* of Bolzano, for example, reported that the "pseudo-religion" thwarted local political authorities' "efforts of penetration and moral elevation." Of the district's 292 inhabitants, there were only two members of PNF, no "Young Fascists" (boys), three *avanguardisti* (teenage boys), and only four members of the girls' branch of the "Young Italians."[141] The *questore* of Trento lamented that the Witnesses opposed "all forms of physical education" and demonstrated "hostility toward the regime's youth organizations."[142] In these cases, a small number of Witnesses had obviously become scapegoats for the regime's failure to win adherents in a province with a large ethnic German population.[143]

---

[139] See Paolo Piccioli, "I testimoni di Geova durante il regime fascista," *Studi Storici* 41:1 (2000): 191.

[140] Capital letters are those of the *questore* of Trento. These exact words are found in many documents prepared by the *questore*, the prefect, and the *carabinieri* of Trento in the files of the *confinato politico* Cesare Torghele (b. Toghele) and others.

[141] *Carabinieri* of Bolzano, September 2, 1936, in ACS, *confinati politici*, b. 705, "Stefenon, Narciso."

[142] *Questura* of Trento, November 6, 1937, in ibid.

[143] This sentiment was expressed by all authorities – *carabinieri*, *questore*, and prefect. See, e.g., *questore* of Trento, October 10, 1936, *confinati politici*, b. 1015, "Torghele, Cesare."

Upon Mussolini's direct orders, police in Canal San Bovo sentenced four church leaders to political exile and approximately twenty others to political probation. The regime's actions provoked the group, whose literature and proselytizing became explicitly anti-Fascist and anti-"totalitarian."[144] In response, police repression escalated, and two of the church leaders were tried by the Special Tribunal. Throughout Italy, particularly in small rural communities in Abruzzo, other groups of Jehovah's Witnesses endured similar persecution and responded in a similar fashion.[145] Once the police had them in custody, they learned that the Jehovah's Witnesses would not, if asked, serve in the Italian military. With the Ethiopian war underway, these "anti-national and anti-militarist ideas" threatened "national defense." One *questore* recounted that while in jail, Jehovah's Witnesses refused to partake in the special meal prepared in honor of the celebration of the thirteenth anniversary of the March on Rome.[146] Following these revelations, more of their coreligionists were sentenced to *confino* for propagating "defeatism" and the "depression of national sentiment and spirit."[147] As the regime cracked down on the Witnesses, they, in turn, reacted with increasing hostility toward Fascism and its militarism.

Evangelicals, Jehovah's Witnesses, and other minor religious groups thus all endured some persecution before the Second World War. In 1939, with the regime's racial laws in place and Europe teetering on the brink of war, Mussolini and Bocchini decided on a coordinated campaign against both groups. Up to this moment, the regime viewed most religious groups outside of the mainstream Protestant faiths as an undifferentiated mass of pacifist, degenerate anti-Fascists. Almost all were referred to as Pentecostal or *tremolante* (trembler) "sects" because the Pentecostals represented the largest and most diffuse of these religions. The Pentecostals, Bocchini mistakenly explained to Italian prefects, rejected the authority of all forms of government, denied the right of governments to declare war, and asserted the moral duty of Christians to embrace pacifism. The entire conglomeration of evangelical religions and the Jehovah's Witnesses represented the same threat to the regime as "the subversive

---

[144] Rochat, *Chiese evangeliche*, 276; Piccioli, "I testimoni di Geova," 193–5.
[145] On the illegality of imprisoning people for months without consulting a magistrate, see Rochat, *Chiese evangeliche*, 282.
[146] *Carabinieri* of Pescara, October 22, 1935, and *questore* of Pescara, November 1, 1935, in ACS, *confinati politici*, b. 355, "Di Censo, Francesco."
[147] *Questore* of Pescara, May 26, 1936, in ibid.

political parties."[148] Accordingly, the OVRA began an investigation of "Pentecostal sects."[149] However, Inspector General of Public Security Pasquale Andriani, the head of the fourth OVRA zone, soon concluded that the Pentecostals posed little threat to the regime. They could even belong to the PNF and readily recognized "earthly authority." They concluded their prayers with "the invocation of the benediction on the king, the head of government, and all persons invested with authority." Moreover, unlike the Jehovah's Witnesses, the Pentecostals would serve in the military. Finally, Andriani addressed the question of their effect on the "health of the race," concluding that the Pentecostals "did not constitute a particular danger from the political point of view."[150]

Ignoring Andriani's conclusions, Bocchini warned public-security officials that the members of both religions lived in a "climate of exaltation," which had a "damaging effect on the mental health of its followers." Finally, while conceding that Pentecostalism was less inimical to Fascism than the tenets of the Jehovah's Witnesses, Bocchini claimed that their greater numbers and wider dispersion throughout Italy exacerbated their deleterious effect on the nation.[151] The impact of repression inflicted on Pentecostals during 1940 through 1943 was partly deflected by their lack of centralized organization. Nevertheless, approximately fifty leaders from cities and provinces in central and southern Italy – Rome, Aquila, Bari, Catanzaro, Avellino, Macerata, Matera, Benevento, and Naples – were sentenced to political confinement from 1940 to 1943. Dozens of others were arrested, imprisoned, and sentenced to probation or other sanctions.[152] The Jehovah's Witnesses, by contrast, were suppressed in a manner comparable only to the campaign waged against the clandestine anti-Fascist movements. During 1939 and 1940, the regime used all means at its disposal against them. The regular and political police, the *carabinieri*, the OVRA, the Special Tribunal, criminal courts, and police commissions identified and punished nearly all adult Jehovah's Witnesses (150–300), together with a few minors. Twenty-eight individuals were sentenced to political confinement, and another twenty-six were tried by

[148] Rochat, *Chiese evangeliche*, 257–8; Piccioli, "I testimoni di Geova," 214–16.
[149] Rochat, *Chiese evangeliche*, 258–60.
[150] Andriani, January 3, 1940, 1–3; excerpted in Rochat, *Chiese evangeliche*, 292.
[151] Bocchini to prefects, "Setta religiosa dei 'testimoni di Geova' o 'studenti della Bibbia' ed altre sette religiose i cui principi sono contraria alle nostre istituzioni"; Rochat, *Chiese evangeliche*, 264–6.
[152] Rochat, *Chiese evangeliche*, 266–72.

the Special Tribunal, which condemned them to a total of 186 years in prison.[153]

When examined together, the campaigns against the Pentecostals and Jehovah's Witnesses bring into sharper focus the regime's practice of facilitating the persecution of vulnerable minorities and social outsiders. By punishing a few hundred members of a minority "sect," even one that posed no threat, the regime garnered support from Catholics, Fascists, and ordinary citizens. Historian Giorgio Rochat attributes the change in policy around 1935 to the regime's pursuit of more radical, dynamic policies in the foreign and domestic spheres in an attempt to create "a new type of Italian, aggressive and obedient, of uniform mentality, manners, and comportment."[154] The Catholic Church clearly provided an important impetus for the campaigns against the groups, but the existence of the Jehovah's Witnesses and the Pentecostals also blatantly contradicted Mussolini's project of constructing a rigidly hierarchical, disciplined, uniform society that was fully integrated into state institutions. Moreover, the foreign origins of the two religions made their practitioners seem suspicious, alien, and even traitorous in a Fascist state that was ultranationalist and xenophobic. The regime also clearly practiced discrimination and persecution for its own sake. The persecution of an extremely small, utterly defenseless religious minority served to create yet another distinction between those who belonged in Fascist society and those who did not, between the nation and the antination. Although only a few Italian communities experienced the actions taken against religious minorities, the regime risked nothing by assaulting these groups. For Mussolini, no minority was too small or inconsequential to persecute.

Official Fascist Racism

The cynical motives that led Mussolini to persecute a few hundred loyal, law-abiding Pentecostal Italians perhaps shed some light on his motives for introducing anti-Semitic racial legislation. Beginning in 1938, a series of laws stripped Italian Jews of basic civil rights, expelled them from the party, prohibited state employment (including the military, civil service,

---

[153] Piccioli, "I testimoni di Geova," 219–20, 294–8. For a list of all *confino*, prison, military tribunal, and Special Tribunal sentences inflicted on Jehovah's Witnesses and other evangelicals, see the list in Rochat, *Chiese evangeliche*, 321–9.

[154] Rochat, *Chiese evangeliche*, 245.

and schools), barred students from attending public schools and univer-
sities, and forbade marriages between Christians and Jews and domestic
employment of Christians in Jewish homes. Jews also could not own or
manage companies of a certain size. Legislation in 1939 banned or greatly
limited their participation in many professions, such as law, medicine,
engineering, accounting, agronomy, and midwifery. Between 1939 and
1942, Jews were prohibited from making their livelihood as street vendors, private teachers, and artists. In 1942, the regime removed Jews from
private industries related to the war.[155]

Prisons and political confinement did not play a leading role in the
implementation of the racial laws. Instead, the regime launched a hateful, sustained campaign of legal discrimination. Italian Jews, many of
them Fascists, were fully assimilated and solidly middle class. In cities
throughout the north, they inhabited elite social, political, and economic
circles. Consequently, their position as "social outsiders" had to be manufactured through propaganda and discrimination. Mussolini intended
the racial laws to be a painful experience for Jews and the non-Jewish
Italians around them. And it was. The vast majority of "Aryan" political
detainees and prisoners could count on someday being released, provided
they ceased their "anti-Fascist" activities or behavior and submitted to
the regime. The strategy behind the attack on Italian Jewry, by contrast, aimed not to change them or their behavior but to identify all Jews
and systematically exclude them from the Italian nation. Once this campaign had begun, it is hard to imagine how Mussolini could have ever
"amnestied" or "pardoned" them. To the contrary, the trend went in the
other direction: Italians of Jewish descent who received exemptions lost
them over time. Fascist policies and propaganda were intended to place
Jews beyond the pale, separating an "alien" minority from the "Aryan"
Italian nation. Sooner or later, presumably, the regime would have had
to find a "solution" to its newly manufactured "Jewish problem." In
the end, it was the Nazi Final Solution, implemented in part by Fascist
collaborators, that ended what Mussolini's regime had begun in 1938.

As with other Fascist policies, the regime used the repressive apparatus
to punish violations of and protests against the legal prohibitions imposed
on Jewish Italians. For example, Jews deprived of their livelihood who

---

[155] For the racial laws, see Michele Sarfatti, *The Jews in Mussolini's Italy: From Equality to
Persecution* (translation of *Gli ebrei nell'Italia fascista. Vicende, identità, persecuzione*),
trans. John and Anne Tedeschi (Madison, 2006); and Susan Zuccotti, *The Italians and
the Holocaust: Persecution, Rescue, and Survival* (Lincoln, 1996).

attempted to circumvent restrictions on economic activities were condemned to *confino politico*. After the introduction of the ban on working as street vendors, a Jew from Rome's ghetto paid an "Aryan" to obtain a vending permit. Roman police caught on and assigned him to three years of *confino*.[156] Additionally, Jewish Italians who had been Fascists, feeling betrayed, criticized the regime's anti-Semitic turn and were punished by the police. More than custodial police sanctions, however, Italian Jews were subject to constant harassment and discrimination in their daily lives. "Aryan" Italians informed state and party authorities about Jews who violated the discriminatory legislation by employing Catholics as domestic servants, practicing prohibited professions (medicine, law, and street vending), owning radios or telephones, and attempting to attain Aryan status or exemption from the racial laws by bribing state officials or receiving backdated baptismal certificates. Police usually investigated the charges and, when necessary, enforced compliance. Italians suspected of assisting Jews or criticizing the racial laws were also targeted by denouncers.[157]

Just like the politically compromised and "social outsiders," Italian Jews were now vulnerable to denunciation for trifling acts of anti-Fascism. Ines Levi, for example, was an Italian Jew who converted to Catholicism in 1920. Because of the racial laws, she lost her job working as a stenographer in Modena. She applied to the state for an exemption from discrimination but was denied. Economic circumstance forced her out of her apartment and into a boardinghouse run by two sisters. One day, according to a statement by Levi's landladies, a child asked her where she hung her portrait of the Duce. Levi allegedly replied, "You put it in the bathroom; that's its proper place." The two sisters also reported that Levi had said, "by the end of the year the Italians will see what the Jews are capable of," allegedly referring to the likelihood of the Axis losing the war and Italy's Jews getting their revenge against "Aryans." Investigating Levi, the police learned that she had always been loyal to Fascism. After being sentenced to political confinement, she appealed to Mussolini for an act of clemency, calling attention to the fact that her father, Vito Levi, was a "Fascist of the first hour." Her sister, Anita Levi,

---

[156] ACS, *confinati politici*, b. 973, "Spizzichino, Cesare." Only one case of this nature came up in the random sample. There were also two cases of Jews being assigned to *confino politico* for "money laundering" as a result of the special surveillance conducted on Jewish communities after the racial laws. See b. 391, "Fano, Ugo"; and b. 319, "De Angelis."

[157] Franzinelli, *Delatori*, 156–7.

had also been a correspondent for the prominent publication *Regime fascista*, in Rome, until she was fired in 1938. Finally, she absolutely denied saying the things attributed to her, explaining that the two sisters were retaliating for a dispute over rent.[158] Such police measures inflicted on Jews, whether for violations of the racial laws or other political offenses, reveal how badly state racism compromised their position within society.[159]

Official anti-Semitism also became ubiquitous throughout the Fascist police bureaucracy. As if Mussolini had turned a switch, police and *carabinieri* now began to include the "race" (Aryan or Jewish) of all persons under investigation. *"Ebreo"* (Jew) became one more, albeit very important, designation stamped on the front of "personal files," just like the labels "Communist," "Socialist," "ex-convict," or "pederast." Whereas most Communists deemed "irreducible" or "unrepentant" were political militants who had chosen to fight Fascism, being Jewish was not a defiant stance or an act of resistance. Even homosexuals could keep a low profile and at least hope the police would leave them alone. Moreover, Jewish detainees already in custody, whose religion had previously been irrelevant to state authorities, suddenly became Jews "unworthy of consideration."[160] The anti-Semitic legislation, like so many of Mussolini's policies, thus reverberated throughout the police apparatus, the state bureaucracy, the *confino* system, and Italian society.

With Italy's entrance into the war in June 1940, Mussolini ordered the internment of foreign-born Jews, anti-Fascists, and other "dangerous" individuals. This new practice brought even harsher consequences for Italian Jews denounced by Aryan Italians. In addition to six thousand foreign Jews, four hundred Italian Jews were interned as "anti-Fascists." Police officials – Political Police Chief Guido Leto and Police Chief Carmine Senise among others – personally ordered the internment of individual Italian Jews who had been denounced for trifling, petty "political" matters.[161] Jews were clearly more vulnerable than ever, and ordinary Italians and police officials knew it. After 1939, denunciations blamed Jews for the war. Banned from military service, Jews were then

---

[158] See file in ACS, *confinati politici*, b. 565, "Levi, Ines."
[159] For further examples of the use of *confino politico* to uphold or repress public criticism of the racial laws, see Dal Pont and Ghini, *Gli antifascisti al confino*, 155–6.
[160] Prefect of Littoria, October 1938, *confinati politici*, b. 883, "Rosner, Eugenio."
[161] See Franzinelli, *Delatori*, 160.

accused of shirking their duty and betraying their country. As conditions in Italy grew worse, Italian anti-Semites blamed the "Jewish–Masonic conspiracy."[162]

Unfortunately, the worst was yet to come for Italian and foreign Jews in Italy. When it did arrive after September 1943, the racial laws and the repressive apparatus had already deprived Jews of substantial material resources and social bonds useful for avoiding capture by the Germans and their Italian collaborators. The police state apparatus also provided the gestapo with a Jewish census, containing the names and addresses of all Italian Jews. Finally, the regime's political policing system had cultivated the surveillance and denunciatory practices that would deliver many Jews to the German authorities.[163]

In recent decades, historians have struggled to understand how a regime so apparently devoid of anti-Semitism could suddenly turn on its Jewish citizens, many of whom were loyal Fascists. The first serious studies of the question pointed to Hitler, arguing credibly that Mussolini intended to bring his regime into line with his new German ally.[164] A subsequent line of interpretation examined how, after the invasion of Ethiopia, the experience of empire – of Italians ruling over Africans – brought the issue of race to the fore. In Mussolini's view, the Italians had not developed a sense of racial superiority. They had not learned to be "masters." The racial laws, therefore, were pedagogic, implemented to instill Italians with the sense of racial superiority requisite for an imperial people.[165] A third view, which emerged in the 1980s, presented the racial laws as part of the Fascist regime's "totalitarian turn" and the creation of the new *uomo fascista*. According to this reading, the Jews – as bourgeois, materialist devotees of the liberal state – stood in the way of the fascistization of Italian society. Moreover, the process of excluding them from the nation, Mussolini believed, would teach the Italians a difficult lesson, forcing "Aryans" to pitilessly persecute their racially inferior

[162] Ibid., 143–60.
[163] Fargion, *Il libro della memoria*; Fargion, "The Persecution of Jews in Italy"; and Michele Sarfatti, *Mussolini contro gli ebrei: cronaca dell'elaborazione delle leggi del 1938* (Torino, 1994).
[164] Renzo De Felice, *Storia degli ebrei sotto il fascismo* (Turin, 1961); Meir Michaelis, *Mussolini and the Jews* (Oxford, 1978).
[165] Luigi Preti, *Impero fascista: africani ed ebrei* (Milan, 1968); Gene Bernardini, "The Origins and Development of Racial Anti-Semitism in Fascist Italy," *Journal of Modern History* 49 (1977): 431–53.

former compatriots.[166] Most recently, Michele Sarfatti has documented the undercurrent of anti-Semitism within the Fascist movement and the steady deterioration of the rights of Jewish communities as Mussolini's dictatorship adopted Catholicism as the official religion of state.[167] This latter line of inquiry emphasizes how the suppression of individual rights, and the adoption of a homogenous, normative national, or Fascist identity – ethnically Italian, nationalistic, Catholic, heterosexual, virile, and so forth – progressively excluded ethnic and religious minorities and social outsiders from the nation. In theory and in practice, Fascist dynamism depended on cleansing the nation of its enemies, whether they were political subversives, career criminals, homosexuals, Pentecostals, or Jews. The internal logic of Fascism thus required individuals or groups to play the part of the "antination." The Fascists targeted the most obvious minorities or outsiders first, but soon others, even law-abiding, assimilated minorities, like the Pentecostals and the Jews, fell victim to the violent Fascist project of constructing a "national society."

Parallel War and the Failure of Fascism

Italy entered the Second World War on June 10, 1940, attacking France just days before the Germans took Paris. By contributing "a few thousand dead" to this presumably short war, Mussolini hoped to earn himself a place at the peace table. In light of Germany's astonishing successes, Italians could reasonably have expected the Axis to win the war during 1940 or 1941. Still, there were doubts.[168] "Who knows how it will turn out," mused a sixty-year-old hairdresser, Virginio Crema, in the fall of 1940.[169] The police continued to punish such trifling offenses, often committed by socially marginal individuals. During the next year, Italy's position became more difficult. Italian military campaigns failed virtually everywhere – in the Balkans, Africa, and the Mediterranean. By the end of 1941, Italy counted the Soviet Union and the United States among its enemies. Even before the disastrous defeats suffered by the Axis at El

---

[166] Renzo De Felice, *Mussolini il duce*, II; and also the new edition of Renzo De Felice, *The Jews in Fascist Italy: A History*, trans. Robert L. Miller and Kim Englehart (New York, 2001).

[167] Sarfatti, *Jews in Mussolini's Italy*.

[168] Eleven percent of sentences (41/388) were for "defeatism" during the Second World War, not including "economic defeatism."

[169] Prefect of Bolzano, November 7, 1940, in ACS, *confinati politici*, b. 295, "Crema, Virginio."

Alamein and, later, Stalingrad, many Italians had begun to accept defeat and the impending failure of Fascism. On the afternoon of April 17, 1942, on a street in the city of Foggia, a single sheet of paper slipped out of the coat pocket of Olga Trandafilo, an eighteen-year-old student at the Istituto Superiore Professionale. Before it even hit the ground, the paper was snatched up by Michele Lecci, a young Fascist employed in the offices of the regime's youth organization. Lecci quickly glanced at the paper, which contained a list of real movie titles with mocking references to the regime, its policies, the military, and the war effort (Table 4).[170]

Lecci informed a local police commissioner, who questioned Trandafilo. She told police that her brother had brought the list home from work, and she was on her way to show it to some friends. Through further interviews and interrogations, police painstakingly reconstructed the list's meanderings through the workplaces, homes, and social gatherings of various white-collar workers in Foggia. In the end, the police assessed each individual's responsibility for reproducing and disseminating the list, and condemned three men, all in their early forties, to *confino politico*, and six younger people (four women and two men) to political probation.[171] As it turned out, the list of films did not originate in Foggia. It had been circulating throughout banks and other white-collar offices throughout Italy since at least January 1942.[172]

The widespread dissemination of the document perhaps merely represented a need for humor during bleak times. However, it also reveals a fact about the regime's myths and hagiography, which many Italians came to appreciate during 1942. Mussolini's propaganda and rhetoric had incorporated Fascism's institutions, policies, and milestones into a grand narrative of national transformation, which would eventually culminate in a European conflict. Just as the triumphant realization of Mussolini's totalitarian project depended on victory over Britain and France, defeat would signal its abject failure. Now, in 1942, the Axis faced a vastly more powerful coalition of enemies, and Italy had been subjugated

---

[170] See list "Filmi di Attualità," in report of Maggiore Comandante Ermanno Belucci (*carabinieri*), November 6, 1942, and report of *questore* to prefect of Foggia, May 5, 1942, in ACS, *confinati politici*, b. 93, "Berardi, Raffaele."

[171] *Questore* to prefect of Foggia, May 5, 1942, in ACS, *confinati politici*, b. 93, "Berardi, Raffaele."

[172] Earlier that year, two midlevel bank employees in Montepulciano (Siena) were sentenced to *confino politico* for copying and distributing the same list; *questore* to prefect of Siena, March 24, 1942, and enclosed list, "Biennale di Venezia – I Grandi Films," in ACS, *confinati politici*, b. 653, "Menchini, Enrico." See also Mimmo Franzinelli, *Delatori*, 99–100.

TABLE 4. *List of Satirical Film Titles (1940)*

Original	English Translation
Il pirata sono io	I am the pirate
I miserabili	Les miserables
Paradiso perduto	Paradise lost
Eterna illusion	Eternal illusion
Non me lo dire	Say it isn't so
Non è una cosa seria	Nothing serious
Alba tragic	Tragic dawn
I nostri parenti	Our relatives
Zona di guai	Danger zone
Non ti conosco più	I don't know you anymore
Uomini sul fondo	Men on the bottom
Un caso disperato	A desperate case

Hitler	Hitler
Gli Italiani	The Italians
Impero	Empire
Vincere	Winning
Vinceremo	We will win
Fascismo	Fascism
28 Ottobre	October 28
I tedeschi	The Germans
La bonifica	Land reclamation
Starace	Starace
Squadra navale italiana	Italian naval squadron
Autarchia	Autarky

to its German ally. It had become apparent that Fascism had failed, and the Axis would lose the war.

The strains of war soon brought an expanded rationing regime, price fixing, and prohibitions. The basic caloric allotment for Italians was among the lowest in Europe, comparable to and, by 1942, lower than even that of the Poles under Nazi occupation.[173] The system of rationing in Italy was poorly organized and corrupt, often failing to deliver even the meager daily caloric allotment of one thousand calories. As a result, means of supplementing one's diet had to be found. Some rural Italians could rely on homegrown produce and livestock, but for urban populations, and for products that could not be produced at home, extreme scarcity created a black market with inflated prices. In his memoir, Mussolini's wartime chief of police, Carmine Senise, claimed that the political police spent more time investigating speculators and profiteers during the Second World War than repressing anti-Fascism.[174] Though Senise proffered this claim by way of self-exculpation – during his tenure, he contended, the police largely stayed out of the nasty business of political repression – it is nevertheless true that the repression of "antinational" economic activity became an increasingly important task. As during the 1930s, agricultural producers and distributors continued to divert their products to the black market.[175] Fascist and other state officials accepted bribes and made illegal profits from the rationing system.[176] Small shopkeepers hoarded or skimmed foodstuffs, selling them illegally.[177] And in the north, after the German military had installed itself in most strategic cities, small vendors often sold eggs, meat, and other foodstuffs to German soldiers who could afford black-market prices.[178]

The police also prosecuted famished Italians who justifiably blamed their dire condition on a regime whose foreign policy and failed domestic

---

[173] See Clough, *Economic History*, 278.

[174] Carmine Senise, *Capo della Polizia*, 87.

[175] For large-scale hoarding and price fixing, see personal file of "Tranchese, Giacomo," in ACS, *confinati politici*, b. 1021.

[176] See case of "Calascibetta, Renato," in ACS, *confinati politici*, b. 173.

[177] Francesco Icardi, a PNF member in Alassio (Savona) who ran a store, was caught selling eggs at inflated prices. The police caught him in a sting operation in September 1941, with an undercover officer posing as an ordinary Italian in search of eggs on the black market. See personal file of "Icardi, Francesco," in ACS, *confinati politici*, b. 529. See also the case of Luigi Vandano, a PNF member and bar owner in Chieri (Turin), who was arrested and sentenced in March 1942 for selling gelatin at inflated prices; ACS, *confinati politici*, b. 1051.

[178] See the case of "Fede, Giulio," in ACS, *confinati politici*, b. 397. In August 1942, Fede, a PNF member and store owner, was caught selling prosciutto to German officers at inflated prices in Ascoli (Ascoli Piceno).

mobilization had reduced them to penury and starvation. For instance, in October 1941, a crowd gathered in a shop in Molfeta (Bari) to listen to the daily radio bulletin. When it was over, an illiterate manual laborer with one maimed hand exclaimed, "We're starving, and the Government should know that [the bread ration] is not enough. They should cut the head off that one in Rome, because he's making us die of hunger."[179] Arrested at his home, he admitted what he had said and reiterated that he was "exasperated by the insufficient ration assigned him."[180] In another representative case, in November 1942, a factory worker in Sesto San Giovanni (Milan) yelled in the factory cafeteria, "we work fourteen hours a day with a little broth, and the money isn't enough." The *questore* of Milan described the worker as "neurotic," "impulsive," and "dangerous to public order, especially for the repercussions his attitude could have on the mass of workers."[181] Mussolini and Bocchini sent him to the Castel di Guido, a workhouse outside of Rome. Ordinary Italians also blamed corruption among state and party officials for exacerbating their circumstances. In Naples, in December 1942, a white-collar worker accused local authorities of skimming flour rations to make sweets for themselves and, consequently, was sentenced to one year of political exile in the province of Campobasso. No matter that the police investigation suggested that he was correct.[182]

In the second half of 1942, the turning of the military tide in Africa and Russia, the landing of the Anglo-American forces in north Africa, the bombing of Italian cities, the growing authority of the German military in Italy, and the deep unpopularity of the war on the home front left Mussolini depressed and physically ailing. Figures within government and the Fascist Party openly talked of replacing their Duce and suing for a separate peace with the Allies. Toward the end of 1942, Mussolini staged a short-lived political comeback. Speaking to the Directorate of the Fascist Party on January 3, 1942, the anniversary of his 1925 *coup d'ètat*, Mussolini declared that Italian people now had "the chance to show what it is made of." Refuting the idea that Fascism had "changed things only on the surface," Mussolini predicted that the Italians would "stand firm and astound the world."[183] Contrary to Mussolini's projection, Fascism

---

[179] See reports of the *questore* and *carabinieri* of Bari, October 29, 1941, in ACS, *confinati politici*, b. 547, "La Forgia, Domenico."

[180] See *questore* of Bari report, October 29, 1941, in b. 547, "La Forgia, Domenico."

[181] *Questore* to prefect of Milan, January 10, 1943, in ACS, *confinati politici*, b. 829, "Principi Guido."

[182] See ACS, *confinati politici*, b. 403, "Ferrarese, Mario."

[183] Quoted in F. W. Deakin, *The Brutal Friendship* (Garden City, 1966), 132.

had not radically remade the Italians. Instead, the home front fell apart. In March 1943, in Turin and Milan, workers in war industries went on strike and occupied factories. The strikes were organized by Communist cells, but Fascists and anti-Fascists participated in them, including members of the Fascist Militia (MVSN) unit organized for monitoring the political behavior of FIAT workers.[184] The government and party were losing their grip on Italian society. On April 1, Roberto Farinacci, the Ras of Cremona, wrote to Mussolini that "the Party is absent and impotent.... And now the unbelievable is happening. Everywhere, in the trams, the theatres, the air-raid shelters... people are denouncing the regime, and not only this or that party figure, but the Duce himself. And the most serious thing is that no one reacts. Even the police do not function, as if their work was now useless."[185] In response to the strikes and deteriorating public order, Mussolini threatened "draconian" measures. He blamed the party and the police, replacing Carmine Senise with a new police chief.

Perhaps predictably, Mussolini blamed Italy's failures on the moral character and physical condition of his own people, both the Italian masses and the bourgeoisie. Speaking again to the Party Directorate at Palazzo Venezia on April 17, Mussolini assessed the internal situation. He extolled the morale and dedication to victory of the soldiers, their families, and the Fascists. The rest belonged to the "inferior category." He ranted, "It is composed of all those who are physically and mentally below par and who are blind, lame, toothless, feeble-minded, shirkers, people lacking in some quality." Finally, there were "the middle classes and their attitude, a topic which enrages many Fascists," because the bourgeoisie was "rich and cowardly at the same time."[186] In the end, Mussolini continued to blame the mass of physically and mentally "inferior" Italians, together with the complacent bourgeoisie, for Italy's failure to realize Fascism's goals. By this time, police were sentencing ordinary Italians to political confinement for saying what everyone was thinking. In April 1943, a seventeen-year-old worker in Forlì mocked Mussolini's slogan *"vincere e vinceremo!"* (We're winning and we shall win!) with *"perdere e perderemo!"* (We're losing and we shall lose!).[187]

From 1935 onward, Mussolini increasingly deployed the apparatus of political repression for the purpose of "fascistizing" Italy, devoting

---

[184] Ibid., 225.
[185] Ibid., 227.
[186] Ibid., 319.
[187] ACS, *confinati politici*, b. 205, "Carlini, Bruno." For other examples, see b. 173, "Caldera, Luigi"; (1943) b. 289, "Cosentino, Gennaro"; b. 481, "Gilbertini, Rosina."

considerable personal energy to the task. Countless documents concerning common, often poor, downtrodden Italians were stamped "conferred with the Duce" or "seen by the Duce." Mussolini also scribbled on and signed many documents. Bocchini and his replacement, Carmine Senise, were the primary handlers of these cases, but both men met with Mussolini to discuss them on a daily or, at the very least, weekly basis. The very personal nature of Mussolini's administration of these cases must be understood within the context of his intention to effect a moral and even anthropomorphic renovation of Italian society. Vacillating between biting excoriations of the Italian people and chauvinist exhalations of their strength and superiority, between calls for harsh repression and frequent "generous" clemencies, Mussolini subjected thousands of unfortunate Italians to his obsessive bureaucratic paternalism.

The victims of the campaign against newly invented political crimes were predominately lower and lower-middle class, socially marginal, or poor. Relatively few were involved in organized anti-Fascism or deliberate opposition to the regime. Although some were explicitly critical of the regime's policies, reading their police files makes it clear that these Italians were also punished for moral failings and behaviors that did not conform to Mussolini's vision of Fascist society. Understanding how and why these groups were persecuted must take into account local contexts, but Mussolini's animosity toward them, expressed by designating them "political" threats to the nation, was meaningful and consequential. At the center, in Rome, Mussolini established a politics of repression, setting the parameters of unacceptable behaviors. In doing so, he encouraged and enabled local authorities, Fascists, and ordinary Italians to denounce and suppress these "anti-Fascist" behaviors in their own communities.

7

Ordinary Fascist Violence

Another phenomenon that provoked the hostility of citizens to the regime
was the thirst for overreacting, for excessive force that overcame all party
hierarchs, from top to bottom.... Hierarchs big and small saw no other
mode of affirming their authority than assuming and illegally exercising
powers entrusted to the organs of the State, often reaching the point of
invading the sphere of the personal liberty of citizens. It even reached
the point that party authorities believed it was their right to intervene in
conflicts of a personal nature.

Carmine Senise, Chief of Police (1940–1943)[1]

A disagreement with the head of the local *fascio*, even an apolitical one, is
enough to legitimize a confino sentence. What counts is not the text of the
written law, but the ability to apply it whenever one pleases.

Emilio Lussu, Lipari escapee[2]

Federico Fellini's film *Amarcord* tells a nostalgic, semiautobiographical
story about coming of age under Fascism in a seaside town resembling
Rimini. Well into the film, a high-ranking Fascist, the province's *federale*,
makes an official visit to the town. That night, as the festivities are winding
down, the Socialist hymn, the *International*, suddenly becomes audible.
Rushing into the central piazza, the Fascists discover that someone has
placed a gramophone in the bell tower of the church. Clearing the piazza
with menacing shouts, the Fascists fire their pistols up at the night sky.

---

[1] Senise was the regime's vice-chief of police during the 1930s and served as chief of police
between 1940 and 1943. Senise, *Capo della polizia*, 42–3.
[2] Emilio Lussu, *La Catena*, 44.

Bullets ricochet off the church bell, clinging and clanging, until the gramophone finally receives a fatal blow and plummets into the cobblestoned piazza below. The Fascists then march off singing the Fascist fight song *All'armi siam fascisti*.[3] In the next scene, the Black Shirts are back at their headquarters, interrogating the usual suspects: ex-Socialists, anarchists, subversives. One of these unfortunates is Aurelio Biondi, a hot-tempered Socialist with a habit of wearing a red tie on the occasion of Fascist celebrations. Dragged from his home in the middle of the night and placed under a bright, naked lightbulb, Aurelio unconvincingly denies knowing anything about the gramophone. He has never, he claims, "involved himself in politics." The Fascists then ask him to drink a "toast" to the *patria*: several glasses of castor oil. He refuses, and two younger Fascists then force the oil down his throat with slaps and punches. Aurelio goes home in a sorry state. He is convinced, moreover, that one of his own sons has betrayed him. After several humiliating hours in the bathroom, Aurelio walks out into his hallway, screaming, "If the one who informed is who I think he is, he better move to another continent!" His sons lie in their beds, giggling with nervous fear.[4]

Many of the quotidian vexations of the lived experience of Fascism, so colorfully captured by film directors, novelists, and poets, have been taken for granted, but rarely studied, by scholars. Ordinary violence and bullying are simultaneously everywhere and nowhere in the history of Fascism. The same can be said of the creeping influence of party-state authority, which seeped into relationships between friends, neighbors, family members, and strangers. During the 1930s in particular, the Fascist regime's policies of political and social control began permeating broader sections of Italian society and shaping the minutiae of everyday life. No longer confined to the venues of conflict between Fascists and anti-Fascists, the politics of ordinary violence metastasized to communities throughout the Italian peninsula, infiltrating public spaces, the work place, and even the family home. Personal relationships and social interactions became political. The threat of physical attacks, institutional confinement, and financial ruin loomed over even the most mundane events.

The Nationalization of Fascist Violence

Many studies have suggested that squad violence and "pockets of illegality" persisted throughout Italy, often on the margins of the Fascist Militia

---

3 First verse: To arms, to arms / we are the *fascisti* / terror for the *comunisti*.
4 *Amarcord*, DVD, directed by Federico Fellini (1973; Italy: New World Cinema, 2006).

(MVSN) , into the late 1920s and early 1930s.[5] In such cases, Fascist Ras, together with their cronies and clients, continued to rule towns, small cities, and neighborhoods as private fiefdoms, engaging in a wide array of illegal activities, ranging from extortion to physical attacks. Local and central authorities often turned a blind eye to this type of criminality, but in special circumstances, larger political forces compelled police and *carabinieri* to investigate and prosecute Fascists. Over the course of the regime, the political winds regularly shifted, most commonly in response to Mussolini's appointment of a new party secretary. During these periods, Fascists at the national and provincial levels engaged in factional struggles, smear campaigns, and denunciatory practices in order to win political offices and administrative positions. New men attained positions of power, and the supporters of the outgoing Fascist Party (PNF) secretary were thrown out, often leading to their expulsion from the party and economic ruin. But the disgraced Fascist hierarch and his supporters never completely dropped out of the game. Political rehabilitation, and opportunities for revenge, always remained possible. Mussolini alone arbitrated this politics of "cannibalism." These shifts in political power thus led to serious, sometimes violent conflicts, as ambitious party men sought to capitalize on a changing political landscape.[6]

Such settings prompted provincial authorities to begin exposing the criminal activities of embattled or defeated Fascists. In 1929, for example, the Ras of Milan, Mario Giampaoli, a violent, corrupt "true believer," fell from power. Police then punished several of his cronies for the widespread use of physical violence, torture, blackmail, and even rape and murder.[7] In the early 1930s, Leandro Arpinati, the former Ras of Bologna, was disgraced and punished when Achile Starace, an enemy, became party secretary. Arpinati, a former party secretary, lost his position as undersecretary of the Interior Ministry and was stripped of his party membership before being sent off to *confino* on Lipari.[8] Back in Bologna, Arpinati's lackeys fell one by one under a barrage of accusations: cocaine use, corruption, nepotism, gambling, and illegal violence.[9]

---

[5] See, among others, Bosworth, *Mussolini's Italy*, esp. 250–5; Bartolini, *Fascismo antislavo*, 75; Valleri, "Dal partito armato," 39; Piccioni, *San Lorenzo*, 90, 105, 107; Marco Palla, *Firenze nel regime fascista, 1929–1934* (Florence, 1978), 152–3.

[6] Corner, "Everyday Fascism," esp. 200. These factional conflicts have been the subject of recent research; in addition to Corner, see Lupo's *Il fascismo* and Bosworth's *Mussolini's Italy*.

[7] See Bosworth, *Mussolini's Italy*, 93–4, 206–9.

[8] Ibid., 279–80.

[9] Ibid., 251–3.

This type of changing of the guard occurred on a smaller scale in many Italian communities. In Gallarate, a small industrial textile center forty kilometers northwest of Milan, *carabinieri* described how for ten years, up until 1934, Marcello Padovani – a "*squadrista* of the first hour" and secretary of the local *fascio* – and his clique of Fascists had "held the city under a regime of terror" with "the pretext of defending who knows what Fascist principle." Padovani's innumerable "acts of violence and extortion," motivated solely by profit and personal feuds, only attracted the attention of authorities when he was found to have embezzled tens of thousands of lira from the local PNF's welfare coffers.[10] His corruption, rather than his "reign of terror," led to his downfall and the rise of new political leadership. Thus, Fascists who systematically inflicted terror might be exposed and prosecuted only if they lost internecine struggles within the party or committed some serious act of malfeasance against the party or state.[11] Moreover, the winning faction was likely to wield its newly acquired power in the same corrupt fashion. As Bosworth explains, "It is very likely that for every individual expelled from the party and punished by the regime, many more were not but went on embodying corruption, brutality, patronage, familism and localism and being the little Farinaccis of the suburbs."[12]

Although the regime suppressed Fascist criminality in some circumstances, it by no means discouraged Fascists and militiamen from actively repressing banned behaviors. Outside of state public-security forces, the PNF and MVSN were the central conduits through which Mussolini's police state sought to penetrate and control Italian society. During the 1930s, moreover, the PNF extended its influence over much of the Italian peninsula, becoming a truly national mass party. Mussolini's appointment of Achille Starace as PNF secretary in 1931 in many ways signaled Fascism moving beyond its northern origins. Born near Lecce, in Puglia, Starace was the first party secretary from the south, an important fact, at least symbolically. Though he participated in the early Fascist movement in the north, Starace had strong ties to Puglia and served informally as a sort of liaison or power broker who worked to strengthen southern Fascism, particularly in Puglia and Sicily.[13] More importantly, as party secretary, he oversaw the expansion of the PNF's membership. Under the

[10] *Carabinieri* of Milan (Gallarate/Varese) to prefect of Varese, July 2, 1934, in ACS, *confinati politici*, b. 733, "Padovani, Marcello."
[11] For other examples, see Bosworth, *Mussolini's Italy*, 250–5.
[12] Ibid., 250.
[13] Lupo, *Fascismo*, 83, 173, 182–3.

previous two secretariats of Giovanni Giurati and Augusto Turati, joining the PNF was voluntary and admission was highly selective. Between 1927 and 1932, entry to party rolls was either closed or severely restricted, and 230,000 members were purged.[14] Under Starace, by contrast, membership became automatic for many young men: every year the *"leva fascista"* initiated members of the Fascist youth organizations – the Balilla (ONB) and, from 1937 onward, the Italian Youth of the Lictors (GIL) – into the PNF proper. Belonging to the party also became obligatory for state employment, eligibility for social services, and other benefits. For many, the saying went, the PNF card stood for "Per Necessitá Familiare" (For Family Necessity). Accordingly, party membership increased from 825,000 in 1931 to more than two million in 1936; it would reach almost five million by 1939.[15] Additionally, Italians joined party organizations – the labor syndicates, the *fasci femminile* (women's section), the youth groups, the Dopolavoro – by the millions. The influence of the party also broadened geographically. Fascism, if measured by recruitment rather than "true" political faith, was no longer a phenomenon of the Po Valley, Venezia Giulia, Tuscany, Puglia, and a few major cities. By the 1930s, southerners joined the PNF at roughly the same rate as northerners. Geographically speaking, the party was everywhere.[16]

The PNF also insinuated its structure more deeply into Italian communities. By the mid-1930s, the party had divided up cities into district groups (Gruppi rionale), which were then subdivided into "sectors" and, finally, "nuclei." The purpose of these entities, according to PNF statutes, was "to make increasingly intense and diffuse the capillary activity of the party."[17] With new party units came new leadership positions (district chief, sector chief, nucleus chief), which served to "find a place for the old Fascists and to give a fragment of the party's power to the zealous Fascists as a reward for their loyalty and their dedication to the organization." The regime's intention was to monitor and more directly rule the population, "so that every single family, every single individual could be known, accounted for, organized, and controlled."[18] Although perhaps falling short of this goal, these structural reforms had a significant effect, particularly in urban areas. "Fascist surveillance is well organized at the local level," a Communist agent wrote about Florence during the

---

[14] Ibid., 385.
[15] Ibid., 386.
[16] Marco Palla, "Lo stato-partito," 23–5.
[17] Art. 58 of the *regolamento* of the PNF.
[18] Gentile, *Via italiana al totalitarianism*, 188–9.

mid-1930s. "For quite some time, on each street," he reported, "there is a Fascist charged with following the latest news about what occurs on the street, private matters of the residents, and, above all, about those individuals who are not Fascists."[19]

The expansion and deeper penetration of the PNF and the MVSN into Italian society throughout Italy led to a nationalization of politicized conflict and violence. Party and militia members wielded a great deal of coercive power, playing important formal and informal roles in state policies of political and social control.[20] In larger urban areas – Rome, Turin, Milan, Genoa, and Naples – small groups of Fascists and militiamen formally patrolled the streets of their districts from evening until dawn, giving particular scrutiny to public spaces, such as piazzas and parks, and establishments that served alcohol. Militiamen were also sometimes assigned "special surveillance service" in areas that had experienced suspicious political activity – graffiti, leaflets, anti-Fascist songs, and so on. The militia's Provincial Investigative Offices (UPI) officially served as collection points for political denunciations. Informally, however, Italians delivered information and gossip to Fascists and militiamen of all ranks.[21] Police frequently contacted local party officials for information about the attitudes and behaviors of individuals in their communities.[22] Finally, the MVSN's UPIs and local PNF offices conducted their own investigations into anti-Fascist activities, mainly criticisms of the regime, before turning a case over to the police.[23] In 1935, for example, an anonymous person reported to a local MVSN office that Guido Cimini, a "habitual criminal" known for having a "strange and unstable" character, regularly engaged in criticisms of Mussolini and his economic policies at a bar in Milan's historic center. An agent from the MVSN's UPI went in plain clothes to the bar and found Cimini, dressed in a ragged pinstriped suit coat with a

---

[19] Ibid., 189.

[20] Of 447 files of political detainees sampled from the period 1932–43, at least 44 involved members of the PNF, 37 involved the MVSN, and 2 involved both the PNF and the MVSN. Put another way, of the 166 cases in which people brought anti-Fascist behaviors to the attention of the police or *carabinieri*, 83 involved the PNF or MVSN and 83 involved ordinary citizens.

[21] For examples involving the MVSN, see ACS, *confinati politici*, b. 253, "Cimini, Guido"; b. 565, "Levi, Ines"; b. 577, "Lori, Ercole"; b. 583, "Lupi, Umberto"; b. 727, "Orioli, Alessandro"; and for the PNF, see b. 173, "Caldera, Luigi"; b. 211, "Caturan, Giuseppe"; b. 685, "Montebello, Sergio"; b. 769, "Pellegrino, Pietro"; b. 1027, "Trombetta, Enrico."

[22] These contacts are implicit in the language of most police reports. For a more explicit example, see the case of "Santurri, Mario," in ACS, *confinati politici*, b. 913.

[23] See ACS, *confinati politici*, b. 253, "Cimini, Guido"; b. 901, "Sala, Carlo."

dirty, scoop-necked undershirt beneath. The UPI agent began talking to Cimini, who immediately asked for money to support a fantastical plan to steal weapons, start an insurrection, and "destroy the current political order." After discovering the "plot," which authorities recognized as nothing more than "fruit of [Cimini's] imagination," designed only to put money in his pockets, the MVSN informed the police, who immediately arrested and sentenced him to the Ventotene confinement colony.[24]

For Fascists and militiamen of all ranks, the most common form of political policing was spontaneous action, rather than formal patrolling or surveillance duty. In their daily lives, Fascists reacted to behaviors they interpreted as suspicious or anti-Fascist. Such incidents almost always occurred in the same types of spaces: taverns, piazzas, parks, streets,[25] and occasionally boardinghouses, public dormitories, soup kitchens, and working-class apartments.[26] For example, on an August night in 1937, in Rome's Piazza Coronari, a small square near Piazza Navona, a group of Romans were lingering until almost three in the morning, enjoying a carousel still in operation at that late hour.[27] According to a police report, a forty-six-year-old sector chief of the PNF named Armando Cecconi, a

---

[24] *Carabinieri* of Milan (Interna) to comando generale, April 15, 1935, ACS, *confinati politici*, b. 253, "Cimini, Guido."

[25] For the militiamen acting in public spaces, see ACS, *confinati politici*, b. 3, "Acciari, Adolfo"; b. 48, "Baffico, Pietro"; b. 113, "Bicocchi, Cesare"; b. 427, "Forzato, Aristide"; b. 457, "Gariglio, Romildo"; b. 457, "Garnerone, Pietro"; b. 469, "Gesmundo, Giovanni"; b. 469, "Gheffoli, Andrea"; b. 475, "Piovano, Giacomino"; b. 571, "Loi, Giovanni"; b. 653, "Meloni, Francesco"; b. 661, "Mervi, Francesca"; b. 679, "Molinari, Giovanni"; b. 703, "Napoli, Vincenzo"; b. 739, "Palermini, Pasquale"; b. 823, "Pradal, Germano"; b. 841, "Radan, Francesco"; b. 853, "Refrigeri, Amedeo"; b. 877, "Romazin, Giovanni"; b. 991, "Tamagni, Umberto"; b. 991, "Tamburnini, Guglielmo"; b. 1045, "Valsecchi, Ferruccio"; b. 1063, "Viali, O."; b. 1069, "Violetta, Giovanni"; b. 1069, "Viotto, Antonio"; b. 1081, "Zadnik, Giuseppe," b. 1087, "Giacinto Zanetti."
For Fascists acting in public spaces, see ACS, *confinati politici*, b. 83, "Bellodi, Viglielmo"; b. 93, "Berardi, Francesco and Raffaele"; b. 98, "Berrini, Giuseppe"; b. 118, "Biondi, Aldo"; b. 168, "Buttarello, Biagio"; b. 301, "Cudini, Carlo"; b. 319, "De Angelis, Mario"; b. 445, "Galbier, Vittorio"; b. 469, "Gezzele, Giuseppe"; b. 505, "Grazioli, Martino"; b. 529, "Ienuso, Cristoforo"; b. 541, "Kinder, Ermano"; b. 559, "Leggi, Ruggero"; b. 613, "Marangon, Tullio"; b. 679, "Molinari, Oliviero"; b. 727, "Orecchia"; b. 763, "Patrioli, Angelo"; b. 799, "Pinna, Giovanni"; b. 811, "Rinaldo Pogliani"; b. 823, "Prampolini, Giovanni"; b. 877, "Romano, Pasquale"; b. 877, "Romanzin, Giovanni"; b. 955, "Sinigaglia, Licurgo"; b. 961, "Soleschi, Pietro"; b. 991, "Talatin, Antonio"; b. 1045, "Vallino, Giovanni"; b. 1051, "Vattovani, Andrea"; b. 1075, "Voccoli, Ribelle"; b. 1075, "Volgger, Alfonso."

[26] ACS, *confinati politici*, b. 28, "Tancredi, Angelini"; b. 83, "Bellini, Mario"; b. 193, "Caporelli, Giuseppe"; b. 505, "Linceo, Graziosio."

[27] *Questore* (Palma) to prefect of Rome, September 13, 1937, in ACS, *confinati politici*, b. 559, "Leggi, Ruggero."

civil servant in Rome's municipal government, happened to be passing by and "deemed it appropriate, in the interest of public quiet, to make the carousel cease operating and disperse the citizens, inviting them to return home, being that it had become quite late." To this end, Cecconi first went to collect his PNF subordinates, all younger men in their mid-twenties, some of whom also belonged to the MVSN. Notably, at three in the morning, most of them were already in uniform "on duty" at the nearby party headquarters on Viale Coronari. Entering the piazza, the "squad" of Fascists first approached the operator of the carousel, telling him to shut it down, and then "requested that the public to return to their own homes." The police chief of Rome reported, "While of course all complied with their request, one unknown man cast a look of disdain and provocation at them, and even mumbled incomprehensibly. This caught the attention of the aforementioned Fascists who, without demonstrating any animosity... repeated their request, as he appeared rather intoxicated from wine." To their insistence that he leave and go home, the man allegedly responded: "Who are you? What do you want? I'll go wherever I want, because I'm free and couldn't care less about the law." The man's confrontational attitude led the Fascists to attempt to take him to the local police station. However, the report continued, "the unknown rebel, not tolerating such an injunction, refused to move, and it was then necessary to resort to force."[28]

At the police station, the man identified himself as Ruggero Leggi, a fifty-four-year-old tinsmith whose name appeared in the police registry of known anarchists. His file revealed that he had been sentenced to political probation between 1928 and 1930 and had eighteen prior criminal offenses ranging from threatening authorities to drunkenness. Though unmarried, Leggi lived with his sister-in-law, Teresa Alciati, on via del Governo Vecchio, just minutes from Piazza Coronari. Ruggero's brother had died, and he and Teresa had lived as husband and wife for the past fifteen years. They had one daughter together in addition to Teresa's four children. According to the police commissioner, Ruggero Leggi drank heavily, often squandering his wages in taverns. He was "impulsive and violent," and though considered of "scarce culture," he was "intelligent enough to present a threat during public events." The police commissioner also noted that Leggi had deserted during the First World War. Additionally, as with so many "subversive women" buried inside the police files of their men folk, Ruggero's nieces also fell under scrutiny.

[28] See Americo di Clemente, "Verbale di fermo," in ibid.

Police alleged that two of them led "the life of libertines," taking "lovers" from all over Rome. In the eyes of authorities, all of these details severely compromised Ruggero. Although he begged for leniency in the name of his five dependent children, he was condemned to three years of political internment, spending one year in the Tremiti internment colony and two more in exile in the town of Bultei (Sassari) in Sardinia. During his absence, Teresa and her children suffered financially, falling behind in the rent. Her late husband's pension allowed her to eke out a living, but Ruggero's wages were sorely missed.

The actions of Sector Chief Cecconi illustrate how the party's growing presence affected daily life in one small part of a large city. Cecconi was exercising his duty, or his prerogative, as sector chief, to police the behavior of persons in his *rione* (neighborhood). Merely displaying resistance to Cecconi's will constituted a political offense. How the other Romans enjoying a night in late August, during Italy's traditional summer holiday (*ferragosto*), experienced the tense and ultimately violent incident is a matter of speculation. Were the spectators white-collar workers like Cecconi, or working class like Leggi? Did they applaud or abhor the Fascists taking Leggi into custody? Whatever the case, the dynamics of social power engendered by the Fascist state obligated Leggi – a working-class anarchist, allegedly inebriated at three in the morning – to defer to the will of Cecconi. Clear to all must have been that the consequences of defying the Fascists were real physical violence – however mild – and then institutional punishment. Cecconi's Fascists may or may not have terrorized the Romans in Piazza Coronari, but they unquestionably asserted their state-backed authority over the neighborhood's inhabitants and demonstrated the consequences of resistance.

The ubiquitous presence of Fascists in public spaces, announced by uniforms, insignias, and long-standing reputations, was a source of fear and intimidation. Countless anecdotes and reminiscences attest to the sense that the party was "everywhere." In many cases, the mere appearance of Fascists provoked hostile remarks from disgruntled or drunken Italians, leading to confrontations.[29] On a street in Turin, late one November night in 1938, a drunken, homeless, unemployed mechanic encountered Fascists belonging to the local *gruppo rionale* and proclaimed that "he wasn't afraid of anyone."[30] In that same city in October 1939, another drunken,

---

[29] Lidia Piccioni found that in San Lorenzo, a common political offense was Italians simply telling Fascists that they were not afraid of them. Piccioni, *San Lorenzo*, 106.
[30] ACS, *confinati politici*, b. 1045, "Vallino, Giovanni."

unemployed mechanic exclaimed to a group of Fascists, "the Militia and the Party don't scare me at all, and I don't give a damn about ranks."[31] Such expressions of "not being afraid" of Torinese Fascists suggest that there was something to fear. The MVSN there, as in many other cities, had developed a reputation for engaging in beatings, torture, and even the occasional homicide.[32] In July 1940, for example, on the outskirts of Turin, two eleven-year-old boys played popular songs on a guitar and a harmonica inside a *trattoria* while a few patrons sang along. Several MVSN vice-squad chiefs entered the restaurant, and one of them, Arturo D'Elia, demanded that the boys stop because "the nation was in mourning due to the loss of Marshal [Italo Balbo]" (the Ras of Ferrara, Quadrumvir of the March on Rome, and Governor of Libya), who had recently died in an airplane crash. To sing songs at this moment was "to profane the memory of the Hero." To the vice-squad chief's attempt to force patriotic reverence for a fallen Fascist on his fellow citizens, a fifty-four-year-old mechanic named Antonio Viotto responded, "just another dead asshole." Vice-Squad Chief D'Elia immediately attacked Viotto, punching him in the face and jumping on top of him. A few bystanders attempted to stop the attack, but D'Elia picked up a chair and smashed it over one of their heads, leaving a bloody gash. At this point, a military officer who happened to be present ordered the vice-squad chief to stop and eventually succeeded in removing him from the premises. D'Elia then accused the military officer and other witnesses of "not being Fascists." The lieutenant brought D'Elia back to MVSN headquarters, and then "described the incident verbally to the centurion [MVSN commander]... leaving it to him to refer the information to his own superiors."[33] Vice-Squad Chief D'Elia's involvement in the incident having ended, the local *carabinieri* searched for and arrested Antonio Viotto, who resided in the center of Turin. By his own admission, Viotto spent most of his nights drinking in taverns and conducting a "disordered life." He had also incurred several citations for public drunkenness. For his "offense to a High Personality," he was sentenced to two years of political exile, which he spent in a small village in the southern province of Cosenza.[34]

---

[31] ACS, *confinati politici*, b. 313, "D'Angelo, Mario."

[32] Canali, *Le spie*, 77–8; Franzinelli, I *tentacoli*, 241–3; Dunnage, "Surveillance and Denunciation in Fascist Siena," 256.

[33] *Carabinieri* of Torino (Esterno), "Incidente tra borghesi, militi e un ufficiale del Reggio Esercito," July 6, 1940, in ACS, *confinati politici*, b. 1069, "Viotto, Antonio."

[34] See *questore* (Murino) to prefect of Torino, August 12, 1940; and Antonio Viotto to Duce, November 14, 1940, in "Viotto, Antonio."

Combing the margins of police files looking for such incidents certainly does not uncover the true scope of the illegality and violence that Fascists inflicted on some Italian communities. State and party authorities had no incentive to commit to writing every crime and abuse perpetrated by local Fascists, who were after all operating under the watch of the police, *carabinieri*, *podestà*, and prefects. In many communities, Fascists and militiamen conducted their own "investigations" and roughed up, beat, and intimidated people as they pleased, without the police ever getting involved. One PNF *federale* in the Po Valley boasted that his Fascists dealt with enemies "in our usual fashion." On the occasion of the regime's many national celebrations, parades, and ceremonies, Fascists beat up people for trifling offenses – not taking off one's hat, reading a foreign newspaper, and other seemingly innocuous acts.[35] In Rome's San Lorenzo neighborhood, local Fascists brought "suspects" to PNF headquarters, where they were interrogated, roughed up, and sometimes, like the unfortunate Aurelio Biondi in Fellini's film, forced to drink castor oil. In 1938, for example, a blacksmith with a reputation for listening to broadcasts from Spain was forced "to drink a mixture of oil and petroleum." Finally allowing him to leave, the Fascists "followed him, beat him, and hurt him gravely."[36] In Venezia Giulia, virulent Fascist antislavism, ongoing "denationalization" policies, and Slavic resistance created a tense, violent atmosphere, unlike anyplace else in Italy. Even speaking a Slavic language in public could provoke an altercation. In 1936, to offer just one example, Alojz Bratuz, the director of a Slovenian choral group, celebrated Christmas with songs sung in Slovenian. Afterward, outside the church, a group of Fascists abducted the director and four singers, taking them to a secluded area, beating them, and forcing them to drink machine oil. Six weeks later, Bratuz died.[37]

Further immunizing the perpetrators of ordinary violence from punishment was the predictable fact that the victims of attacks, extortion, and other crimes committed by Fascists were unlikely to file a complaint with authorities, who were often themselves complicit in Fascist misdeeds. What, after all, were the *carabinieri* and police doing in small cities like Gallerate during the many years in which low-level Ras like Padovani were presiding over regimes of criminal terror? Moreover, denouncing Fascist illegality sometimes attracted unwanted attention to

[35] Corner, "Everyday Fascism," 213.
[36] Piccioni, *San Lorenzo*, 90, 105, 107.
[37] Bartolini, *Fascismo antislavo*, 75–6.

the complainant, potentially resulting in some type of police sanction. In a small Ligurian town, an agricultural laborer named Giovanni Battista Violetta walked into an *osteria* and ordered a bottle of wine, pouring a cup for everyone at a table except Candido Marazzo, whom Violetta knew to be a militiaman. Violetta then allegedly offered the following toast: "This is how the militiamen must be treated. All cheats who do nothing."[38] Militiaman Marazzo stormed out of the tavern but waited outside. Later, as Violetta was walking home, Marazzo attacked him with numerous blows to the head, seriously injuring his eye. For the militiaman, the matter was settled. The next day, Violetta went to the hospital to seek medical treatment. During the examination, he told a doctor what had happened. The doctor reported the incident to the *carabinieri* and encouraged Violetta to seek out a lawyer. It is revealing that a medical doctor assumed that the police and judicial authorities might actually take action against Violetta's attacker. When the militiaman discovered that charges might be pressed, he went to the *carabinieri* and denounced Violetta's political offense against the MVSN, ten days after the fact.[39] The police interviewed Violetta's drinking companions, all of whom confirmed the substance of the militiaman's story, though with wildly differing versions of the alleged insult. Perhaps some tried to mitigate Violetta's situation, remembering his generosity. In any case, for his "outrageous and provocative" words and his "anti-regime sentiments," Violetta was sentenced to political confinement. It was unlikely that authorities would side with Violetta in this dispute: sixty-two-years-old, poor, alcoholic, and separated from his wife for thirty years, Violetta was, according to the police, "indifferent to the regime." Although "in public" he was "held to be an anti-Fascist," he had no history of committing political "offenses."[40] Fascists were therefore not only rarely sanctioned for assaults on citizens, but such attacks were also fully condoned, with the police only concerned about whether to punish the victim. It seems highly probable, moreover, that most such incidents were never reported. In certain circumstances, Fascists could punch, slap, kick, and rough up people without much fear of official remonstrance, let alone prosecution. Victims of such aggression, if they attempted to report it to police, were often punished for their "provocative antifascist behavior."

---

[38] *Questore* to prefect of Savona, June 19, 1941, in ACS, *confinati politici*, b. 1069, "Violetta, Giovanni Battista."

[39] See Violetta's statement to police (Daniele Piu and Vincenzo Marcello), June 26, 1941, in ibid.

[40] *Carabinieri* of Genova (Albegna) to *questore* of Savona, May 29, 1941, in ibid.

In addition to possessing an implicit license to physically attack their fellow citizens in certain circumstances, Fascists could also call on the police to inflict sanctions on anti-Fascists or enemies. In absolute terms, this type of political denunciation became more common in the years after 1934. Moreover, during this period, the Ministry of the Interior received complaints about Fascists of all ranks threatening ordinary people with political confinement and other sanctions. In theory, Fascists had no authority to inflict such sanctions; in practice, many Italians understood that an accusation launched by a Fascist could well result in some sort of punishment. The problem was so acute that Undersecretary of the Interior Ministry Buffarini Guidi sent multiple missives to provincial authorities urging them to reign in the practice of Fascists using *confino di polizia* as an "instrument for threatening" people.[41] At issue was not the involvement of party members in denouncing or repressing anti-Fascist acts but simply the phenomenon of Fascists threatening people with sanctions in order to intimidate them, often in terms that suggested that the party, rather than the state, held jurisdiction over *confino* sentences.

When Fascists made political accusations against ordinary Italians, police investigated the charges, usually interviewing many witnesses. The police sometimes scrutinized Fascists' motives and, in a small percentage of cases, turned the tables, punishing a Fascist instead for "false denunciation."[42] In most cases, however, public-security authorities conducted a crude political arithmetic, weighing the accuser's Fascist credentials against the political standing and moral character of the accused. Police and *carabinieri* gave great weight to any claims made by Fascists in good standing. Where there was uncertainty, authorities obviously sided with party members. In Vicenza, for example, a young Fascist named Italino Fossa denounced Mario De Angelis for criticizing Mussolini's foreign policy. In the community, many speculated that Fossa had acted against De Angelis because Fossa and his friends had taken exception to De Angelis's courtship with a local woman, Silvana Poluzzi. Police reported that De Angelis had in the past been viewed as "politically suspect" but noted that recently he "always engaged in good political conduct" and was well liked by local Fascists, with whom he spent a great deal of time. Nonetheless, Fossa, the young Fascist, was "respected

---

[41] Buffarini Guidi to prefects, May 22, 1937, and July 29, 1938, in ACS, MI, Massime, b. 17, fasc. 2, sf. 3.

[42] See ACS, *confinati politici*, b. 457, "Garnerone, Pietro"; b. 499, "Gozzi, Arturo"; also, Franzinelli, *Delatori*, 14.

as a serious young man, committed to the party, to which he has devoted much of his time." Disregarding suspicions of a personal vendetta, the police accorded Fossa's complaint greater credibility and sentenced De Angelis to two years political exile in the south.[43]

The Private Sphere

In addition to sowing intimidation and fear in public spaces, members of the party and militia also used their position atop Fascism's hierarchical society to their advantage within the private sphere of the home and family.[44] Party members projected state repressive policies into the private sphere in two senses. First, Fascists who suspected that anti-Fascist activities were occurring inside someone's residence – listening to forbidden radio broadcasts, singing Socialist hymns, denigrating the regime – simply entered the home, forcibly if necessary, without a warrant or any official authorization whatsoever.[45] Second, the regime's institutions and policies created the potential for turning the most intimate of personal relations into sites of politicized conflict.[46] Long-standing animosities between members of nuclear and extended families were summarily resolved by political accusations and institutional punishment.

For example, Giuseppe Caporelli and Anna Antonucci lived with three of their five children in the Rione Regola, one of the central districts of historic Rome, near the Tevere, Palazzo Farnese, and Campo de' Fiori. Fifty-six years of age, unemployed, and alcoholic, Caporelli had a reputation for "mistreating" his wife and children. His wife, Anna Antonucci, who earned fifteen lira per day as a vegetable vendor in the Campo de' Fiori market, resented having to support her abusive husband. The dynamic within the family began to change around 1930 following the engagement of their daughter Iole to Renato Polini, a member of the militia. The young Fascist, with whom Anna had a "close relationship," served as a counterbalance to Giuseppe. Before long, Polini had apparently become

---

[43] ACS, *confinati politici*, b. 319, "De Angelis, Mario."

[44] Chief of Police Senise makes this same claim in his memoir (*Capo della polizia*, 42–3).

[45] For instances of Fascists barging into homes, see ACS, *confinati politici*, b. 83, "Bellini, Mario"; b. 108, "Bianchi, Augusto"; b. 505, "Linceo Grazioso"; b. 823, "Pradal, Germano."

[46] Though less common than other forms of conflict, politicized interfamilial conflict occurred, particularly involving a family member who was violent, alcoholic, or abusive, or over an inheritance, marriage, or money. E.g., ACS, *confinati politici*, b. 63, "Barenghi, Renzo"; b. 83, "Bellini, Mario"; b. 331, "De Lisio, Agostino"; b. 499, "Gozzi, Arturo."

"the absolute and despotic master of Caporelli's house." Giuseppe, as might be expected, detested his unemployed future son-in-law, who had no profession or trade, viewing him as an overgrown child.[47] One day in late November 1931, upon returning home, a drunken Giuseppe asked his wife for something to eat. Anna, who was playing a card game with her children, Renato Polini, and several neighbors, "rudely" told her husband that a man who did not work did not deserve to eat. Incensed, Caporelli retorted that his wife dared talk to him with such insolence only because of the presence of Polini, who "being a militiaman," enjoyed "the protection of Mussolini." The young Fascist, claiming this statement to be "false and offensive," immediately went to the local public-security commissariat with Caporelli's wife, Anna, in tow. "Identifying himself as a militiaman," Polini "reported that Caporelli had pronounced offensive phrases directed at His Excellency the Head of Government." Later that night, Caporelli was arrested, and in the morning, police interviewed witnesses, all of whom confirmed the young Fascist's accusations against Caporelli. The police proposed Caporelli for political confinement, deporting him to Lipari shortly thereafter.

In subsequent weeks, following Caporelli's appeal of the sentence, a more complex picture emerged. The *questore* of Rome remained convinced that Caporelli was a subversive: though he had not engaged in political activity recently, Caporelli had once attended a Socialist meeting some thirty-four years earlier, in 1897! Moreover, the local Fascists of Regola had received anonymous denunciations – perhaps even made by Polini – that Caporelli regularly blamed Mussolini for unemployment among workers, leading them to "die of hunger."[48] Caporelli's neighbors, interviewed by the police, also reported that just days before his arrest, Caporelli had expressed hope that "the king would die and the Fascist Regime would crumble."[49]

The *carabinieri*, who had opposed the original sentence, conducted their own investigation, which yielded markedly different conclusions. The whole affair, one officer argued, had made a negative impression among the inhabitants of Regola. An anonymous tip from a local Fascist – from the same *gruppo rionale* of Regola – revealed that Polini had been expelled from the MVSN for "reprehensible conduct." Yet Polini still

---

[47] *Carabinieri* of Rome, February 24, 1932, in ACS, *confinati politici*, b. 193, "Caporelli, Giuseppe." See also *questore* of Rome (Cocchia) to MI, December 4, 1931, in ibid.
[48] *Questore* (Cocchia) to prefect of Rome, December 11, 1931, in ibid.
[49] *Questore* to prefect of Rome, December 11, 1931, in ibid.

regularly donned the militia uniform and "committed acts of violence and abuse for strictly personal motives." As for Anna Antonucci, "the public voice" largely blamed her for the incident. When talking to friends, she "did not hesitate to show her happiness . . . at her success in finally being rid of her husband." Her children, including her daughter Iole, Polini's fiancée, told the *carabinieri* that their mother and Polini pressured them to say bad things about their father. The *confino* sentence was thus "an error," and its annulment would be "viewed positively by the public."[50] In his appeal, Giuseppe declared himself to be an "authentic Italian" and "admirer and supporter of the Fascist Faith," sent away for an entirely private matter: his objection to the marriage of Polini to his daughter Iole. He denied that he was a "subversive" or otherwise "antinational," and claimed that he knew nothing of politics.[51] Nonetheless, he spent eleven months on the island of Lipari until his inclusion in the amnesty granted for the tenth anniversary of the March on Rome.

One of the central issues in Caporelli's case concerned the legitimacy of Polini's exploitation of Fascist coercive power to resolve conflict within the most private of spheres, the nuclear family. Despite the *carabinieri*'s objections, the police put the weight of the state behind Polini's efforts to dispose of his future father-in-law. The Roman police chief took no account of Polini's violent reputation, or the apparent fact that he falsely and illegally continued to present himself as a member of the MVSN. In this case, the police chief, and state authorities more generally, simply sided with the Fascist aggressor, thereby validating everything the community already believed about Polini and the regime. The assumptions that shaped this politicized domestic dispute reveal how merely belonging to the militia – or falsely presenting oneself as a Fascist – might intimidate one's family, neighbors, and acquaintances.

The incident also furnished a very public example to the residents of Regola. A former militiaman notorious for violence and corruption, and a vegetable vendor who bitterly resented her husband, successfully manipulated the politics of ordinary violence to have Giuseppe Caporelli arrested and confined. Although domestic, the confrontation occurred, in effect, in full view of neighbors and friends, who were later interviewed. The local section of the PNF weighed in, both as a source and depository of political denunciations. People in Regola talked about what had happened to Giuseppe Caporelli and why. Neighbors and witnesses confirmed that

---

[50] *Carabinieri* of Rome, February 24, 1932, in ibid.
[51] Caporelli to Appeal Commission, March 15, 1932, in ibid.

Caporelli had made anti-Mussolini statements – what better way to separate oneself from a suspected political criminal – but they also expressed dismay that Polini and Antonucci were able to call upon the apparatus of political repression to send Caporelli off to an island camp. If the tensions inside Caporelli's family had never boiled over in this manner, leading to a political denunciation, we would have little empirical evidence of this dynamic of social power. It must be assumed, however, that many more familial relationships were affected by the presence of a bullying Fascist or another skilled practitioner of the Fascist politics of ordinary violence.

The Patronizing State

Fascists also exercised coercion by means other than resorting to physical and institutional punishment. During the 1930s, party membership became a prerequisite for public employment, state teaching positions, academic and sporting competitions, and, at least unofficially, preferential treatment in many other spheres of daily living controlled by the PNF. The goal of this expansion of party authority was to discipline, organize, and regiment the Italian population – to solidly integrate the individual into the totalitarian mass society. However, by their very nature, party organs were exclusive. Not everyone could belong. Of the party-state institutions, the militia exercised the strictest discipline over the ideological commitment of its members. The party practiced a degree of selectivity. But within every community there lived former Fascists who had been purged from the rolls or would-be Fascists who were refused admission based on some personal shortcoming. The youth organizations provided a fairly certain path to future PNF membership, but some poor families could not afford the cost of the uniform and the dues. Only the Dopolavoro operated according to sufficiently superficial political requirements as to admit virtually anyone, yet organized leisure provided only recreational diversions, without any of the power, special material advantages, or preferential treatment enjoyed by Fascists in good standing.[52] Citizens who did not belong to party organizations, for whatever reason, were essential to the Fascist style of rule. Without have-nots, there could be no haves.

Italians who had been rejected by the party or somehow left out of the Fascist *inquadramento* (coordination) of the nation harbored resentments – some because they had failed in their efforts to join the

---

[52] Palla, "Il stato-partito," 23–5.

party; others because the presence of Fascists in everyday life served as a constant, sometimes humiliating reminder of their own marginal socio-economic status, not to mention their powerlessness to change it. Some of them, even ordinary, powerless party members, chafed at the banal political conformity of Fascist society, and sometimes they lashed out. In January 1938, in an *osteria* in a rural community in the province of Vicenza (Veneto), Tullio Marangon invited two men to drink with him. When his companions began singing the Fascist hymn *Giovinezza*, Marangon started belting out the Socialist anthem *Bandiera rossa* in a "provocative manner." The bar owner and other patrons made him stop, but he continued to criticize the regime, and his drinking companions threatened to tell the police. Marangon responded that he had been a Fascist since 1927 and left. On his way out the door, he sarcastically declared that he was going out to look for "subversives" in their town, mocking the pointless obsession with "anti-Fascism" in rural Italy of the 1930s.

The *carabinieri* soon arrested Marangon and began an investigation, learning that he had only attended school through the fourth grade, but had remained in the Fascist youth organization until 1936, when he became a party member in the *leva fascista*. However, according to authorities, he had "always demonstrated an insufficient understanding of Fascism," skipping meetings and failing to pay party dues.[53] *Carabinieri* searched his father's home but found nothing incriminating. His brother, authorities noted, was an enthusiastic member of the Fascist youth organization, a fact that reflected well on the family. Marangon's father was viewed as a bit of an anti-Fascist but had altered his behavior, in part by giving his children a proper "Fascist education." In sum, the Marangon family had attempted to adapt to Fascism but with only partial success. Although his brother held promise, Tullio was deemed unworthy of the party card. Sentenced to political exile in the south, Marangon left his pregnant new wife at home with his father and brother.

Membership in the PNF often represented a path to social promotion, because Fascists controlled some of the funds, contracts, appointments, and other resources that flowed from Rome to the provinces.[54] Many Italians became, in essence, "professional" Fascists. Former *squadrists*

[53] *Carabinieri* of Verona (Vicenza Esterna), to *questore* and *carabinieri* of Vicenza, January 14, 1938, in ACS, DGPS, *confinati politici*, b. 613, "Marangon, Tullio."
[54] Corner, "Everyday Fascism," 207–8.

and enthusiastic younger party men found lucrative, influential positions within the "parallel bureaucracy" that administered welfare agencies, the syndicates, labor boards, state contracts, and all of the party organizations.[55] With great power and resources came great corruption. Throughout the 1930s, police sentenced "squadrists of the first hour" and other Fascists to political confinement for falsifying records, embezzling funds (from the Dopolavoro, Ente Opere Assistenziali [EOA], and other party-state agencies), accepting bribes for employment, overlooking irregularities in rationing, and awarding state contracts.[56] These sanctions served not necessarily to root out such activities but also to combat the general public's view of Fascists as corrupt, clientelistic, depraved opportunists, which many were.[57]

Even when conducting their business honestly, or legally, local Fascists exercised an enormous amount of discretionary power. The party controlled the labor exchanges that provided work permits (*libretti di lavoro*) and found jobs for the unemployed. Local Fascists discriminated against workers who did not join the party, failed to take part in parades and ceremonies, or had a reputation for criticizing the regime.[58] The same was true regarding welfare. During the Great Depression, the regime created a party-run welfare agency, the EOA, which unified a variety of state-sponsored charities. The "district groups" (*gruppi rionali*) of the PNF operated the local EOA offices, distributing food, clothing, firewood, and other aid according to a "rigid and monotonous calendar of public ceremonies."[59] In most communities, the EOA delivered inadequate aid in an inefficient and often corrupt fashion while discriminating against anti-Fascists and other broadly defined categories of enemies.[60] Moreover, the regime in no way modernized or rationalized the system

---

[55] Maruccia Salvati, *Il regime e gli impiegati: la nazionalizzazione piccolo-borghese nel ventennio fascista* (Rome, 1992).

[56] For corruption, see ACS, *confinati politici*, b. 68, "Barra, Caracciolo"; b. 173, "Calascibetta, Renato"; b. 183, "Campi, Paolo"; b. 757, "Pasini, Mario"; b. 763, "Patriarca, Giovanni"; b. 889, "Rota, Giovanni"; b. 901, "Sagone, Salvatore"; b. 955, "Simonetti, Oreste."

[57] Corner, "Everyday Fascism," 210–11.

[58] Ibid., 213–14.

[59] Daniele Grana, "La prevenzione del dissenso: la politica assistenziale del fascismo," in *Regime fascista e societá modenese: aspetti e problemi del fascismo locale, 1922–1939*, ed. Lorenzo Bertucelli and Stegano Magagnoli (Modena, 1995), 127.

[60] David G. Horn, "L'Ente opere assistenziali: strategie politiche e pratiche di assistenza, in Betri, ed., *Il fascismo in lombardia*, 479–90.

of distributing aid to the poor. Chronically underfunded, the EOA functioned mainly as a propaganda device, providing handouts rather than
the social security net of the modern welfare state.[61] These shortcomings
ultimately led to the dissolution of the EOA in 1937. The state then took
over welfare activities from the PNF, with the goal of making welfare
distribution more professional and less corrupt.[62]

In order to receive aid, Italians had to apply to the EOA. Local Fascists then prepared evaluations of the applicants, determining whether
they were eligible or worthy of assistance. Political repression and state
assistance thus potentially constituted "the two faces of the same political
strategy."[63] In some neighborhoods where most residents had histories
of anti-Fascist activity, few received any favors from Fascists. As one resident of San Lorenzo put it, "every time I signed up, they never called
me."[64] However, welfare was not systematically denied to all politically
suspect groups. State coercion and welfare policies targeted some of the
same groups – the poor and the working classes. Many detainees and
their families had received financial assistance, food, furniture, and medical care courtesy of the PNF or Mussolini, sometimes even during their
confinement.[65] At the same time, these handouts were discretionary car-
rots (Figure 10).

Though tens of thousands of poor, working-class Italians received
financial and material assistance from the regime, they were not necessarily won over by it. In the face of crushing poverty – particularly acute
during the Great Depression – token assistance was insufficient compen-
sation for the loss of political rights and basic individual freedoms. Moreover, Fascists expected that recipients appear grateful, often leading to
resentment. These tensions, always smoldering just beneath the veneer of
everyday conformity, are revealed by the case of a crew of manual laborers
digging an irrigation ditch in a small town in the Veneto, near the Adriatic
coast. The foreman, a Fascist named Giovanni Toffanello, chastised one
laborer, Tullio Agostini, for working slowly. Agostini responded, "Go

---

[61] Marco Soresina, "Mutue sanitarie e regime corporativo," in Betri, ed., *Il fascismo in
    lombardia*, 261–303.
[62] Horn, "L'Ente opere assistenziali," 479–90.
[63] Daniele Grana, "La prevenzione del dissenso," 125.
[64] Piccioni, *San Lorenzo*, 92
[65] See, e.g., ACS, *confinati politici*, b. 1099, "Zorat, Giuseppe"; b. 451, "Galotti, Gaes-
    tano"; b. 253, "Cimini, Guido"; b. 475, "Giacomelli, Venero"; b. 769, "Pellicci, Gino";
    b. 955, "Sinigaglia, Licurgo"; b. 18, "Alvi, Alceste"; b. 8, "Agostini, Tullio"; b. 3,
    "Acciari, Adolfo."

FIGURE 10. Fascist or opportunist? In the midst of the Great Depression, a child gives the Fascist salute after receiving a "Pacco del Duce," a charitable handout that normally consisted of food, distributed by the local branch of the PNF, 1930. *Source:* Copyright © Fototeca AAMOD/Database Fotoarchivi and Multimedia, Rome 2010.

to hell, you and Mussolini." An incensed Toffanello reminded Agostini of the kindness of the party and the Duce, who had provided assistance to his destitute family in the past. Agostini's sixty-nine-year-old father was a widower, with one son, Tullio, two daughters (ages twenty-seven and eighteen), and a four-year-old niece under his care. The family lived and slept on the floor of a one-room dwelling. The previous year the PNF had given the family two new beds and a photograph of the Duce. On another occasion, they received financial assistance from the EOA. To Toffanello's reminder of the party's generosity, Agostini responded, "In my room I don't have pictures of saints, I have a photograph of Mussolini, and every morning, just after I wake, I spit in the face of that coward who stands in the way of justice and has ruined us all."[66] Agostini thus had kept the picture of the Duce, but not necessarily because he was grateful.

[66] *Questore* to Provincial Commission of Padova, August 21, 1935, and *carabinieri* of Este to *questura* of Padova, August 19, 1935, in ACS, *confinati politici*, b. 8, "Agostini, Tullio."

For a poor manual laborer, living in a region of classic agrarian Fascism, the party controlled the only possibilities for alleviating dire financial straits. Agostini was unfortunately not party material. He had requested membership in May 1935, but the local PNF never even bothered to respond to his request. Following his exchange with Toffanello, one day after his thirty-second birthday, Agostini was arrested by the *carabinieri*, who first tried to initiate criminal charges against him for expressing "aversion to the person of His Excellency, the Head of Government and the Party." When that failed, provincial authorities proposed him for political confinement. In his recommendation, the police chief of Padova reported that Agostini, in addition to not belonging to the party, had never done military service due to a chronic skin fungus. At the same time, he had neither expressed "ideas contrary to the regime" nor was he "psychically abnormal."[67] For Agostini, the PNF played an obstructive and coercive role in most important aspects of everyday life. The PNF had blocked his path to party membership, given him a job digging ditches, and provided a small amount of aid to his family. Giovanni Toffanello, whose position as a foreman and a Fascist were one in the same, expected Agostini to be grateful to Mussolini and the party. But he was not, and for that, Toffanello sent him down the path to confinement and further hardship. For poor peasants like Agostini, it was perhaps no wonder that two beds and a cash handout failed to compensate for a lack of "justice" and financial "ruin."

After 1945, some Italians recalled that Fascist rule induced feelings of fear and terror. Italians who witnessed acts of denunciation, physical violence, and summary arrests may have been terrified, particularly those individuals who belonged to vulnerable political or social groups. For the victims of and witnesses to the *squadrist* terror of the early 1920s, such incidents of state violence may have brought residual fear to the surface, a reminder that *squadrism* had merely been institutionalized. Ordinary Fascist violence, though considerably circumscribed relative to the golden era of *squadrismo*, still operated in the gray zone between legality and illegality. Higher-ranking Fascists, who had neither law enforcement training nor any real legal jurisdiction to arrest anyone, engaged in behaviors that were essentially illegal. Militiamen, who had some jurisdiction to take custody of individuals, engaged in all sorts of criminal activities. The police, who were responsible for filing charges with judicial authorities,

---

[67] *Questore* to Provincial Commission of Padova, August 21, 1935, in ibid.

nevertheless tolerated these activities, in large part because the Fascist regime had very explicitly created "fields of action" outside the rule of law.[68] By its very nature, this gray zone of illegality had no clearly defined limits, but there was nevertheless a line, established arbitrarily by state and party authorities, that Fascists and militiamen could not traverse. Police and judicial authorities regularly sanctioned Fascists for abusing their authority – corruption, embezzlement, assault, bribery, extortion, and so on. However, state authorities punished Fascists usually only when the political winds shifted, or when a Fascist had otherwise fallen into disfavor. Meanwhile, many other violent, illegal acts fell within the range of acceptable behaviors or were committed by Fascists whose power and position rendered them beyond reproach.

Ordinary Fascist violence was not a phenomenon solely of the 1930s. In Fascist strongholds and recalcitrant working-class neighborhoods, *squadrist* tactics had persisted throughout the 1920s and into the early 1930s. Moreover, most of the documented instances of real physical violence from the 1930s occurred in these same areas: the Po Valley, northern cities, Puglia, Naples, and a few other places. But, importantly, the scope and nature of state-backed coercion changed significantly during Fascism's second decade in power. Above all, politicized conflict no longer pitted Fascists against anti-Fascists. Fascists used their power to maintain public order and neighborhood respectability, resolve family disputes or petty jealousies, punish rebelliousness against Fascist conformity, and generally advance their own interests. This shift meant that Fascists, with the backing of the state, began persecuting Italians with little or no past involvement in politics, whose vulnerability was usually tied to a party affiliation from the distant past, a lack of "enthusiasm" for the regime, their status as "social outsiders," or else a personal or professional conflict with a Fascist. In the 1930s, the PNF also controlled or held influence over a wider array of state institutions. Fascists and militiamen could increasingly rely on police commissions to respond to denunciations by inflicting political confinement or probation. Moreover, the role of local PNF offices in distributing welfare, jobs, and other favors furnished Fascists with additional tools of coercion and discrimination. Finally, although there were perhaps fewer incidents of physical violence in, for example, southern communities, provincial police commissions

---

[68] I borrow this term from Stephen Kotkin, *Magnetic Mountain: Stalinism as a Civilization* (Berkeley, 1995), 21.

throughout Italy were far more active during the 1930s than the 1920s, as shown in earlier chapters. Therefore, with its wider geographic diffusion and deeper social penetration, the various forms of ordinary Fascist violence were nationalized and, in turn, began to encroach on the lives of more and more Italians.

8

The Politics of Everyday Life

With the arrival of Fascism, my paese was divided in two; Fascism divided people, ruined friendships. On one side there were the real Fascists, and on the other there were those who were forced to be Fascists, the "meal ticket" [Fascists]. Here in Barolo, we weren't free to speak any more. In the tavern we were always careful, we always looked over our shoulder before we spoke: one wrong word was enough to get you into trouble.

a peasant from Barolo[1]

For some Italians, discerning and navigating the dangers and opportunities presented by state-backed coercion constituted a way of life. This new form of politicized conflict varied in intensity and form according to region, locality, and class. But whether in Trieste or Trapani, similar patterns of repression emerged involving the same types of spaces, actors, and dynamics of state-backed social power. In this sense, Fascist political violence thus contributed in part to the nationalization of the Italians. One of an Italian's first "national" experiences was learning to appreciate the machinations of the authoritarian state apparatus and the boundaries of expected political behavior. For Italians who transgressed these boundaries, among the possible grim outcomes were a punch in the face, institutional confinement, discrimination in the labor market or state welfare, financial ruin, social ostracism, or mere intimidation and fear. Moreover, in order to protect themselves against politicized attacks, and to curry favor with party-state authorities, many Italians joined the party, enrolled their children in the youth organizations, attended patriotic

---

[1] Nuto Revelli, *Il mondo dei vinti: testimonianze di vita contadina* (Turin, 1977), cxi.

celebrations, contributed their gold to the *patria* during the war in Ethiopia, and otherwise exhibited behaviors they hoped would conform to the Fascist state's *inquadramento* (coordination) of the nation. Although many were no doubt sincere, patriotic Italians, or even good Fascists, the fact remains that party membership and other proregime behaviors created real political and social capital. Conversely, failing to join the National Fascist Party (PNF) or participate in public celebrations compromised Italians in the watchful eyes of state authorities. Thus, even if they were merely bending to the regime and regurgitating its propaganda, many ordinary Italians lived their daily lives in accordance with – or rebelling against – behaviors dictated by the national government. Living a life of calculated political conformity penetrated and shaped the individual psyches of many Italians on some level, particularly those who felt vulnerable to assault, state punishment, discrimination, or social ostracism.[2]

Ordinary Italians, Dangerous Places

Within the system of party-state violence and coercion described in the previous chapter, ordinary Italians were empowered to use the politics of repression, setting in motion predictable processes that caused others to be punished. These aggressors often knowingly took advantage of the vulnerability of "politically compromised" individuals and "social outsiders." At the same time, they did so within the "fields of action" established by a formidable network of institutions and individuals who were either empowered or obligated to repress certain behaviors. Aside from the police state and its network of informants, the PNF and the Fascist Militia (MVSN) were the institutions most responsible for extending state violence into ordinary life. Among Italians who did not belong to the party, awareness of the real or potential presence of Fascists, public-security officials, or informants promoted political conformity and silence. The proprietors and employees of bars, hotels, brothels, and other businesses were pressured to provide information about their patrons to the police

---

[2] Alf Lüdtke notes how "[German] fascism's everyday face" consisted of "socially understood languages, discourses, and codes," which generated forms of pragmatic "everyday thinking and action." Although I am not examining strategies of resistance here, such a framework for social action existed in Italy. See his "Introduction: What Is the History of Everyday Life and Who Are Its Practitioners," in *The History of Everyday Life: Reconstructing Historical Experiences and Ways of Life*, ed. Alf Lüdtke (Princeton, 1995), 3–40.

or else risk losing their licenses to operate. Other actors dependent on the party or state for employment – civil servants, state employees, teachers, party bureaucrats, syndicate officials, officers in the armed forces – multiplied the effect.

Within this constellation of real and potential informers, ordinary Italians made choices: to pass information on to the police, lie or tell the truth when questioned, corroborate accusations, or otherwise extend or withhold cooperation. Some Italians, secure in their conformity to Fascism, denounced and accused with abandon, often for totally self-serving purposes. Their motives sometimes included genuine patriotism, a belief in Fascism, or a sense of duty, but more commonly they used denunciation and informing in order to get ahead, secure their interests, carry out vendettas, settle grudges, and shape their environments. For others, it was precisely their political or social vulnerability under Fascism that led them to report suspicious or anti-Fascist activities to authorities. Whatever the case, people within and outside of coercive institutions adopted the strategies and lexicon of Fascism in their dealings with the state, strangers, co-workers, acquaintances, and family. To use repressive institutions successfully, and to avoid falling victims to them, Italians had to develop at least a rudimentary understanding of Mussolini's main policies and larger goals. The consequences of failing to do so, or intentionally disparaging the regime, could well be police sanctions or real physical assaults by Fascists. Although ordinary Italians and public-security officers may not have truly internalized the Fascist projects of "social improvement" (*bonifica sociale*) or "national regeneration," they did externalize or act on it.[3] Moreover, as practitioners of ordinary political violence, they exhibited behavior promoted by the regime, thereby extending the scope of authority exerted by Fascist coercive institutions further into everyday life.

A recurring feature of instances in which ordinary Italians fell victim to party-state repression was that of place. From north to south, in small towns and big cities, everyday political conflict consistently unfolded in the same politically and socially significant spaces – taverns, piazzas and streets, trains and trams, public parks, brothels, jails, shops, public dormitories, open-air markets, courtyards in working-class apartments, and

---

[3] I borrow this distinction from John Connelly, "The Uses of Volksgemeinschaft: Letters to the NSDAP Kreisleitung Eisenach 1939–1940," *Journal of Modern History* 68 (1996): 899–930.

the work places of manual laborers.[4] Where these episodes unfolded tells us much about who was involved. Political conflict occurred in the spaces inhabited by the poor and the working classes, or wherever they came into contact with better-off social classes or state authorities. Movie theaters, sporting events, museums, upscale restaurants, social clubs, private parties, automobiles, professional offices, the homes of the well-off, and other tony venues did not feature prominently in the files of political detainees.

Bars and taverns (*osterie, trattorie, bettole*) provided the most common backdrop for police operations, politicized conflict, and real Fascist violence. This pattern certainly owed to the popularity of *osterie* as sites of working-class fraternization and the fact that drunkenness often leads to spontaneous conflict. However, particularly during the first half of the twentieth century in Europe, bars were also politically important. They provided semiprivate meeting places beyond the gaze of state authorities.[5] Although reconstructing the political significance attached to specific *osterie* is difficult, police regularly referred in general to "notorious" taverns, "infamous places," and establishments "of dubious political standing."[6] No wonder that the police recruited bar owners and employees as informants. And no wonder that so many bar owners acquiesced: the police controlled business permits, which they could summarily revoke or fail to renew. Moreover, at the risk of losing their operating license, bar owners were also forbidden from hiring persons of bad "moral and political conduct."[7] For the proprietors of such establishments, failure to cooperate fully with authorities had potentially serious consequences. The owner of one bar kicked out five patrons for singing *Bandiera rossa* (Red Flag), but did not report the incident to local authorities. When police found out anyway, the owner, who was a member of

---

[4] Of the 549 cases sampled (and of at least 167 cases involving some sort of denunciatory practice by individuals outside of the public-security corps), 64 involved incidents that took place in establishments that were serving mainly alcohol (*trattorie, osterie,* cafes); 36 occurred in piazzas or streets; 13 in trains, trams, or transit stations; 39 in the workplace; 17 in private homes; 3 in apartment common areas; 5 in public dormitories; 20 in shops or markets; and 7 in jail. Most of these incidents occurred in the 1930s and early 1940s.

[5] Paul Steege, Andrew Stuart Bergerson, Maureen Healy, and Pamela E. Swett, "The History of Everyday Life: A Second Chapter," *The Journal of Modern History* 80:2 (2008): 363.

[6] *Carabinieri* of Milano (Varese) to *questore* of Varese, June 7, 1943, in ACS, *confinati politici,* b. 685, "Mascetti, Giovanni."

[7] Art. 168 of the *Regolamento per l'esecuzione del T.U. delle leggi di P.S.,* cited in Giovanni Verni, "Il perfezionamento dello stato di polizia," in Palla, ed., *Lo stato fascista,* 389.

the local PNF directorate, had his bar and hotel shut down for two weeks and was sanctioned by the party. Other factors added further layers of meaning. In this case, the hotel was located in Belluno, a northeastern province formerly part of the Austrian Empire. As the prefect explained, "considering that we are dealing with a border area, previously subjected to Austrian rule and in which undoubtedly there are still many unenthusiastic individuals, a salutary example, even if harsh, was necessary."[8] In a different, ethnically homogenous region, the same incident may not have led to such a harsh punishment for the hotel proprietor. In Belluno, however, the party was weak, and the loyalties of ethnic Germans were suspect.

After taverns and *trattorias*, the most common site of political conflict was the piazza and, more generally, the street. The Fascist conquest of power was as much about dominating politically meaningful public spaces as controlling the levers of state power. Moreover, once control of the Italian piazza had been won, Fascists repeatedly reasserted their dominance through parades, ceremonies, symbols, and shows of force. Fascist domination was "performed" repeatedly on national and local stages, often spontaneously. Piazzas and streets were therefore heavily policed by public-security agents and Fascists. The appearance of graffiti, posters, leaflets, and other forms of "anti-Fascist propaganda" in piazzas led to stepped-up surveillance and the questioning of suspects. Even a casual conversation about Hitler's foreign policy could lead to denunciations and police sanctions.

Another site of political conflict, the train, offered a degree of mobility that was clearly unsettling to a regime hoping to assert strict control over its population. The working classes used public transit in their daily lives, and anti-Fascist militants traveled around the peninsula by train under false identities. Undercover political police who had studied the dossiers and photographs of leading anti-Fascists patrolled large train stations and policed major lines.[9] Railway employees – who were state employees and members of the Fascist syndicates – often passed information about suspicious passengers or blatantly anti-Fascist behaviors on to authorities. Party members, state employees, and ordinary Italians served similar functions. For example, in August 1938, on the short train ride to Rome from Ostia Lido, a port and beachfront town, a drunken passenger with

---

[8] Reports of prefect of Belluno May 5, 1930, and *carabinieri* of Bolzano, June 15, 1930, in ACS, *confinati politici*, b. 739, "Palla, Felice."
[9] Franzinelli, *I tentacoli*, 247.

a history of mental illness, Augusto Brancaleone, subjected his wife to a monologue about the high "degree of liberty" experienced by women in France and Barcelona, "especially with regard to sex." He also expressed "admiration for democracy."[10] Another passenger, the head archivist at the offices of the Roman prefecture, immediately reported the incident to the police. Brancaleone was arrested and sentenced to two years on Le Tremiti. The Roman police chief believed that Brancaleone's mental illness, alcoholism, and criminal record made him a candidate for "common" confinement, but the content of his offense and "indifference to the regime" prompted Bocchini to designate him a "political" detainee.

Just as working-class districts were subject to intense measures of surveillance and repression, factories and other work sites were rife with paid informants, Fascists, and militiamen, who funneled information to state and party authorities. The regime used this intelligence to gauge public opinion, break up anti-Fascist cells, and quash political dissent. In the mid-1930s, Police Chief Bocchini instructed prefects and police chiefs to encourage militiamen to take a more active role in extracting information from "the factories, the syndicates, the *dopolavoro*, etc."[11] Within this environment, employees used political accusations and informing against their co-workers to resolve conflicts, curry favor with authorities, protect themselves from recriminations, and demonstrate their loyalty to the regime.[12] In 1941 in Aosta, a factory worker named Natale Tagliavini claimed that Antonio Basso, his co-worker, had said that he hoped the English and French would win the war and that "it would be better if Mussolini were dead."[13] Two young workers, both Fascists, later confirmed the substance of the conversation, although they initially

---

[10] *Carabinieri* of Rome, September 12, 1938, ACS, *confinati politici*, b. 148, "Brancaleone, Augusto."

[11] Quoted in Carucci, "Arturo Bocchini," 91.

[12] Workers denounced fellow workers, often when there was personal enmity between them or when one or more workers envied an individual's position or salary. Superiors also denounced workers to the police. Both the police and management, moreover, employed paid informants. Under interrogation, workers seemed to tell what they knew, most likely to avoid being implicated in the matter. For examples of work place denunciation, see ACS, *confinati politici*, b. 8, "Agostini, Tullio"; b. 23, "Amelotti, Pietro"; b. 58, "Banco (Bantrovic)"; b. 68, "Barosi, Italo"; b. 73, "Basso, Antonio"; b. 78, "Bazzi, Pietro"; b. 128, "Bonati, Armando"; b. 199, "Caradente, Sicco"; b. 343, "Denucci, Dante"; b. 433, "Frangini, Giulio"; b. 463, "Gay, Luigi"; b. 499, "Govoni, Guglielmo"; b. 799, "Pinna, Giovanni."

[13] ACS, *confinati politici*, b. 73, "Basso, Antonio"; especially *carabinieri* of Aosta, October 31, 1940, and prefect of Aosta, November 11, 1940.

denied hearing anything. Police authorities had some trouble determining whether Basso had really said such things, or if the whole matter was invented by Tagliavini. The two men did not have "good relations" at work and were frequently heard arguing "for reasons inherent to work and about the correspondence of [their] salaries." Police interviewed many witnesses, but none would confirm Basso's version of the story. Basso was particularly vulnerable to this type of political accusation. He was not a member of the PNF, had never taken part in "patriotic or political manifestations," had little education, was "a rather unsociable character," and had not "performed military service... due to a thoracic deficiency."[14] Politically unengaged and socially unpopular, Basso lacked political merit in the eyes of authorities. The Provincial Commission of Aosta sentenced him to two years, and he was sent to the Pisticci labor colony. As he languished there, earning just enough money for his own survival, his wife and two children suffered economically and physically. The prefect of Aosta, who expressed concern about the condition of the family, referred Basso's wife for assistance from the local welfare office, but what scant help they received was insufficient. Basso's absence, according to the prefect, had reduced the family to "impoverished economic conditions and precarious health."[15] Whether true or not, Tagliavini's accusations nevertheless struck a vicious blow in a long-standing conflict between co-workers, the reverberations of which wreaked havoc on Basso's family.

To characterize all Italians who gave over information to the police as selfish, vindictive, petty tyrants would be incorrect. In many cases, it was the person who was ultimately punished who had put bystanders in danger rather than the other way around. The manifold practices of formally involving citizens in the institutions of coercion – through the party, business permits, obliging schoolteachers to inform about their students – not only offered opportunities for informing, but it also exerted tremendous pressure to inform. When confronted with a drunken person shouting anti-Mussolini slurs, to remain silent was to risk punishment. To deny to police that such a blatant act had occurred was to bring political suspicion upon oneself. A proprietor, patron, or passerby who listened passively to an anti-Fascist diatribe might well be accused by the police of complicity, attracting unwanted attention and even sanctions. Thus, for example, in Genoa, a man was sentenced to political confinement

[14] *Carabinieri* of Aosta, October 31, 1940, in ibid.
[15] Prefect of Aosta, January 13, 1941, and February 18, 1941, in ibid.

for having "tacitly approved" of criticisms of Mussolini's foreign policy "with gestures of his head" in a piazza.[16] Authorities never considered that the man might have silently disagreed, nervously nodding his head out of politeness. In many cases, police reproached, without necessarily sanctioning, entire groups of people for not having forcefully objected to some slander of the regime. Within this context, Italians, even those who might have shared the sentiment underlying anti-Fascist statements, experienced pressure to inform authorities, cooperate in investigations, or at least attempt to separate themselves from the authors of such ill-advised acts. Even the most militant anti-Fascist might be unwilling to jeopardize his freedom and the integrity of his clandestine organization to protect a drunken fool. Although it is true that many Italians too eagerly doomed others to suffer Fascist persecution, it also appears that the authors of public anti-Fascist outbursts, slanders of the Duce, and other "subversive" acts exposed their unwitting fellow citizens to unwanted police scrutiny, suspicion, and sanctions. Acting without hesitation to inform the police or a party official, or recounting all that one had witnessed when questioned, separated a "bystander" from foolish or ill-considered behavior. It was an act of self-preservation, a refutation of a future charge of guilt by association or inaction. Whatever one's moral judgment of these actions, they nevertheless served to extend the authoritarian power of the Fascist state further into everyday life. Fear and apprehension drove witnesses to protect themselves and, by doing so, substantially advanced the state's aspiration to see and hear all.

In perhaps the majority of cases involving ordinary Italians, however, the Fascist regime's thorough involvement of individuals and spaces in the exercise of state-sponsored coercion created countless possibilities for bringing about grim but definitive resolutions to everyday social interactions and conflict. Italians brazenly condemned their fellow citizens to suffer prison, internment, exile, or probation for opportunistic or vindictive motives. In particular, social outsiders – denigrated in police reports for their alcoholism, criminal precedents, lack of work ethic, mental instability, sexual promiscuity, lack of devotion to family, and immorality – were vulnerable to denunciation by Italians who authorities deemed "of undisputed Fascist faith," "favorable to the regime," and "lovers of order." These denouncers were often veterans, patriotic, gainfully employed, hardworking, and from stable, "peaceful" families.

---

[16] *Questore* of Genova, April 3, 1939, in ACS, *confinati politici*, b. 523, "Gusella, Secondo."

When these two subsets of Fascist society interacted with one another, "upstanding" citizens were implicitly empowered to exploit the smallest transgressions by social outsiders, or, worse, to simply concoct some offense. Read more cynically, ordinary people were additionally, or even primarily, trying to use these everyday circumstances to punish "bad behavior" and then disguising their motives behind the "anti-Fascist" behavior of their victims. It was irrelevant whether their victims were actually "culpable" as perpetrators of specific forms of banned political behavior. Nor are their real motives (Fascism or, perhaps, neighborhood respectability) easily discernible. The key to such uses of Fascist coercion was that they skillfully employed multiple social expectations for multiple effects. For example, on a spring night in Naples in 1941, a thirty-two-year-old sailor named Salvatore Paciucco ate dinner with his family and then went out drinking.[17] Hours later, Paciucco turned up at a café, drunk, with cuts and bruises on his face from falling down. After ordering a glass of wine, he began verbally harassing the barman and generally causing trouble. Several customers – an accountant, an elementary schoolteacher, a merchant, a shopkeeper, a soldier, and a draftsman – alleged that after receiving his change from the barman, Paciucco spit on a coin bearing the image of the king and said, according to varying accounts, "Italians disgust me," or "the Italian people are disgusting," or perhaps even "Italian money is disgusting." The five customers then "accompanied" Paciucco directly to the local *carabinieri* headquarters. Revealingly, the barman, who was closest to Paciucco, reported hearing nothing of the sort. In his version, Paciucco had only remarked that he was "more of a gentleman" than the barman. Perhaps the bartender alone told the truth, or maybe he felt either sympathy for Paciucco or disdain for the regime (or his other customers). Judging from the social class of the café's patrons, the impetus to report Paciucco's behavior may have stemmed from more than just love of country. A drunken, crude sailor, stumbling around a café and insulting the bartender, was no doubt offensive to a group of middle-class, professional Neapolitans. Instead of denouncing him for mere public drunkenness or sending him home, they used his alleged insult to the *patria*, perhaps even as a mere pretext, to punish his vulgar behavior. Paciucco spent a year and a half in the province of Cosenza as a political exile. Immediately after his release, he was arrested again, in a drunken stupor, for "insulting" a group of Fascists.

---

[17] *Questore* to prefect of Naples, May 27, 1941, in ACS, *confinati politici*, b. 733, "Paciucco, Salvatore."

Subversive Women

The deep diffusion of state violence into Italian society during the 1930s had an acute effect on poor, unmarried or separated women whose "morality" was suspect in the eyes of authorities and the public. The "subversive women" found buried inside the police files of male anti-Fascists during the 1920s moved into the foreground as targets in their own right during Fascism's second decade in power. Rather than accusing these women of merely being anti-Fascists, police almost invariably alleged that they were "loose" and "immoral." Of the relatively few women sentenced to political confinement during the 1930s, most, police throughout the Italian peninsula alleged, had engaged in prostitution.[18]

A typical case was that of Angelina Buzzetti, a "subversive housewife" (*casalinga sovversiva*) resident in Sanremo, whom police sentenced to live in a small village in the south for one year. Buzzetti had been separated from her husband for more than ten years. Police blamed her failed marriage on her "sleazy moral conduct." She allegedly had "intimate relations with many people" and recently began prostituting herself. Finally, she passed countless hours at the municipal casino, gambling away funds inherited after her mother's death. Police already knew Buzzetti, having "repatriated" her in 1936 to Milan, her place of birth, due to her "immoral conduct." Authorities frequently resorted to "repatriation" in order to deal with troublesome outsiders. After some time, Buzzetti was allowed to return to Sanremo. In May of 1940, she was arrested following a denunciation made by a gardener named Carlo Barbero, "a war invalid, wounded for the Fascist cause," who frequently spoke with Buzzetti, hearing her criticize Mussolini for the Matteotti murder, the invasion of Ethiopia, the alienation of France and England, and his relationship with his daughter (which she alleged was sexual). For her poor "moral conduct" and the "words pronounced against the Duce and the directives of the Regime," the police chief recommended that Buzzetti be sentenced to *confino* "in order to put her in a position in which she cannot harm society."[19]

---

[18] Virtually all women sentenced to political confinement from the sample during the 1930s and 1940s – with the exception of a few militant anti-Fascists – were called prostitutes by the police. ACS, *confinati politici*, b. 133, "Bonomi, Maria"; b. 168, "Buzzetti, Angela"; b. 661, "Mervi, Francesca"; b. 373, "Dori, Agata"; b. 805, "Pistritto, Lucia."

[19] *Questore* (Triola) to prefect of Imperia (Berio), June 19, 1940; *carabinieri* of Sanremo to commissariato of Sanremo, May 28, 1940, "Oggetto: Buzzetti Angelina," in ACS, *confinati politici*, b. 168, "Buzzetti, Angelina."

The vulnerability of poor, marginalized women to these types of accusations was heightened in certain regional contexts. In Trieste, the regime's campaign of "Italianization" left its citizens of Slavic origin distinctly disadvantaged. In 1942, a drunken man named Felice Cosmina asked Francesca Mervi, the cleaning lady at a tavern, for a liter of wine, using terms she claimed were offensive. In response she muttered, "this race of Italian delinquents." An argument ensued inside the tavern, and a Fascist *capo nucleo* later reported the incident to the secretary of the local PNF. Police soon began an investigation. In their report, authorities described Mervi as a "subversive prostitute . . . infected with syphilis" whom police had "repatriated many times." Police noted, "Although she is of Slavic origin," she had not previously been cited for inappropriate political behavior. In her statement, Mervi said that she did not mean to offend all Italians, only Cosmina. Although acknowledging that Felice Cosmina was inebriated, police described him as "an element of good Italian sentiment" who belonged to the PNF, having come out of the party's youth organizations. Moreover, Cosmina was "devoted to the Regime and to our institutions."[20] The distinction police made here between *us* (our institutions) and the implied *them* (Slavs) undoubtedly reflected the official prejudice at work in such matters.

Although men were the primary actors in implementing the state's policies of repression, women often passed information on to authorities through their husbands, fathers, brothers, and boyfriends. Just as women were damaged collaterally by the confinement sentences inflicted on their menfolk, women who wielded political violence sometimes did so through male intermediaries. On an August morning in 1936, in a small town sixty kilometers north of Venice, a fifty-year-old housewife named Tranquilla Depellegrin was doing laundry in the courtyard of the home of Leone Tonelli, a wine distributor.[21] Seated at a table in the courtyard, drinking wine, was Giusppe Torresan, a miner. As Depellegrin began doing her wash, a younger woman, thirty-one-year-old Maria Tuma, appeared and struck up a conversation, asking Depellegrin if she wanted help. Depellegrin thanked her but declined Maria's offer. Giuseppe Torresan suddenly interrupted their conversation, exclaiming "you're still a girl, hardly fit for work." He continued, "But soon the millionaire *signori*

---

[20] *Questore* (E. Messana) to prefect of Trieste, March 9, 1943; and *carabinieri* (Monfalcone) to *questore* of Trieste, February 5, 1943, in ACS, *confinati politici*, b. 661, "Mervi, Francesca."

[21] *Carabinieri* of Bolzano (Trento), September 15, 1936, in ACS, *confinati politici*, b. 1015, "Torresan, Giuseppe."

who don't do their own wash will be finished. Very soon the prole-
tariat will take over Italy – the *signori* and the priests will have to all be
killed. The women will belong to everyone and the mothers won't know
their own children. The Italian government is the most disgusting there
is because it protects the *signori*." Offended or frightened by Torresan's
rant, Tuma immediately left the courtyard to tell her fiancé, Dr. Giovanni Bertol, a notary and a member of the MVSN (both positions were
underlined in the police report). Bertol telephoned the authorities, and
a *carabiniere* officer soon arrived and arrested Torresan. For his "grave
statements" he was assigned to five years political exile in the mainland
south.

The Power of the Powerless?

It would be tempting to view society under Fascism as starkly divided
between haves and have-nots. Police-state repression intensely targeted
the poorest, most marginal groups. At the same time, state-organized
political coercion flowed in many directions. A worker whose union
had been repressed might nonetheless approve, for example, of the arrest
and confinement of a drunk or a homosexual prostitute in his neighborhood. Poor people who had been victimized by the wealthy or the
politically powerful occasionally (though rarely) extracted some measure
of revenge. Merchants who tampered with their scales or inflated their
prices were sometimes punished. In general, authorities took advantage
of any opportunity to sanction or rid communities of individuals who
were universally maligned.

The treatment of suspected pedophiles offers one such example. In a
few cases, the suspect was a Fascist, even the head of the local youth organization – hence, at least ostensibly, the political nature of the sanction.[22]
However, in other cases involving men suspected of raping or sexually abusing children, it was not the crime but the punishment that was
political.[23] When dealing with criminal behaviors that were difficult to
prosecute, and shameful for victims' families to speak about, police chose
to summarily remove the suspect from the community. A pharmacist
who repeatedly sexually molested and raped a young girl in the southern province of Matera left the girl's family "profoundly disturbed" and
caused "strong indignation among the community." The man's relatives

---

[22] *Questore* to prefect of Venezia, September 12, 1937, in ACS, *confinati politici*, b. 103,
"Berton, Giuseppe."
[23] ACS, *confinati politici*, b. 148, "Brancaleone, Pietro"; b. 229, "Ceccarelli."

paid the girl's family off; in return they agreed to not to press charges. Police doubted that criminal proceedings would lead to a guilty verdict anyway. In 1921, the same man had been charged for raping a young boy several times but was absolved for "insufficient proof." The outcomes in both of these cases left the community angry, and the police called for an "exemplary punishment" against the man. Although the pharmacist belonged to the PNF, his membership was barely mentioned in the documentation and seemed to have little import within the community.[24] Instead, by sentencing the man to political confinement, provincial police officials wanted "to give the precise impression to the population . . . that the regime, through its institutions, energetically defends its citizens, even with regard to the moral health of the family."[25] In such cases, punishment carried substantial political overtones in that it demonstrated the regime's commitment to act against criminals without regard for the niceties of due process.

Subaltern groups and social outsiders, the very same people so often victimized by the regime, were also on occasion able to employ the politics of ordinary violence for their own purposes. Take, for instance, the case of a brothel located in Portoferraio, the island of Elba's port city. Pierino Alessi, an agricultural laborer with a criminal history, known for being "an immoral individual" with a "violent character," regularly visited the *casa di tolleranza* (literally, "house of tolerance," the official name of state-licensed brothels), most often to see a woman named Alba. Alessi often refused to pay her, and occasionally threatened Alba and the establishment's proprietor with physical violence. One spring evening in 1942, in the brothel's waiting room, Alba and the customers sang the song *Vincere* (Win), referring to Italy's armies fighting the Allies in Africa and the Balkans. A drunken Alessi menacingly approached Alba, jumping up and down, with his hands in the air, making *la corna* (a sign of bad luck), "in order to make her and the others present understand that it was absurd to think of winning." Later that evening, according to another prostitute, Alessi "manhandled" (*malmenato*) another customer, Asterio Arnaldi, saying to him: "The Duce is very clever, but more than that he is stupid, because with kids like you, he won't win the war." Although Alessi's actions clearly had political significance, the employees of the brothel spoke more in their statements about his violent and unruly behavior. The proprietor had had enough and reported Alessi to the local office of

the *carabinieri*, who arrested him days later.[26] Thus, the employees of
a brothel were able to rid their workplace of a threatening, bothersome
man. Whether these actors were staunch supporters of the regime and
its policies or not, they nevertheless implemented and benefited from the
Fascist politics of repression.

For every seemingly just, or at least not entirely undeserved, punishment, there was an equally unjust consequence. Pierino Alessi's ill-fated
visit to the brothel not only led him to be sentenced to political confinement but also left his wife and two children in a dire situation. Despite
his alcoholism and "immoral conduct," he was their sole source of suste-
nance. With Pierino confined on the island of Ustica – now a mixed colony
for political and common detainees – his family fell into what Alessi's wife
Maria described as "disastrous economic conditions," a fact confirmed
by authorities.[27] Maria made several pleas to the police for subsidies.
Mobilizing the regime's jingoism for her own cause, she signed one letter
"Vincere! Vinceremo!" (We're winning, and we shall win). In granting
Maria three hundred lira, the police chief and prefect of Livorno noted
that Alessi was an "indigent ex-combatant" and "a veteran of the war of
1915–18."[28] Conferring with Mussolini, Police Chief Senise granted the
subsidy, writing "ex-combatant, two children" in pencil in the margin.
Citing Alessi's status as a veteran, the prefect recommended that Alessi,
at his own request, be transferred to the mainland, where he could work.
In the margin of this request, which was rejected, someone, presumably
Senise, had scribbled "ex-convict, violent."[29] Although issued a clean bill
of health in April, when he was first arrested, Alessi was suffering from
"organic deterioration" by the end of the summer.[30]

The Politics of Everyday Life

Late at night on August 22, 1937, Alceste Alvi, the Roman anarchist
discussed in Chapter 3, walked out onto the Ponte Quattro Capi, the
bridge that connects Tiber Island to the Trastevere district. He climbed
up onto the wide stone railing and threw himself into the surging waters

---

[26] *Questore* (Pennetta) to prefect of Livorno (Manlio Binna), May 20, 1942, in ACS,
confinati politici, b. 13, "Alessi, Pierino."
[27] Maria Procchieschi to *questore* of Livorno, September 8, 1942; prefect of Livorno to
MI, June 22, 1942, in ibid.
[28] Prefect of Livorno to MI, June 22, 1942; telegram, prefect of Livorno to MI, May 25,
1942, in ibid.
[29] Telegram, May 25, 1942; and Alessi to MI, August 18, 1942, in ibid.
[30] See Dr. F. Gambassi and Dr. Ugo Costa, May 24, 1942, "Oggetto: Alessi Pierino"; and
director of Colony, Ustica, to MI, September 27, 1942, in "Alessi, Pierino."

of the Tiber.[31] Vittorio Villanucci, a fisherman, witnessed Alvi's leap and moved his boat out into the river. Reaching Alvi, he pulled him to safety and brought him to the hospital.[32] Alvi had attempted to kill himself in a moment of deep despair, brought on in no small part by the havoc political confinement had wreaked on his life. Since leaving Ponza in 1935, he had been almost continuously unemployed. He had for years suffered from a severe ulcer, and his wife Maria Bonacci had now gone completely blind. Before Alceste's first arrest, the couple lived in an apartment in Trastevere and both were steadily employed, he as a stone mason and she as a washerwoman. Now they were homeless, living on the streets or in public dormitories.[33] In the wake of his suicide attempt, Alvi wrote several letters to Mussolini. He asked for economic assistance, but one letter begged the Duce to lift the oppressive police surveillance that, he believed, prevented employers from hiring him. Alvi received one cash handout, but the police refused to drop the surveillance, continuing to note Alceste's comings and goings up until his death in June 1941.[34]

Perhaps more remarkable than Alvi's continued physical and economic decline in the years after his release from confinement was his apparent political conversion. Alceste Alvi, previously described as one of the most "terrible subversives" in Trastevere, hated by local Fascists and persecuted by the regime, now declared himself a devoted follower of Mussolini. In his final letter, addressed to "Benito Mussolini, Founder of the Empire and Duce of Fascism," Alvi claimed that "for years" he had believed in the Duce's "sublime and authentic leadership," which had created "an Imperial Italy." He promised, he wrote, to "obey your orders, which represent discipline, so that we Italians might become, as you have made us become, the most feared and respected men in the world, and to fight in your name when you command me, ready even to die for your greatness and that of my Italy."[35] In dozens of letters addressed simply to the Interior Ministry during his six years of confinement, neither Alvi nor his wife ever praised Mussolini or the Fascist regime. In fact, Alvi's letters were defiantly formal and free of the submissive tone that the regime required of detainees requesting pardons. As the police had always claimed, Alvi was at that time "irreducible" and "unrepentant." Though perhaps insincere, Alvi's newfound adulation of Mussolini

---

[31] The Tiber flooded in the fall of 1937, and the water level was already high in August.

[32] *Questore* of Rome to CPC, August 31, 1937, in ACS, CPC, b. 82, fasc. "Alvi, Alceste."

[33] See "notizie per il prospetto biografico Alvi Alceste," January 26, 1938, in ibid.

[34] See Alvi to Mussolini, (date illegible) January 1938, and April 6, 1939; and "Notizie per il prospetto biografico Alvi Alceste," July 16, 1941, in ibid.

[35] Alvi to Mussolini, April 6, 1939, in ibid.

and the regime's achievements represented one man's understanding of what Mussolini and police officials *wanted* to hear. In this sense, Alvi was attempting to demonstrate that he understood what it meant to be a "good" Italian in the Fascist era: the rejection of subversive ideologies, faith in and devotion to Mussolini, belief in the greatness of Italy, gratitude for the empire, and promises of obedience, discipline, and willingness to sacrifice one's life for the *patria*. Years of confinement, economic deprivations, and poor health, caused almost entirely by Mussolini's regime, had induced Alvi to adopt this language of political conformity.

For ordinary Italians, understanding the regime's values and political program was an essential skill for survival. The consequences of criticizing or thwarting the regime's policies could be severe. Moreover, expressing one's enthusiasm for the regime – by writing letters, making public statements, and, most importantly, joining party organizations and participating in political celebrations – potentially established some degree of immunity from the politics of ordinary violence. Moreover, welfare, jobs, and other patronage and favors were awarded according to the party-state's assessment of an individual's comprehension of, adherence to, and enthusiasm for Fascism. Italians understood this aspect of life under the regime. Thus, the letters written by detainees and their families reflect everyday formulations, however superficial, of what Fascism meant to ordinary people. Common to virtually all letters were expressions of reverence for Mussolini. Greetings and salutations listed Mussolini's many titles (Duce of Fascism, Founder of the Empire) and pledged undying devotion. The tone ranged from formal respect to fanatical worship. "Duce," wrote one detainee, "you see all things most clearly. Your penetrating gaze is not susceptible to falsehoods, because God created in you the omniscient genius, the regenerator, the comforter... all in just one man, whose example, in a day not far off, all the world will copy."[36] Italians attempting to convey some sense of the ideology and mission of the Fascist regime focused primarily on the "strengthening" and "elevation" of the Italian people so that they might be "feared" and respected by foreigners. Giuseppe Maranzana, the unemployed maestro from Potenza, who remarkably happened to be carrying a small metal effigy of the Duce in his pocket at the time of his arrest for insulting Mussolini, expressed his admiration for "Fascism, which has always been the most important factor in the well-being, social justice, and moral and material elevation of

---

[36] Antonio Viotto to Duce, November 14, 1940, ACS, *confinati politici*, b. 1069, "Viotto, Antonio."

the Italian people in all of the world."[37] Antonio Viotto, the unemployed mechanic who was assaulted by a militiaman for insulting Italo Balbo, asked to be returned home "to dedicate himself to the strengthening and wellbeing of Italy." He had always harbored "sincere Italian sentiment" and dreamt of seeing the "dear *Patria*" "stronger, respected, feared, and admired by all the world, for the glory of the House of Savoy, for Your great heart, . . . and for the good of all the Italian people." Viotto promised to "love Italy" and keep alive "the flame of Imperial and Fascist Italy."[38]

In addition to explaining their sincere belief in Fascism, supplicants to the Duce offered examples of their adherence to the new Fascist order. This meant, above all, belonging to the party. Detainees and their families gave full accounts of who had joined the PNF and its subsidiary organizations, making sure to mention if a family member had been a "Fascist of the first hour" or a *squadrist*, had participated in the March on Rome, or had joined before or during the Matteotti crisis.[39] Fascism – an ideology that purported to promote national cohesion and unity – developed a system of discrimination that distinguished between "Fascists and non-Fascists, between Fascists of the first and the last hour, between *diciannovisti* [1919ers] and *ventottisti* [1928ers]" and between "real" and "meal-ticket Fascists."[40] Under the dictatorship, Italians understood this unofficial, yet rigid hierarchy of political merits. Luigia Balocco, the mother of a twenty-five-year-old detainee, wrote letters to police authorities and the queen, identifying herself as a "Fascist woman of the *fascio femminile*" and "one of the first women in the town to give her wedding band to the *Patria*." Of her five brothers, four fought in the Great War, and the fifth, youngest brother was with Gabrielle D'Annunzio at Fiume, for which he received a certificate for having "done his duty." Her husband joined the party in 1927. He also belonged to the MVSN and had recently been called up for service. Her son, the political detainee, joined the Balilla (ONB), the Fascist youth organization, in January of 1927 and "without interruption passed to the *Fasci Giovanili di Combattimento*." She begged, "Therefore, do we not thereby deserve a little bit of mercy?"[41] Family members of detainees also worked through the party

37 See Giuseppe Maranzana to Commission of Appeal, August 25, 1938, in ACS, *confinati politici*, b. 613, "Maranzana, Giuseppe."
38 Letter to Duce, July 28, 1941, in ACS, *confinati politici*, b. 1069, "Viotto, Antonio."
39 E.g., see the case file of "Tranchese, Giacomo," in ACS, *confinati politici*, b. 1021.
40 Salvatore Lupo, *Il fascismo*, 28.
41 See Luigia Balocco to queen, June 10, 1940, and to Mussolini, April 4, 1942, in ACS, *confinati politici*, b. 63, "Bardina, Carlo."

in their attempts to win a pardon or sentence reduction. Letters from family members to Rome often featured the seal of the local party and a short note from the party secretary or another local official approving of a detainee's return. Meanwhile, Italians who were not members of the party were left to explain why. During his days of hard work and long nights of drinking, Antonio Viotto explained, he did not have "the time to consider the importance of joining the National Fascist Party." Alceste Alvi, the Roman anarchist, admitted to Mussolini that he did not belong to the party but only because he had been led so far astray by "the ideas of false prophets." One eleven-year-old girl, whose only living parent had been sentenced to confinement, wrote that her father did not become a Fascist because he was too busy making "sacrifices for the *patria*."[42]

Many Italians petitioning Mussolini or other officials placed particular emphasis on their children's Fascist upbringing, particularly if they were enrolled in the regime's youth groups. One worker from Vercelli repeatedly promised to "observe and obey all of the laws emanated from the Fascist Regime" and swore that he would "raise a Fascist family."[43] Maria Lafasciano, the illiterate wife of a suspected Communist in Corato (Bari), described how her children, who had no bread to eat and would soon be homeless, nevertheless continued "to go to school so that tomorrow they will be children worthy of the Great *Italia*." She exclaimed, "Duce, they are even members of the Opera Nazionale Ballila!" She included a picture of the children, in their uniforms. Lafasciano's children, like many other offspring of political detainees, also wrote letters, swearing their loyalty to the regime. In their letters, other children similarly revealed their understanding of the regime's emphasis on youth and the potential of the next generation, the only Italians born and raised under Fascism. The twelve-year-old daughter of one detainee wrote to Mussolini, identifying herself as a "*Giovane Italiana*, a child of the new generation" to which she was "proud to belong," and she renewed her pledge of "infinite devotion" to Mussolini.[44] A nineteen-year-old political detainee promised that "in the future, I will be a great young Fascist and I will always be ready to defend my country."[45] The three children of one detainee, all members of the Italian Youth of Lictors (GIL), the Fascist youth organization that replaced the ONB in 1937, wrote, "we want to

[42] See ACS, *confinati politici*, b. 517, "Gubernati, Alberto."
[43] See Buccia to Mussolini, September 14, 1937, and to MI, January 8, 1938, in ACS, *confinati politici*, b. 108, "Buccia, Bianchetto."
[44] Alda Bianchi to Mussolini, October 19, 1938, in ibid.
[45] See Giuseppe Altoni to Mussolini, April 10, 1938, in ACS, *confinati politici*, b. 18, "Altoni, Giuseppe."

be worthy of this society in which we live and to be faithful believers in your ideology."[46]

As mothers and wives desperately described their unbridled enthusiasm for the regime, or, more pragmatically, their perfect conformity to Fascism, they revealed a certain exasperation or disbelief that the charge of anti-Fascism could have been successfully leveled against their sons and husbands. They had done everything the regime expected of them. In Palermo, Giuseppe Graziano, a worker confined for allegedly expressing support for the Spanish Republic, begged for release, so that he might return to his wife and four children and "educate them in the school of Fascism and love of the Patria." His children were "always among the very first, most diligent and enthusiastic members of the regime's youth organizations."[47] In a letter to Mussolini, Graziano's wife Teresa swore that her husband was responsible for enrolling the children in the ONB, making sure that their uniforms were always clean and in perfect condition. To prove their membership, she included all of the children's *tessere* (party cards). Her husband was so happy, she informed Mussolini, to have two *piccoli italiani*, one *figlio della lupa*, and one *piccola italiana*. "How," she asked the Duce, "could one call a man like this subversive?" By enrolling their children in the youth organizations, Giuseppe and Teresa Graziano felt they had paid their political dues. Both of them closed their letters with "I salute you Romanly" (*romanamente*), a reference to the salute that had become obligatory for Fascists and state officials.[48]

To corroborate their claims, Italians sent in photographs, party membership cards, ticket stubs to the Decennale exhibit in Rome, and other material evidence of their adherence to Fascism. Maria Caiazzo, a woman from a town near Mount Vesuvius, whose husband, a "Fascist of faith of the first hour," had been arrested, sent in a picture of herself and her six children, the three oldest boys dressed in the uniforms and fezzes of the Fascist youth.[49] Giovanni Pinna, a mechanic from Nuoro province (Sardinia) included a group photo of at least a hundred people celebrating the victory in Ethiopia and Declaration of the Empire. In the center,

---

[46] Aldo, Oscar, and Flora Amici to Mussolini, January 25, 1941, in ACS, *confinati politici*, b. 23, "Amici, Natale."

[47] See Graziano to Benito Mussolini, January 13, 1938, in ACS, *confinati politici*, b. 505, "Graziano, Giuseppe."

[48] Teresa Graziano to Mussolini, January 21, 1937, in ibid.

[49] Maria Caiazzo to Duce, August 13, 1941, Caiazzo to prime minister, September 1, 1941, Caiazzo to Donna Rachele, September 12, 1941, in ACS, *confinati politici*, b. 1021, "Tranchese, Giacomo."

two people are dressed as Ethiopian farmers, in black face, and there is a giant effigy of the Negus. To prove he was there, Pinna circled himself, seated near the back of the piazza.[50] Francesco Guadioso, suspected of various economic transgressions, sent in a picture of his seven children, all dressed in the uniform of the party or the Balilla, all standing around his understandably exhausted, bedridden wife.[51]

Not everyone experienced daily life under Fascism as a minefield of political conflict and violence. The historian George Mosse once told an anecdote about traveling by train in Italy in 1936. With a *carabinieri* within earshot, the people in Mosse's compartment were telling Mussolini jokes. Coming from Nazi Germany, Mosse was terrified, but the *carabinieri* entered the compartment and recounted a few jokes of his own.[52] For Mosse, life under the Fascist regime seemed benign. And relative to being Jewish in Nazi Germany, it was so. But it is likely that authorities cared little about Mosse and his travel companions – who were riding in first or second class. Fascist Italy's totalitarianism was riddled with holes, public and private areas where social class, group solidarity, regionalism, and other factors insulated people against state repression. Nevertheless, within the archipelago of spaces targeted by the regime, the patterns of Fascist political violence created a formidable array of ordinary vexations.

Violence and coercion forced many Italians to be constantly mindful of the regime's institutions, policies, and propaganda. The distribution of punishment, patronage, and pardons depended in part on whether Italians exhibited certain behaviors and avoided others. Thus, many aspects of everyday life – ordinary conversations with neighbors, child rearing, leisure time, attire, sexuality, reproduction, and countless other facets of existence – carried a certain political valence. That ordinary people were aware of the importance of belonging to the party and agreeing with the regime's propaganda might not seem extraordinary. But in a society in which so many felt themselves neither Italian nor "political" during the early part of the twentieth century, the regime's forcible integration of individuals into the political life of the relatively young nation was something very new. For many Italians, the politics of ordinary violence constituted a shared national experience.

---

[50] Picture in ACS, *confinati politici*, b. 799, "Pinna, Giovanni."
[51] ACS, MI, *confinati politici*, b. 463, "Gaudioso, Francesco."
[52] George Mosse, *Nazism: A Historical and Comparative Analysis of National Socialism* (New Brunswick, 1978), 104–5.

Conclusion

Days before the Grand Council of Fascism deposed him on July 24, 1943, Mussolini met with his police chief, Renzo Chierici, to discuss the system of police confinement and civilian internment. Allied bombings had made provisioning the island colonies virtually impossible, and public-security officials recommended the evacuation of the detainees to mainland camps. The problem was not small: Ustica held 2,500 people, Lipari 500, Ponza 700, Ventotene 833, and Tremiti 594. Unfortunately, Chierici reported, the mainland camps administered by the Interior Ministry were completely full.[1] During the previous three years of war, the sites of confinement, internment, and concentration had multiplied, until all of Italy was honeycombed with camps and other settlements of internees. In addition to the five thousand *internati* and *confinati* on the islands, the Interior Ministry had interned or otherwise confined in provinces throughout Italy another fourteen thousand political suspects, ex-convicts, gypsies, foreign Jews, enemies nationals, and civilians from occupied territories.[2] Castles, villas, schools, abandoned buildings, and other sites held anywhere from a few dozen people to hundreds or thousands. For example, between 1,500 and 2,000 foreigners, mostly Jews, lived in barracks behind barbed wire in the concentration camp at Ferramonti, in Basilicata.[3]

[1] Renzo Chierici to DGPS, July 21, 1943, in ACS, MI, Massime, fasc. "Corrispondenza relative allo sgombero delle colonie di confino," b. 25.
[2] Capogreco, *Campi del Duce*, 66–7, gives the total population of Interior Ministry internees and *confinati* at just under 20,000.
[3] An overview of all of these sites can be found in ibid., 179–249.

Italy had become the Fascist archipelago. When the regime began interning civilians en masse in 1940, it deployed the very same normative practices, facilities, and personnel that constituted the *confino di polizia* system.[4] Police held internees in the same cells, deported them in the same trains, and exiled or interned them in the same camps and island colonies as the *confinati*. Detainees were sometimes even unaware that they were *internati* (internees) rather than *confinati*.[5] The only difference was that the prefect did not bother convening a Provincial Commission regarding internees; instead, the police arrested people whose names appeared on lists compiled and updated over the course of the dictatorship. In sum, upon Italy's entrance into the war in June 1940, peacetime confinement morphed effortlessly into wartime internment – which is really to say that Italy already had a wartime system of internment for most of Mussolini's rule.

Parallel to the Interior Ministry's system of confinement and internment camps, Italian military authorities ran prisoner of war camps (approximately 70,000 prisoners). Additionally, the military interned or deported into the interior of Italy tens of thousands (60,000–100,000) of Slovenian, Croat, and Montenegrin civilians; some were Italian citizens from Venezia-Giulia, while others were former citizens of the "ex-Yugoslav" territories annexed by Italy during 1941 and 1942. Many of these internees lived in a state of "free internment" (exactly like mainland *confino*) or under minimum security regimes in large buildings. Others were sent to camps, which often held between three and six thousand internees, located in the Italian provinces of Padua, Gorizia, Perugia, Sassari, Udine, Treviso, Arezzo, Perugia, and Savona, and in the newly annexed territories around Fiume and the Dalmatian coast. Generally speaking, conditions in the military camps were far worse than in those operated by the Interior Ministry, with mortality rates of up to nearly 20 percent.[6] Like the Interior Ministry, the military had already developed practices of mass civilian internment before the Second World War. In the early 1930s, in Cyrenaica, the western province of Libya, the Italian military interned nearly one hundred thousand civilians, mostly in six

---

[4] Ibid., 58–65.

[5] Ibid., 8–9.

[6] Capogreco estimated that a total of 100,000 Slovenians, Croats, and Montenegrins were interned or deported into the interior of Italy (in the same manner as mainland *confino*) by Interior Ministry and military authorities (ibid., 78). Detainees died mainly of hunger and exposure. Conditions were the worst in camps located in occupied Yugoslavia. See ibid., 251–76, esp. 255–6, 269–70.

large camps.[7] This aspect of the campaign to "pacify" Cyrenaica, according to General Badoglio, might have resulted in "the destruction of the so-called submissive population," but it absolutely had to be pursued to its end, "even if the entire population of Cyrenaica" had to "perish."[8] Tens of thousands died from starvation, disease, and summary executions.[9] Years later, in Ethiopia, after the official end of hostilities, the military decimated the Ethiopian political and intellectual class, the real and potential backbone of resistance to Italian rule.[10] Italian authorities deported hundreds of higher-level Ethiopian nobility and functionaries to *confino* in Italy, while sending other "ordinary" patriots, intellectuals, educated persons, and their families to concentration camps such as Danane[11] and Nocra.[12]

At their meeting in July 1943, Police Chief Chierici informed Mussolini that in order to evacuate the island populations, the General Directorate of Public Security (DGPS) planned to build two more large concentration camps in central Italy, one in Arezzo, another in Siena. But the work would take too long, at least two months. Consequently, Mussolini directed Chierici to begin transferring the island populations to the jurisdiction of the military camps. Mussolini's arrest on July 25 put the matter

---

[7] Rochat, "La repressione della resistenza in Cirenaica," 33–50. These six camps, named after the cities and villages where they were located, were Marsa Brega (pop. 21,117), Soluch (pop. 20,123), Sld Ahmed el Magrun (pop. 13,050), el Agheila (pop. 10,900), Agedabia (pop. 10,000), and Abiar (pop. 3,123). Mortality rates during the first year were 25%, 30%, and up in many camps; Angelo Del Boca, *Gli Italiani in Libia*, vol. 2: *dal fascismo a Gheddafi* (Rome, 1986–8), 179–89.

[8] Badoglio to Graziani, June 20, 1930; quoted in Rochat, "La repressione della resistenza in Cirenaica," 61.

[9] Based on 1923 and 1936 census data, Rochat estimates that a minimum of 30,000 and a maximum of 70,000 people died; ibid., 82–3.

[10] In addition to internment, prison, and deportation, the Fascist colonial administration also resorted to massacres of suspect groups. For the massacre of hundreds of coptic monks and others after the attempted assassination of the Italian General Rodolfo Graziani, the viceroy of Africa Orientale Italiana (AOI), see Giorgio Rochat, *L'attentato a Graziani e la repressione italiana in Etiopia 1936–1937*, in Rochat, *Guerre italiane in Libia e in Etiopia. Studi militari 1921–1939*, 177–214.

[11] Approximately 6,000 men, women, and children who "resisted" the Italian conquest of Ethiopia passed through Danane, and many accounts report that up to one-half perished from malnutrition, malaria, and other diseases. The Danane camp operated until the British drove out the Italians in 1941. See Del Boca, "Un lager del Fascismo: Danane," 60; see also Nicola Labanca, "L'internamento coloniale italiano," in Di Sante, ed., *I campi di concentramento in Italia*, 60.

[12] The concentration camp/prison island of Nocra, located in the Red Sea off the coast of Massawa (Eritrea), was considered much worse than Danane by contemporaries; Labanca, *In marcia verso Adua* (Turin, 1993), 282–4.

up for reconsideration.[13] With the fall of Fascism, former police chief Carmine Senise and other police officials began to dismantle the *confino di polizia* system, releasing the "least" dangerous island detainees, though at a tortuously slow pace. Meanwhile, many detainees, the "most dangerous" ones, were transferred directly to military concentration camps. The process was chaotic. In September 1943, when the Allies announced the armistice, thousands of internees, including ex-*confinati*, remained in camps, which were liberated by the Allies in the south, taken over by the Germans in the north, or simply dissolved by Italian authorities. In the north, under German occupation, ex-detainees went on to fight in the resistance, die in Nazi massacres, suffer or die in German concentration camps, or, like most Italians, wait out the war.

The bloody fratricide that followed Mussolini's fall from power was in part the product of the brutality of German occupation. However, Fascists and anti-Fascists alike carried out executions, massacres, and reprisals in order to settle long-standing scores. In many communities in the north, the regime's supporters finally had to pay for the blood pact they had made with Mussolini and the squads in the early 1920s. Many of the men summarily executed by partisans were the very same *squadrists*, and their patrons, who had killed and terrorized Socialists and trade unionists in the early 1920s.[14] Twenty-years of ordinary violence had neither erased the memory of squad terror nor diminished the desire for revenge. On the other side, as the authority of the Fascist party-state broke down, *squadrists* old and new could now lethally suppress Fascism's opponents and enemies. The violence of twenty years of Fascism – so carefully confined within the real and metaphorical archipelagos of domestic repression and warfare – had now flooded society with unspeakable force and brutality. The atrocity and suffering of occupation and civil war represented the legacy of Fascist rule, rather than some horrible deviation in the regime's trajectory.

If the "Fascisms" of 1919, 1922, 1926, 1935, or 1945 had a unifying ideology and program, it was violence. The orthodox history of Italian Fascism invariably suggests that violence disappeared after 1925 or 1926, only to remerge in 1935 in the form of outwardly directed military violence. During this history's "lost" decade, roughly between 1925 and 1935, the dictatorship allegedly limited itself to "traditional police state

---

[13] Chierici to DGPS, July 21, 1943.
[14] Crainz, *Padania*, 191–2.

methods."[15] This book has attempted to show that such a reading of the regime's history rests upon a misunderstanding of the ideology and economy of violence at work during Mussolini's rule. However muted relative to the years of *squadrismo*, Fascist violence continued to operate under Mussolini's party-state. Domestically, whether during the era of *squadrismo* or under the Fascist regime proper, violence was carefully calibrated, selective, highly personal, and insidious, if seldom lethal. It operated within and exploited the parochialism of Italian towns – Fascists knew which buttons to push in small, tightly knit communities.

At the center, Mussolini intended Fascist state violence to make the people of the Italian peninsula and islands into Fascists or, at the very least, Italians. The goal of domestic violence was not simply to eliminate a few "degenerate" groups but also to force Italians to behave according to the central tenets of the Fascist state: authority, centralization, hierarchy, and discipline. The persecution of enemies, "social outsiders," and other "others" also served multivalent forms of Fascist pedagogy. The victims of political sanctions served as living reminders of the various behaviors that Mussolini, the police, and Fascists had deemed anti-Fascist or un-Italian. Moreover, the involvement of ordinary Italians in the implementation of violence and discrimination against minorities, whether they were Slavs, Pentecostals, or Jews, would, Mussolini believed, teach Italians to be disciplined, martial imperialists – that is, to be Fascists.

At the very least, Fascist violence inside of Italy helped the regime to assert greater control over the peninsula and its people, thereby contributing to a coercive process of "nation building." The central state created a national politics of ordinary violence, which Fascists and other Italians used to resolve political, social, economic, and personal conflicts in their everyday lives. Most Italians had to learn how to contend with this mechanism of Fascist rule, whether they were its perpetrators, its victims, or some position in between. Cultural historians have deemed *confino di polizia* a central "site of memory" for Italians.[16] Even today, all those who were alive when Mussolini was in power remember *il confino*. They invariably speak of it in two seemingly contradictory ways. The *confinati*, most will say, were *gente per bene* (good, respectable people).

[15] Frank Vollmer, "Revolutionary Discipline through Totalitarian Consensus: Dynamistic Modernism and Violence in the Political Culture of Italian Fascism," in ed. Gerhard Besier et al., *Fascism, Communism, and the Consolidation of Democracy*, 11–32.

[16] Gianfranco Porta, "Il confino," in *I luoghi della memoria: simboli e miti dell'Italia unita*, ed. Mario Isnenghi (Rome-Bari, 1996), 439–60.

They were the prominent anti-Fascists, exiled to places like Lipari, who had degrees and titles before their name – *Onerevole, dottore, ingenere*, and the like. Popular memory thus associates *il confino* with the repression of respectable, bourgeois men of principle – people for whom many Italians had retained a degree of respect or even sympathy. At the same time, Italians also recall that "when there was Mussolini, the law was obeyed," otherwise "you were sent to *confino*." Memories of *il confino* thus also evoke the regime's authoritarian policies toward criminals, troublemakers, and social outsiders. Mussolini "cleaned up the piazza," getting rid of vagabonds, con men, alcoholics, ex-convicts, pimps, loan sharks, *mafiosi*, and other "dregs" of Italian society. If the local baker had rigged his scale to cheat his customers, Mussolini took care of him, too. Finally, despite this regime of public order, many ordinary Italians did not feel safe, for they too felt menaced by the state. The regime's authoritarian practices of confinement, harassment, and discrimination were often deployed selectively against specific groups (e.g., homosexuals and Jehovah's Witnesses), but just as often they cast a wide net, striking at the poor, unemployed, and vulnerable, which is to say the majority of the Italian population in the mid-twentieth century. Here too, probably even more so than the regime's menacing secret political police, the OVRA, *il confino* acted as a symbol of the complex culture of repression the regime imposed on Italian communities. In this sense, *il confino* is not only a site of memory; it also implanted and shaped memory. Many Italians remember the National Fascist Party (PNF), the parades, the donation of wedding rings to the cause of Ethiopia, and other hallmarks of Fascist rule precisely because of "what would happen" if they did not participate. If a poor, married woman with four children did not give her wedding band to the party in support of the Ethiopian War, what consequence might befall her down the road? What about her children? Due to the nature of Mussolini's rule, the answer was: anything could happen. Repressive policies were fluid – uncertainty prevailed. Thus, it was always better to conform. Over many acts of collaboration, participation, and conformity hung the dark shadow of discrimination and ordinary violence.

If today some elderly Italians will insist that there was no crime under Mussolini, and that the Duce cleared the rabble from the piazzas, the post-1945 Italian Republic's official, anti-Fascist political culture and the historical profession have (until very recently) largely ignored the Fascist regime's persecution of apolitical "grumblers," habitual criminals, drunks, ethnic minorities, homosexuals, the unemployed, midwives, the mentally ill, and other categories of "social outsiders."[17] The postwar Italian Republic was founded on the principle of opposition to Fascism, and most anti-Fascist scholars interested in the repressive nature of Fascist rule focused their efforts mainly on identifying incidents of open opposition and dissent in the archives of the Fascist police. By contrast, historians unsympathetic to anti-Fascism have devoted little attention to policing, informing, denunciation, and coercion, arguing that the regime had no real system of mass repression.

This book has argued a third line, that any account of Mussolini's dictatorship that makes claims about Italian society must start by acknowledging that violence was at the heart of the regime's ideology and methods. Police and Fascists no doubt made opposition and dissent nearly impossible, and those Italians who chose to engage in anti-Fascist activities suffered dire consequences. However, whether or not Italians opposed Fascism, the regime needed to inflict violence, repression, and discrimination against internal enemies. Without this violence, there would be no Fascism. To be successful, every "Fascist" policy and every utopian goal required state-sponsored discipline, coercion, and violence. Such was the Fascist style of rule.

Historical memory of how greatly Fascism relied upon persecuting social outsiders and subaltern groups has been repressed for so long in part because the victims were often too marginalized or embarrassed to talk about it. In popular culture and the historical profession, the only "true" victims of Fascism were the anti-Fascists. Italian Jews and historians also eventually felt comfortable talking about the regime's anti-Semitic policies. But during the postwar period, with whom would a young homosexual talk about his years in political confinement? An ex-convict? A prostitute? An illiterate, alcoholic farm worker? Most anti-Fascists, and many Italians I suspect, saw nothing wrong with rounding up certain categories of social outsiders and "dregs" of society. The memoirs of most anti-Fascists reflect outrage only at the fact that the regime had "mistakenly" labeled this "rabble" political. For the anti-Fascists, the Manchurians were "false politicals," who had trespassed "unlawfully into a pasture reserved for others."[18] If anti-Fascists did not discern the illiberal injustice inflicted on ordinary criminal suspects and social

---

[17] Exceptions are Luisa Passerini, *Fascism in Popular Memory: The Cultural Experience of the Turin Working Class* (Cambridge, 1987); Rochat, *Regime fascista e chiese evangeliche*; and Benadusi, *Nemico dell'uomo nuovo*.

[18] Spinelli, *Lungo monologo*, 115.

outsiders, then who did? For many Italians, the regime's authoritarian treatment of such groups may have constituted an important trade-off for lost political rights and lower wages. Consequently, the complicity of so many Italians in denouncing and informing on vulnerable social groups no doubt reinforced the postwar silence surrounding this aspect of life under Fascism. Finally, the Italian Republic conducted no meaningful purge of the Italian police, judiciary, and other state agencies complicit in repression, coercion, and discrimination.[19] The same police officials who helped keep the regime in power were responsible in the postwar period for determining who received reparations as "victims of Fascism." Only Italians with impeccable anti-Fascists credentials qualified.[20]

In the postwar period, the repression of historical memory also occurred with regard to Fascist war violence. A very small minority of historians began researching the Italian military's war crimes in the late 1960s, but important figures in Italian society continued to deny atrocities, such as the use of poison gas in Ethiopia, with an almost absurd degree of obstinacy.[21] However, the current scholarly interest in Fascist war crimes and concentration camps has marked an important turn in the study of Fascism, for it has led scholars to direct their attention at perhaps the most essential feature of Mussolini's regime: violence. Fascist war violence, inflicted upon other groups, deployed far more brutal tactics than the police state or even the *squadrists*, in large part because the victims were racially "inferior" others. But colonial and military campaigns *were* still ideologically and programmatically bound up in the same larger domestic project of fascistizing, nationalizing, or simply disciplining the Italian population. State-backed violence at home always rose in direct proportion to military violence inflicted on foreigners and racial others. In Rome, beginning in 1935, Mussolini increased the size of the political confinement system and also dilated the definition of political crime to

---

[19] Franzinelli, *I tentacoli*, 411–84.

[20] Many personal files of political detainees contain postwar documentation from the years 1956–7 regarding their applications to receive indemnities for the persecution they suffered under Fascism. In many cases, police officials were clearly attempting to obstruct reparations, claiming that detainees were criminally dangerous ("dangerous subversive," "anarchist") or suffered no documentable illness (when they clearly had). Most "Republican police" used the same terms as the "Fascist police" in order to describe former political detainees, mainly because these police officials were the same people. E.g., see ACS, *confinati politici*, b. 183, "Camponeschi, Carlo"; b. 259, "Civita, Riccardo"; b. 403, "Ferrarese, Mario"; b. 619, "Marchina, Angelo."

[21] See the essays in Angelo Del Boca, *I gas di Mussolini. Il fascismo e la guerra d'Etiopia* (Rome, 1996).

include many behaviors unrelated to organized opposition. At the local level, apparent success in Ethiopia emboldened old-guard Fascists and young zealots to confront citizens whom they suspected were opposed or indifferent to the regime. Then, at the first sign that a war was going badly, whether in Spain or the Balkans, Fascists – from Mussolini to Farinacci – began to look with suspicion at the Italian people, sensing the betrayal of Italy's worst elements. Mussolini demanded "increased vigilance" over the behaviors of Italians. At the local level, discussions of foreign policy and war often turned violent. Militiamen and Fascists attacked people because they felt "provoked" or "insulted" by sidelong glances and grumblings. Just as squad violence was born out of a desire to extirpate the internal enemy after the First World War, Mussolini's new wars – in Spain, Ethiopia, Albania, France, Yugoslavia, Greece, and North Africa – rekindled Fascist impulses to shore up the home front.[22] After all, for many Fascists, Italy's "internal enemy" had never been fully dealt with. Socialists, Communists, anarchists, Anglophiles, Francophiles, homosexuals, defeatists, shirkers, and other degenerates, still undermined the war effort. Finally, Mussolini and other gerarchs meant for Fascist war violence to serve the same transformative purpose as domestic violence. Brutal warfare would teach Italians to hate, hurt, and annihilate their enemies pitilessly.[23] Violence inflicted on Italians, either at the front or in Allied bombing raids, would teach the weak a lesson, and harden the strong.[24]

Piero Caleffi was the provincial secretary of the Italian Socialist Party in Mantua. Attacked by *squadrists* in the early 1920s and later imprisoned by the Fascist regime several times, Caleffi went on to fight in the resistance and was captured by the Germans and deported to the Mauthausen concentration camp. Caleffi recalled,

> It seemed that the satanic creators of this unworldly world were the tools of a superhuman logic, that of a ruthless god who wanted to thin out a guilty and wretched humanity, too numerous to still be obedient and submissive. But, in truth, never as now had the link seemed more clear between the first [prison] sentence and the first humiliating beatings at home in 1923, during the first Fascist reaction, and the horrifying world in which I now found myself. Whether consciously or not, the Fascists were the precursors to the extermination camps.[25]

[22] See Salvatore Lupo, *Il fascismo*, 435–6.
[23] See Ruth Ben-Ghiat, *Fascist Modernities*, 173.
[24] Gentile, "Un gregge di rammolliti."
[25] Piero Caleffi, *Si fa presto a dire fame* (Milan, 1968), 155.

Although historians and social scientists might dispute the claim of a direct link between Fascist *squadrismo* and Nazi industrial killing, Caleffi instinctually perceived certain fundamental similarities in the Fascist and Nazi projects. Particularly for the opponents and victims of Fascism, the Nazi regime represented a similar, if more extreme, evil.[26]

Born in the wake of the First World War, and exhibiting an authoritarian impulse to (continue to) mobilize and control all, Fascism was the first anti-Bolshevik revolutionary movement to seize power in Europe, or the world for that matter. Although the extent to which Fascism was revolutionary is certainly debatable, undeniable is that Fascism (whether it was revolutionary or reactionary) was born out of spontaneous, illegal paramilitary squad violence, organized at the grassroots level. The Black Shirts were not merely anti-Marxist, however, and they proceeded to compromise the integrity of the liberal state, bringing Mussolini to power. They pressured Mussolini's government to persecute political opponents en masse, and he obliged them, leading to the creation of a political police, militia, and complex system of confinement, punishment, and discrimination. This new, modern system of police-state rule, together with Fascism's totalitarian aspiration to create a new *uomo fascista*, served as a model for movements and regimes in other societies, as they rejected liberalism in the face of Europe's interwar crisis of modernity. Adolf Hitler, among others, understood the importance of the Fascist model, frequently acknowledging his debt to Mussolini and his movement. "The brown shirt," he once conjectured, "might perhaps not have arisen without the black shirt."[27] In the horrible history of Europe's "era of violence," Fascist Italy thus established a precedent that was recognized by perpetrators and victims alike.[28]

---

[26] Many of the political detainees discussed in this book met a horrible end under German occupation: Mario Magri, who spent most of his adult life (17 years) in the *confino* camps and villages, was murdered by the Nazis in the infamous Fosse Ardeatine massacre outside of Rome; Roberto Barsotti, the secretary of Pisa's Communist Party (discussed in ch. 3), was executed by the Germans in 1944.

[27] Quoted in MacGregor Knox, *Common Destiny: Dictatorship, Foreign Policy, and War in Fascist Italy and Nazi Germany* (Cambridge, 2000), 53.

[28] On the "era of violence," see Ian Kershaw, "War and Political Violence in Twentieth Century Europe," *Contemporary European History* 14: 107–23.

Bibliography

Archival Sources

Archivio Centrale dello Stato (ACS)
   Ministero dell'Interno (MI)
      Direzione Generale della Pubblica Sicurezza (DGPS)
         Divisione Affari Generali e Riservati (AGR)
            Ufficio Confino Politico (UCP)
            Fascicoli personali confinati politici (*confinati politici*)
            Massime (M)
            Casellario Politico Centrale (CPC)
         Divisione Polizia
            Confinati comuni

Newspapers

Manchester Guardian
New York Times
Il popolo di Roma
Il popolo d'Italia
Review of Reviews
Il Sole 24 Ore

Published Works

Abse, Tobias. "Italian Workers and Italian Fascism." In *Fascist Italy and Nazi Germany: Comparisons and Contrasts*, ed. Richard Bessel. Cambridge: Cambridge University Press, 1996, 40–60.
———. "The Rise of Fascism in an Industrial City: The Case of Livorno 1918–1922." In *Rethinking Italian Fascism. Capitalism, Populism and Culture*, ed. David Forgacs. London: Oxford University Press, 1986, 52–82.

Adler, Franklin Hugh. "Why Mussolini Turned on the Jews." *Patterns of Prejudice* 39:3 (September 2005): 285–300.

Alberghi, Pietro. *Il Fascismo in Emilia Romagna: dalle origini alla Marcia su Roma*. Modena: Mucchi editore, 1989.

Amarcord. DVD. Directed by Federico Fellini. 1973; Italy: New World Cinema, 2006.

Anfosso, Luigi. "Domicilio Coatto." In *Enciclopedia Giuridica Italiana*, ed. Pasquale Mancini. Milan: Società editrice libraria, 1898.

Ansaldo, Giovanni. *Il giornalista di Ciano: diari, 1932–1943*. Rome: Il Mulino, 2000.

_____. *L'antifascista riluttante: memorie del carcere e del confino, 1926–27*. Bologna: Il Mulino, 1992.

Aquarone, Alberto. *L'organizzazione dello Stato totalitario*. Turin: Einaudi, 1995.

_____. "Violenza e consenso nel fascismo italiano." *Storia contemporanea* 1 (1979): 145–55.

Aquarone, Alberto, and Maurizio Vernassa, eds. *Il regime fascista*. Bologna: Il Mulino, 1974.

Arendt, Hannah. *The Origins of Totalitarianism*. New York and London: Harcourt, 1994.

Baris, Tommaso. *Il fascismo in provincia: politica e società a Frosinone*. Bari: Laterza, 2007.

Bartov, Omer. *Mirrors of Destruction: War, Genocide, and Modern Identity*. Oxford and New York: Oxford University Press, 2000.

Benadusi, Lorenzo. *Il nemico dell'uomo nuovo: l'omosesualità nell'esperimento totalitario fascista*. Milan: Feltrinelli, 2005.

_____. "Private Life and Public Morals: Fascism and the 'Problem' of Homosexuality." *Totalitarian Movements and Political Religions* 3:3 (2004): 171–204.

Ben-Ghiat, Ruth. *Fascist Modernities: Italy 1922–1945*. Berkeley: University of California Press, 2004.

_____. "A Lesser Evil? Italian Fascism in/and the Totalitarian Equation." In *The Lesser Evil: Moral Approaches to Genocide Practices*, ed. Helmut Dubiel and Gabriel Gideon. London and New York: Routledge, 2000, 137–53.

Berenbaum, Michael, and Abraham J. Peck, eds. *The Holocaust and History: The Known, the Unknown, the Disputed, and the Reexamined*. Bloomington and Indianapolis: Indiana University Press, 1998.

Bergonzini, Luciano. *La resistenza a Bologna: testimonianze e documenti*. Bologna: Istituto per la Storia di Bologna, 1967.

Bernardini, Gene. "The Origins and Development of Racial Anti-Semitism in Fascist Italy." *Journal of Modern History* 49 (September 1977): 431–53.

Besier, Gerhard, Francesca Piombo, Katarzyna Stoklosa, eds. *Fascism, Communism, and the Consolidation of Democracy*. Berlin: Lit Verlag, 2006.

Bidussa, David. *Il mito del bravo italiano*. Milan: Il Saggiatore, 1993.

Bosworth, R. J. B. *Mussolini's Italy: Life under the Fascist Dictatorship, 1915–1945*. New York: Penguin, 2005.

_____. *Mussolini*. Oxford University Press, 2002.

_____. *The Italian Dictatorship: Problems and Perspectives in the Interpretation of Mussolini and Fascism*. New York: Hodder, 1998.

Bridgman, Jon, and Leslie J. Worley. "Genocide of the Hereros." In *Genocide in the Twentieth Century: Critical Essays and Eyewitness Accounts*, ed. Samuel Totten, William S. Parsons, and Israel W. Charny. New York and London: Garland Publishing, 1994, 3–31.

Broszat, Martin. *Anatomy of the SS State*. Trans. Richard Barry, Marian Jackson, and Dorothy Long. New York: Walker and Company, 1965.

Busoni, Juares. *Nel tempo del fascismo*. Rome: Editori Riuniti, 1975.

Caleffi, Piero. *Si fa presto a dire fame*. Milan: Mursia, 1968.

Campbell, Ian L. "La repressione fascista in Etiopia: il massacro segreto di Engecha." *Studi piacentini* 24–5 (1998–9): 23–46.

Campbell, Ian L., and Degife Gabre Tsadik. "La repressione fascista in Etiopia: la ricostruzione del massacro di Debrà Libanòs." *Studi piacentini* 21 (1997): 79–128.

Canali, Mauro. *Le spie del regime*. Bologna: Il Mulino, 2004.

_____. *Il delitto Matteotti: affarismo e politica nel primo governo Mussolini*. Bologna: Mulino, 1997.

Capogreco, Carlo Spartaco. *I campi del Duce: l'internamento civile nell'Italia fascista, 1940–43*. Turin: Einaudi, 2004.

_____. "I campi di internamento fascisti per gli ebrei, 1940–1943." *Storia Contemporanea* 22 (August 1991): 663–882.

_____. *Ferramonti: La vita e gli uomini del più grande campo d'internamento fascista, 1940–45*. Firenze: La Giuntina, 1987.

Carbone, Donatella. *Il popolo al confino: la persecuzione fascista in Basilicata*. Rome: Ministero per i beni culturali e ambientali, 1994.

Carbone, Salvatore, and Laura Grimaldi. *Il popolo al confino: la persecuzione fascista in Sicilia*. Rome: Ministero per i beni culturali e ambientali, 1989.

_____. *Il popolo al confino: la persecuzione fascista in Calabria*. Cosenza: Lerici, 1977.

Cardoza, Anthony. *Agrarian Elites and Italian Fascism: The Province of Bologna, 1901–1926*. Princeton, NJ: Princeton University Press, 1982.

Carucci, Paola. "Il Ministero dell'Interno: Prefetti, Questori e Ispettori Generali." In *Sulla crisi del regime fascista, 1938–1943: La società italiana dal 'consenso' alla Resistenza*, ed. Angelo Ventura. Venice: Marsilio, 1996, 21–73.

_____. "Arturo Bocchini." In *Uomini e volti del fascismo*, ed. Ferdinando Cordova. Rome: Bulzoni, 1980, 65–103.

_____. "L'organizzazione dei servizi di polizia dopo l'approvazione del testo unico di pubblica sicurezza nel 1926." *Rassegna degli archivi di Stato* 36 (1976): 82–114.

Casali, Luciano. "E se fosse dissenso di massa?" *Italia contemporanea* 144 (1981): 101–20.

Checchia, Giuseppe. *Misure di polizia e misure di sicurezza*. Naples: Tipomeccanica, 1934.

Ciano, Galeazzo. *Diary, 1937–1943*. Trans. Robert L. Miller and Umberto Coletti-Perucca. New York: Enigma, 1980.

Clough, Shepard B. *The Economic History of Modern Italy.* New York: Columbia University, 1964.

Coletti, Alessandro. *Il governo di Ventotene: stalinismo e lotta politica tra i dirigenti del PCI al confino.* Milan: La Pietra, 1978.

Corner, Paul. "Everyday Fascism in the 1930s: Centre and Periphery in the Decline of Mussolini's Dictatorship." *Contemporary European History* 15 (2006): 195–222.

————. "Italian Fascism: Whatever Happened to Dictatorship?" *Journal of Modern History* 74 (June 2002): 326–7.

————. *Fascism in Ferrara, 1915–1925.* London: Oxford University Press, 1975.

Corner, Paul, and Giovanna Procacci. "The Italian Experience of 'Total' Mobilization, 1915–1920." In *State Society and Mobilization in Europe during the First World War,* ed. John Horne. Cambridge: Cambridge University Press, 1997, 223–40.

Corso, Guido. *L'ordine pubblico.* Bologna: il Mulino, 1979.

Corvisieri, Silvio. *La villeggiatura di Mussolini: il confino da Bocchini a Berlusconi.* Milan: Baldini, 2004.

————. *All'Isola di Ponza.* Rome: Il mare, 1985.

Courtois, Stéphan, ed. *The Black Book of Communism: Crimes, Terror, Repression.* Trans. Jonathan Murphy and Mark Kramer. Cambridge, MA: Harvard University Press, 1999.

Crainz, Guido. *Padania: Il mondo dei braccianti dall'Ottocento alla fuga dalle campagne.* Rome: Donzelli, 2007.

Dall'Orto, Giovanni. "Il paradosso del razzismo fascista verso l'omosessualità." In *Nel nome della razza: Il razzismo nella storia d'"Italia, 1870–1945,* ed. Alberto Burgio. Bologna: Il Mulino, 1999, 515–28.

Dal Pont, Adriano. *I lager di Mussolini: l'altra faccia del confino nei documeti della polizia fascista.* Milan: La Pietra, 1975.

Dal Pont, Adriano, Alfonso Leonetti, Pasquale Maiello, and Lino Zocchi. *Aula IV: Tutti i processi del Tribunale Speciale fascista.* Milan: La Pietra, 1976.

Dal Pont, Adriano, and Simonetta Carolini, eds. *L'Italia al confino: le ordinanze di assegnazione al confino emesse dalle Commissioni provinciali dal novembre 1926 al luglio 1943,* 4 vols. Milan: La Pietra, 1983.

Davis, John A. *Conflict and Control: Law and Order in Nineteenth Century Italy.* Basingstoke, UK: Macmillan Education, 1988.

Deakin, F. W. *The Brutal Friendship.* Garden City, NY: Anchor Books, 1966.

De Felice, Renzo. *The Jews in Fascist Italy: A History.* Trans. Robert L. Miller. New York: Enigma Books, 2001. [*Storia degli ebrei italiani sotto il fascismo.* Turin: Einaudi, 1993.]

————. *Mussolini l'alleato, 1940–45, 2 vols.* Turin: Einaudi, 1990–7.

————. *Mussolini il duce, 2 vols.* Turin: Einaudi, 1974–81.

————. *Mussolini il fascista, 2 vols.* Turin: Einaudi, 1966–8.

————. "La situtazione dei partiti politici antifascisti alla vigilia della loro soppressione seconda la polizia fascista." *Rivista storica del socialismo* 25–9 (1965): 65–79.

De Grazia, Victoria, and Sergio Luzzato, eds. *Dizionario del Fascismo,* 2 vols. Turin: Einaudi, 2002.

_____. *How Fascism Ruled Women: Italy, 1922–1945*. Berkeley: University of California Press, 1992.

_____. *The Culture of Consent: Mass Organization of Leisure in Fascist Italy.* Cambridge and New York: Cambridge University Press, 1981.

Del Boca, Angelo. *I gas di Mussolini. Il fascismo e la guerra d'Etiopia*. Rome: Editori Riuniti, 1996.

_____. "Un lager del Fascismo: Danane." *Studi Piacentini* 1 (1987): 59–70.

_____. *Gli Italiani in Libia*. 2 vols. Rome: Laterza, 1986–8.

_____. *Gli italiani in Africa Orientale*. 4 vols. Rome and Bari: Laterza, 1976–84.

Delle Donne, Enrica Robertazzi. "Origini del fascismo a Salerno, 1919–1924." In *Mezzogiorno e fascismo: atti del Convegno nazionale di studi promosso dalla Regione Campania, Salerno-Monte S. Giacomo, 11–14 December 1975*, ed. Pietro Laveglia. Naples: Edizioni Scientifiche Italiane, 1978, 212–34.

De Luna, Giovanni. *Donne in oggetto: l'antifascismo nella società italiana, 1922–1939*. Turin: Bollati Boringhieri, 1995.

Delzell, Charles F. *Mussolini's Enemies: The Italian Anti-Fascist Resistance.* Princeton, NJ: Princeton University Press, 1961.

De Rossi, Giovanni Maria. *Ventotene e S. Stefano*. Rome: Guido Guidotti Editore, 1999.

Di Michele, Andrea. "Un prodromo emblematico: l'italianizzazione forzata del Sudtirolo, 1922–43." *Qualestoria* 30:1 (2002): 37–43.

Di Sante, Costantino, ed. *I campi di concentramento in Italia: dall'internamento alla deportazione, 1940–1945*. Milan: FrancoAngeli, 2001.

Dolfin, Giovanni. *Con Mussolini nella tragedia: diario del capo della segretaria particolare della duce, 1943–44*. Milan: Garzanti, 1949.

Domenico, Roy Palmer. *Italian Fascists on Trial, 1943–1948*. Chapel Hill: University of North Carolina Press, 1991.

Dunnage, Jonathan. "Mussolini's Policemen, 1926–1943." In *Policing Interwar Europe*, ed. Gerald Blaney. New York: Palgrave Macmillan, 2006, 112–35.

_____. "Policing Right-Wing Dictatorships: Some Preliminary Comparisons of Fascist Italy, Nazi Germany and Franco's Spain." *Crime, Histoire et Sociétés/Crime, History and Society* 1 (2006): 93–122.

_____. "Social Control in Fascist Italy: The Role of the Police." In *Social Control in Europe, vol. 2: 1800–2000*, ed. Clive Emsley, Eric Johnson, and Pieter Spierenburg. Columbus: Ohio State University Press, 2004, 261–80.

_____. "The Policing of an Italian Province during the Fascist Period: Siena, 1926–1943." In *Conflict and Legality. Policing Mid-Twentieth Century Europe*, ed. Gerard Oram. London: Francis Boutle, 2003, 23–41.

_____. *The Italian Police and the Rise of Fascism: A Case Study of the Province of Bologna, 1897–1925*. Westport, CT: Praeger Publishers, 1997.

Ebner, Michael. "Dalla repressione dell'antifascismo al controllo sociale. Il confino di polizia, 1926–1943." *Storia e problemi contemporanei* 43 (2006): 81–104.

_____. "Terror und Bevölkerung im italienischen Faschismus." In *Beiträge zur Geschichte des Nationalsozialismus, vol. 21: Faschismus in Italien und Deutschland: Studien zu Transfer und Vergleich*, ed. Sven Reichardt and Armin Nolzen. Göttingen, Germany: Wallstein, 2005: 201–24.

_____. "The Persecution of Homosexual Men under Fascism, 1926–1943." In *Gender, Family, and Sexuality: The Private Sphere in Italy, 1860–1945*, ed. Perry Willson. Basingstoke, UK: Palgrave Macmillan, 2004, 139–56.

Fiori, Giuseppe. *Antonio Gramsci: Life of a Revolutionary*. Trans. Tom Nairn. New York: Verso, 1990.

Fitzpatrick, Sheila. *Everyday Stalinism. Ordinary Life in Extraordinary Times: Soviet Russia in the 1930s*. New York and Oxford: Oxford University Press, 1999.

Fitzpatrick, Sheila, and Robert Gellately, eds. *Accusatory Practices: Denunciation in Modern European History, 1789–1989*. Chicago and London: University of Chicago Press, 1997.

Folino, Francesco. *Ferramonti, un lager di Mussolini: gli internati durante la guerra*. Cosenza: Brenner, 1985.

Fornari, Harry. *Mussolini's Gadfly: Roberto Farinacci*. Nashville: Vanderbilt University Press, 1971.

Francescangeli, Eros. *Arditi del popolo: Argo Secondari e la prima organizzazione antifascita, 1917–1922*. Rome: Odradek, 2000.

Franzinelli, Mimmo. *Squadristi*. Milan: Mondadori, 2003.

_____. *Delatori. Spie e confidenti: l'arma segreta del regime fascista*. Milan: Mondadori, 2001.

_____. *I tentacoli dell'Ovra: agenti, collaboratori e vittimi della polizia politica fascista*. Torino: Bollati Boringhieri, 1999.

Gabrielli, Gianluca. "Africani in Italia negli anni del razzismo di stato." In *Nel nome della razza: il razzismo nella storia d'Italia, 1870–1945*, ed. Alberto Burgio. Bologna: il Mulino, 1999, 201–12.

Garosci, Aldo. *Storia dei fuorusciti*. Bari: Laterza, 1953.

Gellately, Robert. *Backing Hitler: Consent and Coercion in Nazi Germany*. Oxford and New York: Oxford University Press, 2001.

_____. *The Gestapo and German Society: Enforcing Racial Policy, 1933–1945*. Oxford and New York: Oxford University Press, 1990.

Gellately, Robert, and Nathan Stoltzfus, eds. *Social Outsiders in Nazi Germany*. Princeton, NJ, and Oxford: Princeton University Press, 2001.

Gentile, Emilio. *The Sacralization of Politics*. Trans. Keith Botsford. Cambridge, MA: Harvard University Press, 1996. [Culto del littorio. Rome: Laterza, 1998.]

_____. *La via italiana al totalitarianismo: Il partito e lo stato nel regime fascista*. Rome: Nuova Italia Scientifica, 1995.

_____. *Storia del partito fascista, 1919–1922: movimento e milizia*. Bari: Laterza, 1989.

_____. "The Problem of the Party in Italian Fascism." *Journal of Contemporary History* 19:2 (April 1984): 251–74.

Getty, J. Arch, Gábor T. Ritterspoon, and Viktor N. Zemskov. "Victims of the Soviet Penal System in the Pre-war Years: A First Approach on the Basis of Archival Evidence." *The American Historical Review* 98:4 (October 1993): 1017–49.

Geyer, Michael, and Sheila Fitzpatrick, eds. *Beyond Totalitarianism: Stalinism and Nazism Compared*. New York and Cambridge: Cambridge University Press, 2009.

Ghini, Celso, and Adriano Dal Pont. *Gli antifascisti al confino,1926–1943*. Rome: Editore Riuniti, 1971.

Gibson, Mary. *Born to Crime: Cesare Lombroso and the Origins of Biological Criminology*. Westport, CT: Praeger, 2002.

Gissi, Alessandra. "Un percorso a ritroso: le donne al confino politico 1926–1943." *Italia contemporanea* 226 (March 2002): 31–60.

Goretti, Gianfranco. "Il periodo fascista e gli omosessuali: il confino di polizia." In *Le ragioni di un silenzio: la persecuzione degli omosessuali durante il nazismo e il fascism*. Verona: Ombre Corte, 2002, 64–74.

Gramsci, Antonio. *Lettere al carcere*. Ed. Antonio Santucci. Palermo: Sellerio, 1996.

Grana, Daniele." La prevenzione del dissenso: la politica assistenziale del fascism." In *Regime fascista e societá modenese: aspetti e problemi del fascismo locale, 1922–1939*, ed. Bertucelli and S. Magagnoli. Modena: Mucchi editore, 1995, 121–41.

Hacket, David, ed. *The Buchenwald Report*. Boulder, CO: Westview Press, 1995.

Horn, David G. *Social Bodies: Science, Reproduction, and Italian Modernity*. Princeton, NJ: Princeton University Press, 1994.

———. "L'Ente opere assistenziali: strategie politiche e pratiche di assistenza." In *Il fascismo in Lombardia. Politica, economia, societá*, ed. Maria Luisa Betri. Milan: FrancoAngeli, 1989, 480–90.

Ipsen, Carl. *Dictating Demography: The Problem of Population in Fascist Italy*. Cambridge: Cambridge University Press, 1996.

Isneghi, Mario, ed. *I luoghi della memoria: simboli e miti dell'Italia unita*. Rome-Bari: Laterza, 1996.

Italy. Ministero della Difesa. *Tribunale Speciale per la difesa dello Stato*. 17 vols. Rome: Ministero della Difesa, Ufficio storico dello Stato Maggiore dell'Esercito, 1980–99.

———. Ministero di Grazia e Giustizia. *Progetto preliminare di un nuovo codice penale*. 4 vols. Rome: Tipografia delle Mantellate, 1927.

———. Ministry of Justice. *Lavori Preparatori del Codice Penale e del Codice di Procedura Penale*. 4 vols. Rome: Tipografia delle Mantellate, 1927–30.

———. Ministry of the Interior. *Bollettino della Scuola Superiore di polizia e dei servizi tecnici annessi*. Rome: Ministero dell'Interno, Direzione Generale della Pubblica Sicurezza, 1927–39.

———. Ministero di Grazia e Giustizia. Direzione Generale per gli Istituti di Prevenzione di Pena. *Statistica degli Istituti di Prevenzione e di Pena e dei Riformatori*. Rome: Istituto poligrafico dello Stato, 1928–37.

Jacometti, Alberto. *Ventotene*. Milan: Mondadori, 1946.

Jensen, Richard Bach. *Liberty and Order: The Theory and Practice of Italian Public Security Policy, 1848 to the Crisis of the 1890s*. New York: Garland, 1991.

Kaminski, Andrzej. *I campi di concentramento dal 1896 a oggi*. Turin: Bollati Boringhieri, 1997.

Kershaw, Ian. "War and Political Violence in Twentieth Century Europe." *Contemporary European History* 14 (2005): 107–23.

Knox, MacGregor. *Common Destiny: Dictatorship, Foreign Policy, and War in Fascist Italy and Nazi Germany.* Cambridge: Cambridge University Press, 2000.

———. *Mussolini Unleashed, 1939–1941: Politics and Strategy in Fascist Italy's Last War.* Cambridge: Cambridge University Press, 1999.

———. "Conquest, Foreign and Domestic, in Fascist Italy and Nazi Germany." *Journal of Modern History* 56:1 (March 1984): 1–57.

Kogon, Eugen. *The Theory and Practice of Hell: The German Concentration Camps and the System behind Them.* Trans. Heinz Norden. New York: Farrar, Straus and Company, 1954.

Koon, Tracy. *Believe, Obey, Fight: Political Socialization of Youth in Fascist Italy, 1922–1943.* Chapel Hill: University of North Carolina Press, 1985.

Kotek, Joel, and Pierre Rigoulot. *Le Siècle des Camps. Détention, concentration, extermination: Cent ans de mal radical.* Paris: JC Lattés, 2000.

Kotkin, Stephen. *Magnetic Mountain: Stalinism as a Civilization.* Berkeley: University of California Press, 1995.

Labanca, Nicola. *In marcia verso Adua.* Turin: Einaudi, 1993.

Lafon, Xavier. "Les îles de la mer Tyrrhénienne: entre palais et prisons sous les Julio-Claudiens." In *Carcer: Prison et privation de liberté dans l'antiquité classique. Actes du colloque de Strasbourg (5 e 6 décembre 1997),* ed. Cécil Bertrand-Dagenbach, Alain Chauvot, Michel Matter, and Jean-Marie Salamito. Paris: De Boccard, 1999.

Lautman, Rüdiger. "The Pink Triangle: Homosexuals as 'Enemies of the State'." In *The Holocaust and History: The Known, the Unknown, the Disputed, and the Re-examined,* ed. Michael Berenbaum and Abraham J. Peck. Bloomington and Indianapolis: Indiana University Press, 1998.

Laveglia, Pietro. "Fascismo, antifascismo e resistenza nel salernitano." In *Mezzogiorno e Fascismo, Atti del convegno nazionale di studi promosso dalla Regione Campania, Salerno-Monte S. Giacomo, 11–14 December 1975,* ed. Pietro Laveglia. Naples: Edizioni Scientifiche Italiane, 1978, 342–70.

Lazzero, Ricciotti. *Il partito nazionale fascista.* Milan: Rizzoli, 1985.

Leto, Guido. *Ovra: fascismo, antifascismo.* Bologna: Cappelli, 1951.

Levi, Carlo. *Christ Stopped at Eboli.* Trans. Frances Frenaye. New York: Farrar, Straus, and Giroux, 1989.

Levy, Carl. *Gramsci and the Anarchists.* Oxford and New York: Berg, 1999.

Lupo, Salvatore. *Il fascismo: la politica in un regime totalitario.* Rome: Donzelli, 2000.

———. *Storia della mafia: dalle origini ai nostri giorni.* Rome: Donzelli, 1993.

———. "L'utopia totalitaria del fascismo, 1918–1942." In *Storia d'Italia. Le regioni dall'Unita ad oggi. La Sicilia,* ed. Maurice Aymard and Giuseppe Giarrizzo. Turin: Einaudi, 1987, 373–482.

Lussu, Emilio. *La Catena.* Milan: Baldini and Castoldi, 1997.

Lyttelton, Adrian. *The Seizure of Power: Fascism in Italy, 1919–1929.* London: Weidenfeld and Nicholson, 1987.

———. "Fascism in Italy: The Second Wave." *Journal of Contemporary History* 1:1 (1966): 75–100.

_____. "Fascism and Violence in Postwar Italy: Political Strategy and Social Conflict." In *Social Protest, Violence and Terror in 19th and 20th Century Europe*, ed. Wolfgang Mommsen and Gerhard Hirschfeld. London: Macmillan, 1982, 257–74.

Maccari, Mino. *Visita al confino: a Ponza e a Lipari nel 1929*. Marina di Belvedere, Cosenza: Cultura Calabrese, 1985.

Magri, Mario. *Una vita per la libertà. Diciassette anni di confino politico di un martire delle fosse ardeatine*. Rome: Editore Ludovico Puglielli, 1956.

Maiocchi, Roberto. *Scienza italiana e razzismo fascista*. Scandici: La Nuova Italia Editrice, 1999.

Malefakis, Edward. "La dictadura de Franco en una perspectiva comparada." In *Franquismo: El juicio de la storia*, ed. José Luis García Delgado. Madrid: Temas de Hoy, 2000, 11–68.

Mallmann, Klaus-Michael, and Gerhard Paul, eds. *Die Gestapo: Mythos und Realität*. Darmstadt, Germany: Wissenschaftliche-Buchgesellschaft, 1995.

Mancini, Enzo. *Isole Tremiti: Sassi di Diomede. Natura, storia, arte, turismo*. Milan: Mursia, 1979.

Mann, Michael. *Fascists*. Cambridge: Cambridge University Press, 2004.

Mannari, Enrico. "Tradizione sovversiva e comunismo durante il regime fascista, 1926–43: Il caso di Livorno." In *Annali della Fondazione Giangiacomo Feltrinelli*, vol. 20: *La classe operaia durante il fascismo*, ed. Guido Sapelli. Milan: Feltrinelli, 1979–80: 837–74.

Manotti, Brunella. "Un universo sommerso. Frammenti di vita di 'sovversive' parmensi." In *Nella rete del regime. Gli antifascisti del Parmense nelle carte della polizia, 1922–43*, ed. Massimo Giufredi. Rome: Carocci, 2004, 136–64.

Manzini, Vincenzo. *Trattato di diritto penale italiano secondo il codice del 1930*, vol. 7. Turin: Unione tipografico–editrice torinese, 1936.

Markevitch, Igor. *Made in Italy*. Lausanne, Switzerland: Mermod, 1946.

Mason, Tim. *Nazism, Fascism, and the Working Class*. Cambridge: Cambridge University Press, 1995.

Massara, Katia. *Il popolo al confino: la persecuzione fascista in Puglia*. Rome: Ministero per i beni culturali e ambientali, 1991.

Matteotti, Giacomo. *The Fascisti Exposed: A Year of Fascist Domination*. New York: Fertig, 1969.

Michaelis, Meir. "The Holocaust in Italy: Areas of Inquiry." In *The Holocaust and History: The Known, the Unknown, the Disputed, and the Reexamined*, ed. Michael Berenbaum and Abraham J. Peck. Bloomington and Indianapolis: Indiana University Press, 1998, 439–62.

Missori, Mario. *Governi, alte cariche dello stato, alti magistrati e prefetti del Regno d'Italia*. Rome: Ministero per i beni culturali e ambientali, 1989.

Misuri, Alfredo. *Ad Bestias! Memorie d'un perseguitato*. Rome: Edizioni delle catacombe, 1944.

Molfese, Franco. *Storia del brigantaggio dopo l'Unità*. Milan: Feltrinelli, 1964.

Morgan, Philip. "The Prefects and Party-State Relations in Fascist Italy." *Journal of Modern Italian Studies* 3:3 (1998): 241–72.

_____. "I primi podestà fascisti: 1926–32." *Storia contemporanea* 3 (1978): 407–23.

Mosse, George. "Toward a General Theory of Fascism." In *The Fascist Revolution: Toward a General Theory of Fascism*, ed. George Mosse. New York: Howard Fertig, 1993, 1–44.

———. *Nationalism and Sexuality: Middle-Class Morality and Sexual Norms in Modern Europe*. Madison: University of Wisconsin Press, 1988.

———. *Nazism: A Historical and Comparative Analysis of National Socialism*. New Brunswick, NJ: Transaction Books, 1978.

Musci, Leonardo. *Il confino fascista di polizia. L'apparato statale di fronte al dissenso politico e sociale*. Milan: La Pietra, 1983.

Mussolini, Benito. *Opera Omnia*, 35 vol., ed. Edoardo and Duilio Susmel. Florence: La Fenice, 1951–63.

Naimark, Norman M., ed. *Fires of Hatred: Ethnic Cleansing in Twentieth Century Europe*. Cambridge, MA: Harvard University Press, 2000.

Nello, Paolo. *Dino Grandi: la formazione di un leader fascista*. Bologna: Mulino, 1987.

———. "La violenza fascista ovvero dello squadrismo nazionalrivoluzionario." *Storia contemporanea* 13:6 (December 1982): 1009–25.

Neppi Modona, Guido. "Carcere e società civile." In *Storia d'Italia:i documenti* vol. 5, no. 2, ed. Ruggiero Romano and Corrado Vivanti. Turin: Giulio Einaudi editore, 1973, 1901–98.

Noce, Teresa. *Rivoluzionaria professionale*. Milan: Aurora, 2003.

Nye, Robert A. *Crime, Madness, and Politics in Modern France: The Medical Concept of National Decline*. Princeton, NJ: Princeton University Press, 1984.

Orsi, P. L. "Una fonte seriale: i rapporti prefettizi sul'antifascismo non militante." *Rivista di storia contemporanea* 2 (1990): 280–303.

Ottolenghi, Gustavo. *Gli italiani e il colonialismo: i campi di detenzione italiani in Africa*. Milan: SugarCo, 1997.

Pagano, Alessandra. *Il confino politico a Lipari, 1926–1933*. Milan: Franco-Angeli, 2003.

Palla, Marco. "Lo stato-partito." In *Lo stato fascista*, ed. Marco Palla. Milan: RCS Libri, 2001, 1–78.

———. *Firenze nel regime fascista, 1929–1934*. Florence: Olschki, 1978.

Passerini, Luisa. *Fascism in Popular Memory: The Cultural Experience of the Turin Working Class*. Cambridge: Cambridge University Press, 1987.

———. "Donne operaie e aborto nella Torino fascista." *Italia Contemporanea* 151–2 (1983): 83–109.

Payne, Stanley G. *A History of Fascism, 1914–1945*. Madison: University of Wisconsin Press, 1995.

Peregalli, Arturo, and Sandro Saggioro. *Amadeo Bordiga: la sconfitta e gli anni oscuri, 1926–1945*. Turin: La Grafica Nuova, 1998.

Persichilli, Gina Antoniani. "Disposizioni normative e fonti archivistiche per lo studio dell'internamento in Italia, June 1940–July 1943." *Rassegna degli Archivi di Stato* 38 (1978): 95–112.

Petersen, Jens. "Violence in Italian Fascism, 1919–1925." In *Social Protest, Violence and Terror in 19th and 20th Century Europe*, ed. Wolfgang Mommsen and Gerhard Hirschfeld. London: Macmillan, 1982, 275–99.

Petrini, Davide. *La prevenzione inutile: illegittimità delle misure praeter delictum.* Naples: Case Editrice Jovene, 1996.

Petrosino, Dario. "Come si costruisce uno stereotipo. La rappresentazione degli omosessuali nell'Italiano di Leo Longanesi (1926–1929)." In *Nel nome della razza: Il razzismo nella storia d'Italia, 1870–1945,* ed. Alberto Burgio. Bologna: Il Mulino, 1999, 503–14.

———. "Traditori della stirpe: il razzismo contro gli omossessuali nella stampa del fascismo." In *Studi sul razzismo Italiano,* ed. Alberto Burgio and Luciano Casali. Bologna: Clueb, 1996, 89–107.

Piccioli, Paolo. "I testimoni di Geova durante il regime fascista." *Studi Storici* 41:1 (January–March 2000): 191–229.

Piccioni, Lidia. *San Lorenzo, un quartiere romano durante il fascismo.* Rome: Edizioni di storia e letteratura, 1984.

Picciotto Fargion, Liliana. "The Persecution of Jews in Italy, 1943–1945: A Chronicle of Events." In *The Jews of Italy: Memory and Identity,* ed. Bernard D. Cooperman and Barbara Garvin. Bethesda: University Press of Maryland, 2000, 443–54.

———. *Il libro della memoria: Gli ebrei deportati dall'Italia, 1943–1945.* Milan: Mursia Editore, 1991.

———. "Jews during the German Occupation and the Italian Social Republic." In *The Italian Refuge: Rescue of Jews during the Holocaust,* ed. Ivo Herzer, Klaus Voigt, and James Burgwyn. Washington, DC: The Catholic University Press, 1989, 109–38.

Ponziani, Luigi. *Il fascismo dei prefetti: amministrazione e politica nell'Italia meridionale, 1922–26.* Catanzaro: Meridiana, 1995.

Preti, Luigi. *Impero fascista: africani ed ebrei.* Milan: Mursia, 1968.

Rabaglietti, Giuseppe. *Le funzioni di polizia giudiziaria della Mvsn e delle sue specialità militizia forestale, stradale, ferroviaria, postelegrafonica, portuaria e confinaria.* Turin, 1933.

Rapone, Leonardo. *Antifascismo e società italiana, 1926–1940.* Milan: Edizioni Unicopli, 1999.

———. "L'Italia antifascista." In *Storia d'Italia, vol. 4: Guerre e fascismo,* ed. Giovanni Sabbatucci e Vittorio Vidotto. Rome-Bari: Laterza, 1997, 501–60.

Reibel, Carl-Wilhelm. *Das Fundament der Diktatur. Die NSDAP-Ortsgruppen, 1932–1945.* Paderborn, Germany, Munich, Germany, Vienna, Austria, and Zürich, Switzerland: Schöningh Verlag, 2002.

Reichardt, Sven. *Faschistische Kampfbünde: Gewalt und Gemeinschaft im italienischen Squadrismus und in der deutschen SA.* Cologne, Germany, Weimar, Germany, and Vienna, Austria: Böhlau, 2002.

Reichardt, Sven and Armin Nolzen, eds. *Beiträge zur Geschichte des Nationalsozialismus, vol. 21: Faschismus in Italien und Deutschland: Studien zu Transfer und Vergleich.* Göttingen, Germany: Wallstein, 2005.

Rempel, Gerhard. *Hitler's Children: The Hitler Youth and the SS.* Chapel Hill: University of North Carolina Press, 1989.

Revelli, Nuto. *Il mondo dei vinti: testimonianze di vita contadina.* Turin: Einaudi, 1977.

Richards, Michael. *A Time of Silence: Civil War and the Culture of Repression in Franco's Spain, 1936–1945*. Cambridge: Cambridge University Press, 1998.

Rochat, Giorgio. "L'attentato a Graziani e la repressione italiana in Etiopia 1936–1937." In *Guerre italiane in Libia e in Etiopia. Studi Militari: 1921–1939*, ed. Giorgio Rochat. Paese, Italy: Pagus, 1991a, 177–214.

————. "La repressione della resistenza in Cirenaica, 1927–1931." In *Guerra italiane in Libia e in Etiopia. Studi militiari, 1921 –1939*, ed. Giorgio Rochat. Paese, Italy: Pegasus, 1991b, 29–98.

————. *Regime fascista e chiese evangeliche: direttive e articolazioni del controllo e della repressione*. Turin: Claudiana, 1990.

————. *Il colonialismo italiano. Documenti*. Turin: Loescher, 1973.

Rodogno, Davide. *Fascism's European Empire: Italian Occupation during the Second World War*. Cambridge and New York: Cambridge University Press, 2006.

Rossi, Ernesto, ed. *No al fascismo*, 2nd ed. Turin: Einaudi, 1963.

Rotelli, Ettore. "Le trasformazioni dell'ordinamento comunale e provinciale durante il regime fascista." *Storia contemporanea* 1 (1973): 57–121.

Sacco, Leonardo. *Provincia di confino: la Lucania nel ventennio fascista*. Fasano di Brindisi, Italy: Schena, 1995.

Salvati, Maruccia. *Il regime e gli impiegati: la nazionalizzazione piccolo-borghese nel ventennio fascista*. Rome: Laterza, 1992.

Salvatori, Luigi. *Al confino e in carcere*. Milan: Feltrinelli, 1958.

Salvemini, Gaetano. *La Terreur Fasciste, 1922–1926*. Paris: Gallimard, 1930.

Santomassimo, Gianpasquale. "Classi subalterne e organizzazione del consenso." In *Storiagrafia e fasciscmo*, ed. Guido Quazza et al. Milan: FrancoAngeli, 1985, 99–116.

————. "Antifascismo popolare." *Italia contemporanea* 140 (July–September 1980): 39–69.

Sarfatti, Michele. *The Jews in Mussolini's Italy: From Equality to Persecution*. Trans. John and Anne Tedeschi. Madison: University of Wisconsin Press, 2006.

————. "The Persecution of the Jews in Fascist Italy, 1936–1943." In *The Jews of Italy: Memory and Identity*, ed. Bernard D. Cooperman and Barbara Garvin. Bethesda: University Press of Maryland, 2000a, 412–24.

————. *Gli ebrei nell'Italia fascista: vicende, identità, persecuzione*. Turin: Einaudi, 2000b.

————. *Mussolini contro gli ebrei: cronaca dell'elaborazione delle leggi del 1938*. Turin: Silvio Zamorani, 1994.

Schnapp, Jeffrey T., Olivia E. Sears, and Maria G. Stampino, eds. *A Primer of Italian Fascism*. Lincoln and London: University of Nebraska Press, 2000.

Secchia, Pietro, ed. *Enciclopedia dell'antifascismo e della resistenza*, 6 vols. Milan: La Pietra, 1968–89.

Senise, Carmine. *Quando ero Capo della Polizia*. Rome: Ruffolo, 1946.

Silone, Ignazio. *The Abruzzo Trilogy*. Trans. Eric Mosbacher. South Royalton, VT: Steerforth Italia, 2000.

Sluga, Glenda. *The Problem of Trieste and the Italo-Yugoslav Border: Difference, Identity and Sovereignty in Twentieth-Century Europe*. Albany: State University of New York Press, 2001.

Snowden, Frank. *Violence and the Great Estates of Southern Italy: Apulia, 1900–1922.* Cambridge: Cambridge University Press, 2003.

_____. *The Fascist Revolution in Tuscany, 1919–1922.* Cambridge: Cambridge University Press, 1989.

Sofsky, Wolfgang. *The Order of Terror: The Concentration Camp.* Trans. William Templer. Princeton, NJ: Princeton University Press, 1997.

Sonnessa, Antonio. "Working Class Defence Organization, Anti-Fascist Resistance and the Arditi Del Popolo in Turin, 1919–22." *European History Quarterly* 33:2 (2003): 183–218.

Soresina, Marco. "Mutue sanitarie e regime corporativo." In *Il fascismo in Lombardia. Politica, economia, societá,* ed. Maria Luisa Betri. Milan: FrancoAngeli, 1989, 261–303.

Spadafora, Rosa. *Il popolo al confino: la persecuzione fascista in Campania,* 2 vols. Naples: Athena, 1989.

Spinelli, Altiero. *Il lungo monologo.* Rome: Ateneo, 1968.

Spriano, Paolo. *Storia del Partito Comunista Italiano.* 7 vols. Turin: Einaudi, 1990.

Steege, Paul, Andrew Stuart Bergerson, Maureen Healy, and Pamela E. Swett. "The History of Everyday Life: A Second Chapter." *The Journal of Modern History* 80:2 (2008): 358–78.

Tasca, Angelo. *The Rise of Italian Fascism.* Trans. Peter and Dorothy Wait. New York: Fertig, 1965.

Tosatti, Giovanna. "La repressione del disenso politico tra l'età liberale e il fascismo. L'organizzazione della polizia." *Studi storici* (1997a): 217–55.

_____. "L'anagrafe dei sovversivi italiani: origini e storia del Casellario politico central." *Le Carte e la Storia* 3:2 (1997b): 133–50.

_____. "Gli internati civili in Italia nella documentazione dell'Archivio centrale dello Stato." In *Una storia di tutti: Prigionieri, internati, deportati italiani nella seconda guerra mondiale,* ed. Giorgio Rochat. Milan: FrancoAngeli, 1989, 35–50.

Totten, Samuel, William S. Parsons, and Israel W. Charney, eds. *Genocide in the Twentieth Century: Critical Essays and Eyewitness Accounts.* New York and London: Garland Publishing, 1995.

Treves, Anna. *Le nascite e la politica nell'Italia del Novecento.* Milan: LED, 2001.

Trilussa (pseud. Carlo Salustri). *Lo specchio e altre poesie.* Milan: Mondadori, 1938.

Triolo, Nancy. "Fascist Unionization and the Professionalization of Midwives in Italy: A Sicilian Case Study." *Medical Anthropology Quarterly* 8:3 (1994): 181–259.

_____. "The Angel-makers: Fascist Pro-Natalism and the Normalization of Midwives in Sicily." PhD diss., University of California, Berkeley, 1989.

Valleri, Elvira. "Dal partito armato al regime totalitario." *Italia contemporanea* 32:141 (1980): 31–60.

Valli, Roberta Suzzi. "The Myth of Squadrismo in the Fascist Regime." *Journal of Contemporary History* 35:2 (2000): 131–50.

Vinci, Annamaria. "Il fascismo al confine orientale." In *Storia d'Italia: Le regioni dall'unità ad oggi, vol. 17.1: Il Friuli-Venezia Giulia*, ed. Roberto Finzi, Claudio Magris, and Giovanni Miccoli. Turin: Einaudi, 2002, 377–513.

Villari, Luigi. *Italy*. New York and London: Charles Scribner's Sons, 1929.

Violante, Luciano. "La repressione del dissenso politico nell'Italia liberale: stati d'assedio e giustizia militare." *Rivista di storia contemporanea* 4 (1976): 481–524.

Voglis, Polymeris. *Becoming a Subject: Political Prisoners during the Greek Civil War*. New York: Berghahn Books, 2002.

Vollmer, Frank. "'Revolutionary Discipline' through Totalitarian Consensus: Dynamistic Modernism and Violence in the Political Culture of Italian Fascism." In *Fascism, Communism, and the Consolidation of Democracy*, eds. Gerhard Besier, Francesca Piombo, and Katarzyna Stoklosa. Berlin: Lit Verlag, 2006, 11–32.

Volpe, Francesco. *Ferramonti: un lager nel sud. Atti del convegno internazionale di studi, 15/16 maggio 1987*, 3 vols. Cosenza: Orizzonti meridionali, 1990.

Ventrone, Angelo. *La seduzione totalitaria: Guerra, modernità, violenza politica, 1914–1918*. Rome: Donzelli, 2003.

Wachsmann, Nikolaus. *Hitler's Prisons: Legal Terror in Nazi Germany*. New Haven, CT, and London: Yale University Press, 2004.

Walston, James. "History and Memory of the Italian Concentration Camps." *The Historical Journal* 40:1 (1997): 169–83.

Wanrooij, Bruno. "Italy: Sexuality, Morality, and Public Authority." In *Sexual Cultures in Europe: National Histories*, ed. Frank X. Eder, Lesley A. Hall, and Gert Hekm. Manchester, UK, and New York: Manchester University Press, 1999, 114–37.

_____. *Storia del pudore: la questione sessuale in Italia, 1860–1940*. Venice: Marsilio, 1990.

Zuccotti, Susan. *The Italians and the Holocaust: Persecution, Rescue, and Survival*. Lincoln: University of Nebraska Press, 1996.

Index